Johann S. Weidenfeld

Four Books of Johannes Segerus Weidenfeld

concerning the secrets of the adepts, or, Of the use of Lully's Spirit of Wine, a practical work - with a very great study collected out of the ancient as well as modern fathers of adept philosophy

Johann S. Weidenfeld

Four Books of Johannes Segerus Weidenfeld
concerning the secrets of the adepts, or, Of the use of Lully's Spirit of Wine, a practical work - with a very great study collected out of the ancient as well as modern fathers of adept philosophy

ISBN/EAN: 9783337329822

Printed in Europe, USA, Canada, Australia, Japan

Cover: Foto ©Thomas Meinert / pixelio.de

More available books at **www.hansebooks.com**

FOUR BOOKS
OF
JOHANNES SEGERUS WEIDENFELD,
Concerning the
SECRETS of the *ADEPTS*;
OR,
Of the Use of *Lully's*
Spirit of Wine:
A PRACTICAL WORK.

With very great Study Collected out of the Ancient as well as Modern FATHERS of

ADEPT PHILOSOPHY,
Reconciled together,
BY

Comparing them one with another, otherwise disagreeing, and in the newest Method so aptly digested, that even young Practitioners may be able to discern the Counterfeit or Sophistical Preparations of *Animals*, *Vegetables* and *Minerals*, whether for Medicines or Metals, from True; and so avoid Vagabond Impostors, and Imaginary Processes, together with the Ruine of Estates.

ISAACUS HOLLANDUS.

2. Oper. Miner. Cap. 3. Pag. 420. Vol. 3. Theatr. Chym.

I discours'd you plainly, using no Allegories; should I tell you of *Selbach*, *Kalcabria*, *Manessi*, and of a *red Matter*, or of the Sky-coloured *Muerach*, *Illabar*, and *Calfaria*, or the like, you would not easily apprehend me; but I have opened you the way, and removed every Obstacle; that you may not err.

London, Printed by *Will. Bonny*, for *Tho. Howkins* in *George-Yard* in *Lombard-Street*, MDCLXXXV.

M. Gaster

Authori Sacrum.

(phorum
QUod nemo eſt auſus citior, quod nemo So-
Præſtitit, in calamo claret in orbe tuo
Hactenus in ſophicis ſparſim tumulata tenebris
Ars jacuit, dubiis inveterata ſtrophis.
Fabula naſutis; avidiſq; Tarantula ſtultis;
Oedipus ignaris; & Labyrinthus avis.
Hic aſinum fingebat equum, mox certior alter
Pone aures leporem ſe tenuiſſe putat.
Sic inhians Lapidi, Lapidis vice volvere ſaxum
Conatur chymici neſcia turba gregis.
Hoc quantum tua nunc removendo induſtria
Contribuat, ſophiæ judicat ipſe tyro. (ſaxo
Semiſophiq; tuos pſallent ſine fraude labores,
Veri candoris propria ſigna tui.
Et ciniflona cohors, exſpes, proſtrata, reſumptis
Viribus, antiquum (macte!) ſubibit onus.
Ne vero ſine re ſis infelicior ipſis,
Perge laborantem continuare manum,
Participeſq; Sacro digitos carbone notare,
Ut videant ſibi Te reddere nolle parem.

Quo

Quo tua ſedulitas tibi nomen & omen Adepti
Aſpirante Dei conciliabit ope.
Poſteraq; emeritas cantabit natio laudes
Et referet grates ubere dote pias.

Sic Amico ſuo cecinit

ALBERTUS OTHO FABER,

Reg. Maj. Britannicæ Med. Ordinar.

[ ]

To the Right Honourable

ROBERT BOYLE,

A CHIEF MEMBER OF THE

ROYAL SOCIETY:

Long Life and Health.

THE *Arcanums* of *Paracelsus* being applauded by many men with so many and such ample *Encomiums*, yet not enough, incited me Ten Years since, first to undertake the consulting of *Paracelsus* himself about his Medicines. Two Years thereof had elapsed, in which I turned over his Books day and night, with an indefatigable and invincible Mind, yet with unequal Success, and scarce any Benefit at all: For in the Books of *Paracelsus*, besides the usual way of concealing Secrets, common

to

to the *Adepts*, I found another much greater difficulty withal, yet leſs frequented by the *Adepts*; *Paracelſus*, as Corrector of the *Adepts*, having propos'd to himſelf therein, the inſtructing of not only raw initiated Scholars, but even expert Maſters of the more ſecret *Chymy*, and for this reaſon he abbreviates his Receipts with wonderful Accurtations, Learned indeed to the Learned, but to us ſeem as lame and imperfect; and beſides, they are ſo diſguiſed with moſt intricate Terms of the true *Philoſophical Chymy*, as to illude not only ſhallow, but profound Capacities: Which Impoſſibility (I had almoſt ſaid) of underſtanding, *Paracelſus* aggravates, by intermixing Common with Secret Receipts; which is not for a Scholar, but a moſt experienced Maſter to diſtinguiſh.

But of theſe Difficulties, the firſt and greateſt Obſtacle withal, was my own unhappy Preconception of ſome

certain

Alkaheſt: For being now out of the hope of attaining to the preparation of this Liquor by other mens Books, as well as *Paracelſus* his own *De Viribus Membrorum*, I betook my ſelf to other places, treating of the *Circulatum minus*, and *Specificum corroſivum* (as ſynonimous Terms of the *Alkaheſt* with ſome men) to which I added the *Aqua* or *Oleum Salis*, *Aqua Comedens*, *Aqua Regis*, *Circulatum majus*, and one after another, being perſwaded that ſome one only univerſal *Menſtruum* was intended by all, that I might find the Method of preparing this Liquor in all places compared together, which I could not in each ſeverally; but at length deſpairing, and being overcome by the manifold and almoſt incredible, yet unſucceſsful pains I took, I reſolved to decline *Chymy* and *Medicine*, as Arts too deep for my underſtanding: When behold! on a ſudden the Eyes of my Mind were opened, and I ſaw all theſe things differ, not in name only, but alſo in matter, preparation

 and

and uſe; ſo inſtead of one Liquor *Alkaheſt*, which I ſought for, I found in *Paracelſus* many *Menſtruums*, with the ſeveral Uſes of them all in *Medicine*; now knew I how to prepare, and according to *Paracelſus*, diſtinguiſh things into *Eſſences*, *Magiſteries*, *Aſtrums*, *Arcanums*, and thoſe which he calls the *leſs Medicines*; ſo that which was in *Paracelſus* moſt difficult to be underſtood by others, became more clear to me than any thing elſe; and ſo I obtained the End ſooner than the Beginning: Yet the Joy from thence accrewing, fell ſhorter than expectation; for having tried ſeveral Experiments in vain, I came to underſtand that theſe *Menſtruums* of *Paracelſus* contained ſomething abſtruſe and unknown, to be underſtood, not in the leaſt according to the Letter: whereupon, examining them more exactly, and comparing their Qualities with the Nature of the Liquor *Alkaheſt*, I found a vaſt difference between it and them; for it is ſaid, There is one Liquor *Alkaheſt*, and that univerſal; but many are the *Menſtruums* of *Paracelſus*, that indeſtructible, that deſtructible; that not mixing with Bodies, theſe abiding with them; that preſerves the Virtues of things, theſe alter them; that aſcends after the Eſſences of things in deſtillation, theſe before their diſſolutions, &c. I was at a ſtand ſometime which part to take; one while I wiſh'd for one indeſtructible Liquor, rather than many deſtructible *Menſtruums*, ſuppoſing that one better than many; another while changing my Mind, I deſired the *Menſtruums*, as ſufficient for many Uſes I knew before.

Truth overcame at length, enabling me now to demonſtrate the moſt, if not all the Medicines of *Paracelſus* in *Guido* and *Baſilius*: On the contrary, I perceived the *Arcanums* of *Paracelſus*, (commonly ſo called) as prepared by that Liquor *Alkaheſt*, or the like, to be more and more different, yea contrary to the Authentick: wherefore as to the Preparation of Medicines, I began to abſtain, yea deſiſted from further enquiring into the obſcure Matter, Preparation and Uſe of that Liquor *Alkaheſt*, namely, that which I find deſcribed in one place of *Paracelſus* as a *Medicine*, but not in the leaſt as a *Menſtruum*: Which Obſtacle being removed, I found an eaſie way from *Paracelſus* to *Lully*, *Baſilius*, and other Philoſophers of the ſame Faculty, who I ſaw agreed all unanimouſly in confirmation of the *Paracelſian Menſtruums*; yea Light adding Light to Light, appeared ſo clear, that their preparation, variety, ſimple and literal ſenſe ſhewed themſelves all at once, one only Word remaining unknown, yet expreſſing the univerſal Baſis of all the *Adepts*, and that is *Spirit* of *Wine*, not *Common*, but *Philoſophical*; which being known and obtained, the greateſt *Philoſophical*, *Medicinal*, *Alchymical*, and *Magical* Myſteries of the more ſecret *Chymy*, will be in the power of the Poſſeſſor. In

no

no Books of the *Adepts*, hitherto known of me, have I found any thing rare, that owes not its original Being to this *Spirit*; ſo that I dare affirm, that whatſoever *Chymical Spirits* lower and higher, fixed and volatile, are able to do, the very ſame, and more will this our *Spirit* perform: This it was that moved me to employ all my Study and Endeavours, turning over every Stone in queſt of the *Spirit* of this *Wine*, and continually ruminating upon thoſe abſtruſe, and variouſly diſguis'd Terms whereby they clouded it, as the Key of all Philoſophy, behold the Fame of your great Name welcom'd me to *Wilde*, the Metropolis of *Lithuania*; and obſerving that You in expounding *Natural Philoſophy*, abſtained from all manner of Intricacy, and as the firſt and only Perſon indeed uſing a plain and candid Series of Words in applying common Examples of *Vulgar Chymiſtry*, I rejoyced with my ſelf, thinking, What could not this great man do, if Maſter of

the

the more ſecret *Chymy?* I reſolved with my ſelf therefore to take a Journey into *England*, for your ſake alone, that I might confer with you about the *Menſtruums* as well as *Medicines*, and other *Secrets* of *Paracelſus*; from whom alſo I promiſed to my ſelf very great Aſſiſtance in ſome other things not yet known: Nor indeed has my hope deceived me; for beſides the eaſie admiſſion, common to all Strangers and Foreigners, you have been pleas'd to vouchſafe me a more free Acceſs, received me courteouſly, and commended my Studies, and thereby rais'd my Mind to greater Things: Which Favours do oblige me to Dedicate this part of my Studies to you your ſelf; Earneſtly and Humbly beſeeching you kindly to accept it, and continue your Love and Friendly Countenance to him that is and ever will be

Your Honour's

Moſt Obedient Servant,

J. S. W.

TO THE

STUDENTS

OF THE MORE

Secret Chymy.

UNder Heaven is not ſuch an Art, more promoting the honour of God, more conducing to Mankind, and more narrowly ſearching into the moſt profound Secrets of Nature, than is our true and more than laudable *Chymy*. This is it which ſhews the Clemency, Wiſdom, and Omnipotence of the Creator in the Creatures; which teacheth not only Speculation, but alſo Practice and Demonſtration, the Beginning, Progreſs, and end of things; which reſtoreth our Bodies from infinite Diſeaſes, as by common means intolerable to priſtine health, and diverts our Minds from the Cares and Anxieties of the World (the Thorns and Bryars of our Souls) to Tranquility of Life, from Pride to Humility, from the Love and Deſire of worldly Wealth to the Contempt thereof: And in a word, which raiſeth us from earth to heaven; Yet for all that may we ſay of it

with

with the ſame truth, that amongſt all the Arts, which have yielded any benefit or profit to the World, there is none, by which leſs honour has hitherto accrued to God Almighty, and leſs utility to mankind; for leſt a Science of ſo great dignity and utility ſhould be too common, or ill managed by the ignorant and impious, the prudent Poſſeſſors of the ſame made it their buſineſs ſo to deſcribe it, as to make it known to their Diſciples only, but exclude unworthy altogether from it: But in proceſs of time, the *Adepts* arriving to a greater perfection of Knowledge and Experience, invented ſometimes one, ſometimes another ſhorter Method in their Work, altering Fornaces, Fires, Veſſels, Weights, yea, and the Matter it ſelf; who being thereby alſo conſtrain'd to make new Theories and Terms of Art, according to the new invented Practice, it happened, that the Scholar of one *Adept* underſtood not the new Theory, much leſs the practice of another; which alſo ſometimes happened to the *Adepts* themſelves, thoſe eſpecially, which were under the document of ſome certain Patron in ſome particular Method and Proceſs; for they had not the power of diſcerning further than they had learnt; whereupon they commonly ſuſpected all the Notions of other men, eſpecially thoſe that differed from theirs, though in themſelves good and right, as fallacious and contrary to Nature, or applied other mens Theories, Sentences, and Terms of Art unknown to themſelves, to their own private Proceſs, with which they were acquainted, as I ſhall by many Examples elſewhere declare; by which very thing they involved this Art in ſuch a Chaos of obſcurity, that hitherto neither Maſters nor Scholars have ſcarce had the power of communicating any benefit to the learned World.

It is to be wondred at, but rather lamented, to ſee ſuch imperfect Philoſophical Syſtems, as have been hitherto bequeathed to us by the Maſters of this Art, not ſeldom contradicting both Nature and themſelves, whereas the Miracles of Nature might by virtue of this Art have been truly and plainly without any convulſion or contraction of words expreſſed; in which reſpect I dare, with Philoſophical Licence here affirm, that moſt of the *Adepts* have by their Writings declared themſelves to the World better *Chymiſts* than *Philoſophers*.

For what I pray could they have better done in Medicine, than to have applied themſelves to this Subject, imitating the diligence and induſtry of *Paracelſus*? But alas! amongſt all, I find perhaps three or four, who have been careful and cordial herein; and therefore the leſs to be admired, that this noble and neceſſary Art, has made no greater progreſs, witneſs Common Chymiſtry, where the names of famous Medicines are noiſed about, themſelves being unknown, and Shells given for Kernels.

Lately indeed we had not only hope, but promiſes alſo from the Roſy-Crucian Fraternity, as if they had a mind to make this our Age more happy by their Studies; but no effect being hitherto heard of, we cannot but fear, their fair promises will never be performed.

On the contrary, Experience teacheth, that instead of an universal good derived from the Fountain of this Art, the World hath rather been involved by it in great and many Miseries: for the *Adepts* affirming, yea more than often with oaths confirming, that they in their Writings treated more clearly and truly of the Art, than any other Philosophers, have thereby instigated many young Novices of all Degrees and Faculties, to begin their Chymical Labours according to the Method of their Prescriptions, exposing themselves not only to intolerable Expences, but also being as it were obstinate in a certain confidence of their understanding the Authors genuine meaning, do rather die amongst the Coals and Fornaces, than recede from their Imaginations, once imprinted in them for true: Whereupon some of the more Learned Inquirers ruminating with themselves, how rarely, and with what great difficulty some of the *Adepts* attained to the Art, by the reading of Books only, thought it a point of Prudence to desert the Authors, together with their Books, perswading themselves to be able to find out a nearer and easier way by virtue of their own Genius and Reason, trying, repeating, altering, *&c.* Experiments and Conclusions; but herein were they disappointed of their desired success, no less than as a Mariner

sayling

ſayling without a Compaſs, and ſo ſuch Inquirers would have acted more adviſedly, if they had inquired in themſelves, whether they had overcome all the Difficulties obvious to them, before they applied themſelves to this more ſecret Art, and doubtleſs many of them would have hearkned to the Counſel of *Theobald* of *Hohenland* (who copiouſly deſcribed the Difficulties of this Art collected out of Philoſophers Books) and avoided it, as worſe than the Plague, or a Serpent : *For who of you* (ſaith our Saviour) *intending to build a Tower, will not firſt ſit down, and compute the Charge, whether he has wherewith to finiſh it, leſt having laid the Foundation, and not being able to perfect it, all that beheld it, ſhould begin to deride him, ſaying, That man began to build, and could not finiſh the Building*, Luke 14. 38.

But I am ſenſible that theſe Admonitions will rather be ſlighted than accepted, eſpecially by thoſe who are loath to have the magnificent Towers built by themſelves in the Air, demoliſhed : For notwithſtanding the impoſſibility of removing the aforeſaid difficulties by ſome men, they endeavour to perſwade others, that they can teach them, what as yet they know not themſelves, and ſo will rather perſiſt in deceiving, than deſiſt from that which they know to be Weakneſs and Error : Others think themſelves very able to overcome all manner of difficulties, and therefore it is in vain to diſſwade them from this Art : Others indeed perceiving all the difficulties, and an undoubted incapacity in themſelves of facilitating them, are, though free from all fraud and arrogance, yet by ſome natural or ſecret impulſe ſo incited to this Art, as not to be driven from it by any Argument.

Wherefore having a ſenſe of the frailty which mankind is afflicted with, to them will I dedicate my Studies relating to Medicine. Deceivers I will reſtrain, ſhame thoſe that aſcribe more to themſelves than due; but the true Diſciples of this Art, I will lead by the hand, that they may not for the future be ſubject to the deriſion, reproaches and ſcoffs of Satyrs, together with the loſs of health, as well of Mind as Body, and at length verifie in themſelves the lamentable Prediction of *Geber*, ſaying, *Moſt miſerable and unhappy is he, whom, after the end of his work, God denies to ſee the Truth, for he ends his Life in Error; who being conſtituted in perpetual labour, and ſurrounded with all manner of Misfortune and Infelicity, loſeth all the Comfort and Joy of this World, and ſpends his Life in Sorrow, without any benefit or reward*, Lib. 2. Inveſt. cap. 38. So with the ſame Argument will I vindicate this the beſt of Arts from the Injuries of Defamers, who being deceived, by not knowing the Principles, accuſe it as fraudulent, impoſſible, and ſo ridiculous, as that they deter the Lovers of it, and incite them to vilifie all the demonſtrations and famous Teſtimonies of the ſame; and laſtly, That the Honour and Glory of God hitherto buried in the Aſhes of it, may from thence riſe again, as a

Phœnix,

Phœnix, I will ſet before your eyes, that which you have not been hitherto able to find in ſo many Volumes of this Art, namely, *Diana* naked, or without Cloaths; that is, I will take from her Face and Body, the Vizards of Tropes, Figures, Parables, barbarous Names, *&c.* by which ſhe hath been hitherto diſguiſed, leſt ſhe ſhould be obvious to the knowledge of wicked men. I will expoſe *Diana* to you, namely, the *very Truth* of our Art (with ſo much ſtudy and labour ſought in vain) not covered indeed ſo much as with the Veyl of neceſſary expreſſion, but her moſt ſecret parts ſhall be expoſed to your view, concerning which the *Adepts* gave exceeding caution to their Diſciples, adding a Curſe withal, not to divulge them to the unworthy Rabble. Wherefore if you deſire to know the *Menſtruums* of *Diana*, wherewith the *Adepts* prepared their Philters, the Liquors of Life and Death, if you would know the way how they prepared their Tinctures, either univerſal or particular for Metals; if laſtly, you covet to know how they made pretious Stones, Pearls, perpetual Lights, together with other Secrets of the Art, read the Receipts of the four Books following; Receipts I ſay, which were either not underſtood, or altogether ſlighted by almoſt all of you, becauſe of the ruggedneſs of their Style, which ſometimes alſo you eſteemed vain, falſe, and impoſſible, compiled in a manner meerly to deceive you; yet moſt true, collected not out of trivial vulgar Chymiſtry, but out of the beſt Books of the beſt *Adepts*, the

Trea-

Treasury of *Diana*; Receipts, I say, so concatenated and elaborated by as well the congruity, as wonderful dexterity of the Masters, that where you take away or deny one of them, you cannot but reject all the rest as false: on the contrary, he that owns one amongst all to be true, must repute all the rest true; and consequently vindicate the Authors of them, our most venerable Masters from all the Infamy of Lying and Scurrility. Variety springing out of Unity, the Fountain of Truth, and returning into it, as into its Ocean, illustrates the excellency of those Receipts: I could never yet satisfie my self, whether there be infinite, or only one Receipt in our Chymy, divided into divers parts, and designed for several Uses: Variety I observe in the various and distinct parts of these four Treatises, but Unity in every part, yea in the Individual of every Part, you will always find three confirming one Treatise: In the the First Book of *Menstruums*, you will find also the Medicines of the Second, and Alchymical Tinctures of the Third, and Secrets of the Fourth Book; which very thing is also to be understood of the Second, Third and Fourth Books. Lastly, These Receipts are not only true, but also clear, described by plain and common Words, to be understood not only according to the Letter, but also by their clearness, illustrating and explaining Places more obscure otherwise not intelligible, so that by one only Process you will sometimes explain more than ten Theoretical Books, never explicable but by this Light.

Now

Now these Receipts I was willing to communicate to you, ye *indefatigable Students* of this Art, for the Reasons already given, as also that you may throughly apprehend the *absolute necessity* of *Lully's Spirit* of *Wine* in our *Chymy*, before I treat with you concerning the *Matter* and *Preparation* of it. No man desires that which is unknown to him, or pursues that which he knows not the benefit of: Wherefore I was desirous first to demonstrate the *several Uses* of this Spirit by the Experiments of the *Adepts*, which if you find true, they will be of such service to you hereafter, as to be much to your detriment to be without them; but if false, slight and give no credit to them, but accuse the Masters, the Authors of them, of Lying, Deceit and Villany; but such wickedness I never expect from you, whatsoever Adversaries, the blind and ignorant of this Art, will do, we little regard, and if a *Zoilus* or *Momus* appear according to his Custom, let him chaw the Shell, that is, the homely Style, the slender and slight Observations and Conclusions given upon the Receipts, all which we give him freely; but touch the *Kernel* he cannot.

But if either now or hereafter you reap any joy or benefit by the sight of *Diana*, attribute it not to *Diana*, though of *Ephesus*, nor to me, but to God Almighty, who hath by his Light brought us out of this *Cimmerian* Darkness: The time perhaps will come, wherein I may be further useful and assistant, in procuring liberty for you to embrace.

brace *Diana* in your Arms, as also discourse familiarly with her concerning her *Doves*, *Forest*, *Fountain*, *Milk*, *Aqua vitæ*, &c. for at present you read the Inscription upon her Forehead, *Touch me not.* Wherefore I advise you, not to touch the Secrets of *Diana*, unless you have to try the Fate and Fortune of *Acteon.*

Inscius Actæon *vidit sine veste* Dianam,
Præda suis canibus non minus ille fuit.

Actæon, hunting in the Woods alone,
When he the naked Goddess saw unknown,
He (for who could her Fury stay ?)
Was to her Fury and his Dogs a Prey.

We may indeed behold her,but not embrace her yet a while; for this is permitted to none but *Adepts*, and such as are Masters of the *Philosophical Wine*; but if you object with the Poet,

Quid juvat Aspectus, si non conceditur Usus?
Tis not the Sight, but Use that gives Delight.

To these Things I answer you, That by viewing *Diana* naked,

1. You will find, that all the Secrets of *Chymy* depend upon one only Center of the Art. namely, the *Spirit* of *Philosophical Wine*.

2. You will understand, that all the Preparations of all the Secrets are done according to the signification of the Words.

3. You will perceive, that all Processes of what Method and Matter soever, if not without the *Spirit* of *Philosophical Wine*, are true, and will never be false.

4. What

4. Whatſoever is rare or ſelect, diſperſed here and there by the beſt of the *Adepts*, you will have here pick'd and digeſted into order, ſo, as that there will be nothing wanting, but the enjoyment of them

5. You will moreover have the convenience of chuſing the beſt and ſhorteſt out of all the Proceſſes.

6. Or you will be enabled to find out alſo more of your ſelves, if theſe pleaſe you not.

7. You will ſee that he who hath performed even the leaſt thing in this Art, may conſequently alſo perform the greateſt.

8. One only clear Proceſs will open the underſtanding of more, otherwiſe moſt obſcure.

9. You may know alſo, that the *Adepts* themſelves have been ſometimes in the dark, and oftentimes underſtood not the ſtyle of anothers Writing: That ſome have corrected others, and ſo made the Art more perfect.

10. And to ſay all at once; No man, though never ſo Learned, though never ſo Eloquent, though never ſo ſubtil an Impoſtor, will be able for the future, either by his Authority, Perſwaſion, or ſubtilty, to deceive any man, and drive him out of our common Road into an untrodden Path, except he be willing himſelf.

Nor will you alone be free from the Deceipts of other men, but your own Miſtakes alſo; by which you have hitherto moſt miſerably loſt all, Time, Pains, Money, Health, and what not? You have made your very Life it self vain, unprofitable, and offensive to your selves as well as others.

Yea and such are the glittering Rays of our *Diana*, that I fear they will dazzle your eyes, like as the *Israelites* were at the sight of *Moses* descending from the Mountain.

You will scarce believe me, should I affirm, that the Secrets of the *Adepts* are to be understood and prepared according to the Letter; if you argue it to be improbable that the *Adepts* should have exposed their Mysteries to the view of all men, they themselves having advertised you of the contrary. What then?

Is not this our Art, saith *Artesius, cabalistical, and full of Mysteries? And you Fool believe we teach the Secrets of Secrets openly, and understand our Words according to the Letter; be assured (I am not envious as others) he that takes the Philosophers Sayings according to the common sence and signification, has already lost the Clew of* Ariadnes, *and wanders up and down the Labyrinth, and it would be of the same benefit to him, as if he had thrown his Money into the Sea.* The same thing adviseth *Sendivogius* in the Preface of the twelve Treatises: *I would*, saith he, *have the candid Reader know, that my Writings admit not so much a verbal construction, but such rather as Nature requireth, lest afterwards he should have Cause to bewail the expence of time, pains and cost in vain,* &c. *Because*, as *Arnold* saith in his *Speculum*, *An intention according to the Letter nothing avails, and to operate according to the intention of the Letters*

ters, is the dissipation of Riches. For, saith Geber, *Where we spoke most openly we conceal'd the Art, speaking to an Artist not Ænigmatically, but in a plain series of Discourse.* Yea *Roger Bacon* proceeds further, saying, *When I swear I say true, believe it a lie, that is, as to the Letter, and therefore when I tell you of* Stalks, *understand* Lead, &c. *lib de Arte Chymica*, pag. 56. *All that I say is false, therefore nothing I say is true; wherefore I pray, believe me not; but when I say true, take it to be false; and if this, the contrary: So that which is false will be turned into true, and that which is true, into false: I tell you these things, that you may beware of things that are to be avoided, and believe things credible, in writing properly, I write not,* &c. p. 301. *And though I say, Take this and this, believe me not, operate according to the Blood, that is, the Understanding, and so of all; leave off Experiments; apprehend my meaning, and you will find, believe me being already a lighted Candle*, pag. 345.

These and the like may you alleadge to confirm your Opinion; but give me leave to suggest to you the distinction that is to be made between the Theoretical and Practical Books of the *Adepts*: In the Theoretical Books there is scarce any thing to be understood literally, all things being parabolical, ænigmatical, &c. But in the Practical Books all things are clear and intelligible, according to the Letter: *Philosophical Wine* alone excepted, the foundation and beginning of all Secrets: For example, Take the *magnum Testamentum* of *Lully*, in the Theoretical part of which, is Philosophically, that is, by various Sophisms, described the *Nature, Matter*, and *Preparation* of *Lully's Wine*; but in the Practical part of this *Testamentum*, the *Use* of this *Wine* is declared according to the Letter: From hence will you also easily observe, That those *Adepts* which reject the Literal Sense are rather Theoretical than Practical: We treating at present of the practice of the *Adepts*, or the *Use* of *Philosophical Wine*, will prove that most of the Secrets delivered to us by them, are according to the Letter.

But some of you will urge, that the *Adepts* themselves have even more than often declamed against the Literal Sence of Practice, against the very Descriptions (commonly called Receipts) of Experiments; but let these our Companions know, the *Adepts* wrote against two sorts of Receipts.

The first comprehends the Receipts of Smoak-sellers, Deceivers, wicked men, who pretend they either had them from the Disciple of some *Adept*, or found them in the Walls of some old Cloister or Sepulcher; against whom hear *Dionysius Zacharias*, *Pag.* 781. *Vol.* 1. *Th. Chym.* saying, *Before I left the Colledge of Arts, I entred into familiarity and friendship with many other Scholars; they had divers Books of Chymical Receipts, which being lent me, I transcribed with very great diligence, my private Master, who had also a long time before began to labour in this Art, consenting; so that before I went away,*

away, I had gathered a very large Book of ſuch Receipts, I went preſently with my Maſter to the Place where I was to ſtudy Law, began to turn over my Writings; whereof ſome contained Projections of One upon Ten, others upon Twenty, Thirty; a Third, a half part; for the Red of eighteen Carrachs, twenty, &c. into Gold of Crowns, Ducats, and of the higheſt colour that could be; One was to endure Melting, another the Touch-ſtone, another all Tryals: Of the White likewiſe, one was to be of Ten penny, another of Eleven, another Sterling Silver, coming white out of the Fire, another white from the Touch: In ſhort, I thought if I were able to perform the leaſt of thoſe things greater felicity could not happen to me in this world.

Eſpecially when I read the Inſcriptions of great Perſons before ſuch Receipts; one of the Queen of Navarr, *another of the Cardinal of* Lorain, Turine, *and infinite others, that by ſuch Diſguiſes and Titles, Credit might be given by unwary men.*

Bernhard alſo complains of the ſame Receipts, *pag.* 771. ejuſd. Vol. *If I had had,* ſaith he, *at firſt, all the Books, which I afterwards procured, doubtleſs I ſhould have ſooner attained to the Art, but I read nothing but falſe Receipts, and erroneous Books; beſides I happened to confer with none but the moſt perverſe Thieves, wicked Men, and Impoſtors.*

The other ſort contains Receipts of *Adepts* themſelves, againſt whom ſome other *Adepts* have alſo ſometimes written: As for example, the ſame *Bernhard*, Pag. 748. Vol. Theat. Chym. ſaying,

To withdraw the true Speculators of this Art from common Errors into the right Way, that they may not waste their Wealth, and lose their Labours, Name and Reputation, insisting upon the false Receipts of Books, as those of Geber, Rasis, Albertus magnus, Trames, Lumen, Canonis pandectarum, Demophon, Summa, *and other Seducers,* I *will first declare my own Errors,* &c. And in pag. 750. goes on, I*nfinite is the number of them, whom to write is needless; and there is great plenty of Books written upon this Subject under Metaphorical Words and Figures, so as not to be easily understood by any but the Sons of Art; the reading of which, leads men out of the right way, rather than directs to the Work; in the number of which, are* Scotus, Arnold, Raymund, Johannes Mehung, Hortulanus Veridicus, *&c.*

My Business therefore is to satisfie you, and say, That the Authors of the first sort of Receipts deceive actively, wittingly, and willingly: But the Receipts of the later sort, written by *Adepts* themselves, seduce only passively: And this for two Reasons; either in respect of the *Adept* being less experienced in the Art, and unacquainted with the Practice of his more Learned Consort; for it is impossible for one *Adept*, though never so expert in his Method, to know the various Experiments of all the other, much less the peculiar Theorems, private Meditations, different Denominations of things, *&c.* formed or derived from the same: Or in respect of your selves, who extort from those Receipts, as to the Literal Sound, more, than

the

the *Adepts* themſelves allow, not at all obſerving that the *Spirit* of *Wine* being once and always underſtood, the reſt you will eaſily underſtand. *For knowing this*, ſaith *Flammel*, *in his Hieroglyphicks*, pag. 28. *I perfected the Magiſtery eaſily*; *for having learnt the Preparation of the firſt Agent*, *I following my Book according to the Letter, could not err if I would.* And a little after; *Then following my Book from word to word, I made Projection.* But why theſe? Plenty enough of Examples in this Treatiſe will inſtruct you in all theſe things that are to be underſtood according to the Letter, except *Wine*, *Lunary*, *Vegetable Mercury*, and other things ſynonymous to the Matter of the *Spirit of Philoſophical Wine*, or things prepared by the ſame Spirit, *Vegetable Sal Harmoniack*, *Philoſophical Vinegar*, &c.

For this *Spirit* of *Wine* being prevaricated, the *Adepts* knew, that all the reſt, though never ſo plainly diſcovered to the Sons of Art, could not contribute the leaſt benefit to the Reader; Wherefore I fear not the indignation of the *Adepts*, nor the Anathema's which they thundred out againſt the Betrayers of their Secrets, having herein done nothing more, but (to ſpeak ingenuouſly) leſs, than they themſelves. I have according to my capacity, methodically digeſted thoſe things which were here and there confuſedly diſperſed, but added nothing of my own, and ſo expect neither Honour nor Thanks from you; but this only, that I may know, if our Studies pleaſe; and I ſhall ſupply thoſe things that are here wanting and deſired, ſomewhat more largely;

largely; for I will not refuse to assist you yet further by the industry of my Studies: So that nothing remains, but upon our bended Knees to return most humble Thanks to the *Father* of *Lights*, in vouchsafing us this Art by the Writings of his Servants, and the High Priests of Nature, without which it would be beyond the power of man to arrive to so great a degree of Knowledge.

Now celebrate with me the Urns of our pious Masters, who have for the Welfare of Mankind, rather dispersed, than buried their Talents; and may you oblige your selves to the same good Office, if you have any of their Writings not yet published.

Finally, It is my earnest Suit to the *Adepts* now living, that they would please to employ themselves freely in expounding Nature, correcting Philosophy and Medicine; And lastly, refuting all the deceitful Sects of Philosophers, as well in the Academies, as private Schools, for the advancement of the Glory of God, being singularly eminent in this Art. *So be it.*

The First Book

OF

MENSTRUUMS.

RIPLEY,

Cap. 2. Medullæ Philos. Chym.

We will here demonstrate the clear Practice, how such *Menstruums* as be Unctuous and Moist, Sulphureous, and Mercureal, well agreeing with the Nature of Metals, wherewith our Bodies are to be artificially dissolved, may be obtained.

London, Printed for *Tho. Howkins* in *George*-Yard in *Lombard*-Street, 1685.

The Tranſlator to the Reader.

YOur Buſineſs it is, not mine, otherwiſe than as a Reader, to judge of this Work, but the ample and publick Encomiums of Learned Societies beyond the Seas, already declaring their Sentiments of its Rarity and Excellency, are convictive Authorities far beyond my Opinion; and therefore I ſhall be ſilent: only this I think neceſſary to let you know, that our Author, having little ſpare time himſelf, left his Latine Impreſſion to be by others corrected, which has been the cauſe of many Errors; and indeed in ſome Places ſo groſs, that the Author himſelf could ſcarce retrieve his own Meaning: This to prevent in the Engliſh Tranſlation, he has been pleaſed to uſe all Care to have it exactly import his own Mind. I muſt alſo tell you, that though I have taken no ſmall pains in endeavouring to make this weighty Work ſpeak true and perfect Engliſh, *yet my Copy not being punctually obſerved, you will find many ſmall Miſtakes, beſides the* Errata's *inſerted at the latter end of the Book, which you may pleaſe, as you read, to correct.*

Farewel.

G. C.

A Catalogue of *Menstruums*.

I.

Simple Vegetable *Menstruums* made of *Philosophical Wine* only.

II.

Simple Vegetable *Menstruums* made of Spirit of *Philosophical Wine*, and the hottest Vegetables, Herbs, Flowers, *&c.* being Oyley.

III.

Simple Vegetable *Menstruums* made of Spirit of *Philosophical Wine* and *Oyley Sals, as Sugar, Honey, Tartar Common,* &c.

IV.

Simple Vegetable *Menstruums* made of *Spirit of Philosophical Wine* and *Volatile Salts*, as Sal Armeniack, Salt of Blood, Urine, *&c.*

V.

V.

Simple Vegetable *Menstruums* made of Spirit of *Philosophical Wine*, and *Fixed Salts* of Vegetables and Minerals not Tinging.

VI.

Simple Vegetable *Menstruums* made of the Spirit and Tartar of *Philosophical Wine.*

VII.

XI.

[ ]

XI.

Vegetable *Menstruums* compounded, graduated, made of the compounded Vegetable *Menstruums* impregnated with the Influences of Heaven and Earth.

XII.

Vegetable *Menstruums* compounded, most highly exalted, made of compounded Vegetable *Menstruums* graduated.

XIII.

Simple Mineral *Menstruums* made of the Matter of *Philosophical Wine only.*

XIV.

Simple Mineral *Menstruums* made of the Acid or Saline Essences of Salt.

XV.

XIX.

Mineral *Menstruums* compounded of *Philosophical Spirit of Wine*, and *Acid Spirits* not tinging, Spirit of Vitriol, Butter of Antimony, *&c.*

XX.

Mineral *Menstruums* compounded of the *Spirit* of *Philosophical Wine*, and other tinging things, Vitriol, Cinabar, Antimony, *&c.*

XXI.

Mineral *Menstruums* Compounded, made of Simple Mineral *Menstruums* and *Mercury*, the rest of Metals, and other tinging things.

XXII.

Mineral *Menstruums* compounded of the Philosophers Vinegar, and other Simple Mineral *Menstruums*, and things tinging being first fixed.

XXIII.

Mineral *Menstruums* compounded made of Mineral *Menstruums* compounded, and Metallick Bodies, and other tinging Things.

XXIV.

Mineral *Menstruums* compounded of vegetable and mineral *Menstruums* mixed together.

The

THE PREFACE.

T O *exempt* Diana *from being exposed Naked to the Petulant Lust of Unsatiable Men, as also to the Scorns and Contempt of the Ignorant, as a Common Prostitute; the* Adepts *have taken care not only to cloath, but cover her almost with several sorts of Garments: To this kind of Apparel, Antiquity has been pleased, yet not properly enough, to refer an* Allegory *of the Procreation of Man, deduced from the Analogy of Seed anciently received, however ill applied to the* Mineral Kingdom.

First, They reckon Coition; *Secondly,* Conception; *Thirdly,* Impregnation; *Fourthly,* Birth; *Fifthly,* Nutriment: *If therefore no Coition, no Conception; without Conception, no Impregnation; without which no Birth can be premised.*

Which Disposition the Ancient Morienus *himself confesseth to have been derived to him from Antiquity.* Hermes, *whom they call Father of the* Adepts, *in his* Tabula Smaragdina, *hath described to us the Father, Mother, and Nurse of the* Chymical Infant. *No wonder therefore, that such an Ancient and Easie Doctrine as this, should have found so easie an access to Posterity: it would be besides the Intention and Scope to offer those things, which might be inferred by us against this Analogy of Seed: Here let it suffice to remember only, that the greater part, as also the more ancient* Adepts, *comparing the Chymical Magistery to the Generation of Man, did under the Notion of this* Allegory, *call their Dissolvents* Menstruums, *or* Feminine Seed, *but the Things which were to be Dissolved,* Masculine Seed. My Son, *saith Lully,* The Vegetable Menstruum is of the Nature of a Womans Menstruum, because a Mineral Menstruum proceeds from it by Dissolution, (*of Minerals and Metals*) and is made artificially as Nature requireth; for it hath the property of an incorruptible Spirit, which is as a Soul, and hath the Conditions of a Body, becaufe it generates and produceth Seed as a Woman; therefore we call our D. (*Diffolvent*) Menftrual Blood, or Menftruum, becaufe it is Generative and Nutritive, and makes the faid C, and (C) (*Metals*) grow and increafe, till they be converted into M (*Sulphur of Nature*, or *Philofophers Mercury*) or into Q, (*Tincture*, or *Philofophers Stone*) for as Menftrual Blood perfects the Embryo by nourifhing, and altering one Principle into another, and one Quantity into another, and one Form into another, yet the Principles and Quantities appearing in every Alteration, under divers Forms, differing from the firft Forms themfelves, till a certain Subftance appears in one entire Quantity, dependent upon feveral Matters, which is a Body, with Spirit and Soul, reduced into Action: And thus it is with our Infant (*Philofophers Stone*) Lully, *Diftinct*, 3. *Can.* 4. *Lib. de Effentia*, When K. (*Colour*) appears yellow, then let the Artift know, that the Body of our Infant is formed, made, and compleatly organized, and begins to be prepared for the reception of the vegetable Spirit into it, and Nature continues in that preparation till the yellow K. vanifheth away, and a red K. (*Colour*) appeareth; and then may the Artift be affured that the faid Infant is perfect both in Body and Soul: fo that he may let the Fire alone till it grows cold; which being cold, the Artift will find our Infant round as an Egg; which he muft take out and purifie (for it is a hard Stone in the middle of many Superfluities, as the Infant of a Woman appears after Birth: *Can.* 11. *Diftinct.* 3. *Lib. Effent.*) and let him take and put it into fome clean Glafs Veffel, &c. 3 *Diftinct.* 3 *Part Lib. de Effent.*

Parifinus, Ripley, Efpanietus, *and other later* Adepts, *the Difciples of* Lully, *had this Analogy of Seed from him, being doubtlefs the moft Learned of the Chymical Philofophers.* Of this living Heaven, *faith* Parifinus, Raymund *fpeaks in his Third Book de Quinteffentia, in the Chapter beginning*, *Cælum & Mercurius nofter*; Our Heaven hath the property of an incorruptible Spirit, which is as the Soul of it, and hath the Conditions of a Body in it, generating and producing Seed, as a Woman,

man, and herein it differs from the other Principles (of the Art) It is alſo ſenſual, becauſe it is apprehended by ſenſe, namely, by ſight, taſte and ſmell, as is declared in *the firſt Diſtinction in the Chapter, which beginneth, Præterea eſt principium movendi, ſcilicet, corpus ſive forma : And a little after, ſpeakidg of the aforeſaid living Heaven, he ſaith,* And in this point our Underſtanding knows that D. (*his living Heaven, or Diſſolvent*) hath a Vegetable property, the ſimilitude of which, R and S (*Gold and Silver*) do tranſmit into the Sulphur of Nature, which is the Spirit of Metals, or Stone, or transforming Poyſon, according to the ſignification of *Raymund*, which ſignification he uſeth in his *Alphabetum figuræ arboris Philoſophicæ*, and therein produceth this following Sentence *in Capite de figura Quintæ Eſſentiæ*: As the Vegetative part of the Mother or Nurſe, tranſmits her Likeneſs into the Son, which ſhe generates, which property the Son retains, ſo our Mercury. The Intention of the Philoſopher (*Lully*) is to demonſtrate, that the Philoſophers Sulphur, or Stone, or transforming Poyſon receives all its benefit by the excitation of the vegetative Virtue, which is in this Divine Vegetative Heaven.

The ſame Author in the Continuation of his Doctrine, ſaith, And alſo the Underſtanding knows, that the ſaid Metals R, and S, (*Gold and Silver*) retain the property of Menſtruum, with which they extend their ſimilitudes into exotick ſubſtances, tranſmuting the ſaid ſubſtances into their own kind, which is the reaſon why we call it Vegetable Mercury ; as alſo becauſe it is extracted out of Vegetables. *The ſame thing at the end of the ſaid Chapter he ſpeaks afreſh* : And our Underſtanding alſo knows, that principle is as a Woman conceiving the Mans Seed, and bringing forth in the ſame form and virtue, as it was in the beginning. From whence we neceſſarily conclude, that the Elements of this Stone, namely, Gold, ought to be moved by vertue of a living Quinteſſence, and the aforeſaid Vegetable Heaven, which way I have ſufficiently proved and demonſtrated. *Pariſinus in Lib.* 1. *Elucidarii, pag.* 221. *Vol.* 6. *Th. Chym.*

Ripley *having the ſame Maſter as* Pariſinus, *expounds this Doctrine more briefly, thus* ; As an Infant in the Womb of the Mother, does by the concoction of temperate heat, convert the Menſtruums into its own Nature and Kind, that is, into Fleſh, Blood, Bones, yea, Life, with all other Properties of a living Body; ſo if you have the Water of *Sol* and *Luna*, it will attract other Bodies to its kind, and make their Humors perfect by its intrinſick Virtue and Heat; *Ripl. Lib. de Merc. Phil.*

We, *ſaith Eſpanietus*, to deal plainly and truly; affirm, that the whole work may be perfected by two Bodies only, that is, *Sol* and *Luna*, rightly prepared: For this is that Generation which is performed by Nature with the help of Art, in which the coition of Male or Female is requir'd, and from whence the Off-ſpring more noble than its Parents, is expected; *Sect.* 20. *Arcan. Herm.* *Sol* is the Male, for he yields the active and informing ſeed: *Luna* is the Female; which is called the Matrix and Veſſel of Nature, becauſe ſhe receives the ſeed of the Male into her womb, and nouriſheth it with her Menſtruum, *Sect.* 22. *Arcan. Herm. Phil.* But the Philoſophers do not by the name of *Luna*, mean common *Luna*, which alſo acts the parts of a Male in their (white) work; let no man therefore attempt to joyn two males together, it being wicked and contrary to Nature, nor can he hope for any Offſpring from ſuch a copulation, but put *Gobritius* to *Beja*, Brother to Siſter.

Conjugio junget ſtabili, propriamq; dicabit.

That he may have from thence the noble Son of *Sol*, *Sect.* 23. *Arcan. Herm. Phil.* I would have the Reader know, *ſaith Sendivogius*, that Solution is twofold, though there be many other ſolutions, but of no effect: the firſt is only true and natural; the ſecond violent, under which are all the other comprehended; the Natural is that, by which the pores of the Body are opened in our VVater, that the digeſted ſeed may be injected into its Matrix: But our VVater is Celeſtial, not wetting your hands; not common, but almoſt like Rain: The Body is Gold, which yieldeth ſeed: our *Luna* is not common Silver, which receives the ſeed of Gold. *Tract.* 10. *Novi Lumin.* *Saturn* taking the Veſſel, drew up ten parts of the VVater, and preſently took ſome of the Fruit of the ſolar Tree, and put it in, and I ſaw the fruit of the Tree conſumed and reſolved as

Ice

Ice in warm water. This water is to this fruit, as a VVoman. The fruit of this Tree can be putrified in nothing, but in this water only; for no other water can penetrate the pores of this Apple, but this: and you must know that the solar Tree sprang also out of this VVater, which is extracted from a magnetical virtue out of the Rays of *Sol* and *Luna*, and therefore they have great affinity one with the other: *In the Dialogue of Mercury.*

Now here we in this Book intend to treat of this Feminine Seed, or dissolving Waters of the Adepts. *Great indeed, yea vast is the Treasure of our Chymy; but altogether inaccessible by those that have not the Keys thereof; without which the* Adepts *themselves could neither dissolve nor coagulate Bodies.* If you know not the way of dissolving our Body, it is in vain to operate, *is the Advice of Dionysius Zacharias, pag.* 798. *Vol.* 1. *Th. Chym.* But he that knows the Art and Secret of Dissolution, has attained to the Secret of the Art; *saith* Bernhard, *pag.* 40. *suæ Epistolæ.* For this cause it is, *saith Parisinus,* that the wise men say, To know the Celestial Water, which reduceth our Body into a Spirit, is the chief Mystery of this Art, *in Eluc. pag.* 212. *Vol.* 1. *Th. Chym. For without these Menstruums things heterogeneous can never be perfectly mixed. Coral, though never so finely pulverized, cannot be mixed with the purest Powder of Pearls: Tea Gold mixeth not with Silver (much less with Bodies less perfect) though both be melted together; the Particles of each do indeed touch one another in their extream parts, being in a mass or heap consisting of things heterogeneous, yet they are and do remain all distinct, unblemished and unaltered in their Figures and Properties, no otherwise than as a heap composed of Barley and Oats: But in the more secret Chymy there is no Body, no heterogeneity, but what hath its own peculiar Menstruum, and with which as being homogeneous to it, it runs into one Concrete, rejoycing in the inseparable Properties of either. So long therefore as you intend to joyn Metals with Metals, dry things with dry, without the Menstruums of* Diana, *so long (to use the Phrase of* Espanietus) *do you presume to joyn males together, which is a thing wicked and contrary to Nature. Hearken therefore to* Bernhard, *Pag.* 757. *Vol.* 1. *Th. Chym. Perswading you to* leave Stones and all sorts of Minerals, likewise also Metals *alone,* though they are the beginning and our matter. *Metals are not only the matter,*

ter, but are also call'd by Lully, *the form of the Stone; yet without these Menstruums they signifie nothing.* The Form, *saith he*, which is the Efficient Principle, Former and Transformer of all other Forms of less virtue and power, is described by C, or (C) (*Metals*) cannot of it self only be the Magistery of the greater work, *&c.* Very commodious it is for that Principle to be known, because hereby the Understanding knows it to be one of the two Substances, from which our Infant is produced, having in it the condition of a male, from which proceeds a sperm in the belly of our D. (*Menstruum or Dissolvent*,) Lul. *Dist.* 3. *Lib. Ess.* Heaven or Mercury (*Menstruum*) is the fourth Principle signified by D. It is the Cause and Principle moving C, and (C) from Power to Action, ruling and governing them in its belly, as the VVoman the Infant which she procreates in her Matrix. And in this point knows the understanding of an Artist, that D (*Menstruum*) hath action upon C, and (C) ruling, governing and reducing them into Action, even as the Heavens above do by their motion, bring things Elementary, into action. And an Artist is to understand that of the two substances, of which our Stone is compounded, and by which it is generated, this, namely, D, (*Dissolvent*) is the more principal. *Ibid. In the Book de Medicinis secretis, pag.* 336. *he goes on*; You must know, *saith he*, that hitherto I have not told you the most secret thing and matter of the whole Magistery, which is our incorruptible Quintessence, extracted out of white or red VVine, which we call Celestial Crown, and Menstruum, after the sublimations, putrefactions, and final depuration of it; which Quintessence is indeed the foundation, principal matter, and Magistery of all medicinal things: My Son, if you have it, you will have the Magistery of the whole thing, without which nothing can be done.

But you, My companions, *know, what mean the Menstruums of* Diana; *you know, I say, they are the highest secrets of the more secret Chymy, much more secret than the Menstruums of Women; that the same also were never acquired but by the extream Pains and ingenuity of an* Adept, *most cautiously described, and recommended to us principally as the Keys of the Art: You easily belie[illegible] [illegible]ully, saying,* Without these *Menstruums* nothing can be d[illegible] the Magistery of the Art. *Mag. Nat. pag.* 329. Or *Christo[illegible] Parisinus*, That

That the great secret lies in these *Menstruums*, insomuch if they be not known, nothing can be done as to the transmuting of Metals. *Elucid. pag.* 222. *Vol.* 6. *Th. Chym. Wherefore I think it enough to declare to you in short, that these* Menstruums, *which hitherto you have with so much study, to little purpose sought in the Theoretical Books of* Adepts, *are now offered to you, being found by me, in Practical Books, no longer shrowded with Obscurity, but disrobed, and exposed naked to the sight and understanding of all men: But you have no cause to fear the Spirit of Philosophical Wine which you perceive in any* Menstruum, *it being familiar and most gentle, because Philosophical. Nor have you need of many Conjurations, to make it appear to you; for in all Pages of the Theoretical Books of* Adepts, *it offers it self willingly and expects you, provided you pray to God, that he would graciously vouchsafe to open your Eyes; for without his permission or special appointment, it dares not manifest it self to you. By the* Menstruums *of the* Adepts, *understand not therefore yours, though they be most secret to you, because I fear they are yet but vulgar, which dissolving a dry Body, are transmuted with it into a Salt or Vitriol, not with a true, but seeming coalition and mixture, which a searching Fire easily discovereth, presently separating these same heterogeneous substances again: On the contrary, the unctious* Spirit *of Philosophical Wine does by its Unctuosity mollifie a dry Body, and transmute it not into a Salt or Vitriol, but into an Oyl: It easily joyns things heterogeneous by its own equal temperament, and is by its homogeneity easily joyned with things homogeneous to it, by which also it is augmented, according to that of* Bernhard: No Water dissolveth bodies, but that which is of their species. and which can be inspissated in bodies; for a Dissolvent ought not to differ from that which is dissolved, in matter, but proportion and digestion; *Pag.* 43. *of his Epistles.* For Nature is not meliorated, but by its own nature; our matter therefore can be no otherwise meliorated than by its own matter. Parmenides saith the same, *L. de Alchym. pag.* 768. *Vol.* 1. *Th. Chym. This Spirit of Phylosophical Wine may be united to all things, and is able to unite all things inseparably.* But they that suppose another water, are ignorant and unwise, and will never come to the effect, *saith* Parisinus *in Eluc. p.* 222. *Vol.* 6. *Th. Chym. Of which* Morienus, *pag.* 52. *thus;* As to this Magistery, let Fools seek other things, and seeking err; for they will never attain

to

to the effect of it, till *Sol* and *Luna* be reduced into one body, which cannot come to pass before the Will of God. *Which* Arnold, *if I mistake not, thus expresseth: You will sooner joyn the Sun and Moon in the Heavens, than Gold and Silver in the Earth without our* Menstruums.

But you that have hitherto desired one only universal, immortal, indestructible Menstruum, *I mean, the Liquor* Alkahest. *or* Ignisaqua, *that undeclinable word, instead of one, whereof you never yet knew the Name, Matter, Preparation and Use, behold! I offer a great many kinds of universal* Menstruums, *in their Descriptions more clear, in Virtues equivalent, if not better than this your* Alkahest. *What others have either obscurely, or impertinently said and written of this Liquor* Alkahest, *we little regard, as Opinions and Conjectures. By the* Menstruums *of the* Adepts, *we intend not all manner of Dissolvents, prepared without the Spirit of Philosophical Wine, and only corroding, but not in the least altering the more minute Particles of Bodies: Nor do we understand an immortal Liquor, not permanent with things dissolved in it: But by* Menstruum *we mean a volatile Liquor made several ways of the Spirit of Philosophical Wine and divers things, not only separating Bodies, but also continuing with them, and altering them with the addition of it self, so as to be no more two, nor again, what they were before. For out of this Dissolution (the solemn Wedlock, inseparable Union and Combination of Body and Menstruum) emergeth a new Being, containing the unblemished Properties of the thing dissolved, and the thing dissolving, not at all separable by Art or Nature.*

These Menstruums *I have distinguished into Vegetable and Minerals, not as if the Vegetables were made of Vegetables only, and the Mineral of Minerals, but every* Menstruum, *that hath not manifest acidity, acting without ebullition and motion, is called Vegetable, though it be made of meer Animals or Minerals by the Spirit of Philosophical Wine. On the contrary, a* Menstruum *becomes Mineral, so soon as manifest acidity is mixed either with the Spirit of Philosophical Wine, or a Vegetable Menstruum; for by adding the acidity, it now dissolves Bodies with violence and effervescence. I have subdivided both kinds into Simple and Compound, but not as if the Simple consisted of fewer Ingredients, but because they are of more simple or less virtue. Simple Menstruums tinge Bodies dissolved in them less, but the Compounded more.*

OF

OF
Vegetable MENSTRUUMS.

The First Kind.

Simple Vegetable Menstruums made of Philosophical Wine *only.*

I. The Heaven, Essence, or Spirit of Wine of *Lully*, *Described*, *Can.* 1. *Dist.* 1. *Lib. De Quinta Essentia.*

TAke Wine Red or White, the best that may be had, or at least take Wine that is not any way eager, neither too little nor too much thereof, and distil an *Aqua ardens*, as the custom is, through Brass Pipes, and then rectifie it four times for better purification. But I tell you it is enough to rectifie it three times, and stop it close, that the burning Spirit may not exhale, because herein have many men erred, thinking it ought to be seven times rectified, But my Son, it is an infallible sign to you when you shall have seen that Sugar steeped in it, and being put to the flame burneth awey as *Aqua ardens*. Now having the water thus prepared, you have the matter out of which the Quintessence is to be made, which is one principal thing we intend to treat of in this Book. Take therefore that, and put it in a circulating Vessel, or in a Pelican, which is called the Vessel of *Hermes*, and stop the hole very close with *Olibanum* or *Mastick* being soft, or quick Lime mixed with the White of

Eggs, and put it in Dung, which is naturally most hot, or the remainings of a Wine-Press, in which no heat must be by accident diminished, which you may do, my Son, if you put a great quantity of which you please of those things at a corner of the House, which quantity must be about thirty Load: This ought to be, that the Vessel may not waut heat, because should heat be wanting, the circulation of the water would be impaired, and that which we seek for uneffected; but if a continual heat be administred to it by continual circulations, our Quintessence will be separated in the colour of Heaven, which may be seen by a diametrical Line, which divides the upper part, that is the Quintessence, from the lower, namely, from the Fæces, which are of a muddy colour. Circulation being continued many days together in a circulating Vessel, or in the Vessel of *Hermes*, the Hole, which you stopp'd with the said Matter, must be opened, and if a wonderful Scent go out, so as that no fragrancy of the world can be compared to it; insomuch as putting the Vessel to a corner of the House, it can by an invisible Miracle draw all that pass in, to it; or the Vessel being put upon a Tower, draws all Birds within the reach of its Scent, so as to cause them to stand about it. Then will you have, my Son, our Quintessence which is otherwise call'd *Vegetable Mercury* at your will, to apply in the Magistery of the transmutation of Metals: But if you find not the influx of Attraction, stop the Vessel again, as before; and put it in the place before appointed, and there let it stand till you attain to the aforesaid Sign. But this Quintessence thus glorified, will not have that Scent, except a Body be dissolved in it, nor have that heat in your mouth as *Aqua ardens*: This is indeed by the Philosophers call'd the Key of the whole Art of Philosophy, and as well Heaven, as our Quintessence, which arrives to so great a sublimity, that either with it by it self alone, or with the earthly Stars (*Metals*) the Operator of this work may do miracles upon the Earth.

Anno-

THE *twenty four following Kinds of* Menſtruums *will prove, that amongſt the* Diſſolvents *of the* Adepts, *no one is made without the* Vegetable Mercury, *or Spirit of* Philoſophical Wine; *for it is the foundation, beginning and end of them all: Yea it is according to the various and diſtinct degrees of its ſtrength, ſometimes the leaſt, ſometimes the greateſt of all the* Menſtruums. *It is the leaſt and weakeſt, when it doth by its ſimple Unctuoſity diſſolve only the unctuous or oyly parts of Vegetables, but either reject or leave untouched the Remainder being leſs oyly and heterogeneous to it ſelf: it becomes the ſtrongeſt when we temper its Unctuoſity with Arids, (that is, dry things, not Oyly) for ſo it is made homogeneous to things dry-oyly, and to things meerly dry. In reſpect of which Homogeneity, the Menſtruums of the* Adepts *differ from the common, becauſe they do by reaſon of the ſaid Homogeneity, remain with the things diſſolved inſeparably; yea, are augmented by them, but not with the leaſt ſaturation, tranſmuted and melted into a third ſubſtance, and ſo cannot part without the diminution or deſtruction of their former Virtues. The permanent Homogeneity of Menſtruums with things to be diſſolved, is the reaſon why Eſſences are made with ſimple Vegetable Menſtruums, but Magiſteries with the ſame compounded, and ſo theſe operate more ſtrongly, thoſe more weakly. This is it, to comprehend all in a word, which ſhews us the various kinds of Menſtruums diſtinct one from another in ſo many ſeveral degrees, now to be deſcribed and illuſtrated by our Annotations.*

But that you may more eaſily underſtand the following Receipts and me alſo, I thought it neceſſary to preadmoniſh ſome certain things concerning the Nature and Property of this Spirit of Wine, *leſt you ſhould judge amiſs of a thing not ſufficiently underſtood.*

Firſt, You are not to take the Spirit of common Wine, though never ſo much rectified, for the Philoſophical Spirit of Wine; for ſo the following Receipts of all Menſtruums would be erroneous and ſeducing.

Having occaſion (ſaith *Zacharias*) for a moſt excellent *Aqua-Vitæ* for the diſſolving of a mark or half a pound of Gold, we bought a large Veſſel of the beſt Wine, out of which we did by a Pellican obtain great plenty of *Aqua vitæ*, which was often rectified in many Glass-Vessels bought for that end: then we put one *Mark* of our Gold, being before calcin'd a whole month, and four *Marks* of *Aqua vitæ* into two Glass-Vessels, one Retort entring into the other, being sealed, and both placed in two great round Furnaces: we bought also Coals to the value of thirty Crowns at one time, to continue Fire under it for the space indeed of a whole Year. We might have kept Fire for ever before any congelation would have been made in the bottom of the Vessels, as the Receipt promised, no solution preceding; for we did'not operate upon a due matter, nor was that the true water of Solution, which ought to dissolve our Gold, as appeared by experience, *pag.* 783. *Vol.* 1. *Th. Chym.* Ripley *admonisheth us of the same thing, who saith,* Some think that this Fire (*this Fiery Spirit, of Philosophical Wine*) is drawn from Wine according to the common way, and that it is rectified by distillations often repeated, till its watry Phlegm, which impedes the power of its Igneity, be wholly taken from it. But when such a sort of Water (which Fools call Pure Spirit) though a hundred times rectified, be cast upon the Calxes of any Body, be it never so well prepared, we do nevertheless see, that it is found weak and insufficient as to the act of dissolving a Body, with the preservation of its Form and Species, *Cap.* 2. *suæ Medul. Phil.* Common Wine (*saith he a little lower*) is hot, but there is another sort much hotter, whose whole substance is by reason of its aerity most easily kindled by Fire, and the Tartar of this unctuous Humor is thick; for so saith *Raymund*: That Tartar is blacker than the Tartar from the black Grapes of *Catalonia*; whereupon it is called *Nigrum nigrius Nigro*; that is, *Black blacker than Black*: and this humidity being unctuous, doth therefore better agree with the Unctuosity of Metals, than the Spirit extracted from common Wine, because by its liquefactive virtue Metals are dissolved into Water; which operation the Spirit of (*Common*) Wine cannot perform; which, how strong soever, is nothing else but clear water mix'd with a kind of Phlegmatick Water, where on the contrary, in this our Unctuous Spirit distilled, there is no Phlegmatick aquosity found at all. But this thing being rare in our Parts, as well as other Countries, *Guido Montanor* therefore the Grecian Philosopher found out another unctuous humidity, which swims upon

other

other Liquors, which humidity proceeds from Wine; to the knowledge hereof attain'd *Raymund*, *Arnold*, and some other Philosophers, but how it might be obtained, said not.

> O tortas adeo mentes! assuetaque falli
> Artificum vario rerum per inania ductu
> Pectora! cum duris quid mollia vina metallis?
> Apta epulis, atque apta bibi suavissima vina?
> Hic tamen expressam prœlis torquentibus uvam
> Accipit, & phialæ postrema in parte reponit,
> Cujus in extremo rostrum connectitur ore, *&c.*

Thus facetiously sings the Poet and Adept Augurellus, Lib. 2. Chrys. pag. 206. Vol. 3. Th. Chym.

2. *That you take not any Oyl, though an hundred times rectified, instead of the Spirit of Philosophical Wine; for all oyly matters, whether distilled or expressed, natural or artificial, alone, but much more mixt with other things, as* Alkalies, Acids, *&c. do by distilling, digesting*, &c. *in Bath, Dung, Vapor*, &c. *become thick, pitchy, yea, at length dry, insipid, black as a Coal, and sometimes like a Tyle, capable of being made red hot; which is a manifest sign, that they want rather a Dissolvent, than are themselves Dissolvents.*

3. *It is necessary to observe that the Spirit of* Philosophical Wine *appears in two forms, either like an Oyl swimming upon all Liquors, or like the Spirit of* Common Wine (*to the Nature of which it comes sometimes nearer, and therefore doth from the Analogy borrow its Name*) *not swimming upon watry Liquors, but mixible with them and its own Phlegm; yet separable by simple Distillation, it easily by this means leaving its Phlegms behind it; but if being rectified, and kindled, it burns wholly away, it affords us the common sign of perfect rectification of the common Spirit, but however, they are not two, but one only Spirit, differing in degree of purity and subtilty. Which to prove, is not necessary, examples being obvious to us in almost every Description of the* Vegetable Menstruums.

4. *Lastly, Distinction must be made between the first and second Spirit of* Philosophical Wine, *Father and Son. The first doth in*

its preparation require Laborem Sophiæ, *the most secret, difficult and dangerous work of all true Chymistry. The second is easily made with the former Spirit according to the Rule of perfect Chymistry :* An Essence makes an Essence, a Magistery a Magistery. *Differ they do in Order, not in Nature ; they are both of one Virtue, though of different preparation: for this, as hath been lately said, is of a more easie, that of a mor difficult preparation. Essences they are both, the former artificial, the other natural, in Medecines therefore unequal, though alike in Chymistry , as* Menstruums , *but they are easily distinguished one from the other by their Epithets.* The first *hath these more general Names in the Latine Tongue,* Essentia Vini, Alcool Vini, Mercurius Vini, Vinum Vitæ, Vinum Salutis, Aqua Vitæ, Aqua ardens, Vinum adustum, Vinum sublimatum, *&c. Examples of which you will have in these and the like Receipts :* Take beaten Gold, and let it be resolved into Liquor by the Essence of Wine ; Paracelf. *in Descript. Auri Diaphoret. Lib. 3. de male curatis.* Take Flints, and dissolve them in the *Essence of Wine,* as Salt in Water, *&c.* Paracelf. *in Descript. Essentiæ silicum, cap. 18. de Morbis Tartar. pag.* 327. Take the *Crocus* of *Sol,* and the *Alcool of Wine,* corrected, *&c.* Paracelf. *in Tinct, Croci Solis, lib. de præparat. pag,* 81. The *Alcool of Wine* exiccated or corrected, is, *saith Paracelsus,* when the superfluity of the Wine is taken away, and the *Vinum ardens* remains dry and dephlegmed, without fatness, leaving no Fæces in the Vessel, pag. 507. *But as to this, you will have many more Examples, especially in the following Book of Medecines.*

The Second *Spirit of* Philosophical Wine *hath its Sirnames annexed to these more general Names, indicating the radix of its Original, of which the following Receipts may be for Examples.* Take the Leaves of *Sol* four scruples, of the *Alcool of Wine* drawn from a Pine , from Balm, ana. *&c.* Paracelf. *in descript. Balsami Solis, pag.* 90. *Chyr. major.* The Extraction of Mummy is made by mixing it with the *Essence of Wine* drawn from Celandine, *&c.* Parac. *in descript. Tincturæ Mumiæ, cap.* 10. *Lib.* 3. *de Vita long. pag.* 65. Take the *Essence of Wine* drawn from Celandine, Mercury of *Saturn,* &c. Paracelf. *Lib.* 8. *cap.* 10. *de Tumoribus, Pustulis,* &c. *pag.* 138. *Chyr. major. In these and the like Receipts he does by the* Alcool of Wine, *drawn from the* Pine, Balm, Celandine, *&c. mean the second Spirit of* Philosophical Wine, *or the Essence of those things made with the former Spirit, which also is* *proved out of the fifth Chapter of the third Book of long Life, pag. 63. Where* Paracelsus *calls the Essences of Herbs the* Elixir of Life, *or* the Wine of Health, *made from this or that Herb :* which (*he saith*) will be manifested in the example of Balm. Digest Balm (*with the first Spirit of Philosophical Wine*) a Philosophical Month in an Athanar, then separate so, as that the duplicated Elements may appear apart, and the Quintessence; which is the *Elixir of Life*, will presently shew it self, in *Nepitha* sharp, in *Lolium* yellow, in *Tincium* blackish, in *Lupulus* thin and white, in *Cuscuta* harsh, in others likewise to be judg'd according to the Prescript of Experience. Moreover that Spirit being extracted, and separated from the other, behold the Wine of Health, (*Essence of Balm*) in which the Pseudo-Philosophers have earnestly laboured some Ages, yet never acquired any thing. And a good part of them that followed *Raymund* (*intending to follow him according to the Letter, understanding Wine red or white*) emptied some Butts of Wine in extracting the Quintessence of Wine, but found nothing at all but burnt Wine, which they unhappily used for the Spirit of Wine: sufficient it is to have thus admonished the *Spagyrist*, which way the Quintessence may be had in Herbs.

This twofold, the first as well as second Spirit of Wine may be made not only out of the Vegetable, but the Animal Kingdom also : So is it read of the Aqua Vitæ *and Phlegm of the Wine of Urine, in the 16th. Experiment of* Lully, *and in Paramiro* Paracelsi, *pag.* 57. Many have diligently laboured to find in man his own Health, *Aqua vitæ*, *Lapis Philosophorum*, *Arcanum*, *Balsamum*, *Aurum potabile*, and the like. Which they did rightly; for all those things are in him, as also in the external world. *So also hath he a description of the Liquor of Flesh, pag.* 505. Take of the Liquor of Flesh six ounces, of Mummy, *&c. Here by Liquor, he means the Wine of Flesh, which is proved by* Paracelsus *himself; saying*, Where and according to this it is to be noted, that the Wine of Balm is a Secret in an Asthma : Here also it is to be observed, that by *Pulmonaria*, not the Herb, but the Liquor, that is, the Wine of it hath place in this Cure : *In which words, the Liquor and Wine of* Pulmonaria, *are synonimous. So in Lib.* 8. *de Tumoribus, cap.* 3. *By the* Liquor of Hermodactils. *And cap.* 9. *By the* Liquor of Balm; *and lib.* 9. *cap.* 4. *By the* Liquor

Par-

Parthenion, *And cap.* 5. *By the* Liqnor of Bdellium, &c. *The Wines or Essences of them all ought to be understood. Though neither the first nor second Spirit can be produced out of the dry Kingdom of Minerals (there are indeed some purely Oyly, as* Oleum Petræ, Naphthæ, Carbonum fossilium, Succini, Agathis, &c. *which are reputed Members of this Kingdom, the Oleosity of which notwithstanding differs so little from the Unctuosity of Vegetables and Animals, that scarce deserve to be called Subjects thereof) yet for the same reason that the Essences and Liquors of Vegetables are called Wines, is an Essence of the Mineral Kingdom, sometimes also called the Liquor and Wine of Minerals; so the Liquor or Essence of Vitriol or Copper is called* Wine of the first Metal, *Cap.* 12. *Lib.* 3. *de Vita longa, pag.* 65.

Being now instructed by the light of these Premises, let us come nearer to the Spirit of Wine of Lully, *which we shall find like an Oyl swimming upon its Phlegms, deduced not from the Common, but Philosophical* Aqua vitæ *by Circulation: But all other Essences being made by the help of some certain Essence, this first Essence of Wine alone must by its own virtues emerge its self out of its own fæculencies and impurities: In this respect the making of* Philosophical Wine (*red or white*) *renders the work of all the most secret Chymistry most difficult and abstruse; of which we shall by the Blessing of God) clearly and truly treat in a particular Book; namely, our Fifth. Our purpose at present is to prosecute the Use of this Wine in the making of* Menstruums, *where we find* Aqua vitæ *the first and weakest of all* Menstruums, *which, being by circulation alone reduced into an Oyl, is made much more excellent than before.* Lully's *Receipt is clear enough; yet however we thought it advisable to confirm at least, if not illustrate it with the Receipts of other Adepts.* Johannes de Rupescissa, *a Scholar of* Lully, *had so great an esteem for the first Distinction of his Master's Book of* Essence, *that he made it his own with a little alteration: He hath described the Spirit of* Philosophical Wine *after this manner:*

II. The

2. The Eſſence, Soul or Spirit of Wine of *Johannes de Rupeſciſſa, deſcribed Chap 5. of his Book de Quinteſſentia.*

REpute me not a Liar, in calling *Aqua ardens* a Quinteſſence, and ſaying that none of the modern Philoſophers and Phyſicians have attained to it, *Aqua ardens* being commonly found every where ; for I ſpoke true of a certain : for the Magiſtery of a Quinteſſence is a thing occult, and I have not ſeen above one, and him a moſt approved Divine, that underſtood any thing of the Secret and Magiſtery of it : And I affirm for a truth, that the Quinteſſence is *Aqua ardens*, and is *Aqua ardens*. And may the God of Heaven put prudence in the heart of Evangelical Men, for whom I compoſe this Book, not to communicate this Venerable Secret of God to the Reprobates : Behold now I open the Truth to you. Take not Wine too watry, nor Wine that is black, earthy, inſipid, but noble, pleaſant, ſavoury, and odoriferous Wine, the beſt that can be found, and diſtill it through cooling pipes ſo oft, till you have made the beſt *Aqua ardens* you can ; that is, you diſtill it from three to ſeven times ; and this is the *Aqua ardens* which the modern Phyſicians have not acquired. This water is the Matter out of which the Quinteſſence which we intend principally in this Book, is extracted : becauſe when you have your noble water, you muſt cauſe ſuch a Deſtillatory to be made in a Glaſs-makers Furnace, all entire of one piece, with one only hole above, by which the water muſt be put in and drawn out ; for then you ſhall ſee the Inſtrument ſo compleatly formed, that, that which by the virtue of Fire aſcends, and is diſtilled into the Veſſel through the Pipes, may be again carried back, in order to aſcend again, and again deſcend continually day and night, till the *Aqua ardens* be by the will of God above, converted into a Quinteſſence ; and the underſtanding of the Operation is in this ; becauſe the beſt *Aqua ardens* that can be made, hath yet a material mixture of the four Elements ; therefore it is by God ordained, that the Quinteſſence which we ſeek for, ſhould be by continual Aſcenſions and Deſcenſions ſeparated from the corruptible compoſition of the four Elements; and this is done, becauſe that which is a ſecond time or oftner ſublimed, is more pure and glorified, and ſeparated from the corruption of the four Elements, than when it aſcends only one time, and ſo to a thouſand times, and that which is by continual aſcent and deſcent ſublimed, comes at length to ſo great an altitude of Glorification, as to be almoſt an incorruptible Compound, as Heaven it ſelf, and of the Nature of Heaven; it is therefore called Quinteſſence, becauſe it is in reference to our Body as the Heavens in reſpect to the whole World; almoſt after the ſame manner, ſo far as Art can imitate Nature, in a near and connatural ſimilitude.

Circular Diſtillation therefore being for many days made in a Veſſel of Circulation, you muſt open the hole which is in the head of the Veſſel, which is indeed ſuppos'd to have been ſeal'd with a Seal made of *Lutum Sapientiæ*, compounded of the fineſt Flower and the White of an Egg, and of wet Paper moſt carefully pick'd and mix'd, to prevent the leaſt exhaling. And having opened the Hole, if the Odour (which ought to be ſuper-admirable, above all the Fragrancies of the world) which ſhall ſeem to have deſcended as it were from the ſublime Throne of the moſt glorious God; be ſo great, that ſetting the Veſſel in a corner of a houſe, it ſhall by an inviſible force with the fragrancy of the Quinteſſence (which is wonderful and highly miraculous) attract to it ſelf all people that enter in; then have you the Quinteſſence which you heard of; to which none of the modern Philoſophers and Phyſicians (except him that I excepted before) have ſo far as I have been able to underſtand, attained. But if you find not the Odour and Influence of attracting men, as I ſaid, ſeal the Veſſel as before, and bring it to the heat above deſcribed, in order to compaſs your deſire by Sublimations and Circulations; namely, in finding out this Quinteſſence ſo glorified, into an Odour of ineſtimable fragrancy and ſavour glorified to a wonder, and the influx of attraction before expreſſed; and not only ſo as to yield a wonderful Scent, but alſo to raiſe it ſelf more fully to a kind of incorruptibility: it hath not that heat in your mouth which *Aqua ardens* hath; nor that moiſtneſs, that is, ſuch an Aqueity flowing, becauſe the acute heat of the *Aqua ardens*; and its watery moiſtneſs is by

Sub-

Sublimations and Circulations wholly consumed, and the Terreity will remain apart in the bottom: And the Heaven as well as Stars, of which this our Quintessence is compounded both as to Matter and Form, are not as that which is compounded of the four Elements; but there is but little of it glorified so much even to the highest, fill'd with so noble a form, that the power of Matter cannot aspire to any other Form, and so remains uncorrupted, till the Composition be destroyed by command of the Creator: Nor is the Quintessence which we seek, altogether reduced to the incorruption of Heaven; as neither is Art equal to Nature: yet notwithstanding it is incorruptible in respect of the Composition made of the four Elements, because should it be altogether incorruptible, as Heaven, it would absolutely perpetuate our Body; which the Author of Nature, the Lord Jesus Christ forbids. Now have I opened to you much of the Secret, to the Glory of the immortal God.

Paracelsus extracts his Essence of Philosophical Wine *not out of* Aqua ardens, *but out of* Philosophical Wine *it self: Thus;*

3. The Spirit of Wine of *Paracelsus: Described, Chap. 9. of the Third Book of Long Life, pag. 64.*

YOur Wine being powred into a Pelican, digest in Horse-dung, and that the space of two Months continually, you will see it so thin and pure, that a Fatness, *which is the Spirit of Wine*, will of it self appear in the superficies. Whatsoever is under this is Phlegm, without any nature of Wine; but the Fatness alone being put into a Phial, and digested by it self, is of most excellent energy for long Life.

Guido *used the following Method, little differing from the* Paracelsian.

4. The Essence of Wine according to *Guido*, *Described, Pag.* 1. *Thesaur. Chym.*

TAke White or Red Wine, which is better, distil by *Balneo* till the Matter remain in the consistence of Honey, which being divided into two parts in a duplicated Cucurbit, mixt with the distilled Liquor, and joyn together again, and after the digestion of six weeks, a green Oyl will swim upon the Matter; which separate through a Funnel.

From the Receipts, we think these Things following worthy of Observation.

1. *That the Wine, Red or White, is not Common, but Philosophical, and that is the only thing that is obscure in these four Books; to be understood not according to the Letter, but by Analogy: but* Aqua ardens, Aqua vitæ, Spirit *or* Essence *of a* Philosophical Wine *are the proper Names of it.*

2. *That the* Aqua ardens *of* Philosophical Wine *doth in some things agree with the Properties of* Common Spirit of Wine; *namely, it goes before its Phlegm in distillation: it is rectified as the* Common, *from its Phlegm. Lastly, being rectified, it is known by burning Linnen, Sugar,* &c.

3. *That this* Aqua ardens *doth by Circulation dayly lose its moisture and sharpness; and is at length converted into a swimming Oyl, the Essence and Spirit of* Philosophical Wine. *But who ever reduced* Common Spirit of Wine, *or* Aqua Vitis, *by bare Circulation into an Oyl? Who, I say, hath by continual Circulation brought that Oyl to Driness; so as to be sublimeable as a volatile Salt, and that not but by a strong Fire, as* Isaacus *affirms himself to have experienced, in the Description of his Vegetable Stone? Of which lower in the Third Book.*

4. *That the* Oyl, *or* Essence of Wine *may be divers ways made out of* Philosophical Wine.

5. *That not only the Time, but also the Scent, Colour,* &c. *of the* Essence *are varied according to the variety of Method: The Essence of* Lully *is like Heaven, that is, of a Sky-colour; the Oyl of* Guido *is green.*

6. *That it hath not a Scent so fragrant, unless it hath a Body (especially a Metallick or Mineral) dissolved in it.*

7. *That this Heaven, the first of all* Menstruums, *is also a Medecine; and is called the* Essence *or* Specifick *to a long Life.*

8. *That it is called Heaven for several Reasons by* Lully.

First, *Because it works Contraries, like Heaven.* Our Vegetable *Menstruum*, saith *Lully*, the Celestial Animal, which is call'd Quintessence, preserves Flesh from corruption, comforts things elemented, restores former Youth, vivifies the Spirit, digests the crude, hardeneth the soft, rarifies the hard, fattens the lean, wasteth the fat, cools the hot, heats the cold, dries the moist, moistens also the dry: One and the same thing can do contrary operations. The Act of one thing is diversified according to the nature of the Receiver; as the heat of the Sun, which hath contrary operations; as in drying Clay, and melting Wax: yet the Act of the Sun is one in it self, and not contrary to it self.

Secondly, *Because like Heaven it receives the Forms of all Things.* As the universal Form (*the Macrocosmical Heaven*) hath an appetite to every Form, so the Quintessence (*of Philosophical Wine*) to every Complexion; whereby it is evidently manifest, that the Quintessence of things is said to be of that complexion to which it is adjoyned; if joyned to hot, hot; if to cold, cold, *&c.* This therefore the Philosophers called Heaven; because as Heaven affords us sometimes heat, sometimes moisture, *&c.* so the Quintessence in mens Bodies at the Artist's pleasure, *&c. Distinct.* 1. *Lib. Essentiæ.* To this Heaven we apply its Stars; which are Plants, Stones and Metals, to communicate to us Life and Health, *Ibid.*

Thirdly, *Because like Heaven it moveth all things from power to act.* Therefore Heaven or our *Mercury* is the Cause and Principle moving C (C) (Metals) from power to act: And in this point knows the understanding of an Artist, that D (*our Heaven*) hath action upon C, and (C) ruling and governing, and reducing it into action; as Heaven brings that which is in Elemental things, by its own motion into action, *&c.* For we call it Heaven, by reason of its motion; because as the upper Heaven moves the universal Form, and first Matter, and Elements, and Senses, to compound Elemented Individuals; so

D

D moves C, and (C) and the four Elements to M, (*the Sulphur of Nature, or Philosophers Mercury*) or to Q (*the Tincture*) *Distinct*. 3. *de quarto principio Libri Essentiæ*.

4. *Because like Heaven, it is incorruptible. Aqua vitæ* is the Soul and Life of Bodies, by which our Stone is vivified; therefore we call it Heaven, and Quintessence, and incombustible Oyl, and by its infinite other Names, because it is incorruptible almost, as Heaven, in the continual circulation of its motion, *pag*. 145. *Elucid. Testam.*

5. *Because it is of the colour and clarity of Heaven.* Heaven or our *Mercury* is the fourth Principle in this Art, and is signified by D, of an azure colour and line, and is signified by that colour, because it is celestial, and of a celestial Nature, as we said before in the description of it, *Dist*. 3. *Lib. Essentiæ*,

This Essence Johannes de Rupescissa *calls* Humane Heaven, *for the following Reasons:*

We ought to seek that thing which is to the four Qualities of which our Body is compounded, as is Heaven in respect of the four Elements: Now the Philosophers called Heaven Quintessence in respect of the four Elements, because Heaven is in it self incorruptible and immutable, and not receiving strange impressions, but by the command of God; so also, the thing which we seek, is in respect of the four Qualities of our Body, a Quintessence, in it self incorruptible so made, not hot dry with Fire, nor moist cold with Water, nor hot moist with Ayr, nor cold dry with Earth; but is it a Quintessence able to work Contraries, as the incorruptible Heaven; which, when it is necessary, infuseth a moist Quality, sometimes a hot, sometimes a cold, sometimes a dry: Such a Radix of Life is the Quintessence, which the most High created in Nature, with power to supply the necessity of the Body to the utmost term which God hath appointed to our Life: And I said that the most High created the Quintessence, which is by the Art of man extracted from the Body of Nature, created by God: And I will name it by its three Names attributed to it by the Philosophers: It is called *Aqua ardens*, *Anima*, or *Spiritus Vini*, and *Aqua Vitæ*. And when you have a mind to conceal it, call it it Quinteſſence; becauſe this is its Nature, and this is its Name, the greateſt Philoſophers have been willing to diſcloſe to no man, but cauſed the Truth to be buried with them: And that it is not moiſt as the Element of Water, is demonſtrated, becauſe it burns; which is a thing repugnant to Elementary Water. That it is not hot and moiſt as Ayr, is declared, becauſe dry Ayr may be corrupted with every thing, as appears in the generation of Spiders; but that remains always uncorrupt if it be kept from expiring. That it is not dry and cold as Earth, is expreſly manifeſt, becauſe it is exceeding ſharp, and heats extreamly: And that it is not hot and dry as Fire, is apparent to the Eye, becauſe it infrigidates hot things, and waſtes and eradicates hot Diſeaſes. That it conduceth to incorruptibility, and preſerves from corruptibility, I will demonſtrate by an Experiment; for if any Bird whatſoever, or piece of Fleſh, or Fiſh be put into it, it will not be corrupted ſo long as it ſhall continue therein; how much more will it therefore keep the animated and living Fleſh of our Body from all corruption? This Quinteſſence is the humane Heaven, which the moſt High created for the preſervation of the four Qualities of mans Body as Heaven, for the preſervation of the whole Univerſe. And know of a certain, that the modern Philoſophers and Phyſicians are altogether ignorant of this Quinteſſence, and of the truth and virtue thereof: But by the help of God I will hereafter declare to you the Magiſtery of it. And hitherto I have taught you a Secret, the Quinteſſence, that is, the humane Heaven, *Cap. 2. Lib. Eſſentiæ.*

9. *Laſtly, That many Receipts more obſcure, and otherwiſe intelligible by no man, are by theſe illuſtrated.*

The

The Second KIND.

Simple Vegetable Menstruums *made of the Spirit of* Philosophical Wine, *and the hottest Vegetables, Herbs, Flowers, Roots,* &c. *being Oyly.*

5. The Anima Metallica, or Lunaria Cœlica of Lully; *Described in Composit. Animæ Transmut. pag.* 193. *Vol.* 3. *Theat. Chym.*

FIrst you must know, that the Matter of our Stone, or of all the Stones of the Philosophers, together with Precious Stones, which are generated or compounded by Art, is this Metallick Soul, and our *Menstruum* rectify'd and acuated, or the *Lunaria Cœlica*, which among the Philosophers is called *Vegetable Mercury*, produced from Wine red or white, as is clearly manifest, being revealed to us by God, in our *Figura Individuorum*, *Distinct.* 3. *Libri Quint. Essent.* &c.

But first, it is expedient to draw our *Menstruum* by Art from Death, that is, the Impurities and Phlegm of Wine, by the Office of an Alembick, and to acuate it in distillation with pertinent Vegetables; such as are *Apium sylvestre*, *Squilla*, *Solatrum*, *Carduus*, *Oliandrum*, *Piper nigrum*, *Euphorbium*, *Viticella* or *Flammula*, and *Pyrethrum*, an equal quantity of all, and pulverized. Then the *Menstruum* must be circulated continually for the space of ten days in hot Dung, or *Balneo Mariæ*.

Anno-

THE *Unctuous Spirit of* Philosophical Wine *attracts none but the Unctious natural Essences of Vegetables, as we shall observe below in the Book of Medecines. Essences being thus extracted, as also all other Oyly things, crude or expressed, and all distilled of both Kingdoms, Animal and Vegetable, this Spirit of Wine doth by simple digestion divide into two distinct parts, two Oyls or Fats, whereof one is the Essence of the thing, the other the Body: The Essence so made we named the* Second Spirit of Wine. *Both Essences, this by Division, and that by Extraction prepared, are by longer digestion made one with the aforesaid Spirit of Wine. For those things which are of one and the same purity, and of a Symbolical Nature, are easily mix'd together, and that inseparably, and so an Essence made by an Essence, is joyned to that Essence. And if we protract Digestion further, one of the Fats, namely, the Body less Oyly, and therefore left hitherto, is at length received also into a Symbolical Nature, by reason of which mixtion, not only is the Spirit multiplied, but also made fitter for the Dissolutions of dry things, because the Particles of this Body less Oyly incline to dryness; concerning which way we treat in this Receipt, in the Prescription of which, the Oyl drawn out of Oyly Vegetables, is by distillation together with the Spirit of* Philosophical VVine, *circulated into a Magistery (or double Essence, Natural and Artificial; of which, lower in its place) by which the Spirit of Wine is multiplied, and made more homogeneous to dry Bodies. There is the same* Menstruum, *but a little otherwise described in his Natural Magick. pag.* 358. *thus;* Take *Nigrum nigrius Nigro*, and distil ten or eight parts of the same in a Glass-Vessel, and in the first distillation you must receive only one half; this again distil, and hereof take a fourth part; and the third distillation you must take in a manner all, and so distil that part eight or nine times, and it will be perfect, but not rectified under one and twenty Distillations. Take of this VVater a quarter of a pound, and acuate the same by distilling it with the Vegetables, which are *Apium Sylvestre*; and so of the rest, of which was spoken above in *Anima Transmutationis, in the Chapter which begins, First you must know*, &c. And then put it into a Vessel of Circulation, in hot dung, or in the remains of a Wine-preſs with the preſervation of the Species. Which water is alſo one of the things without which nothing can be effected in the Magiſtery of this Art.

That Menſtruum *which ought to be drawn from the Death of Wine by the Office of an Alembick, acuated with the ſaid Vegetables, and at length circulated, is the Spirit of* Philoſophical Wine, *which is by theſe degrees ſo exalted, as to be by* Lully *deſervedly called the Matter of all the Stones of the Philoſophers, and vertuous Stones (that is, Precious Stones)* Anima Metallica, *and* Lunaria Cœlica, *which alſo is called* Vegetable Mercury, *deduced from Wine red or white.*

The Matter of which this Menſtruum *is made, is called Wine in the former Receipt : the* Menſtruum *muſt be extracted from the Death of Wine : But in the latter it is called* Nigrum nigrius Nigro. *To theſe two* Lully *adds a third ſynonimous, pag.* 1. *Teſt. noviſſimi.* Take red Wine, which we call the Liquor of *Lunaria* and *Nigrum nigrius Nigro. By which ſynonimous Terms none but a Fool can underſtand* Common Wine; *for the common Spirit herefrom diſtilled, is altogether inſufficient to perform ſuch and ſo great things; yea, all the* Arcanums *of the more ſecret Chymy, which we are ſolicitous to deſcribe, would be proſtituted to all men, were this one only Word literally underſtood: by Wine therefore is meant a Philoſophical Secret hidden from all the unexpert.*

It is expedient to draw from the Death of Wine, by the Office of an Alembick, *that is, we muſt rectifie ſo often till it become moſt pure, without the Fæces and Phlegm of Wine, which is by* Lully *called the Death of the Spirit.* It is (*ſaith he*) purged from all its Superfluity, and Phlegmatick corruptible matter, which is its Death, and which mortifies its Spirit, which hath the power of vivifying its Earth; let therefore the corruptible Phlegm be purged and ſeparated from it by a ſubtil method, which I will tell you: For what reaſon? becauſe if it be not well purged, its Earth will never become white, nor will Matrimony be made between the Body and Spirit; and ſo that Spirit is call'd the Spirit of the Stone *in Apertorio.*

The Method of Rectification omitted in the former Receipt, is deſcribed in the latter, as alſo in Epiſtola accurtatoria: *This Rectification of* Philoſophical Wine Sendivogius *underſtood not, as appears*

appears by the Sixth of his Epistles, **Brux.** 25. *Martii* 1646. *Where thus :* The second Article (*my Companion*) of the *Pagesian* work, endeavours to repeat the mysterious way of extracting and preparing *Mercury*, more than needed, the Authority of *Lully* being misunderstood, and the Precepts of other Philosophers ill applied, he commanding the tenth part of his *Magnesia* first ascending by distillation to be saved, as the only useful, and truly Mercurial substance; but the other nine parts proceeding by continuance of distillation, to be cast away as of no use, to this end, that the said tenth part reserved, might at length be restored to the Earth remaining after compleat distillation, (which Earth is foolishly supposed to be the Salt and Sulphur of *Mercury*) and by repeated cohobations, inhumations, digestions and sublimations described by him, united ; but it is a grievous Error, for that which Authors declare concerning the tenth part containing the Spirit, and of inhumations in its own Earth, is otherwise referred than to the extraction and preparation of *Mercury*, as shall be elsewhere in time demonstrated ; nor for the said extraction and preparation of *Mercury* is there any Rule to be used besides the bare distilling of *Magnesia*, whereby the Spirit and Oyl are together elevated to a Siccity even of the *Fæces*, and separation of the Spirit from the Oyl, and rectification of the same Spirit oftentimes repeated : But these things we will in their proper place more amply treat of in the Method of operating.

Parisinus, *a Disciple of* Lully, *will correct* Sendivogius, *who learnt of* Lully, *to rectifie his Spirit of* Philosophical Wine *after this manner.*

Take A (*Chaos, our Vegetable* Mercury, *in which the four Elements are found confused, pag.* 271. *Vol. sext. Theat. Chym.*) and put it in a Vessel to be distilled through Y (*Balneo, pag.* 276.) and in this temperate distillation gather its B. (*Celestial ardent Spirit, pag.* 269.) continue that distillation this way and method till you attain to the Signs declared in our *Apertorial*, and till you know that the said B. is dissolved and separated from its Elemental Nature, continuing this Magistery even to the fourth Revolution : Then put this Celestial fiery Matter into a pure Vessel, and distil slowly with ordinary fire, and take only a tenth part; in the second distillation take half, and in the

 third,

third, two parts of three; and in the fourth, take four parts of five, and more: Then take that last Celestial Water, and distil it three or four times by the Rule abovesaid, taking the whole without any separation appointed. This observe, and admire the necessity of this Mystery and Foundation, and you will understand the reason why dull and ignorant men make the worst Bread with the finest and purest Flower, because they mix the course part with the fine: The same thing happens to presumptuous Artists, who perswade themselves that they are able to find out the beauty of our Quintessence with the exuberated Spirit negligently purified, without an exact separation of the pure from the impure. *in Elucid. pag.* 230. *Vol.* 6. *Theatri Chym.*

Which way notwithstanding of rectification so exactly to observe, there seems to me to be no necessity; rectification of the Spirit being good enough, which way soever done, either with fewer or more cohobations, provided it be separated from the impurities of the Wine, which you will know (*saith Lully*) when it burns a piece of Linnen by reason of its vehement heat, *that is, as elsewhere more clearly, till a Linnen Cloth moistned with this Spirit, and kindled, be wholly consumed. This rectified Spirit is in distilling, sharpned with the oyly Vegetables nominated in the Receipt, the Oyls of which, being nearest to it, it easily carrieth with it, and is impregnated with the same, and acuated by the aridity contained in them: Yet are we not obliged to use these Vegetables only, and no other, or is it necessary to mix all of them together, as if one or two would not suffice. The Oyl of any Vegetable, or drawn out of a Vegetable with the help of the Spirit of* Philosophical Wine, *or already made, and added to the Spirit of* Philosophical Wine, *will here satisfie us. I will give one form or other in confirmation of this kind of* Menstruums; *of which sort is,*

6. The

6. The Aqua Vitæ of Paracelſus, *Pag.* 508. *Tom.* I.

TAke of the *Alcool of Wine* exſiccated three pounds, of the Flowers of Roſemary, Macis, Lavender, of each half an ounce; of Cubebs, Cloves, Cinamon, of each two ounces; of Maſtick, half an ounce; of both ſorts of Storax, half a dram of each; of Doronicum, three ounces; and cohobate ſe ven times.

The following Uſe beſides the Alcool of Wine *exſiccated, teſtifies, that this Water is made with the Spirit of* Philoſophical Wine. Take of the Leaves of Gold, Num. 20. of Pearls not perforated, Granats, Rubies, of each half a drachm; digeſt for a Month: Then take of this Oyl three or four grains with Malago wine, or the water of Majoram or Sage. *This* Menſtruum *is Vinum Eſſatum or Eſſentificatum, or Spirit of* Philoſophical Wine *impregnated with the Eſſences of the Oyly Ingredients, with which* Paracelſus *diſſolves Gold and Precious Stones into a moſt noble Oyl or Elixir, which he ſays is a Secret againſt the ſuperfluity of Womens* Menſtruums. *The Deſcription of this Water being clear, requires no other Light: I will therefore propoſe another Receipt more obſcure.*

7. Another Aqua Vitæ of *Paracelſus*, *Pag.* 115. *Chyr. Min.*

TAke of the waters of Meliſſa, Roſes, Cheirus, Sage, Balſamus, of each one pound: of all the Peppers, Cubebs, Ginger, Cinamon, Maſtick, red Myrrh, Mace, Cloves, of each two ounces; of the Juyce of Honey, half a pound; of rectifi'd Aqua Vitæ, five pound: Let them be all digeſted together for the ſpace of nine days, and after that ſeparated, and diſtilled in a Pelican into a Spirit. Then to this Liquor add an Apple roaſted and broken, and let them be digeſted together with the following Spices upon Aſhes for three days; of which take five grains every day. *The Spices are theſe*;

Take

Take of Cinamon, Cloves, Mace, of each two ounces; of Cheirus, Anthos, of each half an ounce; of Amber, two drachms; of Musk, five grains; of Zibeth, half a drachm; of Ginger, Cubebs, Nutmegs, of each one ounce and half; of Amomus, two drachms; of Zedoary, two ounces and half; of Grains of Paradiſe, one ounce and half. After Digeſtion of them all, ſeparate, and keep the Matter in Glaſs Veſſels very cloſe ſtopp'd.

From the Doſe it ſelf of this Preſcription, it is manifeſt that the operation is meerly Philoſophical; *for if by* Aqua vitæ *he would have underſtood the* Common Spirit of Wine, *it would be altogether ridiculous to give only five grains for a Doſe. We meet with many more* Menſtruums *of this kind, which little differing from the priſtine Nature of the Spirit of* Philoſophical Wine, *were leſs obſerved by ſome* Adepts; *wherefore* Chriſtophorus Pariſinus, *a Noble* Sicilian, *doth not very much commend this acuation of the Spirit of* Philoſophical Wine. Some (*ſaith he*) have made (*the aforeſaid Spirit*) acute with *Vitriol*, which way is very good; ſome with *Nitre*; ſome with *Cinnabar*; ſome with theſe two, ſome with all three; ſome with their Earth, which way diſpleaſeth me, becauſe a thick Unctuoſity and ponderoſity was hereby introduced; ſome uſe *Vegetables*, as Herbs, Roots, Flowers, and Seeds known to you, which have ſtrong (*Vegetable*) Mercuries in them; wherefore they that handled it after this manner, augmented rather its Vegetable Form (*Unctuoſity*) than that they made it more ſoluble. *Pariſinus in Elucidario, pag.* 231. *Vol.* 6. *Theat: Chym. For this reaſon,* Ripley *following the ſame Maſter as* Pariſinus, *believed theſe things to be covered with a Mantle of Philoſophy; for ſo he writes in his Medulla Philoſophiæ. Raymund* ſaith, it ought to be drawn out from the Death and Fæces of Wine for the ſpace of one hundred and twenty days, by continual rotation, in a Balneo of of the hotteſt Dung, and that it muſt be acuated with hot Vegetable things, as *Piper nigrum, Euphorbium, Pyrethrum, Anacardus, Squilla, Solatrum, Apium Sylveſtre,* and ſuch like; for without the virtue of theſe things, as he ſaith, it is not ſufficient to diſſolve Metals, except in a long time; but that nothing of doubt or ambiguity may appear, I ſay, that all theſe things are covered and ſhrowded with a Philoſophical Mantle: For his

his meaning is, that in this Spirit may be had another resoluble *Menstruum*, because without such a resolutive *Menstruum* Solution can never be made: And that resoluble *Menstruum* is generated only from the Metallick kind, and is by our resolutive *Menstruum* produced into act, *Ripley, pag.* 168. *Medul. Philos.* Ripley *did by the resoluble* Menstruum *produced into act by the* Menstruum *resolutive* (*that is, the Spirit of* Philosophical Wine) *mean a certain Mercurial Water; of the Preparation of which lower: where likewise it will appear that by the aforesaid Vegetables* Ripley *thought* Lully *intended running* Mercury; *yet neverthelefs his following* Menstruum *proves, that these Vegetables have been sometimes also taken by him literally.*

8. The Aqua Vitæ of *Ripley*. *Pag.* 338. *Viatici.*

THE *Menstruum* being distilled from the first Fæces, circulate it with the hottest Species, such as are, *Black Pepper, Euphorbium, Pyrethrum, Anacardus, Grains of Paradise,* and the like, for the space of 100 days in Balneo; and after that, distil only half of it, and make your putrefaction with it, &c.

It is here manifest that Ripley *took these* Vegetables, *Not* Argent vive, *because, Circulation being finished, he distilled only one half of the Spirit, as the most subtil part of the* Vegetables; *in which case that Metal* (Mercury) *though dissolved, would remain in the bottom. But whereas* Lully *acuates the Spirit by distilling, and then circulates;* Ripley *does this by circulating, and after that distils. To this* Aqua Vitæ *he sometimes adds Oyls, or Essences either of* Metals *or* Vegetables, *as followeth;*

9. The Compounded Aqua Vitæ of *Ripley*, *Pag.* 343. *Viatici.*

CIrculate the strongest red Wine with known Vegetables, for the space of 120 days, with continual Rotation in Balneo, and then draw only the purest Spirit by distillation; to which put the Oyl of the purest *Luna*, made without a Cor-

Corrosive; and let them be circulated together 100 days more, and then is the Water of the nature of the *Basilisk*, because as a *Basilisk* kills a man at an instant by the Aspect alone, so this Water being put upon *Argent vive* does without any other Fire, suddenly in a manner congeal it into the purest Silver: And note, if the Fire (*Oyl or Essence*) of Celandine be put in, or the Fire of the Flowers of Thyme, after the first Circulation, and they circulated together without the Oyl of *Luna*, the *Argent vive* will be much better congealed, *&c. But that which begets the greater scruple, is the Paraphrase of* Lully *himself upon this place.* We, *saith he*, would not have you ignorant of that you may extract our *Argent vive* (*Veget.*) from its Myne another way: The way (my Son) is to take the Herb which is called *Portulaca marina*, *Apium*, *Squilla*, &c. distil the Fæces which remain calcine, draw off the Salt with the distilled water, and abstract the water from it, purifie the Salt by often dissolving and coagulating, and you will have the Salt of the acuating Vegetable Herbs: These (*saith he*) I meant, when I said, acuate with acuating Vegetables, that is, the Salts, not the simple Herbs: *Wherefore you might say, it follows, that this Receipt of the Metallick Soul hath not at all been described, so as to be understood according to the Literal Sense; but I have my Answer ready, namely, that* Lully *acuated the Spirit of Wine with crude Vegetables also, it is easily proved by the third Distinction of his Book of Essence, in* Figura individuorum, *alledged by him, where he rehearseth the nearest Individuals, acuating the Spirit of* Philosophical Wine, *as are* red Wine, new Honey, Celandine, Flowers of Rosemary, Herb Mercury, red Lilly, Tartar, Mans Blood, and white Wine. *Why he chose these, not others, and these only, it is not my business to answer: that which we learn from thence, is, that he commended two of those Individuals to us before the rest*, Tartar *and* Honey, *of which thus.* There are some Individuals, in which Mercury (*Vegetable*) hath a free Act in some respect, in *Tartar* it hath one free operation only, and in *Honey* two, and this an Artist ought to know, that he may be certified in this Art, and the first Truth thereof. *He prefers* Tartar, *not for the sake of the* Tartar, *but the* Alkali *made from thence, and that he resolves as the best of* Alkalies per deliquium, *and circulates it being purified*

with

with the Spirit of Philosophical Wine, *according to the Doctrine prescribed* in prima Tabula individuorum, *in the* second Experiment, *and in other places. The* Alkali of Tartar *may be supplied with the* Alkalies of Honey, Celandine, *and the rest of the Individuals named by* Lully, *with which the* Adepts *did also sometimes acuate their Spirit of Wine, as shall be declared below in the Fifth Kind of* Menstruums : *But these things make also against the Literal sense of our Receipt, and do prove that the Salts of the* Vegetables, *not the crude* Vegetables *themselves were taken in the Receipt. But though he made choice of* Tartar , *because of the strongest* Alkali *to be from thence prepared, yet did he not for the same reason intimate, that Celandine, the Flowers of Rosemary, Herb Mercury, red Lilly, and mans Blood were better than the rest, because with these he proceeds another way ; for he separates the Elements from them with the Spirit of* Philosophical Wine, *from which he takes only the Fire or Oyl, which he circulates with the Spirit, and so acuates it, as is clearly enough evident* in secunda Tabula Individuorum.

But because Honey *surpasseth not only its own collateral Individuals, but also the* Tartar *it self (for he saith that the Spirit of Wine in* Tartar *hath one, but in* Honey *two free Operations) and therefore attributes his peculiar process to* Honey, *namely, by distilling the whole Comb, the* **Honey** *together with the Wax, with the Spirit of* Philosophical Wine *through an Alembick. Now between both processes of* Honey, *and the rest of the Individuals our Receipt keeps a middle station. If* Honey *be volatilized as to the whole substance, it becomes thereby a Magistery, which being joyn'd to the Spirit of* Philosophical Wine, *yields us a* Menstruum *of the Third kind. But the Fires or Oyls of Celandine, of the Flowers of Rosemary, common white and red Wine, &c. are by separation of the Elements made with the Spirit of* Philosophical Wine, *Essences, which being added to the said Spirit of Wine, do not alter, but multiply it rather, because an Essence is added to an Essence, that is, the second to the first Spirit of* Philosophical Wine. *But if Celandine, the Flowers of Rosemary, as also the Vegetables of our Receipt be distilled with the Spirit of* Philosophical Wine, *it does extract and elevate all their Unctuosity with it self, rejecting the aridity of them, being more simple, subtil, volatile, and less loaded with dry Particles, than the Unctuosity of crude Honey;*

and so by being circulated with the Spirit of Philosophical Wine; *it is made indeed a Magistery, yet more inclining to the nature of an Essence, and therefore less dry, and less altering the Spirit of Wine, than that of* Honey, *and so being now deservedly united with the aforesaid Spirit, it makes a* Menstruum *different from the* Menstruums *of the Third Kind. So the Literal Sense of our Receipt does hitherto stand unmoved. But not to derogate from the Authority of the Author, and his own Commentator* Lully, *it is necessary to suppose, that, the Spirit of* Philosophical Wine *being distilled upon the aforesaid Vegetables, he did sometimes out of the remainder prepare an* Alkali *by calcination, and acuate his Spirit with it, and so make a* Menstruum *of the Fifth Kind.*

From these and the like Receipts, we observe,

1. *That* Wine, Lunaria, Nigrum nigrius Nigro, *the Matter of the* Menstruum *of Vegetable Mercury or Soul of Metals, is not* Common, *but* Philosophical Wine; *nor that the Spirit of this Wine is the Common, but Philosophical* Aqua ardens.

2. *That a* Menstruum *of this kind is the unctuous Spirit of* Philosophical Wine *acuated, that is, tempered with the common Unctuosity of Vegetable Oyls. Mix, digest, and distil any common distilled Oyl with the Spirit of* Philosophical Wine, *and you will obtain a* Menstruum *of the Second Kind much sooner; yea, you will make the same in a moment, if you mix the Essence (Spirit) of* Philosophical VVine *with the Magistery of an oyly Vegetable.*

3. *That one oyly Vegetable (Saffron or Macis) of so many, is sufficient for the acuation of the Spirit of* Philosophical VVine; *nor yet will you err, if you take* Triacle; *which Spirit of* Triacle, *made with this Spirit of Wine, will be a* Menstruum *of this kind.*

4. *That these* Menstruums *are Medecines.*

5. *That these* Menstruums *made out of meer Vegetables, are properly called* Vegetable Menstruums, *tho' some which we call* Vegetable Menstruums *compounded, are by reason of the addition of Metals or Minerals, sometimes by the* Adepts *called* Mineral Menstruums: *so* Lully *in the 34th. Experiment, calls his* Circulatum majus *made of Gold and Silver, the true Mineral* Menstruum. *But we distinguish them from the Mineral* Menstruums, *because*

they

they are corrosive, being prepared with the acidity of Mineral Salts. But these are most sweet, without any Corrosive, and do kindly dissolve things that are to be dissolved.

6. *That a* Menstruum *is call'd the Soul of Metals.* Soul *is diversly taken among the* Adepts.

First, For perfect Metal, Gold or Silver. So Arnold *in Flore Florum*: Philosophers call the Soul a Ferment, because as the Body of man can do nothing without its Ferment or Soul, so is it in the thing propounded; for Ferment is a Substance which converts other things into its own Nature. And you must know, there is no Ferment, except *Sol* and *Luna*, that is, Gold and Silver appropriated to those Planets, &c. Ferment therefore must be introduced into the Body, because it is the Soul thereof. This is that which *Morienus* said, except you cleanse the unclean Body, and make it white, and infuse a Soul into it, you conduce nothing to this Magistery.

Secondly, For Metals, and other things, volatilized with a Philosophical Menstruum. *So* Lully *calls Gold and Silver volatilized in the preparation of his* Circulatum majus, Menstruum, *or animated Spirit.* Take, *saith he, the* animated Spirit of *Sol*, and the animated Spirit of *Luna*, joyn them together, &c. *So the Tinctures of Gold and Silver volatilized by a* Menstruum, *as also of imperfect Metals, are by him called Souls. So in the 20th. Experiment he hath the* Animal Water *of* Saturn; *in the 21th. Experiment, the* Soul *of* Mars. *Tea separating the Elements from all things, he calls the tinged distilled Liquors* Souls or animated Spirits, *because by them is the dead, dry and fixed Earth again revivified, volatilized, and reduced into a* Sal harmoniack. *See the Revivification of the Salt of* Tartar *by its own Water, in the Volatization of it given in the* Second Experiment.

Thirdly, For Menstruums *themselves. For* Menstruums *are the Souls of Metals, by which the Metals, otherwise dead, are animated and revivified: so* Lully *of this our* Menstruum, the Soul of Metals, *pag.* 195. *Comp. Anim. Transm.* Otherwise, *saith he*, Metals cannot be dissolved, unless they be animated with a *Vegetable Menstruum*, by the power of which, Resolution is made in things resoluble. *And in Elucid. Testam. pag.* 145. *Aqua vitæ* is the Soul and Life of Bodies, by which our Stone is vivified. *So also* Ripley *in Libro Mercurii, pag.* 108. *saith*, The Sperm of

 Me-

Metals is also called Metallick *Aqua Vitæ*, because it administreth life and health to Metals, being sick, dead, &c.

Fourthly, For the Unctuosity as well of the Metal as Menstruum. *Of both saith* Ripley, *pag.* 150. *Medullæ Phil.* There is some certain Similitude of the Trinity to be perceived in the Body, Soul and Spirit (*of our Work.*) The Body is the substance of the Stone; the Spirit is the Virtue (that is, the Quintessence, which excites Natures from Death) and the Soul is to be taken for the Ferment, which cannot be had but out of the most perfect Body (*Gold*) in Sulphur (of *Gold*;) there is a Terrestreity for the Body, and in Mercury (*Menstruum*) an aereal serenity for the Spirit; and in both a natural Unctuosity for the Soul: For they are all fermentable in the Unctuosity of the Body, being mix'd and inseparably united with it throughout its most minute parts, by which Soul is the Stone formed, because nothing can be any way formed without it.

7. *That this* Menstruum, *is called Vegetable Mercury, produced from red or white Wine. The Adepts have many Mercuries.*

The First *is, Common Argent vive, running or sublimed.*

The Second *is, The running Mercury of Bodies, extracted out of Metals by the Spirit of Philosophical Wine.*

A Third *is, Any Salt* Alkali, *especially fixed with the Spirit of Philosophical Wine.*

Lully *calcines Celandine, and from thence extracts a Salt; of which thus*; Repeat this Magistery so often, till you have extracted all the Salt, which is the Mercurial Part of that Individual (*Celandine.*) These things therefore being done, take all these Dissolutions (*Lixivia's*) and transmit them through a Filter, or Linnen-Cloth, that they may be purged from Terrestreity; then distilled by *Balneo* congeal, and the moisture being gone over, in the bottom of the Vessel will remain a Mercury or Salt, of a white colour; and by this means you will have extracted out of this Matter a *Mercury*, which hath almost innumerable Virtues of acuating the Vegetable Spirit, drawn from (*Philosophical*) Wine, so as to have the power of dissolving all Metals with the conservation of the Vegetative and Germinative Form.

In Magia Naturali, *He calls Tartar calcined, and impregnated with the Vegetable* Menstruum, *by being four times distilled, then resolved*

resolved per Deliquium, *and coagulated by the Name of Mercury*. And *saith he*, pag. 379, you wil have the Salt of Art, or Testamentary Mercury, without which is nothing done. *Sometimes the Salt, or* Caput Mortuum, *in the separation of the Elements, called exanimated Earth, he calls Mercury. So in* Exp. 6. *The inanimated Earth of Urine, dissolved in Water, filtred and coagulated, he calls Mercury*: Then, *saith he*, Keep our fixed Sal armoniack, our animal Sulphur, our fixed animal Mercury. Lay a little of which, upon a Fire-hot-plate, and if it melt as Wax without fume, it is a sign you have *Argent vive* fixed and perfectly depurated, wherewith you will be able to produce many Experiments. This is that Mercury, which hath afforded us most convenient relief.

The Fourth *Mercury, is either Vegetable or Animal; of which saith* Ripley *in Pupilla, pag.* 300. There are more Mercuries than the two above-said (*Mineral the red and green Lyon*) namely, the Vegetable and Animal Mercury, because both may be extracted out of some Liquors, as out of Blood and Eggs. *Lully Distinct.* 3. *Libri Essentiæ in Figuris & Tabulis Individuorum, describes the Vegetables and Animals, in which are found these Mercuries most readily.* There is, *saith he*, lastly this other Secret of Nature, for the Artist of this Art to know, and really have the knowledge of the Individuals,in which our Mercury is found most easily. Wherefore let the Artists of this Art know, that our Mercury is found in every Elemented Body, yet in some so remote, as to anticipate the Life of Man, before the Artist of this Art can possess it, being extracted, as is expedient: Wherefore we do in that place reveal those things which contain it most nearly. Of this Mercury, *saith Lully, Libro Mercuriorum, pag.* 8. VVhen we say common Mercury, we speak of that which the Philosophers understand;and when we say vulgar,we speak of that which the Rustick understands, and which is sold in Shops: *Which* Ripley *in the 326th pag. of his Concordance, thus expresseth*; VVhen I speak of Mercury, understand Mercury more common than common.

The Fifth is, *The Spirit of* Philosohical VVine, *which* Lully *in Exp.* 3. *calls Vegetable Mercury.* So, *saith he*, will you have a Vegetable Salt extracted from this Individual (*Honey*) which Salt is most precious, and hath the power of acuating the

Vege-

Vegetable Mercury, and diſſolving the two Luminaries, &c. in *Exp. 5. Salts he prepares out of Portulaca, Apium, Squilla, &c.* with all which, *ſaith he*, you may acuate the Vegetable Mercury extracted out of VVine, either joyntly or ſeverally; of which lower in the fifth kind of *Menſtruums.*

The Sixth *is, The* Philoſophical Menſtruum *it ſelf; for our preſent* Menſtruum *is called Vegetable Mercury, produced from white or red Wine.*

The Seventh *is, The animated Spirit or Air of every Body, in the ſeparation of the Elements, which Mercury being a Fire or Oyl, is called Sulphur in almoſt all Receipts.*

The Eighth *is,* Sal armoniack *Vegetable, Animal or Mineral, the Sulphur of Nature, which is alſo called our Mercury, Mercury Sublimate, and Philoſophers Mercury. Neceſſary it is we ſhould obſerve theſe things in the following Deſcriptions of* Menſtruums, *except we would ſome times confound the things themſelves with the Names.*

The Third KIND.

Simple Vegetable Menstruums *made of the Spirit of* Philosophical Wine, *and Oyly, Salts, or (such as can neither be called fixed nor volatile) hitherto called* Essential Salts, *such as are Sugar, Honey, Tartar of Common Wine, and other Vegetables.*

10. The Mellifluous Heaven of *Parisinus. In practica Elucid. p. 231. V. 6. Theat. Chym.*

THe way of acuating this Celestial and Burning B (*Spirit of Philosophical Wine*) is to take of the Substances declared to you what quantity you will: But we take the Substances of Flowers United (*that is, the Substance of New Honey, pag. 269.*) which we put in a Vessel to distill all the Aquosity through Y. (*Balneo Mariæ. pag. 270.*) Then we pour in three parts and more of B upon that Substance prepared after this manner; shutting the Vessel with its Cover, called *Antenotorium*, and put it in Putrefaction for the space of one Natural Day; then with three Distillations by Z. (*Fire of Ashes, pag. 270.*) we distill till we obtain all the Mercurial Part with the whole Juice of the Blessed Substance by that Method, then repeat the aforesaid Magistery with New Substance of Flowers, and making this Regiment four times, at the end of which, you have reduced B solutive from Power into Act by Virtue of the *Manna* of the Flowers United.

Now take a strong Glass Vessel, able to hold as much Water, as as a common Pitcher, with a Neck one ſpan and a half long, to which another Glaſs Veſſel, containing a fourth part only of the Pitcher, muſt be joyned, and well luted: Into this Veſſel put four Pounds of C (*the ſaid* Menſtruum *made of Honey*) to Circulate in *Balneo*, or Horſe Dung, the ſpace of thirty or forty Days, at the expiration of which time, you will have C converted into D (*into the Quinteſſence in its Perfection, drawn from excellent Wine, which is the Form of the Univerſal Body reduced into B, and B into C, and then Circulation to be made. This Quinteſſence is Vegetable, becauſe, all the reſt of the ſharp Waters deſtroying Metals, this alone doth by its Virtue vegetate, augment and multiply them. Wherefore this Water is the Myſtery of Art, becauſe it is Burning, Calcines, and diſſolves Bodies, if it be perfectly rectified, pag.* 269.) But the Sign of knowing, whether this Converſion be made, will be a ſediment in the bottom of the Veſſel, like that, which appears in the Urine of a ſound Man. When the Glorious Body draws nigh, after thirty Days in the end of Perfection, then will you ſee D, or the Quinteſſence in greater clarity and ſplendor than any Diamond. The clarity whereof ſurpaſſes all Precious Things, ſo as that it is difficult to judge, whether that Divine Liquor be in or out of the Veſſel: Then you muſt ſeparate our Heaven from its Sediment or *Hypoſtaſis* with Induſtry, keeping it in a Veſſel well luted in a cold place, that nothing may from thence expire. This Quinteſſence is by the Philoſophers called *Spiritus Vivus*, becauſe it gives Life to humane Bodies, and Metalls, as alſo *Aqua Argenti vivi*, *Aqua Vitæ*, *Aqua Cæleſtis*, *Aqua Divina*, *Stella Dianæ*, *Anima*, *Spiritus Mercurii noſtri Vegetabilis*, *Fumus*, *Ventus*, *Cælum Noſtrum*. To conclude, infinite Names have been given it, which notwithſtanding ſignifies one and the ſame thing.

Annota-

Annotations.

THe *antecedent acuition of the Spirit of* Philoſophical Wine *with Oyly Vegetables, did not ſo well pleaſe* Chriſtopher Pariſinus, *and therefore inſtead thereof he ſubſtituted this, which he found better than the other.* The great Myſtery and Treaſure (*ſaith he*) which we teach you in this Chapter, is, how you ought to make B (*the Cœleſtial and Ardent Spirit*) acute, which we ſignifie by C, wherefore give Ear, for I know not how I ought to propound this Doctrine, leſt this Secret ſhould be proſtituted to all Men: For all the Philoſophers that ever have been, have abſconded this Secret under divers Figures, becauſe without all doubt this is the thing, which is the Principal, or one of the Principal Keys of this admirable Science. This I would have you certainly believe, that B hath no ſolutive Nature actually; but only potentially; for if B were not acuated by the way and means manifeſted to you, it would have no power of Diſſolving: Some made it acute with Vitriol, which way is good enough: Some with Niter: Some with Cinnabar: Some with theſe two, and ſome with all three: Some with their Earth, which way diſpleaſeth me, becauſe this way thick Unctuoſity and Ponderoſity was introduced: Some have uſed Vegetables, as Herbs, Roots, Flowers, and Seeds known to you, which have powerful Mercuries in them; for this Reaſon it is, That they which handled it this way, augmented rather its Vegetable Form, than made it ſolutive: Some uſed Flowers United for acuition, which is the Principal Way, and of our Intention, which is found in the *Alphabetum apertoriale*: Some not knowing the true way of acuating this B, ſpent much time in preparing divers Waters, before they could put any Body into B, as happened to us in the beginning, ſeeking that Practice, which is now manifeſted to you by the Practice of our *Summetta*, which though it hath ſucceeded well, yet with very great Labour. The Myſtery of this diſſolutive part is difficult, and tedious, and therefore I will undertake the Repetition of it; for having made B acute by this Method, which we now manifeſt concerning the ſolution of Bodies, to be perfected without trouble in a little time, you will be certain. But I confeſs, when I was with you at that time, wherein we made the first beginning of dissolving, we did not understand *Raymund Lully* in this dissolutive part; but having read him over again returning to our Studies, Practising, Praying, and Fasting, a perfect Illumination of Mind came to us: this way therefore will I manifest under the Seal of Silence, *pag.* 231. *Vol.* 6. *Theat. Chym.*

Parisinus *doth by these Words make us more assured, that the Spirit of* Philosophical Wine *hath no power of dissolving any but Oyly things, because it is Oyl it self; but in order to dissolve dry things also, it is necessary for it to be acuated, that is, so tempered, as to be made homogeneous also to dry things, and so dissolve them, which to be a Work difficult and tedious, his own Experience proveth: out of many acuators therefore of the Adepts, he chooseth Hony before the rest, whose principal acuating faculty, he calls the great Mystery and Treasure of the Art. For according to* Lully, *the Spirit of* Philosophical Wine *in Honey hath two free Operations, that is, this Unctious Spirit is easily United to the Unctuosity of Honey, and by the same means also easily tempered with the aridity of Honey. In a Word, there are other indeed, yea all the following* Menstruums *stronger than this, but none more easie to be prepared, and better for a young Beginner.* Lully *made the same* Menstruum *after this manner.*

11. The Spirit of Honey of *Lully*. *Cap.* 19. *Lib. Mercur.*

TAke of *Aqua Vitæ*, and put into this Vegetable Humidity a third part of a Honey-Comb, with all its Substance, Wax, and Honey together, ferment, or digest it in a gentle heat for three Hours, and the longer it stands, the better it is: then let it be Distilled in Balneo, and repeat the Distillation and Fermentation nine times, renewing the Comb every second Distillation.

Parisinus *it seems to me learnt not only the Spirit of* Philosophical Wine, *but also the preparation it self of this* Menstruum, *from his Master* Lully, *though the preparation he corrected a little:* Parisinus *digests one Pound of Honey inspissated with three or four Pounds of the Spirit of* Philosophical Wine, *for a Day in Balneo, then Di-*

stilling

ſtilling three times mixeth them together. The Work he repeats three times, ſo as at theſe four times to have joyned four Pounds of Honey together with ſo many Pounds of Spirit, and Circulates both each time. Lully *digeſts the Hony-Comb three Hours with three parts of Spirit, and in two Diſtillations joyns both together : He repeats the Work four times, ſo as in eight Diſtillations to have United four parts of Honey with three of Spirit ; the* Menſtruum *now joyned together, he Diſtills once more, that in nine times or cohobations, he makes his Spirit of Honey.* Pariſinus *made choice of three Ingredients for his Medicine :* The moſt High Creator created three Mines ; among Minerals, one, and that is of *Sol* and *Luna* : among Vegetables, the Wine ; among Animals, the Bee, *pag.* 222. *Elucid. Lully of theſe three thus, cap.* 46. *lib. Mercurior.* Amongſt all Minerals, Vegetables, and Animals, fixed Gold is choſen for the making of Medicines ; and above all the Virtues among Vegetables and Animals, are the Virtues of the Juice, or Broth of *Lunaria*, and the Fly of *Beſena*, which makes Honey.

Pariſinus *in his* Alphabetum apertoriale *hath indeed the ſame way of acuating the Spirit of* Wine ; *but he in the ſame place ſuperadding the Salt of Honey, extracted out of the* Caput mortuum *calcined to the* Menſtruum, *this acuition is referred not to this, but to another Kind.*

But the Honey ſeems to have this ſpecial Priviledge, as if Menſtruums *of this third Kind, could be made of it alone ; yet you muſt know that all Oyly Salts, (as are Sugar Criſtallized, Manna Criſtallized, crude Tartar of common* Wine, &c.) *do on one ſide prove their affinity with Oyly things, but on the other ſide with dry, and ſo do by that their Oleoſity, introduce their own aridity into the Oyly Spirit of* Philoſophical Wine, *but by their aridity temper the Oleoſity of that Spirit. Wherefore the ſame things are to be underſtood of Sugar and Manna, as have been ſpoken of Honey ; one Example or two we will add of crude Tartar, being dryer then the things aforeſaid.*

12. The Spirit of Crude Tartar of *Guido*. *Pag.* 51. *Thesaur.*

TAke of crude Tartar two Pounds, of Spirit of Wine three Pounds, Distill and Cohobate ten times upon its own *Caput Mortuum.*

Paracelsus *prepared this Spirit of Tartar after this manner :*

13. The Spirit of Crude Tartar of *Paracelsus*. *Lib.* 8. *Paragraph, pag.* 505.

TAke crude Tartar, beat and digest it seven or eight times in the *Alcool* of *Wine*, and Distill it into a Liquor, in which is no *Alkali*.

Out of the Receipts we observe the things following:

1. *That the Spirit of* Philosophical Wine *hath in dry things no dissolving faculty without acuition.*

2. *That this acuition is the Mystery of the Art, being difficult and tedious.*

3. *That it is best made with crude Honey, white Sugar-candy, and Manna purified.*

4. *That such* Menstruums *as these are somewhat hard to be made with crude Tartar.*

5. *That* Lully *by* Aqua Vitæ, Parisinus *by the* Celestial *and* Ardent Spirit, Guido *by* Spirit *of* Wine, *and* Paracelsus *by the* Alcool *of* Wine, *meant not common* Aqua ardens, *which if a Man try an experiment with the Spirit of common Wine, he will by his own Experience find the Truth of the Matter confirmed.*

6. *That* Menstruums *of this Kind are the Magistery of Honey, Manna, Sugar, crude Tartar, mix'd with Spirit of* Philosophical Wine, *they are made extempore, thus: Take of the Essence of* Philosophical Wine, *and the Magistery of Hony or Sugar, equal parts of each, mix.*

7. *That these* Menstruums *are Medicaments.*

8. *That*

8. *That not only the Spirit of* Philosophical Wine, *but also the* Menstruums *themselves have been Circulated, by reason of which Circulation the* Menstruums *are called* Circulatums; *and though it be not always expresly declared in Receipts, that they should be Circulated, yet it ought to be understood in all: for this Circulation is the Purification and Melioration of the* Menstruum. By F, *saith* Parisinus, *in* Alphabeto Summetta, *pag.* 9. *mei* M. S s. We mean *Aqua Vitæ* Circulated thirty Days at least, in which Operation it is Purified from its Terrestreity, so as to raise it self to the Celestial Virtue of a Quintessence, which is called our *Heaven*, Influencing upon the Elements such effects, as you may deservedly call miraculous: We therefore Name it *Quintessence* and *Aqua Vitæ*, because it vivifies Bodies. Without this F, no alteration can be made in Bodies, which caution may serve you for a general Rule. It is otherwise called Vegetable Water, whereof we have more than often made mention in several places of our *Summetta*, which we sent you, affirming the difference between F and D to be greater, than between a clear Day and a dark Night, as will appear in the Operation of it in particulars as well as generals, which Virtue proceeds notwithstanding from our Circulation.

The

The fourth KIND.

Simple Vegetable Menstruums *made of Spirit of* Philosophical Wine, *and* Volatile Salts, *such as common* Sal Armoniack, *Salt of Blood, Urine, Soot,* &c.

14. The Spirit of *Sal Armoniack* of *Trismosinus. In Tract, Aquil. nig. pag.* 13. *Aur Veller. Germ.*

TAke of *Sal Armoniack* one Pound, of common *Salt* melted one Pound and a half, being very well pulverized and mix'd, sublime them; the Matter sublimed sublime again with new *Salt*, and that to be repeated so oft, till the *Sal Armoniack* be made like an impalpable Spirit, (*Powder*) then imbibe with the Spirit of (*Philosophical*) Wine, and the Vessel being very close, set it in Balneo to be dissolved; being dissolved decant, and putrify with new Spirit of Wine added the space of eight Days in Balneo, then Distill gently one half in Balneo, and being Distilled pour it again to the remainder, and Distill again, but with a stronger Fire, that all may ascend through the Alembick: Being Distilled, rectifie it so often, till it be without Fæces.

Annotations.

H*Itherto of things Oyly acuating the Spirit of* Philosophical Wine: *now follow those things which are less Oyly, Volatile Salts, which though they seem not to be Oyly, yet that they are so is easily demonstrated by the following preparations of Salts Harmoniack, whose Earths, otherwise most fixed and flowing like Wax, are by the*

the Unctuosity alone of the Menstruum *made Volatile, but this will not now be our inquiry: It sufficeth us to use crude and common* Sal Armoniack, *Salt of Urine, Blood,* &c. *for the acuition of the Spirit of* Philosophical Wine, *which Salts do by their aridity alter their Unctuosity of this Spirit, more than the aforesaid Oyly Matters, and consequently make the Vegetable* Menstruum *stronger. The same Receipt hath* Trismosinus Libro novem Tincturarum in Tinctura Quarta, pag. 59. *as also in* Tinctura Pitrumonsonis Philosophi Angli, pag. 90. *of the aforesaid Book.* Trismosinus *sublimes crude* Sal Armoniack *several times upon Salt fused, to be acuated by the acidity of this Salt, and then the better dissolved by the Spirit of* Philosophical Wine. Geber de investigat. Magist, pag. 284. *Sublimes* Sal Armoniack *with an equal proportion of Salt.* Aristotle *the Chymist perfected this sublimation after this manner, pag. 74. Volum. 3. Theat. Chym.* Take of *Sal Armoniack* one Pound, of *Spuma Maris* six Ounces, of *Sal Gemme*, of *common Salt* and *Alum*, of each two Ounces, grind them all together, and Sift through a thick Hair Sieve, then put the Matter into an Aludel, and sublime, and the Sublimation repeat.

The Sal Armoniack *being thus sublimed, is impregnated with the Spirit of Wine, (not common, for then would the process not succeed, but* Philosophical Wine) *and then dissolved* per deliquium: *For the Unctuosity of this Spirit cannot dissolve the substance of* Sal Armoniack, *being heterogeneous to it, but successively, and by slow degrees. Wherefore this dissolution will better succeed according to the Method of* Lully. Dissolve, *saith he, Sal Armoniack* in the Phlegme of *Vinum* of *Lotium*, (*Philosophical Wine made of Urine*) pass it through a Filter, and remove the Water by Balneo, and the Salt will remain coagulated and white; dissolve again with the Phlegm, and Distil it away by Balneo. Then take such a quantity of *Aqua Vitæ* (*Spirit of Philosophical Wine*) as you have of Phlegm, and pour them together upon the same Salt, and the Vessel being covered with its *Antenotorium* (*Blind Alembick*) set it in Balneo twenty four Hours; the *Antenotorium* being taken away, and an *Alembick* put on, Distill by Balneo with a most gentle Fire, when the Salt is coagulated, congeal it again, repeat the same Magistery, dissolving by turns after this manner, and congealing three times; and so have you reduced the said Salt into a Vegetable Virtue, by the help of the Vegetative Spirit, by which you dissolved and congealed it. Lully *in* Exp. 16. Sal Almoniack *is easily dissolved in the Phlegm of* Philosophical Wine, *and so is by this means sooner joyned with the Unctuous Spirit of* Philosophical Wine, *than if it were immediately cast into this Spirit. That* Trismosinus *knew also this Method, and sometimes made use of it, appears by the following* Menstruum.

15. Another Water of *Sal Armoniack* of *Trismosinus.* *In Tinctura Gereton, pag.* 98. *Aur. Vel. German.*

TAke of *Sal Armoniack Crude* two Pounds, let it be dissolved in *Wine (Philosophical)* Cristallize it, let the Cristals be dissolved *per deliquium*; the solution divide into two parts, one of which distil into the other with a Fire sufficiently strong, rectify the parts being joyn'd together into a strong Water of *Sal Armoniack. The* Sal Armoniack *therefore being dissolved either in the Phlegm of* Philosophical Wine, *(that is, Aqua ardens not rectify'd) or* Philosophical Wine *it self, Cristallized, and resolved* per deliquium, *is either by it self, or with the addition of new Spirit of Wine, Distilled into a Water of* Sal Armoniack.

This Kind of Menstruums *is made not of* Sal Armoniack *only, but also of the rest of the Volatile Salts, thus:*

16. The Gelative Sulphur of *Lully.* *In Exp.* 8.

TAke of the aforesaid animated Spirit (of *Urine*) one part, and of *Aqua Vitæ* perfectly rectify'd four parts, which pour upon the animated Spirit, and forthwith stop the Vessel, that it may not respire, which Vessel must be a large Bottle, which shake and move with your Hands, so in the twinkling of an Eye or Moment, you will see all the Water converted into Salt; but if any part of Phlegm be in the *(Philosophical) Aqua Vitæ*, it will be immediately separated from the Salt in the Form of Water; the *Aqua Vitæ* therefore ought to be very well purged from

from all Phlegm, that, when the work is done, no Matter may remain with the Salt, but be wholly converted, which will be better and more useful, and by this means you will have the Animal and Vegetable Salt, which we will call Coagulative and Gelative Sulphur, because it hath the property and virtue of dissolving the two Luminaries, and reducing them from power to act, their Vegetative and Germinative Form being preserved. Lully *sometimes sublimed this Offa or Pap of Urine, in the Ninth Experiment following, thus:*

There is, *saith he*, besides, another way of Copulating the aforesaid Animal Spirit with the Vegetable Spirit, namely, thus: Take of the Animated Spirit, rectifi'd as above, what quantity you will, and pour it upon three parts of our (*Philosophical*) *Aqua Vitæ* perfectly rectifi'd, which Copulation ought to be made in a Body large and high, to which an Alembick may be suddenly fitted: the said Copulation therefore being made, you must have presently ready some Cotton-Wooll dipped in Oyl, and very well squeezed, wherewith the Mouth of the Distilling Vessel must be forthwith stopped, and it must be let in within the Neck downward, a hands breath, fastened with a strong Flanel thread, that upon occasion you may draw out the said Cotton-Wooll, then put to it an Alembick with a Receiver, very close stopped, and set it in a Furnace of Ashes, giving it at first a gentle heat; but then by degrees increasing the Fire, till it be sublimed: which sublimation you must keep in a Vessel firmly stopped, because with this Salt and other Means you will be able to do Wonders.

Parisinus *in his* Apertorium, *pag.* 15. *M. S. S. mei, doth by this Salt of Urine acuate his C. or Spirit of* Philosophical Wine, *which being acuated, he then Circulates by the way used, and before described in the Circulation of his* Cœlum melleum. Lully *hath also sometimes used the Volatile Salt of Blood, for the making of these* Menstruums, *as in his twelfth experiment.* Take Blood ground (Blood drawn from sound and cholerick Men, dryed on a clean Table, that the Phlegm may be separated from it, and then pulverized, *Exp.* 11.) put it in a Glass Body with a long Neck, and having fitted an Alembick to it with a Receiver, Distil first with a gentle Fire, till the moisture exhale, then encrease the Fire till the Salt be sublimed, which will be very white, gather it warily, and keep it; for it is of very great Virtue and Efficacy. You have, my dearest Son, all the Medicines (*Salts*) which have properties with the two Luminaries, as also with the other imperfect Metals, without which this Art of Transmutation cannot obtain its desired end.

The Things which I observe from the Receipts are:

1. *That by Wine, Spirit of Wine, and* Aqua Vitæ *common, is not meant* Aqua Ardens, *with which it is impossible to reduce or distil common* Sal Armoniack *into a liquid substance, and though it might, yet that* Menstruum *would be Common, not Philosophical, being made without the Spirit of* Philosophical Wine.

2. *That these* Menstruums *are made of all Volatile Salts.*

3. *That the* Menstruums *of this Kind are the Magisteries of Volatile Salts. Mix the Essence of* Philosophical Wine *with the Magistery of any Volatile Salt, and you will in a moment make a* Menstruum *of this fourth Kind.*

4. *That these* Menstruums *may be also made by* Parisinus *his way of* Cœlum melleum, *namely by Circulation, and therefore called Circulatums, common* Sal Armoniack *Circulated, Salt of Urine, Blood, Harts-horn,* &c. *Circulated, or the Water of* Sal Armoniack *Circulated, the Water of the Salt of Blood Circulated,* &c.

5. *That it is very uncertain what* Philosophical Menstruum Trismosinus *meant by Spirit of Wine: For divers* Menstruums *have been by the Adepts signified by the same Name of Spirit of Wine; for the most part they meant the simple Spirit of* Philosophical Wine, *sometimes the same acuated after a different manner, that is, the simple Vegetable* Menstruum. *So* Basil *in his Book of Conclusions, prepares the Oyls of Metals with Spirit of Wine; by which he declares himself to have meant not the simple Spirit, but a simple Vegetable* Menstruum, *in the preparation of the Oyl of Mercury, he commanding this open Metal to be by the Spirit of Wine, rectify'd first with Salt of Tartar, (which* Menstruum *we shall have in the following Kinds) reduced into an Oyl; with the rest of the Metals being more compact, do more require: Sometimes also they did by the Spirit of Wine intend Vegetable* Menstruums *compounded; so* Lully, *among the other Names of* Circulatum majus, *reckons up also* Aqua Vitæ. This *Menstruum*, saith he, the Wise Men called by almost innumerable Names, the *Acetum acerrimum*, which converts Gold into a Spirit;

rit; this is *Aqua Sicca, Aqua Solis, Aqua Vitæ, in Exp.* 25. *Yea, Mineral* Menstruums *also the* Adepts *more than often call by the Name of* Aqua Vitæ. *So* Albertus in suo Composito de Compositis, pag. 939. Volum 4. Theat. Chym. *Distills a Mercurial Mineral Water; of which thus:* Behold, this is the *Aqua Vitæ*, the *Acetum Philosophorum*, and *Lac Virginis*, by which Bodies are resolved into the first Matter.

Though therefore it be uncertain to Divine what Spirit of Wine, out of such a vast number of Menstruums Trismosinus *intended; yet shall we not much err from the Truth, if we take any* Menstruum *whatsoever; either Simple or Compounded, Vegetable or Mineral, instead of this Spirit; for we may with all promiscuously perfect the same Philosophical Work, differing only in degrees, as being stronger or weaker, which common Spirit of Wine makes altogether impossible, and fallacious: Yet notwithstanding Directions there are, which may in this ambiguity make us more certain; as,*

1. *Any ambiguous, or unknown Name of any* Menstruum, *is easily known by its Synonima's, if there be any in the same Book, or other Writings of the same* Adept, *as for Example: If in the Description of the* Ballsamum Samech *of* Paracelsus, *you know not what the* Circulatum minus *is, the Synonima's (produced by* Paracelsus *himself,* Lib. 10. Arch. *in the Description of the* Circulatum majus, *(where it is called* Primum Ens Salis, *and* Arcanum Salis) *denoting moreover the Nature, yea, and preparation of the* Menstruum, *delivered here perhaps less clearly* (quatenus Menstruum) *but elsewhere more plainly under the Title of* Essence *or* Primum Ens) *do put it out of all doubt, that it is the* Arcanum *of common Salt. But I said, Synonima's in the Writings of the same, not of another* Adept, *because oftentimes others intended another thing by these Names, yea that Name which hath in one Book the same signification with the rest, hath commonly in another, though of the same Author, a signification different from them; and therefore that Synonymum must, if possible, be had out of the same Book, which must then be compared both with other Writings of the same Author, and also with the Writings of other* Adepts, *to confirm the meaning of the Author about the identity of the Synonimum, which was doubted of.*

2. *But if there be no Synonima's in Books of the same Author, it is not convenient for this unknown Name to be explicated by the Writings of other* Adepts; *because the* Adepts *themselves have sometimes*

 also

also erred, in giving an explication either better than was fitting, or altogether contrary, to an obscure Name and Place ; yet is it not only lawful, but necessary also, to observe what they say, especially the Scholars or Followers of the same Author ; for though they shew not the Authors Meaning, yet do they their own as to that Matter.

3. *But if Synonima's cannot discover the Name, some expression used in the Receipt will perhaps explain it more easily, provided it be rightly examined by an industrious Observer of those Receipts ; as,*

1. *If it be not known, whether the* Adept *means a Mineral (Acid) or Vegetable* Menstruum, *it must be enquired by the Particulars following:*

First, *Whether that* Menstruum *dissolves Bodies with force or heat, for then it must be Mineral, this Sign betraying the acidity of Minerals Salts : because Vegetable* Menstruums *dissolve Bodies always sweetly, and slowly.*

Secondly, *Whether the dissolution digested for a time be converted into a Black Colour, or Black Powder swimming upon the* Menstruum, *for that signifies a Vegetable* Menstruum, *because the dissolutions of Mineral* Menstruums *do contain Bodies twice dissolved, once with the Spirit of* Philosophical Wine, *wherewith they become Black, then with the corrosive or acid Spirit of Salts : Therefore the Black Powder and Colour are Signs of a Vegetable dissolution, whereto is added a Milky Opacity, common indeed to both* Menstruums, *for all weak or weakened* Menstruums, *containing as it were their aridity less dissolved and precipitated, as also Vegetable dissolutions longer digested after blackness, do become Opacous and Milky, and so continue, till they are made diaphanous and most clear, by drawing of the Phlegm, the acid part, or the Spirit of* Philosophical Wine *being better concentrated : yet these three Signs we never observe in the use of the Mineral* Menstruums.

Thirdly, *Whether the* Adepts *admonish the Operator to beware of air or fume in Operation, or Poyson in the use of the thing already prepared ; for that is a Sign that his* Menstruum *is, or was Mineral, because Poysons derive themselves Originally from acidity, for Pearls and Corals, yea Gold and all other Arids, though otherwise most Innocent, do, by being prepared with a Mineral* Menstruum, *become the worst of Poysons.*

Lastly, *If you see Mineral Bodies distinguished into two Oyls, swimming*

ming distinctly and severally upon the Menstruum, *say, that also was a Mineral* Menstruum, *because this cannot be done by any Vegetable* Menstruum, *though never so strong.*

2. *If it be not known, whether either the simple or compounded Vegetable* Menstruum *is to be taken, we observe the things following as to the use of them:*

First, *If in the dissolution of a Metallick or Mineral Body, a White Body or some residue be left, then may ye know it to be a simple Vegetable* Menstruum, *because it extracts only the Tinctures or Essences of things, dissolving the Oleosity, but not the Aridity of things, on the contrary Vegetable* Menstruums *compounded, as also Mineral* Menstruums, *which are stronger than the Simple, do dissolve the whole Body, not leaving any Fæces.*

Secondly, *If the whole Body of a thing dissolved be turned into Oyl, swimming upon the* Menstruum, *that was a Vegetable* Menstruum *compounded, for that only are they able to do: The simple Vegetable* Menstruums *are not strong enough, but Mineral* Menstruums *are too strong; those therefore dissolve not the whole Body, but these dissolve not only the whole Body, but reduce it, being dissolved into Oyl, not one only, but twofold: So the* Temperatum *of* Paracelsus, (*a* Menstruum *otherwise sufficiently unknown*) *is by use known, to be the* Circulatum majus, *or a Vegetable* Menstruum *compounded, because he reduceth Metals by it into a swimming Oyl, or Magistery.*

Thirdly, *If in the dissolution or digestion of the thing dissolved, you see it made Black, or cast forth a Black Powder, say it was a simple Vegetable* Menstruum, *because Vegetable* Menstruums *compounded, and Mineral, as being stronger, do better retain their Body dissolved in them.*

3. *But the doubt, whether the simple Vegetable* Menstruum, *or Spirit of* Philosophical Wine *is to be taken, length of time alone resolveth; for the sooner Essences are made in the Mineral Kingdom, the stronger are the* Menstruums; *and on the contrary: But in the Animal and Vegetable Kingdoms it is difficult, if not altogether impossible, to discern by the length of time alone the dissolutions of the Bodies as being more opened; of which sort are Oyls, Salts, as also the open Metal Mercury, especially sublimed, being more amply opened by the acidity of Salts.*

The Fifth KIND.

Simple Vegetable Menstruums *made of the Spirit of* Philosophical Wine, *and the fixed Salts of Vegetables and Minerals not tinging.*

17. The Cœlum Vegetabile of *Lully*, made of the Salt of *Tartar*.

In the 34th. Experiment.

TAke the best *Aqua Vitæ*, rectified so, as to burn a Linnen Cloth, as you have seen, operating with me, and therefore no need of amplifying to you the Magistery of this Water: Take therefore of *Aqua Vitæ* four Pounds, and put it in a Glass Urinal (*Cucurbit*) which is very sound; then take of the Vegetable Salt sublimed of the second Experiment (*Volatile Salt of Tartar*) one Pound, grind very well, and put it in the *Aqua Vitæ*, lute the Vessel with its *Antenotorium* (*Blind Alembick*) firmly, with Wax Gummed, that nothing may respire, then putrifie two Natural Days; after that take away the *Antenotorium*, and put on an Alembick with its Receiver, the Joynts being very close, and distill upon hot Ashes. Take notice, that the Receiver must be very large and sound, that it may not be broken by the force of the *Aqua Vitæ*, and thus continue your distillation with a slow Fire, till all be distilled through the Alembick: But if any part of the Salt remain in the bottom of the Vessel, pour it again upon the Water now lately

lately distilled, and distill as before, making the Joynts as close as may be; the distillation repeat in this order, till all the Salt be passed through the Alembick in the Form of clear Water. Then put of the aforesaid Salt one other Pound into an Urinal, and pour the same distilled Water to it; cover the Vessel with its *Antenotorium*, as before, putrifie as before, then distill as before; and when all the Salt is passed over with the Water, take again as before of new Vegetable Salt one Pound, and pass it all through the Alembick again, as before, with the distilled Water; and by this means you will have those four Pounds of *Aqua Vitæ* united with three Pounds of the Vegetable Salt, which hath the power of dissolving the two Luminaries (*Gold and Silver*) and all the other Metals, with preservation of the Vegetable Form. But now we intend to reduce this simple *Menstruum* into a Celestial Form: Take therefore this simple *Menstruum*, and put it in a sound Glass Vessel (*a Circulatory*) four parts of which must be empty, but the fifth full: Stop the Vessel so as not to evaporate, and Circulate in Dung or Balneo sixty Natural Days; and by this Method will you have a clarify'd *Menstruum*, in which you will see a Sediment, wherefore empty the Celestial Water into another Vessel, and have a care that no Sediment pass over with the Water, which you must keep very close in Balneo.

Annotations.

A*S to the facility of preparation, the* Cœlum melleum *of* Parisinus *is better than the rest of the* Menstruums, *but this of* Lully *hath preference among simple Vegetable* Menstruums, *for it is the* Sapo Sapientium, *compounded of fix'd* Alcalies, *and the Unctuous Spirit of* Philosophical Wine. *Fix'd* Alcalies *are not easily joyned with the Spirit of* Philosophical Wine, *but when they are throughly mix'd together, they are easily sublimed into* Sal Armoniack, Sulphurs of Nature, *or* Philosophers Mercuries, *the chief Instruments of the more secret Chymy.*

Lully *having prescribed several Acuators of the Spirit of* Philosophical Wine, *speaks at length of acuating this Spirit with these Salts Philosophically Volatilized:* Let, *saith he*, our *Menstruum*, which is the Quintessence of Wine, be depurated from all Phlegm,

Phlegm, and acuated with the Philosophers *Armoniack*, because it cannot otherwise dissolve Gold, nor Precious Stones: But let the Philosophers *Sal Armoniack* be well purified, that is, sublimed, aud cleansed from all terrestreity and uncleanness, according to the manner of the Philosophers; of which Philosophical *Sal Armoniack* we have indeed treated largely in our Book, *De intentione Alchimistarum*, Dedicated to the most Illustrious King *Robert*, in the Chapter *De Salibus Armoniac*, &c. and in *Clausura Testamenti*, otherwise called *Vade mecum*, in the Chapter which begins, *Partus Veræ Terræ*. There you may read from first to last the Magistery, of making and purifying, together with the Virtues and Energies of this Salt: And know, my Son, that whatsoever we Write in that Chapter, we mean that Salt and nothing else: Read and Peruse that Chapter, because nothing can be done in the Magistery without that Salt, for that is the thing with which we acuate our *Menstruum*, to dissolve as Gold, and Precious Stones, and Pearls, as well for humane Medecines, as for a Metallick and Lapidifick Magistery, and to make Pearls and Precious Stones.

In which Receipt of Lully, *we have the Volatile Salt of* Tartar *given us freely, hitherto sought in vain, with very great pains and cost, of which the Theoretical Philosophers have in their Theories exhibited nothing but what is most obscure.* I speak, *saith Sendivogius*, all things openly; the Extraction only of our *Sal Armoniack*, or *Philosophical Mercury*, I have not so openly revealed: *Send. in Epilogo* 12. *Tract. pag.* 337. *Now, out of his second Experiment alledged, we have the following Description of* Sal Armoniack, *or Volatile Salt of* Tartar, *thus:*

The Volatile Salt of Tartar *of* Lully. *Out of the Second Experiment.*

TAke the best *Tartar*, pulverize, and put it in an Earthen Vessel not glazed, to calcine the space of three Days, or till it be White: Which being done, dissolve it in the *Aqua Vitæ*, first distill'd (*in the Spirit of* Philosophical Wine, *not yet rectify'd*) thus; namely, Put this individual, being calcined and White,

White, into an Urinal, and pour in the *Aqua Vitæ* ſo, as to be ſoven Fingers above it, and cover the Veſſel with it's *Antenotorium* (*Blind Alembick*) and ſet it on a Furnace of Aſhes to ſimper two Hours, then pour that which is diſſolved into another Veſſel carefully, but that which remains undiſſolved dry: then again pour in new *Aqua Vitæ*, and again boyl it upon Aſhes: empty the diſſolution again, as before, and keep it with the other former diſſolution: the mitter remaining in the Veſſel, dry again, and take it out of the Veſſel, becauſe it muſt be again calcin'd, to be the more eaſily diſſolved; which being calcin'd, diſſolve again with new *Aqua Vitæ*, and boyl it upon Aſhes: this diſſolution keep with the other, as above, and repeat this Magiſtery ſo oft, till all this individual be calcined, and diſſolved: then put all the diſſolutions in an Urinal, fitting an Alembick with a Receiver to it, and cloſing the Joynts very faſt, diſtil by Balneo, till the matter be congealed, or till no more will diſtil by that degree of heat, then remove the Receiver, and ſtop it to prevent reſpiring, and then ſet the Urinal upon Aſhes; and if any corruptible part (*Phlegm and unprofitable Earth*) remain with the matter, let it be burnt, and the Veſſel having remained two or three Hours, in a Fire ſomewhat remiſs, and not any thing more diſtilling through the beak of the Alembick, let the Veſſel cool, and then pour the ſame Water (*Aqua Vitæ, or Spirit of* Philoſophical Wine) which you kept before ſtopt in the Receiver, upon the matter again: This matter therefore being diſſolved, diſtil the Water again in Balneo, as before, which having taken away, the Receiver you muſt keep well ſtopt from reſpiring: then ſet the Urinal in Aſhes, and dry the matter; being dryed, diſſolve it in again with the Water which you kept in the Receiver; and if you ſee the diſſolution is not clear and diaphanous, you muſt tranſmit it ſo often through a Filter or Linnen Cloth, and ſo oft diſſolve and congeal it by turns, as before, till it be free from all Terreſtreity, and appear clear and ſplendid: then may you be aſſured, that the impure and corruptible part is ſeparated, and you will ſee the whole matter tranſmuted into an Oyl. But now, moſt dear Son, you muſt proceed to the compoſition of our *Mercury*, and *Sal Armoniack*, the Powers and Virtues whereof are ſo many and ſo great, as ſcarce to be comprehended within the expreſſion of Man. The way of which operation is thus: You must know the weight of the Salt or Oyl, which you beheld in the bottom of the Vessel depurated, and pour to it so much of our Spirit (that is *Aqua Vitæ* rectify'd so, as to burn a Cloth steeped in it) as will be four Fingers above it, or let there be six parts more of the weight of the *Aqua Vitæ*, than is the Salt or Oyl: the whole being mix'd together, put into an Urinal with a Cover or *Antenotorium* well luted, that it respire not: putrifie in Balneo the space of two Natural Days, then take off the *Antenotorium*, and put on an Alembick, with a Receiver, close the Joynts well, and distil in a Furnace of Ashes with a slow Fire: which distillation must be continued till the Beak or Head discover no Veins, but suddenly after the Veins disappear, lay aside the Receiver with the distilled Water (*Spirit of* Philosophical Wine) and stop it close, for now comes the animated Spirit (*Spirit of Wine impregnated with the Essence of* Tartar) which hath the power of vivifying its Body (or *Caput Mortuum*) then continue the same distillation, in the end augmenting the Fire, that if any part of Phlegm remain, it may exhale and be removed by that degree of heat: Lastly, the Vessel being cold, take out the matter and grind it: know the weight of the matter, and pour to it four parts of *Aqua Vitæ* more than is the Earth (*Caput mortuum*) and covering the Vessel close with its *Antenotorium*, putrifie as before, then putting an Alembick to it with a Receiver, well luted, distill as before, in a Furnace of Ashes: the Soul being with its Spirit gone over, with the same Signs of Veins, as before, appearing, repeat the same Magistery three times: For then will you have the Spirit perfectly animated, and the Body exanimated and calcined: This Spirit with the Soul (*of Tartar*) is indeed capable of disposing every Physical operation, but in this place we will use it for the vivifying of the calcined Earth: Take therefore the aforesaid Earth out of its Vessel, and grind it, then put a little of it upon a red hot plate, which if it melt like Wax without fume, is a sign of perfect exanimation; if this sign appear not, this Magistery must be reiterated, till you have obtained that sign. Then know the weight of the Earth, upon which pour a fourth part of the animated Spirit, and the Vessel being covered close with its *Antenotorium*, set it in Balneo two or three days to be congealed, or till it be congealed; which done, re-

move

move the *Antenotorium*, putting on a Head, and diſtill in a Furnace of Aſhes without a Receiver, that if there be any part of Phlegm, it may be from thence removed, for that which comes out from this diſtillation will be inſipid, of no ſavour or eſteem in the Form of Rain Water: Then again pour on a fourth part of the animated Spirit, as before, and congeal in Balneo, as before, then diſtil the Phlegmatick moiſture by Aſhes, as before, and thus repeat the aforeſaid Magiſtery, till the Earth hath drunk up and attracted to it all its animated Spirit, and attain'd to ſuch a ſign, that if you put a ſmall quantity of it upon a Fire-hot Plate, the major part fume away, which will be a ſign that the matter is diſpoſed for the ſubliming of our moſt precious Mercury, which hath the power of diſſolving any Metal whatſoever with the preſervation of its Vegetive and Germinative form. Take therefore the aforeſaid pregnant Earth, and put it into a Bolt-head (*Sublimatory*) with a long Neck, which you muſt lute very well with *Lutum Sapientiæ*, and the luting being dryed, ſet it with the matter into a diſtilling Furnace, adminiſtring in the beginning a gentle Fire, till the Bolt-head grow hot, whoſe Mouth muſt be ſtopped with Cotton-wooll, and continue that gentle heat the ſpace of ſix Hours, then augment the Fire ſomewhat ſix Hours more; but if it begins not by that degree of Fire to ſublime, increaſe the Fire gradually to a more violent degree, till it begin to ſublime, which Fire continue the ſpace of twenty four Hours, at the expiration of which time, the Veſſel being cold, take from thence our Sulphur ſublimed (*the Vegetable Sulphur of Nature*) our Mercury (*Vegetable*) our Heaven (*dry*) our *Sal Armoniack* (*Vegetable*) our Stone not yet fermented, and call'd by many more other Names, whoſe faculty is to acuate its Spirit (*of* Philoſophical Wine) as ſhall be made appear by the Experiments hereafter following:

This Volatilization of the Salt of Tartar *is ſufficiently tedious, yet eaſie and clear, according to the tenour of the Receipt. In the following kind of* Menſtruums, *we ſhall have divers examples of making ſuch* Sal Harmoniacks, *wherefore we will thither reſerve thoſe things which are to be admoniſhed about this way of making the Volatile Salt of* Tartar. Lully *mixeth three pounds of this Volatile Salt with four of the Spirit of* Philoſophical Wine *ſucceſſively by various diſtillations, and reduceth the mixture by circulating ſixty*

Days into the Vegetable Heaven. But here we are to be advised, that the Sal Armoniack *of* Tartar *in its own dry Form is a Vegetable* Menstruum; *and so according to the prescribed method of the Receipt, it is not always necessary to reduce that into a liquid substance; for that and the* Menstruum *made from thence are therein different; because in the making of Heaven, the Unctuosity of the Spirit of* Philosophical Wine *being superadded, and now prevalent, hath absorbed and dissolved the aridity of the* Sal Armoniack; *but this being this way too much diluted in a greater quantity of that* Oleosum, *loseth much of it strength, and becomes less fit for the dissolutions of dry Bodies: But now if the volatile Salt of* Tartar *be a* Menstruum *in a dry form, some have unadvisedly said it serves instead of a* Philosophical Menstruum, *which notwithstanding is rightly and very well said, if a corrosive* Menstruum, *which we call Mineral, be understood, whose place the volatile Salt of* Tartar, *or* Vegetable Menstruum, *may upon several occasions supply.*

Now as this Sal Armoniack *reduced into a liquid substance by the Spirit of* Philosophical Wine, *makes our Vegetable Heaven; so being dissolved with the Spirit of common Wine it makes the Spirit of Wine of* Basilius *dissolved with Vinegar, our Vinegar dissolved with Aquafortis, the Philosophers* Aqua Regis; *and so of many others. At present the aforesaid Spirit of* Basilius *hath its place.*

18. The Spirit of Wine of *Basilius.* *In Fine Libri Revelat.*

TAke generous white-Wine (*common*) and distil after the usual manner, to make a strong *Aqua Vitæ* thereof in a Copper, which rectifie in a Phial, and separate the Phlegm: this *Aqua Vitæ* is thus proved: If it burn all away, and leave no Aquosity behind it, being kindled in a Glazed Vessel; but if any remain, distil yet once or twice, the Joynts being very close, that the Volatile Spirit of the Wine may not exhale: The *Aqua Vitæ* being thus distilled, and exactly rectifi'd (but have a care that in the time of distilling you put not a Candle to it, lest it hurt you) joyn three Ounces of *Tartar* perfectly sublimed with a quantity of this *Aqua Vitæ* in another Phial, so as that the Phial be half full, put an Alembick to it with a Receiver large enough, and distil in *Balneo Mariæ* most gently, because of the Volatile Spirits, a little of the *Aqua Vitæ* being left in the bottom, and as you distil, cool the Alembick with wet Cloaths: thus is the Spirit sooner resolved, and passeth into the Receiver.

This is that Spirit of Wine which Basilius *used in several places, especially in his Conclusions, where by the Spirit of Wine he reduceth as well Metallick as Mineral Bodies into Oyl; Whosoever hath imagined to himself another Spirit instead thereof, must have a care lest he prove the truth of this saying to his own detriment: There is yet indeed another description of that Spirit of Wine* in Appendice Elucidationis; *which notwithstanding differs not from the former, except that in the former description it was read the Volatile Salt of* Tartar; *but here it is read* Sal Armoniack, *perfectly sublimed; but that they are* Synonyma's, *is even now manifest by the Receipt of* Lully: *For whatsoever Salt, either fix'd, or volatile, is joyned with the Spirit of* Philosophical VVine *and sublimed, is called our Volatile Salt, our Sulphur of Nature, and our sublimed Mercury, which may be used promiscuously as Salt Philosophically sublimed; for both those Salts (of* Tartar *and* Sal Armoniack) *were by* Basilius *made perhaps out of one and the same matter: But this his* Menstruum *is not so strong as the* Cœlum Vegetabile *of* Lully; *though prepared out of the same Salt of* Tartar *just as that: For* Basilius *diminisheth the virtue of this Salt, by adding the Spirit of common Wine:* Lully *accomplisheth the same work, but with the Spirit of* Philosophical VVine: *yet* Basilius *sometimes also made his* Menstruum *stronger than the* Cœlum Vegetabile *of* Lully, *by separating the Spirit of common Wine from the* Philosophical Sal Armoniack, *which indeed he performed two ways: First, by kindling the* Menstruum *in a Copper Vessel design'd for this use, to burn away the Spirit of common Wine, but leave the* Vegetable Sal Armoniack *by it self, reduced into a liquid substance. The way is this.*

19. The

19. The Fiery Spirit of Wine of *Basilius*. *In the Place as above.*

TAke the antecedent Spirit of Wine, being fit for this preparation of the Fiery Spirit, make an Instrument of Copper, which may be taken up in the middle, below and above the Holes, as also above the middle of the Vessel, put on an Alembick with a Pipe, let them be all of Copper, except the Receiver, which must be of Glass, which put in a wooden Vessel into Water, and cover it above with wet Cloaths, in the wooden Vessel let there be a passage, by which the Water, when hot, may fly out, and cold be poured on: all things being thus prepared, the Spirit of Wine prepared is put in through the lower Holes, so as to touch the Holes, then is it kindled, and the Mercury is driven upwards through the middle Holes, and resolved by the coldness of the Water, and passeth out of the Alembick into the Receiver: Thus is the true Spirit of Wine prepared, but in the work never cease from refrigerating, and pour on new *Aqua Vitæ*, lest it burn too low. *In the Addition or Appendix of manual operations,* Basilius *described this Spirit thus*: Take Wine burned (*rather Wine to be burned, made of the* Sal Armoniack *of* Tartar, *and Spirit of Common Wine*) which put in a strong Vessel that can endure the flame of Fire, and kindle it with a Match of Sulphur, and forthwith apply an Alembick of Iron or Copper, with a large Receiver, and the true fiery Spirit of Wine is resolved and distilled into a Liquor: this is the true airy and fiery Spirit of Wine.

Secondly, *He impregnates* Calx Vive, *or* Quick Lime, *with the* Menstruum *described in* Numb. 18. *from which he distills a* Menstruum *yet stronger, called* Spirit of Calx Vive. Calx Vive, *saith he*, is strengthened and made more fiery by the pure and not sophisticated Spirit of Wine (*made of* Sal Armoniack *and Spirit of Common Wine* very often cohobated, to which *Calx* add the *Sal alkali* of *Tartar*, the dryed Fæces of the same Salt being also added, from which, being thoroughly mix'd, distil the true *Spiritus Gehenneus*, or Spirit of *Hell*, in which are great Mysteries hidden: the method of acquiring this Spirit I have told you,

you, which obſerve, keep, and accept for a farewel-Gift. *Baſilius in Repet. Lapidis, in Cap. de Calce viva:* Mark, *ſaith he*, in the End of this Book, *De Medicinis ſupernaturalibus.* I told you of the Virtues and Qualities of Precious Stones, but there are alſo found many Stones deſpicable and ignoble, yet of great Virtue, as Experience teſtifies; though the ignorant and unskilful will ſcarce give Credit to theſe ſayings, and cannot conceive thoſe things with their dull Brains, yet will I demonſtrate it by an Example of *Calx vive*, which *Calx* is according to the judgment of the Vulgar, of little value, and contemptible in obſcurity; yet nevertheleſs there is powerful Virtue in it, which appears in the application of it againſt moſt grievous Diſeaſes: but its triumphant and tranſcendent efficacy being in a manner unknown to moſt Men, for the ſake therefore of thoſe that inquire into Natural and Supernatural Myſteries, do I diſcover the ſecrets of this Book: as a farewel alſo will I reveal the Myſtery of *Calx vive*, and declare firſt the way of diſtilling the Spirit of it, which work does indeed require an expert Artiſt, well informed before, in this preparation.

20. The Spirit of *Calx vive* of *Baſilius. In Fine Lib. de Med. Supernatur.*

TAke of *Calx vive* what quantity you will, grind and prepare it on a Marble into an impalpable Powder, whereto pour of the Spirit of Wine (*Menſtruum in Numb.* 18.) ſo much as the pulverized *Calx* is able to imbibe, no Spirit ſwimming upon the *Calx*. Then apply an Alembick, lute well, and put a Receiver to it, abſtract the Spirit from it in a moſt gentle Balneo; this abſtraction muſt be repeated eight or ten times: this Spirit ſtrengthens much the Spirit of the *Calx*, which is thereby made more fiery. Take the remaining *Calx* out of the Cucurbit, grind it very well, and add to it of the Salt of *Tartar* (*Alkali*) a tenth part, and as much as all of the Earth of the Salt of *Tartar*; or matter left in extracting the Salt of *Tartar*, and well dried, diſtil them all being well mix'd out of a Retort well luted three parts of which muſt be empty, in a Receiver large and firm: Take notice, that the Receiver, into which the Beak the Retort is put, must have a Pipe one Fingers breadth, to which another Receiver is to be applyed, in which must be a little quantity of Spirit of Wine (*Menstruum in Numb.* 18.) then distil with a soft Fire, and the Phlegm will ascend into the first Receiver; the Phlegm being distilled, increase the Fire, and then will come a white Spirit, in the Form of the white Spirit distilled from Vitriol (*Philosophical*) which will not descend into the Phlegm, but through the aforesaid Pipe into the other Receiver, there joyning it self with the Spirit of Wine, even as Fire is easily joyned with Fire. Take notice, if this Spirit of *Calx* be not rightly prepared or impregnated with the like Spirit of Wine, by the aforesaid cohobations, it is in distilling mixed with its Phlegm, extinguished, and loseth its Virtue; so difficult a thing it is to drive deeply into Nature, she reserving many things to her self: This Spirit being now mix'd with the Spirit of Wine, take away the Receiver, pour out the Phlegm, and keep the Spirits of the *Calx* and *Wine* wearily: Observe, both these Spirits are separated not without difficulty, for they embrace one another, and in distillation ascend together: Wherefore, if you kindle the Spirits being mix'd and united in a Glass Vessel, the Spirit of *Wine* is burned, but the Spirit of the *Calx* remains in the Glass, which keep diligently. This is a great *Arcanum*, few Spirits do exceed its efficacy, if you knew the use of it, its qualities can scarce be described by way of *Compendium*. This Spirit dissolves Crabs Eyes, and the hardest Cristals: these three distilled together through an Alembick, and many times cohobated, make a Liquor, three drops of which taken in warm Wine, do break and dissolve the Gravel and Stone in Mans Body, this Liquor expells the very root or cause of that Disease without any pain to the Patient: This Spirit of *Calx* at the beginning is of a Sky-Colour, but being gently rectified appears white, transparent and clear, leaving some few Fæces behind it: This Spirit dissolves the most fixed Jewels, and Precious Stones, and on the contrary fixeth all Volatile Spirits by its transcendent heat: This Spirit overcomes all Symptoms whatsoever of the *Podagra*, though never so knotty and tartarous, all which it dissolves and radically expells.

If Spirit of Wine, acuated with Vegetable Sal Harmoniack *be kindled, the Spirit of common Wine is burned, but the* Sal Harmoniack

ack *being incombustible, ascends in the Form of a Liquor, and is called the Fiery Spirit of Wine of* Basilius, *but the same Spirit of Wine joyned with the* Sal Harmoniack *being absorbed by the* Calx vive, *and then distilled into it self, and then kindled, the Spirit of common Wine is indeed consumed by the Flame as before, but the Spirit of the* Calx, *or rather the Vegetable* Sal Harmoniack *ascends not as before, but remains in the bottom of the Glass because more digested, and made more fixed: But for the greater elucidation of these Spirits, we thought good to add another Description of the Spirit of* Calx.

21. The Simple Spirit of *Calx vive* of *Basilius*, *In manualibus Operationibus.*

TAke pure *Calx vive*, burn it in a Potter's Furnace with a most strong Fire, to reduce it to an exact maturity, grind it very fine upon a Marble, and put it in a Cucurbit, pour to it Spirit of Wine made of *Philosophical Tartar* (as I shall teach in my method of making *Aurum potabile*) that the *Calx* may be made like thin Pap; this being done, distil from thence the Phlegm, till the *Calx* be dry, pour on new Spirit of Wine, and draw of: repeat it six times, then grind the matter very curiously, and put it in a Cellar to be dissolved *per deliquium*, and within a few days a Liquor will run from it, which being gather'd and distilled by a Retort in Sand, first sends forth a Phlegm to be kept by it self, after that a Spirituous Liquor, which also keep apart: Now take Cristals pulverized, mix them with the same weight of *Vive* or *Mineral Sulphur*, burn this matter, continually stirring it, till all the Sulphur be burned away, then reverberate in an open Fire the space of three Hours; this done, pour the aforesaid Liquor to this matter. Take also Crabs Eyes, to which also pour the same Liquor of quick Lime in another Glass, let them be digested fourteen Days in a heat strong enough, and from both will ascend an humidity upon the superficies, which decant finely into a little Glass, and rectifie in Balneo, and a Liquor will remain in the bottom; three grains of which administred in Wine have produced very great and admirable effects.

 This

This Medicine cures also radically the Stone of the Bladder and Kidneys, as well in Men as Women.

The Spirit of Wine made of Philosophical Tartar, *which* Basilius *promised to give in his method of making* Aurum potabile, *will confirm all the aforesaid* Menstruums *of* Basilius ; *for those are made of* Sal Harmoniack, *or the Volatile Salt of* Tartar *being divers ways prepared* ; *but this Spirit of* Philosophical Wine *is acuated with the Salt of* Tartar, *not indeed the common* Alcali ; *but that being reduced together with the Spirit of* Philosophical Wine *into a liquid substance : for we are to be admonished that it is not always necessary to make the* Cœlum *or* Heaven *of* Lully, *and the rest of the* Menstruums *of this kind, with the Salt of* Tartar, *as being Philosophically Volatilized, but that sometimes also the same* Menstruum *may be made of the Salt of* Tartar *without the sublimation or reduction of it into the Vegetable Sulphur of Nature, by cohobating only the Spirit of* Philosophical Wine *upon Salt of* Tartar, *till it ascend by distillation in the Form of a Milky Liquor. It is thus done,*

22. The Tartarised Spirit of Wine of *Basilius*. *In manal. Operation.*

THe first thing to be known is that the Philosophers *Tartar*, wherewith the Lock is opened, is not like common Tartar, as most Men imagine, but is another Salt, though springing from the same Fountain : This Salt is the only Key to open, and dissolve Metals, if prepared as followeth. Take the Ashes of a fruitful Wine, and draw a *Lee* or *Lixivium* as strong as may be out of them with hot Water, which evaporate by boyling it to a driness, that the matter may remain reddish, which reverberate in a reverberating Furnace three days, or thereabouts, with an open Fire, till it become white : then dissolve it in Spring-Water, suffer it to settle, decant the clear, filter to separate the Fæces, being filtred, coagulate, and you will have the white Salt of *Tartar*, from which the true Spirit is distilled after this manner : Take Spirit of Wine rectifi'd to the highest degree, and altogether void of Phlegm, (*described in Numb.* 19.) and pour it to the Salt of *Tartar* in a Phial with a long Neck, so as to be three Fingers above it, lute an Alembick to the Phial, fit a Receiver to it, and digest with a gentle heat, then draw off the Phlegm most softly, and the Spirit of *Tartar* is opened by Virtue of the Spirit of Wine, and by reason of reciprocal and admirable love they both ascend together; the Fæces remaining, if any be, as also the Phlegm must be cast away; thus will you have the true Spirit of Wine, wherewith *Aurum potabile* is made.

This truly is a most Noble Menstruum, *so as for its excellency to deserve a higher Place than this among the Simple Vegetable* Menstruums; *whereas it ought to have been more rightly transferred to the seventh Kind of* Menstruums; *but it very much at present Illustrating the* Menstruums *of* Basilius, *and so of greater utility here than there, we will not remove it from hence, yet will we add some examples more clear of such sort of* Menstuums. *Thus it is done,*

23. The Vegetable *Acetum acerrimum*, or *Ignis Adepti* of Ripley, made of *Tartar* calcined. *Pag. 331. Concord. Raym. & Guid.*

TAke the *Tartar* of Wine, and calcine it to whiteness. Take of this calcined *Tartar* one Pound, and being pulverized, put it in a great Glass Cucurbit, and pour to it half a Cup, or a little more of the strongest Spirit of (*Philosophical*) *Wine*, stop the Mouth very close, and let them stand in cold Water twenty four Hours, then put a Receiver to it, and distil in Balneo with an easie Fire, yet so as to be distilled; which easie distillation must be continued, till the Phlegm ascend, which must be known by the taste, then let it cool, and again put new Spirit of Wine to the aforesaid *Tartar*, the same quantity as before, doing all things as before: which work you must repeat fifteen times, but when the Vessel is opened in every Imbibition, above all things have a care of the suddain fume of this *Ignis Adepti*: This work being in fifteen times compleat, lay aside three ounces of this fiered *Tartar* for a part, to multiply the Mercurial Oyl, as lower will appear. Take the other part of this fiered *Tartar*, and distil it in Sand with a most strong Fire, which Fire being so distilled hath a white Colour, and is our

Natura ignita, our *Mercury*, our *Aqua Vitæ*, lastly the Key of our Science.

This Menstruum *is the same, as to the Ingredients and Virtue, with the Vegetable Heaven of* Lully, *but it must be Circulated like that Heaven, in order to lose its milky and duskish Colour, and acquire the diaphaneity and clearness of this. This Receipt hath also* Johannes de Rupescissa, *which it is convenient to compare with this, especially he varying somewhat in Circumstances, by dissolving* per deliquium Tartar *impregnated with the Spirit of* Philosophical Wine *before the distillation of it.*

24. The *Aqua Fortissima* and *Vertuosa* of *Johannes de Rupescissa*. *Cap. 43. Lib. Essentiæ.*

THe most Blessed God, the Creator of Secrets, hath made so many wonderful things in Nature, that neither can our Understanding perceive, some few excepted, nor Tongue express the wonderful things of God without stammering : and among the Secrets, I will reveal to you a Water of Divine Action, and the Magistery of it, is, to take the best white *Tartar* calcined, and put it in an Earthen or Glass Vessel, and pour to it the best (*Philosophical*) *Aqua Ardens* you can get, put on an Alembick, and distil the *Aqua Ardens* very weak, then take it away, being little or nothing worth, except for washing of the Eyes or other parts : Then take you *Tartar*, and you will find it twice as strong, and this you may prove each time by your Tongue ; put other *Aqua Ardens* to it again many times more, because it will be every time strengthned above measure, and you may bring it to so great a degree of strength, that no created action can be compared to it : But if you would make it a hundred times stronger, grind it, and put it upon a Porphyry or Marble, to be converted into Water, which then must be distilled through an Alembick.

There is yet another way of preparing this Vegetable Heaven, not by sublimation of the Alcali, nor cohobation, but simple Circulation, namely by digesting the Alcali of Tartar, *in the Spirit of* Philosophical

phical Wine, *till it swims upon the Spirit of Wine like an Oyl. It is thus done,*

25. Vegetable Mercury acuated with the Salt of *Tartar* of *Lully*.

In Prima Camera Individuorum, dist. 3. *Lib. Essen.*

IN the first Chamber is signified, that our Mercury is in the power of H (*crude Tartar*) and in order to draw it out, the Artist must put the said H into E (*that is, in a Glass-Makers Furnace*) three Natural Days, and there must be a great quantity of it, because but little will be made from thence, which H (*Tartar now calcined*) you must grind subtilly, and put it into H of *Arboris Philosophical* (*into dissolution per deliquium*) upon a Marble, in a very cold place, and covered because of dust; and H will be converted into T, (*oleum per deliquium*) which T must the Artist distil through a Filtre in a Glass Vessel, and the Artist having separated T from H, will be able to extract our Mercury out of the said T two ways. First, by the Magistery of the Chapter beginning, *Non reputes me*, &c. (*by Circulation like the Essence or Spirit of Wine of* Lully.) Secondly, by the Magistery of the Chapter, *Non prætermittam* (*by the separation of the Elements, of which not in this place.*)

Lully *sometimes used the Salt of* Tartar *depurated instead of the Oyl of* Tartar per deliquium, *as in the First Experiment.* You have, *saith he*, another sign more certain of the purification of this Individual (*the Salt of* Tartar) namely, when this most precious Salt will remain in the Vessel upon Fire in the Form of an Oyl, but being removed from the Fire, will suddenly be congealed. But dearest Son! Let not the Prolixity of time be irksome to you, in dissolving and congealing this Matter so often, to take away Corruption, which remaining, it can never be joyned with its Spirit extracted from the most precious, and its nearest Individual, which is the best Wine, freed from all manner of Humidity and Corruption: Then Circulate it in a Circulating Vessel, and so reduce it into a Quintessence, and it will forthwith embrace its Spirit: this Circulation we perform'd at first in thirty days, but afterwards compleated the same in forty days; which Circulation was much better than the the first, because the longer it is circulated, the more is it purify'd, and adepted for any of our Physical Operations, which order when need requires, you also must observe.

Menstruums *of this kind may be divers ways made not only out of the* Alcali *of* Tartar, *but other fix'd* Alcalies *may be also taken instead of that, as proves the following* Menstruum.

26. The Simple Vegetable *Menstruum* produced from the three Individuals of *Lully*.

In Experim. 25.

TAke *Aqua Vitæ* so acute, as to burn a Linnen Cloth, which transmit again through an Alembick, that it may be perfectly rectify'd: Then take the Salt of Celandine, Salt of Mans Blood, Salt extracted from Honey, as you have them above in their Experiments, all which Salts put together in an Urinal (*Cucurbit*) and upon every Ounce of those Salts pour four Ounces of the aforesaid *Aqua Vitæ*, cover it with its *Antenotorium*, (*blind Head*) then having a little time digested put on an Alembick, with a Receiver annexed, lute the joynts well, and distil in Ashes, suffering the Salts to go over together with the Water: If any thing remain, pour to it again its distilled Water, and when all is come over, pour in new Salt again, to wit, one Ounce, and pass it through the Alembick as before. Thirdly, add again another Ounce of Salt, as above, and distil, repeating this Magistery three times, every time adding new Salt: These things being done, Circulate this Water in a Vessel deep and narrow the space of fifty Natural Days, but observe that the Vessel respire not: Circulation being finished, you will in the bottom of the Vessel see a Sediment like the Urine of a sound Man, which will be white; empty the Water warily into another clean Vessel, and be careful that the Sediment pass not over with the Water, but remain in the bottom of the Vessel: stop the Vessel of the Circulated Water so as not to respire, and keep it in Balneo.

The

The preparation of the Salt of Celandine is in the Fourth Experiment. Then take the Ashes of Celandine, gathered in the Month of *May* at full Moon, with its Roots and Flowers, and put them in a Glass Vessel, and thereto pour the water of Celandine distill'd in *Balneo*, that you may from thence extract a Salt; and let the matter boyl two hours in a most soft Fire of Ashes; empty the dissolution into another Vessel, but dry the undissolved Earth; and when the Vessel is cold grind it, pouring again new water upon the Ashes as before; make it boyl, and decant the dissolution, as before. This Magistery repeat, till you have extracted all the Salt, which is the Mercurial part of that Individual: then take all those dissolutions and filtre them, that they may be purged from Terrestreity; then distilling by *Balneo*, congeal; for the Liquor being gone over, in the bottom of the Vessel will remain a *Mercury* or Salt of a white colour; which Salt you must dissolve and by turns congeal three times; and by this means you will have extracted the Mercury out of this matter, which hath virtues almost innumerable in acuating the Vegetable Spirit drawn from Wine, and hath the power of dissolving all Metals with the preservation of their Vegetative and Germenative Form.

The fixed Salt of Man's Blood is thus prepared in the Eleventh Experiment. Take Blood drawn from sound and cholerick men, and put it on a clean Table, and so let it dry that the Phlegm may be separated from it; then take the Blood, grind it very well, and put it into a Glass Body, and with a slow Fire distil the water, which being distilled keep apart; and having augmented the Fire a little but not too intensely, lest the Salt perhaps should sublime; let only the moisture and superfluous Oyl exhale till it will distil no more; then the Vessel being cold, take the burned Earth, put it into a Vessel stopp'd close to keep it from respiring; for in respiring it would vanish away into Smoak: set the Vessel in a reverberating Furnace, but the heat must be exceeding temperate, that the Salt of the Matter which is volatile, and not fix'd, may not exhale; and that the Vessel may not by the violence of the Fire be broken, as hath hapned to us; and let the matter stand in that degree of heat the space of two days, and it will be calcin'd; which done, let the Vessel cool, and being cold, open it; and upon the calcined matter pour its

own

own Phlegm, that is the water, which you distill'd at first; set it boyl upon ashes two hours, that some part may be dissolved, and that which is dissolved decant into another Vessel, and again with new water do as before; and thus repeat till you have extracted all the Salt; then draw off the water by distillation in *Balneo*; and in the Vessel will remain the Salt as white as Snow, of a great many virtues; and if you acuate the Vegetable Fire with it, it will without doubt dissolve the two Luminaries with the conservation of their Vegetative Form: And with it may be made a most excellent *Aurum potabile*, to preserve the radical moisture in men, and expel many diseases.

The Third Experiment *teacheth the preparation of the Salt of Honey, after this manner*: Take new white Honey together with the Comb, put it in a Glass Vessel to putrifie the space of sixty days; then distil, &c. Then take the Earth (*Caput mortuum*) which remained in the Urinal, and being perfectly ground, put it in an Earthen Vessel, made of Valentinian Chalk, or of that which Crucibles are made of; or if you cannot have this Vessel, put the same Earth between two Crucibles, one joyned to the other, and very well luted; then set them in a reverberating or Glass-makers Furnace, and there let them stay four or five days, so will the Earth be white; but if you do this work in a reverberating Furnace, have a care that the Fire be not too violent, for so would the Earth evaporate; and if the Fire be too weak, it will never be calcined, a moderate heat therefore is requisite; thus, no such error can happen as we have met with; for when we began this work, we lost all the Earth by the violence of Fire; but to the purpose; this Earth being calcined, as aforesaid, and the Vessel cold, take it out and grind it; then pour the water which you distilled by *Balneo* to it, and let the matter boyl two hours upon ashes, and empty the water into another Vessel from the Earth, which Earth you must dry with a gentle Fire. Upon the same ashes pour new Phlegm, and let it boyl, as before, decant by emptying and keeping, as before, the dissolution of the Body; and thus repeat the Magistery, till you have evacuated all the most precious Salt out of it, and converted it into water: Then take all those dissolutions, and filtre them through a clean Linnen-Cloth, which water you must distil by *Balneo*; at length in the bottom of the

Vesſel will you have a moſt Precious Salt, or Vegetable Mercury : Which done, know the weight of the ſaid Congelation or Salt, and pour to it a third part of the Water, which you kept before, and which you rectify'd ſeven times in Aſhes, (*the acid Water of Honey*) and ſtop the Veſſel with its *Antenotorium*, and ſet it in Balneo five Days, then having taken away the *Antenotorium*, and put on an Alembick, you muſt with a temperate Fire by diſtillation exhale all the moiſture that will diſtil, and that will be inſipid, for the Earth hath received, and in it ſelf retained the Virtue and Acetoſity of the Water : Then again imbibe the Earth with new Water as before, and repeat the Magiſtery by imbibing, digeſting, and diſtilling ſo oft as before, till the Earth hath attracted and imbibed all its Water: And ſo by the help of the living God will you truly have the Vegetable Salt drawn from this individual, which Salt is moſt precious, and hath the power of acuating the Vegetable Mercury, and diſſolving the two Luminaries, and all the other imperfect Metals : And with this may Metals be reduced into their firſt Matter.

To theſe Salts requiſite for this Menſtruum *of* Lully, *I will add the fifth Experiment, which teacheth to prepare* Alkalies *from* Portulaca Marina, Apium Sylveſtre, Squilla, Euphorbium, Pyrethrum, Roſmarinus, Herb Mercury, Solatrum, Oliandrum, &c. *with all which you may acuate the Vegetable Mercury drawn from Wine, either joyntly or ſeverally.*

This ſort of Menſtruums *is made not only out of the* Alkalies *of Vegetables, but alſo out of Mineral Salts, ſuch as common Salt,* Sal Gemmæ, Alum, &c. *Thus it is made.*

27. *The* Circulatum Minus, *or Water of* Salt *Circulated of* Paracelſus *Lib.* 10. *Archidox.*

TAKE the true Element of Water, or inſtead thereof another Salt which hath not been as yet boyl'd to plain Drineſs, or alſo *Sal Gemmæ* putrified ; pour two parts of the water mix'd with a little Juice of *Raphanus* to it, putrefie in accurate digeſtion, the longer the better ; let it afterward congeal, and putrefie again for a Month; then distil in a Retort, the remainder urge with a strong Fire, that it may melt; reverberate in a Retort, with a continual Fire, dissolve upon a Marble, the water flowing from hence pour to it, and putrefie again; distil again even to an Oleosity; joyn it with the Spirit of (*Philosophical*) *Wine* and that which is impure will fall down, which separate; but let the pure be cristalized in a cold place; pour on again that which is distilled, and cohobate so oft till a fixed Oyl remains in the bottom, and nothing sweet goes over; Digest moreover for a Month, then distil, till the *Arcanum* of Salt pass over through the Alembeck: Nor let long labour grieve you, for this is the third part of all the *Arcanums*, which are hidden in Metals and Minerals; and without which nothing can be made useful or perfect.

The same Circulatum *hath* Paracelsus *described in his* Treatise of reducing Metals into their first matter or running *Mercury*; (*which is the fourth Treatise* in Rosario novo Olimpico Benedicti Figuli(*which Description we thought good to compare with this, that they may illustrate one another.* Take, *saith he*, *Sal Gemmæ* most finely pulverized; put it in a strong Crucible, and increasing the Fire by degrees, melt the Salt, being melted, keep it so for the space of three Hours; the Salt being cold, pulverize it again, and melt it in a new Crucible, according to the aforesaid method, and so proceed five or six times; then to the pulverized Salt, pour so much of the hot Juice of *Raphanus* that it may be dissolved, (*mix the Salt, and squeeze it with a little of the Juice, with a wooden spoon, in a wooden Vessel; being dissolved, strain it through a sleeve, and set it apart; add again a little of the Juice, and repeat till all the Salt be dissolved*) coagulate or draw off the water by an Alembick; reduce the Salt into Powder; putrefie in *Balneo* six days; then distil with an open Fire, like *Aqua Regis*, observing the degrees of Fire, till nothing more ascends; force it with a most strong Fire for an hour that it may be throughly calcined; pulverize the Salt, being yet hot, very small on a Marble, and let it be dissolved by it self in a moist place; putrefie all that is dissolved in *Balneo* three days; then distil gradually, by the Rule of Art, all the Liquor through an Alembick in Sand; the remaining Body being well pulverized dissolve on a Marble, putrefie, and distil as before;

repeat

repeat this three times; the remainder reduce into Powder, and put in a Cucurbit; to which pour these three distilled waters, putrefie five days, and again distil in Sand; thus putrefying and distilling, all the Salt will at length ascend through the Alembick, except a little *Caput mortuum* to be cast away: but the water distilled from the substance of the Salt, putrefie for a Day and a Night, and rectifie twice or thrice, and you will have the water of Salt.

This Menstruum *made of Sea-salt, or* Sal Gemmæ, Paracelsus *made choice of before the rest of the simple* Vegetable Menstruums, *as the best, because according to his Doctrine, it is the Matrix or Center of Metals and Minerals.* Because, *saith he,* being instructed by Experiments, and having in other Books also made mention, that the *primum Ens*, or fifth Essence of the Element of Water, is the Center of Metals and Minerals, and having elsewhere also added, that every product ought to dye in that in which it received life, *In a German Manuscript these Words are thus read,* Das ein iegelich frucht in seiner Mutter, darinnen es das leben uberkommen, sterben muss, *That is, every Fruit ought to dye in the same Matrix in which it obtains its Life,* that afterwards it may receive a new Life better, and so by the deposition of the old Body be reduced into the *primum Ens*, or first Being: The way therefore of extracting the Center of Water, in which Metals ought to depose their Body, will I here add.

This Menstruum *we will explain by its Branches; whereof the* First *is,* Oyl of Salt dissolved per deliquium. *In the first process he dissolves Sea-salt, or* Sal Gemmæ, *in water mix'd with the Juice of* Raphanus, *putrefies, and with a stronger Fire distils; but the* Caput mortuum (*the remaining Salt rather*) *he dissolves on a Marble* per deliquium. *In the second Receipt he dissolves* Sal Gemmæ, *being first five or six times melted in an equal quantity of the Juice of* Raphanus *made hot, then coagulates, putrefies, and distils like common* Aqua fortis; *the remaining Salt reduced into Powder, being as yet hot, he dissolves* per deliquium *in a moist place. Sometimes he does without this stinking Juice of* Raphanus *more compendiously prepare that Oyl of Salt* per deliquium, *and that is, from Salt calcined with* Nitre: The Receipt is to take of common Salt, and the Salt of Urine equal parts, to be by the

Rule of *Alchymy* calcined two hours, then resolved in a Cellar after the usual manner, &c. From this calcined Salt is distilled a Spirit, which resolveth Gold into Oyl; but if it be again extracted, and to the highest degree prepared, a most excellent *Aurum potabile* will be had, but without that extraction (*Distillation*) the Gold is only resolved; then is it a most pure Art for Goldsmiths in guilding, and for Iron-smiths a constant and precious Treasure to guild with; yet they that prepare it ought to be skilful *Alchymists*. Libro de rebus Nat. Cap. 4. de Sale. pag. 190. *That* Paracelsus, *by the Salt of Urine intended* Nitre *is easily proved by what follows.* In what place soever (*saith he*) the Urine of Man or Beast is poured forth, at the same succeeding time is *Sal Nitre* produced; for Urine gathered and prepared into another Salt, is called *Sal Niter. ibidem. But the same Receipt*, Tract. de Sale, pag. 171. *Puts it out of all doubt, being thus described.* Take Salt and *Sal Nitre* in equal proportion; let them be calcined by themselves till they melt, then resolve them into a Liquor.

The Second *is*, The Oyl or Essence of Salt. *In the first process he takes the Oyl of Salt* per deliquium, *and cohobates it so oft with the Spirit of* Philosophical Wine, *till the Salt remains at the bottom in a form of an Oyl, and no Phlegm ascends; but if instead of the Spirit of* Philosophical Wine *any* Vegetable Menstruum *be taken, as for example; the* Menstruum *which we treat now of, being already prepared, or Salt circulated, there is no necessity for the Salt to be dissolved* per deliquium, *but is with less pains reduced into an* Oyl or natural Essence. Though, *saith he*, there are more ways to extract the *Ens primum* of Salt, yet this is most commodious and most expeditious; and after this, there is that other way which we mention'd, speaking of the *Elixir* of Salt, namely, that new Salt mix'd well with the dissolving water, which is the distill'd Spirit of Salt, *the* Circulatum minus *made of Salt, the water of Salt circulated*, (*the* Arcanum *of Salt*, *the* Menstruum *which is now in hand*) must be putrify'd, and distill'd so long, till the substance of the Salt be dissolved, and reduced into a perpetual Oleosity, the Body in the Form of Phlegm being abstracted from it. *The place alleadged is in Lib.* 8. *Archid. de Elixeriis pag.* 31. Take Salt well prepared, most white, and pure, put it into a Pellican, with six times the weight of the dis-

solving

solving water (by the dissolving water is our water of Salt (*circulated*) to be understood. *Lib. 10. Archid. pag.* 38.) Digest them a month together in Horse-dung; then separate the dissolving water by Distillation, and pour it on again; and separate, as before, and that so oft, till the Salt be converted into Oyl. *This way of making the Essence of Salt with the* Circulatum minus, *is much better, and more exquisite than that former preparation performed by the Spirit of* Philosophical Wine, *though* Paracelsus *affirms the former method to be more useful, and more expeditious than the latter; which is to be understood of the use of both, not the preparation: For the Essence of Salt is both sooner and better prepared with some* Circulatum minus, *than with the simple Spirit of* Philosophical Wine; *from which Essence of Salt which way soever made, is prepared the* Arcanum *of Salt; which reason will have more commodious, and more expeditious, in extracting the Essences of things, than the Oyl of Salt, not yet so graduated. In the second Process,* Paracelsus *commands, indeed, the Oyl of Salt made* per deliquium *to be putrefy'd; but as to the means of putrefaction, whether with the Spirit of* Philosophical Wine, *or some simple* Vegetable Menstruum *makes no mention, without which notwithstanding the Salt would not ascend in the Alembick, and if it were distilled, yet would it be of no use in extracting Essences: He putrify'd therefore the Oyl of Salt* per deliquium, *for some time with the Spirit of* Philosophical Wine, *then being putrifyed, distil it with a stronger Fire, the residue of the Salt be again dissolv'd on a Marble, and being dissolved, putrify'd and distill'd it with new Spirit of* Philosophical Wine, *or some Simple Vegetable* Menstruum, *so often, till he had distill'd the whole into Spiritual Water of Salt.*

The third Branch consists in the Reduction of the Essence of Salt into the Arcanum *of the same; for the Natural, (that is,* Saline,) *Essence of Salt, doth by being cohobated sometimes with the Spirit of* Philosophical Wine, *ascend together with it, becomes sweet, and is transmuted into the* Arcanum *of Salt, or Artificial Essence, of which* Arcanums *more in the* second Book of Medecines. *Common Salt therefore distilled with the Spirit of* Philosophical Wine *through an Alembick, is the* Circulatum minus *of* Paracelsus, *the* Aqua salis circulati, *the* Primum ens salis, *the* Arcanum salis, *the* Aqua solvens, *the* Spiritus salis distillatus, *the* Matrix *and* Center *of* Metals *and* Minerals, &c. *It is called* Circulatum, *by reason of the Circulation.*

culation or Digestion of the Essence of Salt for a Month with the Spirit of Philosophical Wine, *or which is more probable, because of the common Circulation of all the Vegetable* Menstruums *for the space of* 30, 40, *or* 60 *Days; after the* Menstruum *was already made, so that this Circulation, though omitted in our Receipt, must be understood in these* Circulatums *of* Paracelsus: *It is not therefore called* Circulatum minus, *as if common Salt had less Virtues in dissolving, than the other Salts, but because it hath those only, and not the quality of tinging superadded, as the greater* Circulatums: *after the same manner as Salt is made a* Circulatum, *may also* Vitriol *be made a* Circulatum, Alum *a* Circulatum, Tartar *a* Circulatum, *&c.* This way also, *saith Paracelsus,* is the *Arcanum* or *Magistery* to be made of Vitriol, as also of all other Salts, *Lib.* 10. *Arch. Cap.* 3. *Pag.* 38.

Lastly, As the saline Essence of Salt loseth its saltness, and becomes sweet by being digested and cohobated in the Spirit of Philosophical Wine; *so the Common Spirit of Salt well mixed and digested with the Spirit of Wine, becomes a sweet* Menstruum. *It is thus done:*

28. The Sweet Spirit of Salt of *Basilius. Lib. Partic. sub Sulphure Solis & Rep. 12. Clav.*

TAke of the Spirit of Salt wholly dephlegmed one part, of the best Spirit of Wine free from all Phlegm, or the Sulphur of Wine, made as I shall tell you lower (*the Description of which we lately had in the precedent Pages*) one half part, fit an Alembick well luted, and distil strongly, so as that nothing remains: To the Distillation add one other half part of Spirit of Wine, and distil, and that repeat three times, putrefie fifteen days, or till it become sweet, which must be done in a gentle Balneo; thus will you have the Spirit of Salt and Wine without any corrosion for extractions.

But though this Menstruum *may deserve its Praises, yet it can scarce be reckoned amongst* Menstruums *of this Kind, where we discourse not of acid Spirits, but fixed Salts; it must therefore be considered as an Appendix of the circulated Salt: to the Illustratino of which it will not a little conduce.*

From

From the Receipts we observe,

1. *That by* Aqua Vitæ, *or Spirit of Wine, the* Adepts *did not in the least intend Common; but Philosophical* Aqua ardens; *for Common* Aqua ardens *will never perform that which is desired in these Receipts; and it being granted, that it seems to perform, yet* Menstruums *so made, cannot be* Menstruums *of the* Adepts, *but Common, of no efficacy or esteem in the more secret Chymy.*

2. *That* Basilius *has indeed sometimes used common* Aqua ardens *for his* Menstruums, *but never by it self, but mixed with Vegetable* Sal Armoniack, *or Philosophical Salt of* Tartar *(that is, with the Spirit of* Philosophical Wine) *volatilized; which Salt, being brought into a liquid substance by virtue of this Spirit, is his* Menstruum; *for he separates again from thence the Spirit of* Common Wine, *either by Flame, or by quick Lime.*

3. *That the greater quantity of* Sal Armoniack *is joyned with the Spirit of* Philosophical Wine, *the stronger are these* Menstruums *made; wherefore* Basilius *his* Menstruums *of this Kind, from which all the common* Aqua ardens *is separated, are to be reputed among the best.*

4. *That these* Menstruums *are the Magistery of fixed Salts, by* Paracelsus *call'd the less* Circulatums, *or* Arcanum *of the* Alkali *of Tartar, Beans, Wormwood, as also common Salt, Alom, Nitre,* &c.

5. *And therefore that these* Menstruums *are Medecines.*

6. *That these* Menstruums *may be made several ways; as these out of the* Sal Armoniack *of* Lully, *by the method of* Paracelsus *his* Circulatums, *and so on the contrary, provided the* Alkalies *or fixed salts be volatilized, and distilled together with the Spirit of* Philosophical Wine *through an Alembick.*

7. *That the Spirit of* Philosophical Wine *is not easily mixed with these Salts, but by certain degrees: First, He extracts the Tincture or Soul from them, that is, the more unctuous parts; which being more volatile than the rest, are then easily distilled into a volatile Tincture, or (to use* Luly's *phrase) into the animated Spirit; then the remaining Earth, being now fixed by the same means, is again volatilized by absorbing the said animated Spirit by degrees, and sublimed into* Sal Armoniack.

8. *That these* Sal Armoniacks *are sublimed with a very strong fire.*

9. *That*

9. *That these Salts are called* Harmoniack, *by reason of the Harmony ar Perfection of their mixtion.* So have you, saith *Lully*, the formal Harmoniack mixtion of all the Elements; wherefore wonder not, if we call it *Sal Armoniack*; for so it is called, because of its exalted and sublimed property the pure and first Matter of Nature, *Lib. Mercur. pag.* 155.

10. *That the volatile Salt of* Tartar, *the volatile Salt of* Wormwood, Carduus Benedictus, *&c. common volatile Salt* (*by* Paracelsus *call'd* Sal enixum) *are rightly term'd* Sal Harmoniacks, Philosophical Vegetable Mercuries, *and* Sulphurs of Nature, *&c.*

11. *That the Spirit of* Salt, Nitre, Vitriol, Aqua fortis, *&c. are by being cohobated with the Spirit of* Philosophical Wine *made sweet.*

The

The Sixth KIND.

Simple Vegetable Menſtruums *made of the Spirit and Tartar of* Philoſophical Wine.

29. The *Cœlum Vinoſum* of *Pariſinus* made of the Salt of *Philoſophical Wine.*

In Appendice Eluc. Pag. 271. *Vol.* 6. *Theat. Chym.*

TAke the Philoſophers firſt Matter, called *Chaos* (*Vegetable Mercury, the Philoſophers Wine*) diſtil its Spirit (*ardent*) and Watery Element (*Phlegm*) in its convenient Veſſel, as we ſhall teach in its proper place, till its Body remain in the bottom like melted Pitch, which by two diſtillations waſh with its Watery Element, then pour its Spirit to it, four Fingers above it, mixing the Matter well, till it be well united, and ſet the Veſſel to diſtil in Balneo with an eaſie heat: then put it into Putrefaction ſix Days in a convenient Veſſel, and diſtil in Aſhes, (*the animated Spirit*) then take other Spirit, (*ardens*) and that being poured to it, put it again into Putrefaction ſix Days, and ſo repeat this Magiſtery, till you ſee that the Spirit has imbibed and extracted the Soul out of the Body, an infallible ſign of which will be, when you ſee its Earth hard and dry: for then may you be aſſured, that the Body is for its health-ſake dead, which you may vivify and make incorruptible, and it will no more fear Death, nor Corruption in this World. Now take the aforeſaid Body, firſt weigh it, then put it in a convenient Veſſel, and pour to it an eighth part of its Spirit (*animated Spirit*) which

which extracted its Soul, then put your Vessel in a Fire of digestion, (which we shall speak of afterwards) and continue the Fire till you see that the Earth hath imbibed its Liquor: then open your Vessel, put on an Alembick, and gather that little sweat, which will have the taste of hot Water: Imbibe now your Matter for a second time with a seventh part of the aforesaid Spirit, which contains the Soul, and proceed in the methodizing of the aforesaid Magistery: Now for a third time imbibe with a sixt part, for a fourth time imbibe with a fifth part, for a fifth time imbibe with a fourth part, and do not multiply the weight of the aforesaid Spirit, but continue it so, observing the aforesaid Method, till the Matter, which hath drunk up its Spirit, and is again united with its Soul, be white. Take now the aforesaid Earth, and put it in convenient sublimation, the lower part of the Vessel being luted below the Matter, and make the pure part sublime from the impure, and so will you have our Mercury, which is clear and shining as a Diamond. This is that which the Philosophers do by divers Metaphors, call the first Vegetable Matter, *Sal Armoniack*, our Mercury, our Sulphur of Nature, whereas notwithstanding 'tis one and the same thing. Take the other Simple Spirit, which you first extracted out of your *Chaos*, that which hath not extracted its Soul, and make it more pure and subtil by the way following: Take of the Vegetable first Matter (*Sal Armoniack*) which you made before, one Pound, and put it in a convenient Vessel in Balneo, till the Matter dissolve it self (*per deliquium*) then putting to an Alembick, distil the superfluous Water, then pour on three Pounds of the aforesaid Simple Spirit (*ardens*) and the Vessel being conveniently stop'd, as will be manifested below, put it into Putrefaction for one Natural Day, after the manner following: Get you a Brass Vessel, about one span and a half broad, and three spans and a half long, which towards the Orifice must have a Copper Bottom pierced with many Holes, the Cover whereof, which is to go into the Vessel, and stop it well, must have one or two Holes: but the Glass Vessels, which you would put to that Copper Vessel, ought to be conveniently covered: in the lower part of those Copper Vessels of Putrefaction must be common Water, those Copper Vessels put upon a Furnace, making a moderate Fire under, by the strength of which the

the fume or vapour of the Water will aſcend, and heat the Veſſels, in which your Matter is; the whole work of our Supream Magiſtery will be matured and prepared by this Method, then diſtil conveniently in Aſhes with a heat, ſcarce unlike to the heat of the Sun, till you have drawn all the Juice from it, then diſſolve the Matter by pouring to it of the aforeſaid Simple Spirit three parts, in reſpect of the Matter, which remained in the Veſſel, after the aforeſaid Juice was abſtracted from it; Repeat the Magiſtery a fourth time, proceeding and obſerving all things exactly as above: So will you have the Spirit of your *Chaos*, which is by the Philoſophers called *Fire depurated*, reduced from power into act with the Virtue of the Vegetable Matter. Take therefore a Glaſs Veſſel, ſtrong, able to contain the meaſure of a common Urne, pure and long, whoſe Neck muſt be ſtrong, and two ſpans and a half long; whoſe Cover muſt be another Glaſs, called *Antenotorium*, with a Neck turned downward, containing the fourth part of a common Urne, to be put into the aforeſaid Veſſel: Into this Circulating Veſſel put four Pounds, and no more, of the depurated Spirit, which you brought from power to action, by Virtue of the Vegetable Matter, as I taught you before, Circulate in Balneo, or Dung the ſpace of ſixty Days, and when Converſion is made of the Spirit deduced from power to action by the firſt Vegetable Matter, then this you will thereby know, that in the bottom of the Veſſel will be a Sediment, like the Urine of a ſound Man: Then will you ſee a Quinteſſence brighter and clearer then a Diamond, which exceeds the Stars in ſplendour, ſo as to be doubted, whether it be contain'd in the Glaſs or not: which you muſt dexterouſly ſeparate from its Sediment, and keep in a Veſſel cloſe ſtopped in a cold place: This is that Virtue which the envious have hidden, and obſcured by innumerable Metaphors, calling it *Spiritus Vivus*, *Aqua Argenti vivi*, *Aqua Vitæ*, *Aqua Celeſtis*, *Aqua Dianæ*, *Anima Menſtrui Vegetabilis*, *Fumus*, *Ventus*, our *Heaven*, *Menſtrual Blood*, *Urine ſublimed*, *Menſtruum*, our *Water of Sulphur*, our *Bleſſed Stone*, giving it infinite other Names, which we mention not here, but have by Experience ſeen and known them to be one and the ſame thing.

Annotations.

M*Ost of the* Adepts *knew no other but this way of acuating the Spirit of* Philosophical Wine, *for they believed there was one only thing, and one only Method: but this is not the last amongst the difficult Methods, nor much different from the* Cœlum *Vegetable of* Lully *made of the* Alkali *of* Tartar. *The* Tartar *of this Wine is less Oyly than common* Tartar, *and therefore adjoyned to this, as a higher Kind; but that we may the better understand the Receipt, 'tis convenient to compare it with its Original, taken out of the last Testament of* Lully.

30. The *Cœlum Vinosum* of *Lully.* *In Testam. Noviss.*

TAke Red Wine, which we call the Liquor of *Lunaria*, and *Nigrum nigrius nigro*, and distil an *Aqua ardens* in Balneo, and rectify it, till it be without Phlegm, which you will know, when it burns a piece of Linnen Cloth, by reason of its heat, which you will make it do in five times, sometimes in three, and having such a sign, divide it into two parts, and keep one part for the making of the *Menstruum*, and with the other part abstract the Soul from the Earth (*a pitchy mass*) by the way which I shall tell you. The way, my Son, is, to distil the Phlegm, till it remain in the form of liquid Pitch, then put to it of the Water (*ardens*) which you rectify'd, so much, as to swim three Fingers above the Matter, and the Vessel being very close, set it in Dung or Balneo six Days to digest, after that distil all the Water, in which is the Soul, upon hot Ashes, then increase the Fire a little, and take out the Oyl, which keep: then pour in of the other Water (*ardens, or Spirit of Philosophical Wine*) as before, and put it in Putrefaction six Days, as before, and then distil in Ashes, first the Water, then the Oyl, and thus continue the Magistery the same way, till you have extracted all the Soul from the Earth, keep it, because it is the animated Water, and keep the Oyl for the Tincture: Then take the Earth being dry and hardned, hardened, and calcine till it grows white, being white, give the Soul in the Water reserved to it. My Son! the way is this, Take the Earth being white and depurated (*Salt*) and know the weight, put it in a Vessel of Glass, and pour upon it an eighth part of the animated Water, the Vessel being very close, and place it in Balneo three days, till you see the ardent Spirit condensed in the Balneo, and rectify it, till it be without Phlegm, then having put on an Alembick, draw off the Liquor without taste, because the Soul hath embraced the Spirit, which is in that part; and imbibe a second time with a seventh part of the animated Water, and digest as before, and distil away the moisture: A third time imbibe with a sixth part, digest and distil away the VVater: A fourth time pour on a fifth part of the animated VVater, as before: The fifth time give a fourth part, and digest as you know; and continue with the fourth part always digesting and drawing of the Liquor, till our Earth be pregnant and white: Then take the Earth being pregnant, and put it in a subliming Vessel luted and very close in a Fire of the third degree, the space of twenty four Hours, and sublime the pure from the impure: And thus my Son will you have the Vegetable Mercury sublimed, clear, resplendent in the Form of a wonderful Salt. Know you must my Son, that the Philosophers and we do call it properly *Vegetable Sulphur*, *Sal Armoniack*, our *Sulphur*, the *Sulphur of Nature*, and many other Names we also give it. Take, my Son, of this *Vegetable Sulphur*, which you made, one Ounce, put it in a Glass Vessel, and pour upon it three Ounces of the VVater, (*Aqua ardens rectifyed to the highest*) revealed to you before, and the Vessel being covered close, put it in Balneo for one Natural Day, then Distil in Ashes, till all ascend that can, then know the weight of the Salt remaining at the bottom of the Vessel, and pour to it three times its weight of the aforesaid *Aqua ardens*, and put it in our Balneo the space of one natural Day, then Distil in Ashes, and thus do three times: Then is all the Vegetable Salt come over the Helm with its own VVater, and mixture is made, and the Water clear, which we call *Simple Menstruum*. My Son! Take a Glass Vessel, which must be white Glass and sound, and it must be a large Vessel, and put into it four Pounds, or six (at most) of this *Menstruum* thus simply dissolved, and the Vessel being well shut and sealed,

put

put it in Balneo or Dung, the ſpace of ſixty Days, and it will in that time be converted into a Quinteſſence exceeding Glorious and Odoriferous, which you will know, when you ſee in the bottom of the Veſſel a Sediment, like that in the Urine of a well Complexioned Youth, and it will be clear and reſplendent, as a Star of Heaven: Keep it in a hot and moiſt place, as is a Balneo, ſeparating it firſt from its Sediment, and ſealing the Veſſel well as may be.

Both Receipts agree in all things, except that Lully *calcines the dead Earth, and by diſſolving in common Water and calcining, purifies it;* Pariſinus *not ſo: this Earth notwithſtanding ſeeming by this way of putrifying to be made fitter for the Reception of its Spirit; The Receipts conſiſt of theſe two parts, the preparation of the Vegetable* Sal Armoniack, *and the Reduction of the ſame Salt into a liquid Subſtance or* Menſtruum: *The preparation of the* Sal Armoniack *is effected by two Operations: In the firſt, the Soul is extracted out of the Body by Virtue of the Spirit, to exanimate and fix the Earth, and make it melt like Wax on a red hot Plate: In the ſecond, the Soul is ſtored to this fixed Earth by times, and this variouſly, to make it Volatile: In both Receipts as well of* Lully, *as* Pariſinus, *the animated Spirit is reſtored to the Earth ſo exanimated, in an eighth, ſeventh, ſixth, fifth, and fourth part of its weight, till it wholly evaporates upon a fiery hot Plate; this method of impregnating, or revivifying the Dead Body will be confirmed and illuſtrated by the*

Vegetable *Sal Armoniack* of *Pariſinus*. *In Apertorio Cap. F. and L. and parte ſecunda Citharæ vel Violettæ, and Cap. 5. Elucid. pag.* 235. *Vol. 6. Theat. Chym.*

OUr Vegetable Mercury is that Principle to be admired above all other things of this Art, which conſiſts in the preparation and ablution of its moſt precious Earth, which is of ſo great Virtue, as not to be comprehended by the wit of any Men, thoſe only excepted, who have attained to the miraculous effects of it. Our purpoſe is to take the matter remaining (*In the*

the distillation of Philosophical Wine) like melted pitch, to which pour of its Death (*Phlegm*) the height of four fingers above it, agitate; that the tincture, or unctuous superfluous part of it may be dissolved, let the matter settle, decant the tincture, to the remaining matter pour new Phlegm, agitating and decanting so oft, till no more tincture ascends, and the Earth remains white, sparkling like a Diamond, which dry in the Sun or some such heat; being dryed and pulverized, pour to it of C, that is, its (*ardent*) Spirit, so much as will swim upon it the space of four Fingers, digest in a blind Head three natural Days, then distil with a slender heat of Ashes, till the Veins disappear, take away the Receiver, stop it well, put another to, distil away all the Phlegm with a Fire somewhat stronger, cool the Vessel, take out the Matter being hardened, pulverize, and putting it in the same Vessel, pour to it of C the breadth of three Fingers, lute, and putrefie three days, take away the blind Head, distil through an Alembick, till the Veins ascend, then change the Receiver, as before, repeat these Operations, till the Earth remain white, and fume not upon a hot Plate: Now take a Phial, put the aforesaid Earth into it, lute well the Neck of the Phial, and set it to digest, or calcine rather in Ashes, and you will have your most precious Earth now fit to receive its Spirit (*animated*) or Soul, with the conservation of its radical moisture. Take this Earth, put it in a round Vessel, a hands breadth deep, broad about the Orifice, and imbibe it with its Soul, or animated Spirit, as we shall declare, cap. L. thus have you so full an Instruction of this Matter, that 'tis impossible for you to err, if you be a faithful Christian. I promised (*he goes on cap. L.*) to give you full direction for the making of all sorts of Sulphurs for our Magistery, that is, Mineral, Vegetable, and Animal Sulphur. Wonder not, that I did first sublime, and vivify the Mineral Sulphur of Nature, I doing this, to give them in order, and that you might the better attend your Practice and Theory: though I know, you are not ignorant, that no dissolution can be made without either Vegetable or Animal Sulphur. Now to our purpose; Take the Vegetable Earth prepared, as I taught you cap. F. imbibe it with its animated Spirit, giving an eighth part of it, (*in respect of the Earth*) cover the Vessel with a Blind Head, digest eight days in Balneo, then lay aside this Head, and draw of all the

the insipid moisture in a gentle heat of Ashes, or of the Sun: then imbibe with a seventh part, digesting in Balneo, and distilling in Ashes, as before; then imbibe with a sixth, then a fifth; lastly a fourth part, and with this quantity repeat the rest of the imbibitions, till the Earth hath drank up two parts and more of its weight: Then take the Earth out of the Vessel, pulverize, and put a little of it upon a red hot Plate, if the greatest part of it fume away, put the powder into a Sublimatory, and sublime the Philosophers *Sal Armoniack*, giving the beginning of Vegetation to both the terrestrial Luminaries (*Gold and Silver*) without which, neither the Vegetable nor Animal Work, yea nothing at all can be done in this Magistery.

This Volatilization of the fixed Earth the Adepts *performed other ways also, not always observing the order of the aforesaid weights of the animated Spirit, in the resuscitation or impregnation of the dead Body: For sometimes they imbibed this exanimated Earth with an eighth part of its animated Spirit so oft, till it became animated again, and was made Volatile. Thus* Lully *made his.*

The Vegetable *Sal Armoniack* of *Lully.*
Libro de materia Vegetabili in practica quarta.

TAke excellent Wine either red or white, distil by the Rule of Art an ardent Spirit, burning Cotton, evaporate the Phlegm till the Matter remain thick, as melted pitch, to which pour of the ardent Spirit so much, as to swim four Fingers above it: digest for a week in Balneo, then distil the animated Spirit by Ashes, to the Earth pour new ardent Spirit, repeating so oft, till the Earth remain dry, and in the Form of powder: Moreover, you must from the Earth distil an Oyl in Ashes with a Fire sufficiently strong, so as that the Earth being laid on a red hot Plate, casts forth no fume. That Oyl, as also the Phlegm are of no value in the present Work. Calcine or Reverberate the said Earth in a close Vessel, to which pour of the animated ardent Spirit an eigth part in an Alembick, digest in Balneo three days, then gently draw off the superfluous moisture, being insipid as common Water, imbibe as before, and continue so oft, till the

Earth

Earth in a close Vessel, to which pour of the animated ardent Spirit an eighth part in an Alembick, digest in Balneo three days, then gently draw off the superfluous moisture, being insipid as common Water, imbibe as before, and continue so oft, till the Earth be made Volatile, which you will know, if a little of it put on a red hot Plate be almost wholly evaporated: This impregnated Earth sublime with a subliming Fire the space of twenty four Hours: The Volatile and sublimed Salt sublime by it self yet twice, which is to be with the ardent Spirit dissolved, distilled, and forty or fifty days Circulated into an Odoriferous Liquor.

Sometimes they impregnated the Earth from the beginning to the compleat saturity of it, with a fourth part of the animated Spirit, thus:

The Vegetable *Sal Armoniack* of *Lully*. *In Apertorio suo.*

TAke of the best Juice of *Lunaria*, that you can find, one Pound or two, and put it into a Vessel with an Alembick, the seams being well joynted and luted, set it in a little Furnace, and underneath make a Fire of one wiek, and with such a gentle heat let the aforesaid Spirits be distilled, and so long, till it begins to make Veins: When therefore the Phlegm begins to shew Veins, then is it a sign, that the Spirit is distilled, which contains in it all the perfection of Life, and then take that distilled Spirit, and keep it very choicely in a Glass well stopt with white Wax, then put another Receiver under the Alembick, and receive the second Water, because it retains yet something of the aforesaid Spirit, though not so strong as the first: distil from that second Water so long, till nothing else comes but Phlegm, which is no otherwise then as common Water, tasting a little, if it has yet any Virtue, than may you distil yet more, but if it be as the other Water pure in taste, then lay aside the Receiver with that second Water, and put another Glass to receive all the Phlegm, distilling so long, till nothing more distils, and then let all the Phlegm be poured away, because it is that, which brings Death to our

Precious Stone, and this the vulgar knows not, but we know. Now have you the Earth, which remained in the bottom of the Veſſel black, like melted Pitch: For that calcination of the Earth cannot be done with a ſtrong Fire, as Sophiſters believe, but it is done by its own Spirit, which keeps it from burning, becauſe its Spirit draws the Soul from its Body, and repels its ſuperfluous Phlegm, and mortifies the Earth, and then vivifies it: Now therefore calcine the aforeſaid Earth in this manner; Take the ſecond diſtilled Water (*Aqua ardens mix'd with Phlegm*) and pour it upon the black Earth (*Pitch*) in its Veſſel, and mix well, till it be diſſolved, becauſe the Earth is preſently diſſolved. Then put on an Alembick, and lute well, and diſtil the Spirit with one wiek, as I told you before, till you ſee Veins, then again ſeparate the Receiver of the Alembick with the Spirits, and ſet it apart, and put another Receiver to, and diſtil on, looking if there be yet any Spirits there, if not, then the Water which is diſtill'd, hath a taſte like hot common Spring Water, which put away again, becauſe ſuch Water is Phlegmatick, which cauſeth Death to our Stone: And after the whole diſtillation take the Veſſel with all the Matter, which you will then find more hard than before, and this is the reaſon, becauſe that Spirit hath attracted the Aereral Soul to it from its Body, it being the place in which the Soul is contained: that Operation repeat ſo oft, till you ſee your Matter calcined in the bottom in the Form of a black Powder, or even ſo long, till you ſee no more Phlegm ariſe, ſo as the laſt Water to be of as great virtue, ſtrength, ſmell and taſte, as the firſt: And you muſt not be ignorant, that in the third diſtillation thoſe two Spirits (*ill and well rectify'd*) are to be mixed together upon their Earth, ſo long, till the Earth and Spirits have thoſe ſigns aforeſaid, namely, the Earth be calcined, and the Spirits yield no Phlegm. Then take the Earth, and with it a fourth part of its weight of the Spirit, and put the Matter into your Veſſel, which we call *Retentorium*, and place it in a Furnace, continuing an eaſie heat ſo long, till the Spirit be altogether coagulated in the Earth. Know Son! that the Body, which was Dead, puts on white Garments, as, if God pleaſe, you ſhall ſee, when you try the things aforeſaid. Son! this muſt you repeat with new Spirit ſo long, till you ſee the Earth altogether white as Snow: and then is the Earth big and impregnated

ted with Eternal clarity, which will bring forth an Infant, according to this way: When the Earth is very white, then Son! take it out of its Vessel, and grind it into a most fine powder, and this do upon a Glass Plate, then again put it into a Vessel, luting the Joynts of it well, and set it on a little Furnace, and kindle a Fire, continuing it for thirty Hours, and in the corners and sides of the Vessel you will find our Infant, born and resuscitated in the likeness of a powder, most white, most fair, and in such clearness, as the Body of Silver: Keep it therefore in high esteem, because it is your *Terra foliata*, and it is called the Spirit of sublimed Bodies, converted into *Terra foliata*; so winto the same the Soul, &c.

Sometimes they impregnated this Earth without observing any weigh t, as thus:

Another Vegetable *Sal Armoniack* of *Lully*. *In Luce Mercuriorum.*

TAke Wine red or white, putrify it in Balneo twenty days at least, that the parts of it may be disunited, and the better separated, then by distillation of Balneo, with a most gentle Fire draw off the *Aqua ardens*, which put in rectification so oft, till nothing of the Phlegm remains: then draw off the Phlegm by distillation with a Fire of Ashes, till a certain matter remains in the bottom of the Vessel like liquid Pitch, and the said Phlegm put apart: then take the said matter, and pour to it of the Phlegm so much, as to swim four Fingers above it, and put it for two days in Balneo, then one day in a Fire of Ashes, that it may boyl leisurely, and you will find the Phlegm much coloured, which empty into another Vessel: set it in Balneo again for two days with new Phlegm, and for one day in Ashes, then empty it into another Vessel, and thus proceed till the Phlegm will be no more coloured, and if Phlegm be wanting, then take the coloured Phlegm, and by distillation draw off one half, or a third part of it by Balneo, and operate with it as before; but when that Phlegm is no more coloured, then will there remain in the bottom of the Vessel an Earth almost white, the Phlegm having attracted all the Oyl out of it: if you would separate them asunder, put them in distillation of Balneo, then the Phlegm only riseth, and the Oyl will remain in the bottom of the Vessel most red. Take this Earth, and pour to the same of Mercury, (*Vegetable, or Aqua ardens*) so as to swim two Fingers above it, and put it in a Fire of Ashes for one natural Day, so as to boyl gently, then draw off (*distil*) the Earth by a Fire of Ashes as before, and put it apart: And of new *Aqua ardens* pour to the said Earth so much, as to swim two Fingers above it, and set it in Ashes for a Natural Day, then draw it off by distilling in Ashes as before: and thus proceed till there be no more Spirit (*elsewhere called Soul*) remaining in the Earth, but all pass'd over with the *Aqua ardens*, which you may know by the Earth remaining in a most impalpable powder, and putting it on a Fire-hot Plate it will yield no smoak, which will be a sign, that it is without Spirit (*Soul*): which Earth put then into digestion in an *Athanor*, and there let it stand ten days in a continued Fire. Then take of the *Aqua ardens*, in which the Spirit (*Soul*) is, and pour it upon the said Earth, swimming one Finger above it, and put it in an *Athanor* for one Natural Day: then set it in Balneo, and by distillation draw off the *Aqua ardens* without the Spirit (*Soul*) the Spirit remaining in the Earth, then pour on other *Aqua ardens*; and thus reiterate, till the Earth hath drank up all its Spirit, which you will know by putting the Earth upon a red hot Plate, because the greatest part of it will turn into Smoak; which Earth digest for six Natural Days in an *Athanor*, then put it in Ashes, increasing the Fire, till by the sublimation the Vegetable Mercury riseth at the sides of the Vessel, and in the bottom remains the *Terra damnata*, which is not an ingredient to our Work: Which Mercury gather speedily, and whilst it is new; after its rising, mix it with its Water for two days, and it becomes a Water which hath wherewithal to dissolve all Metals with the preservation of their Form, and this Water we call *Vegetable Menstruum*.

Animal Sal Armoniacks *may also be made the same way as Vegetable* Sal Armoniacks *thus is made.*

The

The animal *Sal Armoniack* of *Lully*. *In Testam. Novissimo.*

SOn! there is another way of this animal Sulphur of Nature, in which there is most accurate knowledge, as in Vegetables, which you must perform by the method which we shall teach you; and Son! the way is to take the Urine of Young Men of good Complexion, and put it in a Glass Vessel forty days, till it be putrified: then take a Cucurbit, and putting on an Alembick in Balneo for the space of forty hours, distil a clear Water, and the Spirit will remain in the Earth (*the Soul as Pitch*) dry it being well luted, and rectify the Water seven times, and the white Salt (*Volatile*) which it made in every distillation gather warily, that it may not feel the Air, and put it in its Water (*Spirit.*) Then put the Earth and Water (*Pitch and Spirit*) together in Balneo or Dung for four days, then distil in the same Balneo, and put it again upon the Earth, digest and distil again as before four days; then take the Water by it self, and put it in Dung the space of two Natural Days, and distil in Balneo, and again putrify in Dung, and continue this order five times: Then is the Water (*Spirit*) perfectly rectify'd and clear. This work being ended, restore the Water to the Earth (*Pitch*) and set it in Dung, then distil in Balneo, and dry up the Earth and the Alembick being taken off, and another Cover put on, sublime for the space of twenty four hours the animal Sulphur of Nature: Then gather it together, and upon the Earth, which remained, pour its (*animated*) Water, and put it in Dung, and distil in Balneo, dry and sublime as before, repeating, till all the Sulphur be sublimed. Son! We have revealed to you every way of knowing our Vegetable Sulphurs, and also the animal Sulphur, with a Declaration of the whole Magistery. Now, with the help of God, we shew you, that there is one way and means in the animal and in the Vegetable, without any variation.

This Receipt being less clear, in making no mention of the Spirit of Philosophical Wine, *and yet of no worth without it; I will therefore add his sixth Experiment of the rational Animal, where thus:*

Very

Very great, certainly, and incomprehensible Gifts hath the most high God vouchsafed to us; in the acknowledgment of which, our Duty is both Day and Night to love, worship, and revere him with our whole heart, and everywhere extol his Name with all our might: for besides his creating us out of nothing, and redeeming us with his most precious Blood, he hath also made Man partaker of all the Blessings contained in the greater World, and for this reason is called *Microcosm*; for it has by divine inspiration been revealed to us, that all Virtues as well Animal and Vegetable, as Mineral are in Man himself, and this very thing I will prove to be true by this wonderful Experiment: Take the Urine of Boys, which must be from the eighth to the twelfth Year, and no more; which Urine gather from those Boys in the Morning, rising out of Bed, a great quantity of which 'tis convenient for you to have, which must be very well putrified in a Glass Vessel, the Vessel being stop'd, not to respire, two parts of which Vessel must be full, the other empty, and thus ought it to be placed in Horse Dung to putrify, till the Urine grows black, which commonly happens within forty or fifty days: but that the Urine may putrify and grow black in a shorter space of time, this we have had for a secret, and proved it by true Experiment, that mixing and joyning a Cup of *Aqua Vitæ*, (*Philosophical*) but first highly rectified with the aforesaid Urine, will accelerate Putrefaction: Putrefaction being done, put the Urine in an Urinal, (*Cucurbit*) with an Alembick and Receiver carefully stop'd, two parts of which Vessel must be full, but the third empty, and distil in Balneo with a gentle Fire one part of three, or till it produceth Veins in the Head, which Veins being vanished and gone, remove the Receiver, and being very close stop'd keep it with the distilled Water, which is the Mercury (*Spirit*) of it, in a place as cold as you can: then continue the distillation, increasing the Fire, and its Phlegm will be distilled, which requires a stronger Fire to go over the Helm: and thus continue distilling, till the Body appears in the likeness of Honey, or melted Pitch, then let the Vessel cool, and keep the Phlegm, which shall distil: Then take the first Mercury, or first Spirit, which you distill'd in the beginning, and rectify it thus: Put it into a large Cucurbit an Arm and a half high, then put into the Mouth of the said Vessel Cotton enough to stop the

the Mouth of it; which Cotton must be first moistened with Oyl, and pressed out, and tyed to a Hempen Thred, that when you have a mind, you may draw it out of the Neck of the Vessel, and that the Cotton may not fall into the Cucurbit; then put an Alembick to the Cucurbit with a Receiver, the Joynts being very close, besmeared with Wheat-Flower and Linnen Swaths, that is, impasted with the Pap of Flower bound fast to the Neck of the Cucurbit, to keep the Vessels from respiring, which past (*Chymical Lute*) being dryed, put the Cucurbit to a Fire of Balneo, boyling gently, and the matter will be sublimed into a most precious Salt: Yet Son! take notice of this, that the Beak of the Alembick must be large and wide, lest the Salt rising and subliming out of the Cucurbit should stop the Mouth of the Beak of the Alembick, when it flows over into the Receiver; for if so, the Vessels would be broken, as it hath also happened to us, when we brought this Experiment to practice; when you see all the Salt gone over by distillation, there will remain in the Cucurbit a certain Phlegmatick Water, which throw away, as nothing worth; but the Salt empty with care, and keep it in a Glass Vessel very close stop'd, which Salt will be Volatile, and we will use it either for the dissolving of Bodies, or for the making of Medecines. There is also another way of rectifying or purging the aforesaid animal Spirit or Mercury: Take therefore that animal Spirit, and distil by Balneo, and half the Liquor being gone over, remove the Receiver, and throw away that which remains in the Vessel: that which is distilled, distil again, taking two parts of it, what remains in the Vessel throw away again as before, and what is gone over, distil again a third time, and take little less than all of it, and thus will you have the animal Spirit or Mercury perfectly rectify'd, wherewith you may exanimate your Earth, which you had before remaining in the likeness of liquid Pitch: Take therefore that liquid Pitch, or rather Earth dissolved, and pour upon it so much of the aforesaid animal Spirit, as to rise four Fingers above it, the Vessel with its *Antenotorium* lute, with Wax gummed, that it exhale not, then shake the Vessel or Urinal very well, that the Spirit may be incorporated, and the Earth being well joyned with the Spirit dissolved, put it in putrefaction for two Natural Days, then take away the *Antenotorium*, and immediately put on an

Alembick

Alembick with a Receiver, lute well to prevent respiring, and distil by Ashes: Have a care of the fumes when you open the Vessel, for they are exceeding strong. All the Spirit therefore being by distillation gone over, increase the Fire, that the Soul may be imprinted into the distilled Water, and lastly again increase the Fire thus gradually, till some other Salt or Sulphur be sublimed: When no more will sublime, cool the Vessel, and gather the sublimation, and lay it with the animated Spirit lately distilled; then take out the hard and burned matter remaining in the Vessel, and grind it, and pour again to it of new Spirit as above, cover the Vessel with its *Antenotorium* again as above, and putrify, then take away the *Antenotorium*, and putting on an Alembick with a Receiver well stop'd, distil the animated Spirit by Ashes; which being distill'd again as before, increase the Fire at last, that some part of the Oyl may be forc'd over, and the other part of the Sulphur sublimed; but when you see nothing more will distil, nor any thing sublime, suffer the Vessel to cool, and keep the animated Spirit last distilled with the other distilled before: So also, if any part of the Salt ascends by sublimation, mix it together with the aforesaid Spirit as before, and keep them all in a Vessel close stop'd: then again pour new Spirit upon the Earth, so as to rise three Fingers above it, and joyning an *Antenotorium* to it, putrify as before, and then distil in Ashes as before: but when nothing more will distil, increase the Fire as much as possible by adding fuel, that the Earth may be calcined, and in this third Operation converted into a Beretine or ash Colour, then the Vessel being cold, and the Receiver with the animated Spirit taken away, keep it with the rest of the animated Spirit, but put the Earth into a Vessel of Earth or Chalk, which must be sound, and able to endure Fire, covered with the like Vessel, giving it as strong a heat as can be made with wood, and so continue two days, then by that time you will have calcined the Earth; the Vessel being cold, draw out the said Earth, which will be almost white, or of an ash Colour clear and bright, pour so much of its Phlegm upon it, as will swim four Fingers above it, and let it boyl in Ashes four Hours, and then decant the Liquor warily into another Vessel, and keep it; dry the remaining Earth, and pour to it again of new Phlegm as before, then make it boyl as before, then decant as before, and dry the Earth; thus repeat

peat the Magistery till all the Earth is dissolved, or the most part of it imprinted into that Phlegm, which probably will happen in the third or fourth dissolution: if any thing remains undissolved, throw it away, for it is an empty Earth of no Virtue, but the Earth which was dissolved in the Phlegm, pass through a Filtre, and then again through a most fine Linnen Cloth, which done, congeal the dissolution in a most gentle Fire of Ashes, in a Glass Urinal, to which must be put an Alembick with its Receiver: which being congealed, dissolve again in the same Water lately filtred, then pass it through a Cloth again, and lastly congeal it as before: But this Magistery you must reiterate, till it yields no more Terrestreity in the Filtre: Then keep our Physical *Sal Armoniack*, our *Animal Sulphur*, our fixed *Animal Mercury*, whereof lay a little upon a hot Plate, and if it melt as Wax without smoak, it is a sign you have the *Argent vive* fixed, and perfectly depurated, wherewith you will be able to accomplish many Experiments: This is that Mercury, which hath afforded us most seasonable succour, as shall be manifested in the following Experiments.

To this exanimated Earth restore the animated Spirit by various imbibitions, according to the ways described in the preparations of Vegetable Sal Armoniacks, because, *saith Lully*, there is but one way and method in the animal, as in the Vegetable, nothing varying.

But the ways of making these Salts being very tedious, we will for a conclusion add Lully's *way of abbreviation.*

The Vegetable *Sal Armoniack* made by the accurtation of *Lully*. *In Testam. Noviss.*

THis Sulphur (*of Nature*) may, my Son! with the help of God be wonderfully abbreviated, and the way is this: To take our liquid Pitch (*after the Phlegm is drawn off*) and put it into a Cucurbit, in a Fire of the third degree, and extract the Oyl, till the Earth remains dry and burned. My Son! calcine as I have taught you, and purify the Earth, and so separate the

Salt from it, and upon it pour a forth part of the Spirit, which is in the second Water, (*distilled out of the Pitch*) and digest as above; then drawing off the Liquor (*superfluous, insipid, and to be cast away*) pour again a fourth part, digest and dry as before, till the Earth be pregnant, the sign will be, that nothing more (*of the aforesaid Phlegm or Liquor*) will distil, sublime, and you will have the Vegetable Sulphur clean and pure, and of the same Virtue with the first. I charge you, my Son! with the fear of God, not to reveal this most excellent way of abbreviation to any Man.

Parisinus *in his way of making Vegetable* Sal Armoniack, *declares the Oyl extracted out of the Pitch of* Philosophical Wine, *to be superfluous and inconsonant*: Separate, *saith he*, all the superfluous unctuosities, which do burn the perfect and precious Elements mix'd and latent in that Vegetable Matter, and are repugnant to that composition: *and a little after*; After the separation of the superfluous unctuosity, and aereal substance, which blacks and burns the other precious Elements of this composition, pour to it its ardent and celestial Spirit. *Yea*, Lully *himself has in some Experiments before declared, that Oyl, as also the Phlegm of this Wine to be of no Virtue in the present Work: nevertheless in this accurtation of* Sal Armoniack, *he not only useth the said Oyl, and indeed (which you may wonder at) for the abbreviation, of a most tedious labour, but also affirms that* Sal Armoniack *thus prepared, is of the same Virtue with the rest. Sometimes he used also the Water or animated Spirit, together with the Oyl, for present abbreviation, thus:*

Another Vegetable *Sal Armoniack* by the Accurtation of *Lully*.

Lib. de materia Vegetabili in practica septima.

TAke the best red Wine, distil the ardent Spirit, according to Art, so as to burn Cotton, after that the Phlegm, upon the matter remaining in the bottom of the Alembick, being thick as liquid Pitch, pour the Phlegm half a foot above it, let it boyl three Hours, decant the tinged Phlegm, pour on other, repeating

peating so oft, till no more will be tinged, if you have not Phlegm enough, you must draw off the tinged Phlegms in Balneo, which being evaporated, a Vegetable Oyl will remain in the bottom of the Glass, the tincture being drawn out of the Phlegm, the matter will remain like a dry Earth, upon this dry Earth pour of the ardent Spirit the height of four Fingers, let it boyl two Hours, that which is in the mean time distill'd pour again to the Earth, let it settle two Hours, then decant the animated Spirit from the Spirit or Soul of the Earth, pour new Spirit upon the Earth, doing as before, three times: The Earth being black and calcined, put into a Glass with a long Neck, and pour the Vegetable Oyl (*aforesaid*) to it, digest in Ashes ten days, then decant, and put it into an Alembick, to which add a fourth part of the ardent Spirit animated, digest in a vaporous Balneo for twenty four Hours, then continue the superaddition of the other three parts of the animated Spirit every twenty four Hours, then distil away the superfluous, insipid, and useless Liquor gently by Ashes, and augmenting the Fire by degrees, sublime the Volatile Salt, &c.

Hitherto of the various preparations of Vegetable Sal Armoniacks. *We will now proceed to the other part of the* Cœlum Vinosum, *namely, the several ways of reducing these Salts into a liquid substance. The* Adepts *did for the most part distil through an Alembick one part of Vegetable* Sal Armoniack *with three parts of the* Aqua ardens, *to which Liquor they added again one part of the aforesaid Salt, and distill'd, and that they repeated three, and sometimes four times, to make the weight of the Salt and Water equal; for the greater the quantity of the same Salt, the stronger is the quality of the* Menstruum, *then lastly they circulated the* Menstruum, *thereby to make it more pure and excellent: But though this Method was more in use among the* Adepts, *yet either their curiosity or sedulity found out also other ways; so instead of the* Aqua ardens, *wherewith they prepared the Vegetable* Sal Armoniack, *as well as the* Menstruum, *they sometimes took* Aqua ardens *circulated, or the Heaven, or Essence of* Philosophical Wine, *described in* Numb. 1. *It is thus done,*

31. Cœlum

31. *Cœlum Vegetabile* of *Lully* Circulated.
Lib. de materiâ Vegetabili in practica quinta.

TAke the best white Wine, distil the ardent Spirit till it burns Cotton; put this Spirit into a Circulatory two thirds empty, strengthen the Mouth with Wax, and Bury it in hot Dung, with its Mouth downward, for the Spirit to be circulated and digested the space of forty five Days, or till it swims above more pure and clear, (*in the Form of an Oyl, see the Heaven, or Essence of* Philosophical Wine, *in* Numb. 1.) having seen this sign, take out the Glass warily, and with a Needle perforate the Wax, that the impure may flow out, then suddenly turn up the Circulatory, that the pure or more fine may remain, which we call the ardent Spirit circulated, which is of a most delicious Sent: now take the residue, from which the Spirit of Wine was drawn, and distil the Phlegm; and upon the matter remaining like melted Pitch, pour the said Phlegm, so as to swim four Fingers above it, digest two days in Balneo, decant the tinged Phlegm, and pour on other, and that repeat so often, till the Phlegm will be no more tinged, which is a thing useless in this operation: Now the Earth calcine in a Reverberatory, pulverize, put it in an Alembick, and imbibe with an eighth part of the ardent Spirit circulated, digest in Balneo, and distil some certain superfluous moisture by Ashes: continue this imbibition, digestion, and distillation, till the Earth be impregnated with the dry Spirit, which was in the ardent Spirit circulated, of which the sign will be, if it doth almost all evaporate, being a little of it cast upon a red hot Plate: This impregnated Earth being put into a Sublimatory, sublime according to Art into a Volatile Salt, which digest in Balneo two days and more, with six parts of the ardent Spirit circulated, decant the dissolution gently, and if any thing remain undissolved, proceed with it as before, this dissolution circulate thirty days, and it will be a Quintessence to be compared in Virtue with the *Aurum potabile* of the Ancients.

As these Menstruums *are made either weaker or stronger according*

ing to the variety of weight, so also are they more or less pure, by longer, or shorter, or altogether neglected circulation, for some Menstruums *there are of this kind, which the* Adepts *circulated not: For an Example take the following.*

32. The less Vegetable *Menstruum* of *Lully*. *Lib. de materia Vegetabili in practica prima.*

TAke the best Wine (red is the best) two pounds of it, put into a Cucurbit with a blind Head, and luting the joynts well, put it in Balneo, to putrify kindly the space of forty five days, then fit an Alembick to it, and augment the heat, that the ardent Spirit may be distill'd, which rectify thrice by it self, or till it is free from all Phlegm, and burns Cotton; keep this ardent Spirit well stop'd in a cold place: take the matter remaining in the first distillation, and draw off the Phlegm, till it remain thick like liquid Pitch, upon which pour of the *Spiritus ardens* so much, as to be the space of four Fingers above it, digest three days in Balneo, then distil gently by Ashes three days, and by Virtue of a stronger Fire, the ardent Spirit will carry over the Soul with it, which it could not do in Balneo; keep the distillation: To the remaining Matter pour new Spirit, doing so often, till all the Soul be come over, and that you will know, if by being projected in a small quantity upon a red hot Plate, it yields no smoak, because the matter is now deprived of its Soul, which we call dry Earth, which imbibe with an eighth part of the animated ardent Spirit, digest for three days in Balneo, then distil gently in Ashes the superfluous Liquor, being insipid as common Water: make the second imbibition with a seventh part, and so continue doing as before, till the Earth be made heavier by a fourth part of its weight, and it will be disposed to a reduction into a Volatile Salt by the way of sublimation: This Earth therefore being well pulverized, put into a Sublimatory, administring Fire according to Art, and that which you find sublimed white as Snow, is the Volatile Salt, which keep in a Vessel well stop'd: Take of this Volatile Salt one part, of the ardent Spirit six parts, digest in Ashes, and the

dissolution

dissolution is the Vegetable Quintessence apt to dissolve the perfect Bodies of *Sol* and *Luna*, to make an *Elixir*, and other Medicines precious and grateful.

Vegetable Sal Armoniack *dissolv'd in* Aqua ardens *(one part of the Salt to six of the Spirit) makes the present* Menstruum; *but the following is prepared from* Sal Armoniack *resolved* per deliquium.

33. The Vegetable *Menstruum per deliquium* of *Lully*.

Lib. de materia Vegetabili in Practica secunda.

TAke the best white-Wine, putrify it in Balneo twenty days, or longer, then distil the *Spiritus ardens* according to Art, till it burns Cotton; then draw off the Phlegm, till the matter remains in the bottom of the Vessel thick as liquid Pitch, to which matter pour so much of the Phlegm, as will swim four Fingers above it, digest in Balneo two days, and in Ashes one day, decant the tinged Phlegm; pour new Phlegm to the matter, doing as before, till no more will be tinged, and the matter remains at the bottom of the Vessel like a white Earth, upon this Earth pour the height of two Fingers of the ardent Spirit, digest for a day in Ashes, and the Soul which is in the Earth, will enter into the ardent Spirit, decant the ardent Spirit being animated, pour off the ardent Spirit again upon the Earth, doing it so oft as before, till the Spirit draws out no more Soul, and the Earth remains in the Form of a most fine powder, being despoiled of all its Soul, which you will know, if it smoaks not upon a fiery Plate; this Earth digest ten days in Ashes, then put it in Balneo, and pour of the tinged Phlegm so much, as will swim two Fingers over it, distil in Balneo, cast away the distillation as a thing of no Virtue, then again pour the tinged Phlegm upon the Earth, repeating as before, till no Phlegm remains, and the Earth is impregnated with all the tincture that was in the Phlegm: This done, imbibe the Earth with the animated ardent Spirit, digest with an easy heat in Balneo, till the Earth is well dryed, then again imbibe, and so oft as before, till the animated ardent Spirit is absorbed by the Earth, and is made Volatile, which you will know, if a little of it cast upon a burning Plate fumes away for the most part; then put this matter into a sublimatory, and sublime with a subliming Fire, and that which is sublimed, is the Volatile Salt of the Vegetable matter: put that Volatile Salt into a Phial, digest in Balneo for a day, and it will be reduced into a Water, which we call Vegetable *Menstruum*, which is a wonderful dissolvent for the radical dissolving of the two Luminaries.

These Menstruums *the* Adepts *made sometimes not of Vegetable* Sal Armoniack, *but by the way following.*

34. The Vegetable Mercury of *Lully*. *Lib. de Mat. Vegetabili in practica sexta.*

TAke the best odoriferous Wine, put it in a Circulatory large enough, stop the said Vessel very well with Sulphur melted, and putrify in Balneo twelve or fifteen Days, then distil the Spirit and Phlegm according to Art, till the Spirit burns Cotton; upon the matter remaining like liquid Pitch, pour six parts of the Phlegm, digest two Days in Ashes, shaking the Vessel now and then, decant the Phlegm being tinged, pour on other, and doing as before, till it hath extracted all the tincture, and a black Earth remains at the bottom of the Alembick: put the tinged Phlegm in an Alembick, and distil in Balneo, and that which remains at the bottom of the Vessel will be the Vegetable Oyl, pour the ardent Spirit to the height of four Fingers upon the black Earth, distil by Ashes, and that which is distilled will be the ardent Spirit impregnated, to the matter pour new ardent Spirit, repeating as before three times, and at the last increasing the Fire about the end: Calcine the Earth with a Fire of Reverberation into whiteness, out of which extract the fixed Salt with a little of the Phlegm, the fixed Salt being pulverized, put in an Alembick, pour to it the animated ardent Spirit about two Fingers, distil gently in Balneo the insipid and useless moisture, repeat as before, till the animated Spirit ascends without diminution of its Virtue, and then will you have the fixed Salt acuated, which put in an Alembick, and pour to it the

Vegetable

Vegetable Oyl three Fingers high, digeſt in Aſhes for a day, increaſe the Fire, and diſtil whatſoever can aſcend; the diſtillation keep warily, becauſe it is the Vegetable Mercury: But if any of the Salt remains in the Alembick, you muſt repeat the ſame operations, till at length all the Vegetable Mercury paſſeth through the Alembick, which will extract the Tincture of Gold, being calcined with common Mercury and Salt, and laſtly with Sulphur, which is an excellent *Aurum potabile*.

Sometimes they prepared theſe Menſtruums *by cohobation alone, without any imbibition: For Example.*

35. The rectified *Aqua Vitæ* of *Lully*. *In poteſtate Divitiarum*.

TAke Wine, ſeparate the Spirit warily, as ſoon and as purely as you can, becauſe you will never ſeparate it ſo warily, but that it will contain in it ſome of the pureſt part of this Phlegmatick Subſtance, or Water: this Spirit being once ſeparated, is called Mercury, that is, *Aqua ardens*, the ſign of which is, that if you dip a Linnen Cloth in it, it will turn into a flame (*if firſt kindled*) and not be burned, but if you ſeparate often times, (*rectify*) it is called *Lunaria* rectify'd, that is, *Aqua ardens* rectify'd, whereof the ſign is, that a Linnen Cloth dipp'd in it, burns all away: Separate now all the ſuperfluous Phlegm, till none at all remains, and at the bottom will reſide a Pitch; then mix the *Lunaria*, that is, the *Aqua ardens* rectify'd, with that ſubſtance made like ſoft Pitch, ſhaking it well, till it be incorporated, and ſet it to diſtil, and that which goes over, is called Man's Blood rectify'd, which *Alchymiſts* ſeek for. That Blood is alſo called Air or Wind, and of this thing ſpake the *Philoſopher*, when he ſaid *Wind carryed him in its Belly*: from the remainder ſeparate the ſuperfluous Oyl (*called above Vegetable*) by diſtilling it through a Glaſs Alembick, till nothing remains, which Oyl keep apart, till I ſhall tell you; but the reſidue will be a ſubſtance black and dry, which reduce to a fine powder, and mix by little and little with the rectify'd Man's Blood, and let them ſtand together for the ſpace of three Hours, and then diſtil

ſtil, and then this Water is called *Aqua ignea rectificata*, or Fiery Water rectify'd : then calcine the *Caput mortuum* in a Furnace of Reverberation, till it be made like Lime, and this Calx or Lime mix with the Fiery Water rectify'd, and diſtil ſeven times, and then is it called *Aqua Vitæ* rectify'd.

The ſame Menſtruum *hath* Paracelſus *in his Book*, de Elixire Vitæ, *and the Author of the Appendix of the third Volume of* Theatrum Chymicum. *Theſe* Menſtruums *differ not from the aforeſaid made of* Sal Armoniack, *but only in preparation ; in thoſe the whole Earth of the* Philoſophical Wine *is by its own Spirit reduced into a liquid ſubſtance, with which is performed the ſame Work, but after another manner : Hitherto ought to be referred the* Menſtruum *of* Guido, *made thus :*

36. The *Circulatum minus* of *Guido.* *In Theſauro Chymiatrico.*

TAke of the Spirit of (*Philoſophical*) *Wine* one pound, of the Salt of (*the ſame*) Wine four ounces, mix, the Joynts being well luted, diſtil through an Alembick in Balneo, pour back the diſtillation, and cohobate four times, and it will be prepared. Lully *reduceth his* Sal Armoniacks *with ſome difficulty into a liquid ſubſtance: but* Guido *diſtils the Salt of* Philoſophical Wine *by four cohobations into the ſame* Menſtruum : *the cauſe of abbreviation is to be ſought in the preparation of that Salt, which is two-fold, common or ſecret ; of the common, ſaith* Guido *thus :* The ardent Spirit of Wine being diſtill'd, draw off the Phlegm, till the matter remains in the ſubſtance of the thinner ſort of Honey, which will in a cold Cellar yield Criſtals like Nitre, which are called the Salt of Wine, which take out and keep ; the remainder evaporate a little while, and take more, &c. *Of the ſecret way of making this Salt, ſaith* Guido *alſo*, pag. 8. Theſ. Take of the Salt of Wine, and Spirit of Wine, of each four ounces, digeſt the ſpace of eight or ten days, draw off gently in Balneo, and the Phlegm only will aſcend, and you will have ſix ounces of the Salt of Wine, to which Salt add again an equal quantity of its Spirit, and digeſt again ten days, and draw off the Phlegm, pour new Spirit to the remaining Salt, and proceed as above, and thus may you increaſe the Salt of Wine as you please: *This latter way of making the Salt of Wine, is not only the multiplication, and addition as well of the quantity, as quality of it, but moreover is also the volatilization of it: It is no wonder therefore, that the Salt, whose half part was Spirit of* Philosophical Wine, *should so easily ascend with the same Spirit; yet is it to be well observ'd, lest we temper the aridity of the Salt of Wine too much, with too great an addition of Unctuosity, and instead of a* Menstruum *of this Kind, make a weaker of the second Kind.*

What has been declared of Vegetable Menstruums *is also to be understood of animal* Menstruums; *for an Example we will instance.*

37. The animal Heaven of *Parisinus*.

In Apertorio.

TAke the Urine of Children, between eight and twelve Years of Age, of good disposition and health, get that which is good, and a good quantity, and put it in many Glass Vessels, which you must not fill above two thirds, that it may the better circulate: To every ten measures of Urine mix of our C. (*Philosophical Aqua ardens*) half a measure, which must be without any Phlegm, the Vessels being very well sealed with Wax, let them putrefy fifteen days, and then you will find the matter black, and separated from its Terrestreity: And you must know, the longer it remains in putrefaction, the more perfect will be the work, every five days the Dung must be changed: then pour it out into the Vessel, which we described in the Vegetable Work, and the Joynts being well luted, distil till you see the sign, which we spoke of in *Chap. B.* but for a more certain sign, distil only two parts, then take away the Receiver, and put another to, continuing the distillation, till it remains like Syrup or melted Pitch, then take these two parts reserved, and distil by the same Balneo, receiving three parts of four, the remaining fourth cast away, but distil half of these three, and again distil three parts of four parts of this half, which distil twice by themselves, and thus will you have your Flower rectify'd, with which we extract *Acetum acerrimum* out of its own Earth: Take therefore this Earth, being in the form of Syrup, to which pour the

Flower

Flower (*Spirit*) the height of three Fingers, cover the Vessel with a blind Head, and lute the Joynts with gumm'd Wax, put it in putrefaction three natural Days, and shake the matter in the luted Vessel now and then, as is convenient, that the saline parts may the better be dissolv'd; then take away the blind Head, and put on a common Alembick, but have a care in this changing, lest the sharpness of the Salts offend your *Eyes*: then distil gently in Ashes, and when you have by such a heat extracted all the Water, increase the Fire, that the Oyl or Soul of it may ascend also together with the distill'd Water, whereof one part will be sublimed, the other part will stick to the superficies of the Earth, in the form of a white powder, let the Vessel cool, gather the sublimation; being gather'd, put it in its Water, make the Vessel very close, because it contains the animated Flower, (*Spirit*) then take out the dry Earth remaining, reduce it into powder upon a Porphyry Stone, pour to it the Flower (*or Spirit*) the breadth of three Fingers, putrefy three days, distil in Ashes, increasing the Fire with Wood as above, repeat the Magistery, till the Earth remains of an Ash Colour, then calcine it in a Reverberatory, as we taught you in the Mineral Work, in *Chap.* 2. And so you will have the animal Earth prepared, abounding with so great Virtue, as not to be expressed. O absolute power! upon which all other powers depend, into what thing hast thou infused such Virtue? No Man will comprehend so great a secret, none will believe, unless he himself hath seen by Experience, as we have seen. Take the animated Flower, rectify it three times in Ashes, always casting away the Earths, (*Terrestial Fæces*) then distil in Balneo three parts from four, the remainder throw away, this repeat yet once, then distil the whole, so will you have the animated Flower rectifyed. Take now a large Vessel (*a Cucurbit*) and put in the rectifyed Flower, stop the Mouth of the Vessel with Cotton, put on an Alembick with a Receiver, and with a gentle heat of Ashes all or the greatest part will be sublimed in the Form of a most precious Salt, with which (*if you will*) you may acuate our ☾, which then you must circulate according to the *Chap. D. D.* wherewith you may perfect all your operations (which we taught in the precedent Chapters) which you will sooner compleat by this *Menstruum*. But if you desire the animal Sulphur of Nature, it is necessary for you to sublime presently after you have rectify'd the desired Flower, namely, by imbibing the Earth according to the method and order which we declared in the Vegetable Work, that is, with an eighth, seventh, sixth, fifth, and fourth part, sublime and use to do as in the Vegetable Work, to wit, by acuating the animated Flower with its animal Sulphur sublimed, circulating, and doing all things as in the Vegetable Work. Now Son! you see how I love you, having repeated such things over and over, and with such pains, lest you should have occasion to complain of me, and that you should be expert in every thing, in which I perswaded my self you might err; therefore have we in this Chapter repeated and described that, which no Philosopher ever did in his great Volume, and I may easily believe, that no Philosopher has presumed to describe so long and ample a practice, as this of ours; all which proceeds from my paternal affection towards you, by which I would oblige you under the pain of God's wrath, not to reveal it to any one, but rather burn it, as soon as you have reduc'd it into use, as you have more than often promised us: My farther advice is, That you would strenuously endeavour to live according to the triumphant Gospel of Grace and Peace: reject and avoid Evil Societies and Actions, as we have often admonished you; but if you do otherwise, you will not please him, who is the Donor of this Famous Knowledge, of every good Thing, and Grace it self.

From the Receipts we Note.

1. *That those things which were noted in the fifth precedent Kind, may hitherto also be referred, the* Menstruums *of this Kind differing only in matter from the antecedent, these were made of* Philosophical Wine *only, those of the fixed Salts of divers things; but as to the way of subliming, or the way of making Vegetable* Sal Armoniacks, *they both agree in all things.*

2. *That these* Sal Armoniacks *are called Sulphurs of Nature. In the preparation of* Philosophical Wine *there is an Earth found, which is called* Sulphur, *existent in the Vegetable Mercury, coagulating its own Mercury; for the sake of which Earth, they called every other examimated and fixed Earth,* Sulphur; *but the animated Spirit*

Spirit (Essence, Tincture, *&c.*) *they termed Mercury, to be coagulated by this Sulphur, but both of them being reduced into one Body, and sublimed, they call'd Sulphur of Nature,* (not more fixed, but) *sublimed.*

3. *These Salts are call'd Sulphurs of Nature, to distinguish them from Sulphur against Nature, that is, of every Acid.* Fire, *saith Ripley,* differs many ways; for one is a natural Fire, another unnatural, another elemental, and another *contra naturam:* Natural Fire is that which proceeds from the Influence of the Sun, Moon, and Stars, from which are produced the Spirits of burning Waters, the essential vapours of Minerals, as also the Natural Virtues of living things; the unnatural is an occasional Fire, which is called a moist Fire, made artificially by Philosophers: it is also called a Fire of the first degree, which is for the meer temperance of heat called Balneo, Stove or Dunghill; in this Fire is made the Putrefaction of our Stone: elemental Fire is that which fixeth calcines, and burneth, and is nourished by things combustible; Fire against (or contrary to) Nature, dissolves violently, breaks, kills, and destroys the governing power of the Form of the Stone: for it dissolves the Stone into the Water of a Cloud with the destruction of the specifick Form: but it is termed Fire contrary to Nature, because the operation of it is contrary to all natural operations, as *Raymond* asserts: for all things that Nature hath made, this Fire destroys, and brings to Corruption, unless the Fire of Nature be added to it, *&c. Med. Phil. pag.* 135. Wherefore also there are four Fires in our art, namely, the Natural, which is the *Menstruum Sericonis*; the unnatural, that is, Horse Dung, or *Vindemia*, and the like: the elemental, *viz.* maintained by Wood and other combustible things; and the Fire contrary to Nature, that is, all corrosive Waters, made of Vitriol, Salt, and such like things. *Viatic. pag.* 342. *but of these in another place, namely, the fifth Book.*

4. *That these Salts are to be used presently after the sublimation of them.*

5. *That Philosophical* Aqua Vitæ, *though never better rectify'd, yet contains in it some certain superfluous moisture, which it expells, either by being circulated by it self, as in the preparation of* Lully's *Heaven, or imbibed in things fixed, as in the ways of making the said Salts.*

6. That

6. *That a* Menstruum *made of* Lully's *Heaven, with the Essence or Oyl of* Philosophical Wine, *is no stronger than the rest, as to the preparation of the* Sal Armoniack, *though it may be sooner made with this Oyl, than simple* Aqua ardens, *but as the* Sal Armoniack *already made is mixed, and again circulated not with the thin Philosophical Water, but with the Oyl or* Aqua Vitæ *circulated.*

7. *That the divers ways of subliming these Salts do most clearly discover to us as well the Nature of that Spirit of Wine, as of these* Menstruums, *and moreover commends the incomparable Experience of* Lully *in these things.*

8. *Animal* Menstruums, *tho' extracted out of the Urine, and other parts of Man, are nevertheless not properly so called, so long as the matter of that Spirit of* Philosophical Wine *was Vegetable, and only acuated with an animal thing: yea the very Spirit of* Philosophical Wine *made also out of the animal Kingdom, as also acuated, would notwithstanding differ not from the simple Vegetable* Menstruums *in the properties of dissolving, because it would together with the said simple Vegetable* Menstruums, *very much vary from the tinging faculty of the compounded Vegetable* Menstruums, *from which it ought to be distinguished; whereas otherwise it might be ranked among the Vegetable* Menstruums.

The

The Seventh KIND.

Vegetable Menstruums *compounded of the aforesaid Simple* Menstruums.

38. The *Circulatum majus* of *Guido. Pag. 4. Thesauri Chym.*

TAke of the Spirit of (*Philosophical*) *Wine* six Ounces, of the Salt of (*the same*) Wine four Ounces, the Vessel being well stopp'd, distil the Spirit in Balneo, which pour back upon the Salt of Wine, and again distil, and this ought to be done twelve times : then distil for a Month in *Balneo rorido* : Putrefaction being done, take out the matter and distil in a Cucurbit, with an Alembick of two Heads or Beaks, in Balneo, and the Spirit of Wine will ascend through the upper Beak into its Receiver, but the Phlegm through the lower into its Vessel : Take out the Salt of Wine, pour one half of the Spirit of Wine to it, and distil with a Retort into the other part of the Wine, distil yet once upon the remainder, and all the Salt will ascend into a strong *Menstruum* : But if you desire a weaker, add six (*other*) Ounces of the Spirit of Wine, and if you would have it very weak, pour to it a greater quantity of Spirit, but according to the aforesaid weight, it is made our great Vegetable *Menstruum*, or *Circulatum majus*.

Annotations.

H*Itherto of Simple Vegetable* Menstruums ; *now follow those which are said to be compounded, not as if they are compounded of more Ingredients, but because they are stronger than the Simple, as well in their qualities of dissolving, as tinging : The* Menstruums

ums *of this Kind differ not from the former in matter, nor in the method of preparing, but in weight only; for the more aridity you add to the unctuous Spirit of* Philoſophical Wine, *the ſtronger are the* Menſtruums *made.* Guido *made his leſs* Circulatum *of one part of the Salt of Wine, and four parts of the Spirit of Wine; but the greater* Circulatum *he makes of two parts of the Salt of Wine, and three parts of the Spirit of Wine. The greater quantity of the Salt, the ſtronger is the* Circulatum. *The leſs* Circulatums *do extract the Eſſences, or Tinctures of things, but the greater* Circulatums *do diſſolve the whole Body into a Magiſtery, as will appear in the ſecond Book.*

Vegetable Menſtruums *compounded are made alſo, if the ſimple Vegetable* Menſtruums *be taken inſtead of the Spirit of* Philoſophical Wine, *in the Deſcriptions of them all; as thus:*

39. The *Menſtruum acutum* of *Guido. Pag. 8. Theſauri Chym.*

TAke of the Vegetable *Menſtruum* (*Circulatum minus, deſcribed in Numb.* 36.) one Pound, of *Sal Armoniack* (*common*) twelve Ounces, diſtil by a Retort firſt with a weak Fire, then a ſtronger, and the *Sal Armoniack* will in part aſcend, pour it back, and diſtil yet once: then again add twelve Ounces of new *Sal Armoniack*, diſtil ſtrongly in Aſhes, pour back, and cohobate yet twice, and you will have our acute *Menſtruum*.

Sal Armoniack *reduced into a liquid ſubſtance by the Spirit of* Philoſophical Wine, *is a* Menſtruum *of the fourth Kind, but the ſame Salt diſtill'd with the* Circulatum minus *of* Guido, *is made not a ſimple, but compound* Menſtruum, *and the better for adding ſo great a quantity of new* Sal Armoniack. Pariſinus *in the third Kind of* Menſtruums *acuates the Spirit of* Philoſophical Wine *with crude Honey, by which way it is made a ſimple* Menſtruum *of that Kind, but if mixed with its fixed* Salt, *and diſtilled through an Alembick, 'tis made a compound* Menſtruum.

40. The *Cœlum majus* of *Parisinus*. *In Apertorio.*

TAke B, that is, red Wine putrify'd, as you know how, put it in a Glaſs Cucurbit, with its Alembick, and Receiver well luted, and ſet it in Balneo, wherein muſt be ſo much Water, as to ſwim two Fingers above the ſaid *Lunaria*, and diſtil gently, and forthwith you will ſee Veins appear in the Alembick; continue the diſtillation ſo long as they appear, and theſe Veins will be like Tears clear as Criſtal, and when Death (*Phlegm*) comes, which kills the Spirit, the ſaid Veins or Tears will ceaſe, and appear round as Pearls: then take away the Receiver, ſtop it, that the Spirit may not evaporate, and ſet it in a cold place, and ſo have you ſeparated the Soul (*Spirit*) of it, tho' it contains a little of its Death yet in it, and thus continue the diſtillation (*the Receiver being now changed*) till all the odoriferous Phlegm is aſcended, and the matter remains like melted pitch, black and thick, which obſerve not to dry overmuch, but according to the ſaid Signs only: And thus will you have two ferments from our B. beware of revealing to any one this Practice, which we communicate to you under the peril of your Soul, for you would be the cauſe of much Evil in this World, to be committed by the Sons of Iniquity: put it therefore into the hands of Almighty God, who knows the Will of thoſe that live according to his Will, and the triumphant Goſpel, for the Glory of which you have extracted the Form out of B, and the ſame way you may extract from all Individuals Animal and Vegetable. *Cap. ſecundum ſignificatum, per C.*

Take the Soul (*Spirit*) of it reſerved in the cold place, and diſtil half of it in Balneo, or till the precious Veins ceaſe from aſcending, rectify yet twice, obſerving the ſame Rules, but the third and fourth time, ſo ſoon as the Veins appear, leave off diſtilling, and try whether it will burn a linnen Cloth, if not, repeat the diſtillation till it doth: then cohobate by it ſelf four or ſix times in Balneo: And thus have you acquired a way fit for the rectifying of the ſaid Matter or Soul, (*Spirit*) which is of ſo great Virtue, as not to be expreſſed by any Tongue, or the Secrets, which the Eternal God hath vouchsafed to it, recited; as when we were at *Venice*, that Famous City, we both saw some Experiments of it; and so keep it well in a cold place. *Cap. tertium significatum per D. D.* Having declared the method of rectifying and separating our ardent Spirit from its Death, depraving its Virtue and Power: you must now know, that it is not able to dissolve the two Luminaries, and reduce them into action, except it be first acuated, as I shall tell you: Though this preparation is to be taught in general, *in Cap. F.* yet to prevent the loss of time, so soon as you have rectify'd your ardent Spirit, otherwise called the first Flower, I had rather have you forthwith put it into Practice, which we have in this *Chapter signified by these two Letters, D. D.* whereof one denotes the acuition of it, the other its Royal Acuator, that is, Salt extracted out of Honey, by the way which we have oftentimes shewed you, that is, with its most precious Water (*of Honey, or the* Menstruum *described in the third Kind, Numb.* 10.) and though this Water be good enough, yet this Water, being acuated with its most precious Salt, of which you will be more certain, will recompence your Labour, and abundantly sustain you, till you attain to the end of your Labour, the great Medicine. Now to the purpose, Take white Honey of young Bees, put it in Putrefaction in large Cucurbits, with their Alembicks in Balneo, and make it boyl continually for an Hour, the rest of the time let it remain in a temperate heat, and this do for the space of fifteen Natural Days, then pour to the matter so much of C, as to swim the breadth of four Fingers above it, covering the Vessels with the blind Heads, and putting them in Putrefaction three Natural Days; then put on the Alembicks with their Receivers, and the Joynts being well luted, distil in Balneo, and when seven parts of eight are distilled, or (which is a more certain sign) when you see round tears or drops ascend, lay aside the Receivers close stopp'd, that nothing may evaporate, keep them in a cool place, for the acuition of the matter; then continue the distillations in the same degree of heat, till nothing more ascends; but if necessity requires a greater Fire, have a care of making it too strong, and when nothing will ascend by the said Rule, take away also these Receivers, and keep them, because they contain the second Water or Phlegm for the extraction of the most precious Salt:

Now

Now put your matter in Ashes, and distil with a heat of the third degree, the Oyl being distilled, suffer the matter to cool, which being pulverized, reverberate in an Earthen Dish in a Reverberatory for eight Days, or till it be calcin'd enough; the sign will be when you find it of an Ash Colour: then pour of the reserved Phlegm to it so much as to cover it the breadth of two Fingers; the Vessel being covered with a blind Head, keep it in Balneo two or three Days, decant the Liquor, and pouring on new Phlegm, repeat so oft, till you have extracted all the Salt, which will exceed Snow in whiteness: And this is that Salt, wherewith we acuate our simple C, (*the ardent Spirit for a* Menstruum *of the Fifth Kind*) this is that which gives the beginning of Vegetation to both the Luminaries, reducing them into the Nature of a Quintessence: And with the same may you also acuate, and augment its own VVater (*of Honey, or* Menstruum *of the Third Kind*) which hath the power of Vegetating all Minerals. VVith this alone will you support your self in your necessity, so as to be in duty bound, my Son! to give thanks to the absolute power: Be careful not to disclose so great a secret to any Man; for we have now declared it so plainly, that 'tis impossible to add any thing more. Now take your decantations, which you drew off in Balneo, that the Salt may remain most white, which you must dissolve, filtre, and congeal three times, and it will be fit for all your operations. Now let us descend to the practice of acuition. Take of the Salt aforesaid one ounce, to which being well pulverized, pour four parts of C, that is, the first Spirit (*ardent, but because a* Menstruum *of the fifth, and not of this Kind, would be made by this Spirit, therefore is C, being acuated with Honey, or the mellifluous Heaven of* Parisinus, *a* Menstruum *of the third Kind to be taken*) in a blind Head, and the Joynts well luted, putrify the space of two Natural Days, then put on an Alembick with a Receiver, and distil in Ashes: distillation being ended, take a pound of the Salt remaining in the Retort, and add to it four times the quantity of C, putrifying, and distilling in Ashes as before, and the Magistery so often repeat, till all the Salt ascends together with its Celestial Spirit, or C, and by this way may you acuate and multiply as you please: but remember that one part of Salt requires four parts of C, (*in this place, the Cælum mellifluum of* Parisinus.) And you

 must

must know, I tell you no fabulous Stories, but very distinctly declare to you the order of true Practice, yet with this Proviso, That when first you have brought it into action, you would altogether conceal it, considering with how great obscurity the ancient Philosophers delivered theirs, which notwithstanding they had not done, but to restrain the ignorant from being too arrogant, for the same reason also do we desire, that, as we have more than often admonished you, you would keep secret, and in convenient time and place work for your self, and the poor of Jesus Christ. *Cap. quartum significatum per E.* VVe ought to return infinite thanks to the goodness of the Eternal God, in teaching us so bountifully the way of preparing our Heaven, and making us partakers of so admirable and inestimable a favour. Certain it is, when I had compleated this most secret Science, and seen real transmutation the first time, I was in a manner astonished, and often lifting up my Eyes to Heaven, fell prostrate upon the Earth, giving thanks to Almighty God. Now to the purpose: Take a large Glass of such a size, as I shewed you one at *Murarium*, into which put two or three pounds of that *Menstruum*, stop it well, and circulate in Balneo or Horse-Dung, but have a care lest in changing the Dung you impede the circulation, and so let it circulate the space of forty Natural Days, and then you will find your matter clear as Cristal, with a Sediment in the bottom like Silk, which decant warily into another Glass, keep it very close in Balneo, and you will have a Simple Vegetable *Menstruum*, (*if made of the ardent Spirit, and Salt of Honey, but a compound, if prepared with the* Cœlum mellifluum *of* Parisinus *and Salt of Honey*) our Heaven is in Virtue beyond expression, herewith do we truly calcine and dissolve the Luminaries, with the preservation of their radical moisture. This is that which will reduce imperfect as well as perfect Metals from power into action. And though I may seem not to have delineated to you the Form of the Glass, yet I know, and do remember, that I left some of them at your House, and many other of our Cucurbits, which are every one good. Govern your self according to your discretion, we having sufficiently manifested to you the way of Truth in this Chapter.

From

From the Receipts we observe.

1. *That the* Menstruums *of this seventh Kind differ from the former simple* Menstruums, *not in matters, nor in ways of making, but in the weights and use of the Ingredients.*

2. *That these* Menstruums *tinge not their dissolution, which is the property of compound* Menstruums. *Every Vegetable Mercury contains indeed its own tinging Sulphur in its Bowels, sufficient both for it self and others, as will be demonstrated in the third Book, but especially in the fifth, nevertheless we affirm, that every Spirit of* Philosophical Wine *wants Tincture, as being not acuated with things more tinging.*

The

The Eighth KIND.

Vegetable Menstruums *compounded of Simple Vegetable* Menstruums, *and common* Argent Vive, *or other Metals.*

41. The *Ignis Gehennæ* of *Trismosinus* made of the Spirit of *Philosophical Wine*, and Mercury Sublimed.

Pag. 7. *Aurei Velleris Germ.*

TAke of Alum calcined, Nitre, of each two parts, of Salt decrepitated,one part,mix, take of this mixture and Mercury sublimed, of each one pound, sublime by the Law of Art, mix the sublimation with new mixture of Salts, and sublime, and that repeat three times: To this Mercury thus sublimed and pulverized pour the Spirit of (*Philosophical*) *Wine*, and draw it off in Balneo to an oleity, cohobate sometimes, and the fourth time will ascend the Mercury together with the Spirit of VVine, rectify the distillation till it leaves no Fæces, and it will be a VVater burning like Hell-Fire: This VVater rectify again in Ashes, till it ascends without leaving any Sediment; lastly, distil through a Paper seven times double in Balneo, and you will have a VVater truly Spiritual, which keep in a Vessel close stoped, by reason it is very Volatile.

Annotations.

T*He Kind immediately antecedent is indeed computed in the number of the greater* Circulatums, *or Vegetable* Menstruums *compounded, because the* Menstruums *of that Kind do in the power of dissolving excell the other Simple* Menstruums, *but not in Tincture,*

Tincture, which that as well as those do want; but we will now offer those which shall be better; they will not only dissolve, but in dissolving moreover tinge the things dissolved in them, and so make them better; they will not only extract the Essences of things, but transmute whole Bodies into Magisteries: Amongst these, the Vegetable Mercurial Waters, made of common Argent vive, *and simple Vegetable* Menstruums *have priority; for many of the* Adepts *being so taught by Experience, have called common* Argent vive *the open Metal, for it is sooner dissolved than the other Metals; and does by its aridity more temper the unctuosity of the Spirit of* Philosophical Wine, *than the individuals hitherto used in the antecedent Kinds of* Menstruums: *As concerning this matter, hear the Philosophers, and above the rest the great* Paracelsus, *Prince, without question, of all the* Adepts, *who saith,* If you intend to convert Metals into a Magistery, and tinge the whole Body altogether into an Essence, you must take the chief and *open Metal,* to which all the rest have affinity in Nature, and putrify it in its own Matrix, which is situated in VVater, and is call'd the Mother of all Metals, (*Paracelsus his* Circulatum minus *made of common Salt*) purge it from superfluities, and reduce it into its liquid first being, that is, the Metallick *Acetum acerrimum,* the *primum Ens* of Mercury. *Lib.* 10. *Arch. Cap.* 3. *pag.* 37. As a temperate Essence (*he goes on*) is drawn out of Herbs (as out of a Vine, for example) by which very Essence, the like Essence may be extracted out of all sorts of Herbs and Roots, so, as that the Mercury of VVine shews not its own Nature, but the Nature of that with which it is essentiated; for the like reason out of Metals and Minerals, the like Mercury or Spirit is extracted out of the *open* and middle *Metal Mercury. Lib.* 10. *Arch. pag.* 39. *Mercury vive* is the Mother of all the seven Metals, and ought deservedly to be called the Mother of Metals, for it is an *open Metal. Libro de rebus naturalibus, pag.* 87. VVherefore call to mind those things which have been said before of half perfect Natural Things, among which *Mercury vive* is one, which is not brought into compaction, but left in liquidity: Besides you must know, that every generated thing which is *open, as Argent vive,* is like an open House, into which every Man that will may enter, for so lies *Mercury* open, that every Physitian may take what he will from it, but it is not so with Gold, Silver, Tin, &c. for that Gate is shut by coagu-

lation,

lation, till opened, dissolved, and reduced into the first matter by Art, which Metals have indeed many impediments, such as are not in *Mercury*, for it *is open*, and wants nothing but the direction of preparation. *Tract.2. lib. 2. de morbis metallicis. 723.*

Basilius *agrees with* Paracelsus, *saying :* In the beginning of Generation the first of all is *Argent vive*, being *open*, and loosely coagulated, because it hath little Salt communicated to it, and therefore is more Spiritual than Corporeal: the rest of the Metals being derived from its Essence, have more Salt, and therefore are made more Corporeal. *Lib. de rebus natural. & supernat. Cap. 2.*

Chortalassæus *affirms the same saying : Argent vive* is of divers Colours, white, skyish, ash, blackish, one slow, another swift, yet in it self an *open* Metal, and hath a Body easily transmutable. *Cap. pag. 359. Volum. sexti Theat. Chym.*

In searching for Sulphur, despair not, *saith Sendivogius*, I tell you by all that's sacred, it is in Gold and Silver most perfect, but in *Argent vive* most easy. *Pag. 213. lib. de Sulphure. Of the antient Philosophers I will add* Arnold, *who in Lib. 1. Cap. 7. Rosarii, saith :* The Medicine is as well in Metallick Bodies, as also in *Argent vive*, as to Nature, because they are found to be of one Nature, but indeed in these Bodies harder, in the *Argent vive* nearer, but not more perfectly. In *Argent vive* alone it is found more easily and more nearly, not more perfectly, it being the Father of both those Luminaries, and all things fusible, for they are all derived from it, and therefore are they all resolv'd into it, because Nature embraceth its own Nature more amicably, and rejoyceth with it more, than with that which is Heterogeneous. For in it is the facility of extracting that subtil substance.

Among the Metals there is none that sooner mixeth with the Spirit of Philosophical Wine, *and is more easily altered, than* Argent vive, *wherefore the* Adepts *esteemed it as an open Metal ; all other Metals and Mineral Bodies are with very great difficulty dissolved by the Spirit of* Philosophical Wine, *but being once counited with this Spirit, they are as well as Mercury, converted into a third substance, never to be divided into their constitutives, that is, Metal and Spirit ; This open Metal they made more open sometimes by the acidity of Salts ; so* Trismosinus *did sometimes sublime common Mercury for*

his

his Hell Fire: yet principal care must be taken, that such Menstruums *as these made of Mercury sublimate, be by being dulcify'd with longer than ordinary circulation, or repeated cohobations, freed from all the acidity of the Salts; but this operation being full of danger, yea contrary to the Rule of Vegetable* Menstruums, *which excludes every Acid whatsoever, we have therefore thought good to advise young Beginners to use crude Mercury, as safer than sublimate. Instead of these we will therefore commend the* Menstruums *made of crude* Argent vive.

42. The Alchymical Mercury of *Ripley*. *In Concord. Raym. & Guidon.*

TAke of crude Mercury well purged one Ounce, of our Fiery *Tartar*, or former Vegetable Salt reserved *(in the Fifth Kind in Numb.* 23.) three Ounces, grind both together very fine upon a Marble, till they be incorporated, then put the matter in a warm Balneo, and let it be all dissolv'd into a kind of white Milk, put it all upon a Pound of crude Mercury, and let it be all dissolved into the like Milk, and thus do *in infinitum*. This Mercury being dissolved putrify in Balneo, then distil in Ashes first with a gentle Fire, and an insipid Water will ascend, which must be thrown away: then the Fire being more increased, another Water will ascend more thick, which Water indeed dissolves all Bodies, putrifies, cleanseth and fixeth them, at the end with a more vehement Fire will an Oyl ascend of a Golden Colour, which must be preserved for the dissolving of the red Ferment, and for the multiplying of the red Elixir, for it is our peculiar Gold, not yet fixed by Nature.

Elsewhere instead of Tartar fired (that is, the Spirit of Philosophical Wine *dryed in the Salt of* Tartar, *or Vegetable* Sal Armoniack *made of the Salt of* Tartar, *but not yet sublimed)* Ripley *sometimes used some simple Vegetable* Menstruum, *with which he made the exalted Water of Mercury, as followeth.*

43. The exalted Water of *Mercury* of *Ripley*. *Cap.* 12. *Philorcii.*

TAke *Nigrum nigrius nigro*, and diſtil an *Aqua ardens*, and fortify it with *Pepper*, *Squilla*, *Pyrethrum*, *Euphorbium*, *Solatrum*, *Anacardus*, grains of *Paradiſe*, *Staphis-agria*, and the like in acuity: but this is a great ſecret. Take the Water of the fifth fortification, and diſtil, pour it upon Mercury ſo, as to ſwim two or three Fingers above it, ſtop the Veſſel to prevent exhaling, put the Mercury in Balneo to diſſolve for a Month, that which is diſſolved of it empty into another Veſſel, and keep: pour new Water upon the Mercury not diſſolved, and proceed as before, thus continuing, till you have one Pound of Mercury diſſolved: Then put the diſſolution together in Balneo the ſpace of fifteen Days, and after that diſtil, and that which aſcends keep apart in a Veſſel, not to reſpire, and upon the remaining Fæces pour new Water, and proceed by Balneo as above, and this Work continue, till all the Mercury is exalted: But this is not the Work of idle and ſloathful Men. Now this Water thus exalted is by the Philoſophers call'd by many Names, for it is *Lac Virginis, Aqua roris Maii, and Aqua Mercurii*.

Nigrum nigriusnigro, *and* Philoſophical Wine,*we have proved before by* Lully *to be Synonimous: the fortification or acuition of that Water or Spirit, with Pepper, Squilla*, &c. *we taught in the ſecond Kind. Mercury, though an open Metal, is yet hard enough to be diſſolv'd in the aforeſaid* Menſtruum *of the ſecond Kind, but the ſtronger the ſimple Vegetable* Menſtruums *are, the ſooner alſo is it diſſolved; an Example you will have in the following Glorious Water of* Lully, *where Mercury is in the ſpace of ſix days diſſolved in the* Cœlum Vinoſum *of* Lully, *by a* Menſtruum *of the ſixth Kind.*

44. The

44. The Glorious Water of *Argent vive* of *Lully*.
In Teſtamento Noviſſimo.

TAke of common *Argent vive* one Pound, put it in a Glaſs Veſſel, and pour upon it of the Vegetable *Menſtruum* (*above deſcribed in the Sixth Kind in Numb.* 30.) ſo much, as to ſwim four Fingers above it, ſet it in Balneo or Dung ſix Days, and it will be all diſſolved into a Glorious Water, elevate the *Menſtruum* gently by Balneo, and at the bottom of the Veſſel will remain the Light of Pearls, and Soul of Metals: This we meant in the Chapter which begins: *Oportet nos cum eo incipere, & cum eo finire.* Then take of this Glorious Water of *Argent vive* one Pound, and mix it with two Pounds of the Vegetable *Menſtruum*, cœlificated (*of Cœlum Vinoſum, in Numb.* 30.) and it will all become one Water, with which you will diſſolve all Bodies, as well perfect as imperfect, for the Production of our Sulphur.

The ſame way almoſt he prepares that which he calls the incalcinated *Menſtruum.*

45. The incalcinated *Menſtruum* of *Lully*.
In Experim. 34.

TAke common Mercury, brought out of *Spain* in Skins ſeal'd with a *Spaniſh* Seal, to prevent Sophiſtication, force it through a fine Skin, then take the Mercurial Water, extracted from Mercury by the Magiſtery, as we taught you in the Experiment of three Veſſels, as you know, and ſo diſſolve the Mercury; being all diſſolv'd, draw the Water from it by Balneo, and in the bottom of the Veſſel will the Mercury remain in the Form of an Oyl: This therefore we will uſe to be incerated (*circulated rather*) into our Heaven or our cœlificated *Menſtruum*: Take therefore four Pounds of the cœlificated *Menſtruum* (*the Vegetable Heaven deſcribed in the Fifth Kind in Numb.* 17.) and one Pound of the aforesaid Mercury reduced into Oyl, and joyn them together, then will you have at length the incalcinated *Menstruum*, with which you will dissolve the two Luminaries, preserving their Form, and not only preserving it, but also propagating it in *infinitum*.

The Receipt of this Menstruum *is plain, yet must we declare what he means by the Mercurial Water extracted by the Magistery of three Vessels, the Description of which* Menstruum *we read thus* ;

46. The Mercurial Water by three Vessels of *Lully*.

In Experim. 13.

TAke *Spanish* Mercury, which is brought in Bladders with the Seal of *Spain*, that it may not be adulterated; sublime it thus: Take Vitriol dryed from all Phlegm, and common Salt prepared, and decrepitated, or first burn'd in Fire; joyn the Mercury with these two, grinding very well, then sublime in a Vessel, at first with a gentle Fire, then increase the Fire, till it be perfectly sublimed: the Vessel being cold, gather the sublimation carefully, and beware of the fumes, being Venomous; imbibe the sublimation very well with the Oyl of Tartar (*per deliquium*) and quick Lime, then put the matter into a Retort, and administer Fire, till *Mercury vive* is gone over into the Receiver; sublime again as before, with the same new Matters, then as before vivify by a Retort, thus repeat the Magistery four times: Then take this Mercury thus prepared, and make it boyl with (*Philosophical*) *Aqua Vitæ*, being dryed, press it through a Goats Skin: Then take this Mercury, and put it in Vessels (*three Aludells*) which must be firmly and strongly joyned together, and covered on all sides with strong *lutum sapientiæ*, then prepare a Furnace, in which these Vessels may be fitly placed, so as that they may all have equal heat; but the Receiver must by no means feel the Fire, so also the Beak of the first Vessel, through which the Mercury is to pass, must be out of the Furnace: Then give Fire to the said Vessels, so as to be red hot, both within and without, then put in the Mercury through the Pipe on the outside of the Furnace, and presently stop the Mouth of the

Pipe

Pipe with Cotton; and by the ſharpneſs of the Fire, part of the Mercury will in a ſhort time diſtil into the Receiver; but one part in the likeneſs of Water; ſeparate the Water from the Mercury, and keep it, but that which remains quick, caſt again into the ſaid Veſſel as before, ſo oft, till it be through the ſharpneſs of the Fire all converted into Water, empty the Receiver every time into another Veſſel, and keep it well ſtopp'd: Then take of this Water four Ounces, and of the Oyl or Salt of the *firſt Experiment* (*Salt of* Tartar *impregnated with the Spirit of* Philoſophical Wine) one Ounce, make it go over together with the ſaid Salt, diſtilling that Water in Aſhes with a moſt gentle heat at firſt, then in the end increaſing the Fire, till more will not diſtil: Then take new Salt, or Oyl of the ſame *firſt Experiment*, and joyn it with that Water a little before diſtilled, and make it go over again, diſtilling by Aſhes as before; but this Magiſtery you muſt repeat five times, mixing one Ounce of the ſaid Salt or Oyl of the *firſt Experiment* every time with three Ounces of the ſaid Water, diſtilling as before in Aſhes, with the ſame degree of Fire, and the ſame weight as before, as well of the Water, as of the Salt or Oyl: And by this means will you by the help of God, have a Mineral and Vegetable Water united together, which hath the power of diſſolving Mercury, and all Metals, eſpecially the two Luminaries: For the multiplication of this Water you muſt proceed thus; Take one Ounce of Mercury purged, and five Ounces of the ſaid ſharp Water (*now prepared*) joyn theſe two together in a ſmall Cucurbit, lute it well, then will the Mercury be forthwith diſſolved, which diſſolution put in a little Urinal, with an Alembick and Receiver, the Joynts well luted diſtilling in Aſhes, and it will all come over into a Water, ſome Terreſtreity of no moment being left in the bottom of the Veſſel: Then may you this way multiply the ſaid Water as much as you will, *viz.* by taking five parts of it, and one of Mercury purged, diſſolving firſt, and diſtilling through an Alembick as before.

He revivifies Mercury ſublimate, to be purged after the common way, by the Oyl of Tartar, and quick Lime; being now purged, he digeſts it in Aqua Vitæ, *that is, Philoſophical; for common Spirit of Wine would be here of no effect; wherein this digeſtion with Philoſophical* Aqua Vitæ, *much of the permanent unctuoſity ſticks to the Ar-*

gent

gent vive, *altering it exceedingly; then he puts it into divers Aludels, joyned together, and to the Receiver, and made red hot, in order to be converted into a Mercurial Water: The way of distilling by Vessels red hot, I find in many places to have been much in use among the* Adepts, *but whether they contrived this way for the abbreviating, or more exquisite way of operating, or for what other cause, I know not.* Basilius, Lib. particularium, in particul. Solis, *distils not Mercury, but Gold often extinguished in the Philosophical* Aqua Vitæ *through a hot Vessel into a red Liquor.* Take of *Aurum fulminans, saith he,* one part, of the Flowers of Sulphur three parts, calcine with a gentle Fire till the Sulphur be consumed, the red hot matter extinguish in the Spirit of Wine, acuated with some drops of the Spirit of Tartar (*the Vegetable* Menstruum *made of the Salt of Tartar*) decant the Spirit, and the powder dry at the Fire, to which being dryed, add again three parts of the Flowers of Sulphur, calcine and quench as before: This Work repeat six times, that the powder of the Gold may be made like Butter, soft and fat, which must be carefully dryed, because it melts with a little Fire, this powder being a little heated put into a Retort with a Pipe, and made red hot, and the Pipe being presently stopp'd, distil the red drops falling into good Spirit of Wine put before into the Receiver.

If the Gold being divers times extinguished in the Spirit of Philosophical Wine *is made soft and fat, why might not this be also done in common Mercury, digested according to the Receipt, in the same Spirit of Wine? But suppose* Lully *propos'd it only to himself, to reduce* Argent vive *into a common acid Liquor, yet does he out of this, with the addition of the Salt of Tartar of the first Experiment, make a Vegetable* Menstruum *of the Fifth Kind, with which he dissolves common* Argent vive, *and reduceth it into a Mercurial Water: then he dissolves common Mercury by this Mercurial Water, and draws it off so, as to remain in the Form of an Oyl; which Oyl of Mercury being dissolved in the Vegetable Heaven, he circulates, and being circulated, calls it the incalcinated* Menstruum. *If instead of the Oyl of Mercury you take crude Mercury reduced into the true first matter of Mercury, and acuate the Vegetable Heaven with this Mercurial* Sal Armoniack, *you will make the same, yea a much better incalcinated* Menstruum. *The way of making the Sulphur of Nature of common* Argent vive *is this following.*

The

The Mercurial *Sal Armoniack*, or Mercury of the Mercury of *Lully*. *In Experim.* 18.

TAke Mercury being twice ſublimed with Vitriol and Salt, put the ſublimate upon an Iron Plate, being firſt very well pulverized, add to it two Ounces of Tin calcined, then ſet it in a moiſt place,and it will be diſſolved : ſublime again,and lay it upon an Iron Plate as before, and it will be all diſſolved, and thus may you diſſolve as much Mercury as you pleaſe: then take this Water, and rectify it ſeven times in Aſhes, or till it will yield no more Terreſtreity, then diſtil it in Balneo with an eaſie heat, and diſtil one part of ten, which is of no uſe, being Phlegm, which it contracted in the moiſt place, then know the weight of the Water remaining in the bottom, and to every four Ounces put one Ounce of the Vegetable Salt of the *firſt* or *ſecond Experiment*, being both of the ſame ſtrength, then diſtil in hot Aſhes with an Alembick and Receiver well luted, which being all diſtill'd, add new Salt to it again, obſerving the ſame weight as before, of the Salt as well as Water, then diſtil again as before, and this ſame way diſtil four times, to every diſtillation adding new Salt as before, and diſtilling in Aſhes, and ſo will you have a Mercurial Water fit for all Phyſical Operations: Then take common Mercury, waſhed with Vinegar and Salt, and ſtrained through a Goats Skin, put it in a Veſſel, and if there be one Ounce of Mercury, add four Ounces of the aforeſaid Mineral Water, and having put on a blind Head in Aſhes, let it boyl gently, and it will in a ſhort time be all diſſolved, empty the diſſolution into another Veſſel warily, that if any Terreſtreity be left in the bottom, it may be ſeparated from the ſaid diſſolution, as a thing of no effect : you may this way diſſolve as much Mercury as you will. Then take the aforeſaid Mercury diſſolved, and putrify thirty Days in Balneo or hot Dung, which muſt be changed every ten Days, that the heat may endure, and not be extinguiſhed : having putrify'd, remove the Veſſel, and putting on an Alembick to, with an Urinal

nal and Receiver well luted, distil all the Water in Balneo, and the Mercury will remain in the Vessel white as Snow, then pour to it so much of this Water, which you now distilled, as to be four Fingers above it; the rest of the Water keep in its Vessel well stopp'd in a cold place, then putting a blind Head upon its Vessel, and sealing the Joynts, putrify a Natural Day, then taking away the blind Head, and putting on an Alembick with a Receiver close luted, distil in Ashes, and increase the Fire, that the Soul may pass over into its distilled Water; lastly, distillation ceasing, let the Vessel cool, take away the Receiver, and keep it well stopp'd, for that which is distill'd therein is the animated Spirit; but to the matter remaining in the Vessel, that is, the Urinal, pour again of the distilled Water so much as will swim four Fingers above it, and having put on a blind Head, putrify as before, and taking away the blind Head by turns, and putting on an Alembick with its Receiver, wherein you kept the other part of the animated Spirit, the Joynts being well luted, distil again by Ashes, and lastly increase the Fire, for the Soul to go over into the distilled Water as before, then the Vessel being cold, keep the animated Spirit in the Receiver as before, well stopp'd, and to the matter remaining in the bottom pour again new Water as before, and putrify as before, distilling in Ashes, pour the Spirit into the same Receiver, where you kept the other: thus repeat the Magistery, till the Body remains dead, black, and void of all moisture, which you will prove by this sign; take a little of this black Body or Earth, and lay it upon a hot Plate, and if it fumes not, nor flyes away from Fire, then take that Earth, and put into a little Glass-Globe wel luted, and the Mouth well stopp'd; set in a reverberating Fire the space of twenty four hours; then remove that calcined Earth, and put it in hot ashes very well stopp'd to prevent the attracting of any moisture: Then take the animated Water, and rectify it seven times in Ashes, which animated and vivifyed Water divide into two parts, whereof one we will use for the vivifying of the Earth, the other for the dissolving of *Sol* and *Luna*: Then take one part of the said Water, and know the weight of the Earth reserved before, grind first, put it in an Urinal, then pour upon it of the aforesaid Water a fourth-part of its weight, and joyning a blind Head to it well luted, set the Vessel in Bal-

neo,

neo, not to touch the Water of the Balneo, but for the matter to be heated by the vapour only, and so let it remain four days; then having taken away the blind Head, and put on an Alembick, distil in Ashes with a gentle heat like that of the Sun, and an insipid Liquor will flow over, which cast away, as nothing worth; then again imbibe with a fourth part of the animated Spirit as above, digesting as above, and distilling the Liquor by Ashes as above: This Magistery thus repeat, till the whole Body hath re-assumed its Liquor or Soul, and remains white as Snow, which Body take out, dry, and grind; being ground, put it into a small Cucurbit, strongly luted with *lutum sapientiæ*, and the Mouth of the Cucurbit stopp'd with Cotton, and set the Vessel in a Furnace of Ashes; but take notice, if the Fire be too violent, the matter will turn into Oyl, and cannot be sublimed, besides there will be danger of breaking the Vessel, as has happened to us, and therefore we are willing to advise you to continue an easy heat, till the matter be sublimed: This also observe, that this way of subliming may also be done in the Fire of an *Athanor*, but then the matter will not be sublimed in less than the space of three or four days; which sublimation will indeed be most white, as the Scales of Fish, or as Talk: Then warily take out the *Magnesia*, the first matter of our common Mercury, our *Sal Armoniack*, our *Sulphur*, which keep in a small Cucurbit, well stopp'd in Ashes, warm as the Sun, but that which remains in the bottom, and cannot be sublimed, cast away, because of no efficacy, its precious Seed being vacuated.

Here he dissolves Mercury with calcined Jupiter *upon an Iron Plate* per deliquium, *with which he cohobates the Vegetable Salt of the* first *or* second Experiment (*Salt of Tartar impregnated with the Spirit of* Philosophical Wine, *or sublimed into a Vegetable* Sal Armoniack) *in equal weight (yet by degrees) through an Alembick; (instead of this* Menstruum *may be taken the Vegetable Heaven of* Lully) *with this* Menstruum *he dissolves common* Argent vive, *and reduceth it into a white Oyl, out of which Oyl he draws the animated Spirit, repeating the Work, till the Earth of the Mercury remains black, fixed, and without fume on a hot Plate: This exanimated and reverberated Earth he revivifies, by imbibing it with a fourth part of the animated Spirit seven times rectify'd, till it becomes white and volatile, which then he sublimes into a Mercurial*

Sal Armoniack, *the making of which differs not from the antecedent Descriptions of the* Sal Armoniacks; *but if it be mixed with four parts of* Lully's *Vegetable Heaven, that which is call'd the incalcinated* Menstruum *is made from thence, and so much the stronger, as that* Sal Armoniack *is stronger than the Oyl of Mercury, but if this first matter of Mercury be circulated according to its time, you will make a* Menstruum *deserving the Name of* Mercurial Heaven. Guido *prepares the incalcinated* Menstruum *not from common Mercury, but the Mercury of Metals,* Sol *or* Luna.

47. The *Menstruum* of *Guido* for Precious Stones.

Pag. 92. Thesauri. Chym.

TAke of the Vegetable *Menstruum* acuated (*described in the Seventh Kind in Numb.* 38. *or Numb.* 39.) four parts, of the Oyl of the Mercury of *Sol* or *Luna* one part, mix. *He elsewhere* pag. 84. *describes the Oyl of the Mercury of Metals thus:* Take of the Mercury of *Sol* (*a Description of which we shall have lower in the third Book*) three Pounds, of the red Lyon (*Gold sublimed, of the preparation of which in its place in the second Book*) twelve Ounces, or equal weight, mix very well, put it in a Cucurbit with its Alembick, lute well, and increasing the Fire by degrees, sublime, and the Mercury will ascend partly quick, partly in the form of a white or Ash-Colour'd Sublimate, and about the lower part of the Glass, of a citrine Colour, mix the quick Mercury again with the Sublimate, and again sublime, and that so oft, till all the Mercury is sublimed, which being so sublimed, put into Phials of a large bottom, and in every one eight Ounces, to putrify in Balneo six weeks, and then six weeks in *Balneo rorido*, and the sublimed Mercury of *Sol* will be resolved into a black Oyl, which rectify through an Alembick, first with a weak Fire, then a stronger, lastly most strong, so will you have the Oyl of the Mercury of *Sol.*

But besides Mercury, that open Metal, Menstruums *of this Kind may be also made of the other Metals, though more compact, an Example of which we have in the* Lunar Menstruum *of* Lully.

48. The *Lunar Menstruum* of *Lully. In Experimento* 24.

TAke common Mercury, and wash it with Vinegar; when the terrestreity of it is taken away, let it run through a Goats Skin, then put it into those your Vessels, of which you had a Form before, (*in Numb.* 46.) put the Mercury in those Vessels, and distil with repetition, till it turns all into Water, as I taught you above; then take four Ounces of this Mercurial Water, and therein dissolve one Ounce of the Vegetable Mercury of the *second Experiment* (*Salt of Tartar sublimed, or Vegetable* Sal Armoniack *made of the Salt of Tartar*) pass it through an Alembick together with the aforesaid Mercurial Water, then in every four Ounces of the Water, dissolve one Ounce of Mercury as before prepared, (*that is Vegetable*) putrify eight days, then distil by Ashes, increase the Fire at last, that so it may pass into that which was distilled, in which dissolve half an Ounce of Silver cupellated, then putrify three Days, then distil in Ashes, and lastly increase the Fire a little, that all the clearness, or whiteness of the *Luna* may go over by an airy resolution in this distillation.

He extracts not the whole Silver, but the more Volatile part of it, (*called in the ways of making* Sal Armoniack, *animated Spirit*) *by the* Menstruum *of three Vessels already described in Numb.* 26. *with the Description of it there declared, you may explain those things which are more obscure in the present Receipt. He sometimes joyns the animated Spirit of* Luna, *and the animated Spirit of* Sol *together, and by circulation reduceth them into an admirable* Menstruum, *after this manner;*

49. The *Circulatum majus* or *Acetum acerrimum* of *Lully*.
In Experimento 25.

TAke the simple Vegetable *Menstruum* of three individuals, *described before in Numb.* 26.) then take *Luna*, calcine it with Mercury, then take principal care to remove all the Mercury from the calcined *Luna*, and the same way calcine *Sol* with *Mercury*, then let all the Mercury be taken wholly from it: these two Bodies put into Glass Dishes each by it self apart, and to them each by it self apart pour clarifyed Honey, mixing the Calxes of the two Bodies very well with the Honey upon Ashes so as to boyl, then take the Honey from the Calxes, by washing them in hot distilled Water, and the Calxes will remain in the bottom of the Vessel, then mix the Calxes with the Honey again, boyling as before, and mixing with a Spoon as before, and thus repeat your Work three times as well in the Calx of *Luna*, as *Sol*: Then take these two Bodies being calcined and washed, and put them into a Vessel of solution severally, and pour upon them of the former cœlificated *Menstruum*, (*of the three individuals*) so much as will swim three Fingers above it, cover the Vessel with a blind Head, luting the Joynts well with wax gummed, that it may no way respire, set it in Balneo for a Natural Day, so as to boyl gently, then for two other Days put it upon Ashes, and let it boyl gently as before, then empty that part of *Sol*, which was dissolved into another Vessel by it self, which solution will be of a yellow Colour: So also take out the dissolution of *Luna* by it self apart, and pour it into another Vessel, each of which dissolutions keep in each Vessel as before in Balneo, but the dissolution of *Luna* will be of a Sea or Green Colour; the undissolved Earth as well of *Sol* as *Luna* dry upon Ashes:. Which done, pour again to each, of the new circulated *Menstruums*, and the Vessel being covered with a blind Head as before, set it in Balneo, and make it boyl gently as before, and continue the same boyling upon Ashes, lastly decant the dissolution of each Body as before into its Vessel, wherein the other dissolutions above were kept by themselves apart: But this Magistery you must repeat,

repeat, till all the *Sol*, and all the *Luna* are dissolved; these dissolutions putrify by themselves apart the space of forty Days, after putrefaction put the dissolutions severally into two Urinals, with Alembicks and Receivers stopp'd, and the Joynts being well luted, distil first the whole *Menstruum* in Balneo, but the Bodies will remain in the form of an Oyl, then again pour upon them so much of their Water lately distill'd, as to swim three Fingers above the Matter, cover the Vessel with a blind Head, and putrify twenty four Hours, then take away the blind Head, and put on an Alembick with a Receiver, and luting the Joynts, distil with a gentle Fire in Ashes; lastly increase the Fire somewhat, that the air (*the animated Spirit*) may pass over into the Water, last of all likewise force it with a stronger degree of heat, till the Fire (*the Soul being more viscous*) ascends over into the air; the Vessels being cold, pour again the new reserved Water to the remaining Matter, the animated Spirit of each Body being first luted in its Receiver, to prevent respiring, cover the Urinal again with a blind Head, putrifying as before, and lastly distil in Ashes as before, last of all as before, increase the Fire; thus repeat the Magistery, till both the Bodies of *Sol* and *Luna* are by an airy revolution transmitted severally through the Alembick: But if these Bodies will not entirely come over by distillation (a little indeed will remain, which keep for the rest of the Experiments) then take the animated Spirit of *Sol*, rectify it oftentimes by it self in Ashes, but be sure not to take away any of the Terrestreities, which will every rectification remain in the bottom of the Vessel, but rather pour back the distilled Water always to the same Fæces, till you have performed the Work seven times compleat: And observe the same order in rectifying the Water of animated *Luna* reserved before. This done, joyn these two Waters together, which Conjunction is called the Conjunction of *Father* and *Mother*, *Male* and *Female*, *Man* and *Woman*: And thus will you have the *Menstruum majus*, the *Animal*, *Vegetable*, and *Mineral*, being joyned together, and these three reduced into one substance you must circulate sixty Days in a Vessel so luted, as not to respire; Circulation being compleated, you will have the *Menstruum majus* brought to action, the power of which is so great, as not to be related: This therefore is that admirable *Menstruum* which dissolves all Bodies, with

the

the preservation of their vegetative and transmutative Form: This, I say, is that *Menstruum* containing in it such odour and fragrancy, that nothing can be compared to it: This lastly is the resoluble *Menstruum*, which is by the Wise call'd by almost innumerable Names, the *Acetum acerrimum*, which converts Gold into a Spirit: This is the *Aqua Sicca*, *Aqua Solis*, and *Aqua Vitæ*; Parisinus *made this* Menstruum, (*which he otherwise calls the greater Mercury, or compounded* Menstruum) *by this method.*

50. The *Circulatum majus* of *Parisinus*. *In Apertorio. Cap. G.*

TAke of the best calcined *Luna* three Ounces, of *Sol* also calcined according to Chapter H, (*in which the Calcinations of Metals are after the common way described*) two Ounces to each, being put by its self in its Glass, pour of Circulated, or the simple Quintessence (*acuated with Honey, or the* Cœlum mellifluum *described in Numb.* 10.) the height of four Fingers, the Vessels with their blind Heads put in Balneo two Days, and in Ashes two more: when you see the Waters in some measure tinged, decant them, and the dissolutions keep by themselves in Balneo well stopp'd, to the undissolved Calxes pour again of E, digesting, decanting, and repeating so often, till the Bodies of *Sol* and *Luna* be reduced into a liquid substance, then distil the Composition (*Dissolution*) of *Sol*, and the Composition of *Luna* in Balneo, and the Bodies will remain in the bottom of the Glass like an Oyl; but to the Waters drawn from the said Luminaries in Balneo, put Vegetable Sulphur, according to the weights of the *Sol* and *Luna*, and it will in the space of two Days be dissolved in Balneo; so soon as the said Sulphur is dissolved in every of its Vessels, pour every one to its Metallick Oyl, but to avoid Error, you must know that your dissolved Sulphur is that which we taught the preparation of in Chapter L, namely, that which is extracted out of (*Philosophical*) *Wine*, otherwise called, *Sal Armoniack*, put the Vessels in Putrefaction eight Days, then draw off the Waters in Balneo every one by it self, then pour of new Water the height of two Fingers, cover the Vessels with blind Heads, and digest for a Day in Balneo, then put on

common

common Alembicks, and diſtil the Waters gently in Aſhes, then increaſe the Fire, that the air may alſo aſcend into the Waters; the Veſſels being cold, pour new Water to each remainder, cover them with blind Heads, digeſt in Balneo for a Night, then diſtil in Aſhes, and this repeat as before, till you have extracted all the Liquor of the two Luminaries; keep the Earths, and if a little of it be caſt upon a red hot Plate, and burns not, it is an infallible ſign, becauſe the ſaid Earth is deprived of its Soul; keep theſe two Earths mix'd together in digeſtion of Aſhes, for the receiving of their Mercuries, (*the diſtilled Airs or Eſſences*) as we ſhall teach in Chapter L. (*in the way of making the mineral* Sal Armoniacks, *or Metallick of Gold and Silver*). Now take the Liquors of both the ſaid Luminaries, that is, their Souls or Mercuries, already paſs'd through an Alembick, and joyn them together, diſtilling through an Alembick in Aſhes; if any ſlimy Earth remains, add it to the former Earths reſerved, and this do ſix times, always removing the ſlimy Earth: Take a large Veſſel or Cucurbit, with an Alembick made all of a piece, in which pour your compounded *Menſtruum*, ſtopping the Mouth with a Glaſs Stopple, luted with the white of an Egg, quick Lime, and courſe Paper, which being dryed, lute then with our *Bitumen*, made of an equal quantity of Pitch, Wax, and Maſtick, and Circulate in a Sophical Balneo, as we ſhewed you at Mr. *Angelo*'s Houſe in the Famous City of *Venice*, when we made the ſimple Circulated *Menſtruum*, and let it be Circulating forty Natural Days, which being expired, you will ſee our *Menſtruum* or *Mercury* clearer than Criſtal, and more odoriferous than any Perfume: This *Menſtruum*, my Son! hath the power of diſſolving the two Luminaries, and reducing them from power to action; and you muſt know that by this alone, yet with the addition of its red or white ferment, you will by Circulation make particulars of great projection: This is that which our Captain *Raymund Lully*, in his *Epiſtola Accurtatoria*, ſpoke of, ſaying, Having diſſolved *Sol*, and drawn the Water from it in Balneo, then know the Gold is made Spiritual, and irreducible into its former Body, to which if you add a hundred parts of common Mercury, it will congeal it into true Gold: Moreover, my Son! if the ſaid Gold congealed into a Gum be diſſolved in ſome Water, and given to a Patient of what infirmity ſoever,

he

he will in a very few Days return to his good temperament; it removes whiteness of hair, and all other signs of Old Age, restores former Youth, and preserves health even to the time prefixed by the Eternal God: Know also, that should I describe all the Miracles (and indeed they may well be called Miracles) and all the effects performed by this Mercury, which, as I remember, I sufficiently declared to you by Word of Mouth, and explained the various Sayings of our Captain in the *Book of Quintessence* then, &c.

From the Receipts we observe.

1. *That these* Menstruums *are stronger than all the antecedent, as being acuated with better arids, or dry things, and therefore do not extract the Essences, but dissolve the whole Body into a Magistery.*

2. *That these* Menstruums *are the Magisteries of Metals and Minerals, and therefore Medecines.*

3. *That they are made many several ways now known to us.*

4. *That the* Sal Armoniacks *of Metals are made the same ways as Vegetable* Sal Armoniacks.

5. *That every one of them is properly called Philosophers Mercury, or Mercury of the Mercury of Gold, Silver, Iron,* &c. *sublimed; the Mercury of Antimony, common Sulphur,* &c. *sublimed, because like common Mercury sublimed, it is most easily resuscitated by hot Water or Vinegar, into the running Mercury of Gold, Silver, Iron, Antimony,* &c. *as we shall be better assured by Examples of the following Books.*

6. *That simple Vegetable* Menstruums, *do as being permanent Waters, continue also with things Metallick, and stick most perfectly to them, not for Medicines only, but also for the making of precious Stones, yea Tinctures, as well particular as universal: As to the simple Vegetable* Menstruums, *extract the Essences of Vegetables, and the same compounded, that they do make Magisteries for a Medicinal use, we shall easily agree; but for the unctuous, and most inflamable Spirit of* Philosophical Wine, *made of combustible Vegetables and Animals, to be a constitutive to any Chymical Tincture, seems to be an assertion altogether Paradoxical; for which cause are we to be admonished, that the* Adepts *rejected every Combustible Vegetable and Animal, as a thing useless*

for

for their Tinctures, but never despised the purify'd Elements of Vegetables and Animals, made incombustible, or acquiring incombustibility in the process it self, though they have declared them to be (without the ferment of the Stone) insuffitient, as also Metals alone without these Menstruums, *being therefore mix'd with Metals, they make Tinctures as well particular as universal for Metals, Witness* Ripley, *saying :* If you have a mind to make Gold and Silver by the Philosophical Art, you must for that purpose take neither Eggs nor Blood; but Gold and Silver, which are Naturally and Prudently, and not Manually calcined, for they produce a new Generation increasing their Kind, as all other Natural Things: But suppose a Man might with benefit effect it in things not Metallick, in which are Colours found in Aspect pleasant, as in Blood, Urine, Eggs, and Wine, or in half Minerals taken out of Mines, yet would it be necessary for the Elements of them to be first putrifyed, and joyn'd in Matrimony with the Elements of perfect Bodies. *Libro. 12. portar. portu.* 1. The *Elixir, he proceeds*, is not to be made of Wine, as Wine, nor of Eggs, Hair, or Blood, as meerly Eggs, Hair, or Blood, but of the Elements only, and therefore we are to seek, in order to obtain the Elements in the excellency of their simplicity and rectification; for the Elements, saies the Philosopher *Bacon* in his *Speculum*, are the Roots and Mothers of all things living: But the Elements of the things aforesaid are not Ingredients to the making of *Elixirs*, but by the Virtue and Commixtion with the Elements of Spirits (*whereof he recites four, Argent vive, Sulphur, Arsenick*, and common *Sal Armoniack*,) *and Metallick Bodies*, and so, as *Roger Bacon* saies, they are Ingredients, and do make the great *Elixir. Mid. Phil. Chym. Cap.* 3. We, *saith he further*, take neither of the first Principles, they being too simple, nor of the last, they being too gross and fecualent, but only the middle, in which is the tincture and true Oyl, separated from any unclean Terrestreity, and Phlegmatick Water; therefore saith *Raymund* thus: The unctious Liquor is the near Matter of our Physical *Argent vive :* And though those Bodies, in which those Mercuries are hidden, be sold openly by *Apothecaries* at a low Price, according to the saying of the Philosopher in this manner: Our Sulphurs we have from the *Apothecaries* at a mean Price, yet if you understand not the Art of separating the Elements, according to the Doctrine of *Aristotle*, in is Epistle to *Alexander*, in the Book of the *Secrets of Secrets*, where he saith, Separate the subtil from the gross, the thin from the thick, and when you have drawn Water out of Air, Air out of Fire, and Fire out of Earth, then have you the full Art: except, I say, you understand this, you will do little or nothing in my Work. *Pupilla Alchym. Pag.* 298. *It appertains not to this place to prove these things by more Examples, it is enough to have instanced these few by way of anticipation, the following Books treating more copiously of this Truth.*

7. *That the Name* (Hell Fire) *the* Menstruum *of* Trismosinus, *is the proper and common Name of Mercurial* Menstruums: *for most of the* Adepts *do affirm Mercury to be of a most hot, yea Fiery Nature: some few deny, accounting it the coldest Metal.*

Amongst the Affirmers was the great Paracelsus, *saying*: We find Mercury to be inwardly of the greatest heat, and no way to be coagulated, but by the greatest cold. *Libro. 6. Archid. magic.* Whoever think Mercury to be of a moist and cold Nature, are convinced of an open Error, it being of its Nature most hot and moist, by reason of which it always and perpetually floweth; for if it was of a moist and cold Nature, it would be like frozen Water, and be alwaies hard and solid, and it would be necessary to melt it by the heat of Fire, as other Metals, which indeed it requires not, having a Natural Liquation and Flux through its own heat, which keeps it in a perpetual Fluxion, and makes it quick, that it can neither dye, nor be congealed. *Cœlum Phil. Sect. de calore merc. pag.* 124. No Name can be found for this Liquefaction (*Fluxion of Argent vive*) much less the Original of it, by which it may be called, and no heat being so vehement, as to be equivalent to it, Hell Fire ought to be compared to it. *Cœlum Phil. can.* 1. 121. Basilius *taught the same, saying*: The Fiery Spirit of Sulphur being invisibly incorporated in Mercury, therefore it presers it self in Fluxion, not to be coagulated, &c. For Mercury is a meer Fire, and therefore cannot be burned by any Fire; no Fire toucheth it so, as to destroy it, for either, &c. *Currus triumph. Antimonii, Pag.* 40.

And Sendivogius: I Mercury am Fire, &c. My Spirit and the Spirit of Fire love one another, and so far as able, one accompanies the other, &c. If any Man knows the Fire of my Heart, he sees Fire is my Food, and the longer the Spirit of my Heart eats Fire,

Fire, the fatter it will be, the Death of which is afterward the Life of all things, &c. I am Fire within, Fire is my Food. *Dialog. Mercurii Pag.* 515. *Volum.* 4. *Theat. Chym.*

Ripley *did by the most hot things of* Lully (*acuating the Vegetable* Menstruum, *without the Virtue of which things, it would not be able to dissolve Metals, but in a long time*) *understand Mercury :* I am, *saith he,* forc'd to say, that all these things which *Raymond* speaks (*of things most hot*) are covered with a Philosophical Veil, for his Saying is, That dissolution must be made with Spirit of Wine, but his intention also is, that in this Spirit (*of* Philsophical Wine) may be had another resoluble *Menstruum,* which is only of the Metallick Kind. *Medul. Phil, Pag.* 168. For that is *Raymund*'s Water, which *Mary* the Prophetess speaks of, saying, Make your Water as a running Water, by Divine Inspiration. extracted out of the two Mineral and Vegetable *Zaiboth.*(*Mercuries*) that is, circulated together into a Cristalline Water, &c. because, as saith *Raymund,* there being in Mercury a Point of Igneity, by the power of which is dissolution made, it is requisite to animate it with the Water of Vegetable Mercury, otherwise it can dissolve nothing: And this is the Water containing all those things which you want, and by Virtue thereof are Pearls made. And this Vegetable Water being compounded, doth by Virtue of the Mercury (*Mineral*) presently dissolve all Bodies, and by reason of its Vegetability (*Vegetable* Menstruum) revivify every Body, and by its attractive Virtue, (*Symbolical Nature*) produce an Oyl from every Body, and Mercury draws to it self its like, that is, the Mercury of a Body. Of this Water, saith *Raymund, in Compendio Art. Transm. ad Regem Robertum :* You know, most Serene Prince, that our Stone is made of nothing but *Argent vive* alone, that is, compounded of Vegetable and Mineral: And therefore said the ancient Philosophers, the Stone is made of one thing only, that is, *Argent vive, Viatic. pag.* 345.

Mercurial Waters are called Ignes Gehennæ, *by reason of this Fiery Nature of* Argent vive, *the corrosive Specifick was because of the Mercurial Water call'd by* Paracelsus Ignis Gehennæ. *Libro. de Specif. Pag.* 29. *The* Circulatum majus, *prepared from Mercury, he calls a living Fire, most extream Fire, and cœlestial Fire.*

 If

If you would bring into action, *saith he*, (the Life of *Antimony* hidden in its *Regulus*) you must resuscitate that Life with its like living Fire, or Metallick Vinegar, with which Fire many of the Philosophers proceeded several ways, but agreeing in the Foundation, they all hit the intended Mark, &c. Yet that Fire, or Corporal Life in common Mercury is found much more perfect and subline, which manifestly proves by its flowing, that there is a most absolute Fire, and cœlestial Life hidden in it; wherefore whoever desires to graduate his Metallick Heaven (*the Arcanum Lapidis, or Antimonii*) to the highest, and reduce it to action, he must first extract the first liquid Being, as the cœlestial Fire, Quintessence, and Metallick *Acetum acerrimum* out of the Corporal Life, (*common Mercury*) &c. *Libro*. 10. *Archid. Cap*. 6. *Pag*. 39.

Amongst the Deniers, who judge Mercury to be of a cold Nature, is first Bernhard, *illustrious for Learning as well as Linage, saying:* Whereas Mercury is compounded of the four Elements, they therefore being heated by the common and general Causes, the Natural heat is excited by its own motion, by such motion as this are the Fire and Air in Mercury moved likewise, and by little and little elevated, these Elements being more worthy than the Water and Earth of Mercury, nevertheless moistness and coldness are predominant, &c. *Lib. Alchym. Pag*. 766. *Volum*. 1. *Theat. Chym*. *Argent vive* being most cold, may in a short time be made most hot, and may the same way be made temperate with things temperate by the Ingenuity of an Artist. *Epist. ad Thomam, Pag*. 57. *Art-Aurif*. *Arnoldus de Villa Nova* in the Book, call'd *Rosarium*, is observed to have declared, that crude Mercury, that is, *Argent vive*, which is by its Nature cold and moist, may by sublimation be made hot and dry, then by revivification made hot and moist like the Complexion of Men, &c. The said *Arnold*, though a Reverend Doctor, and Ingenious in other Sciences, yet perhaps handled Experiments in this Art without the Doctrine of Causes; but he saith, that in the first Purgation, the crude Spirit (*Argent vive*) is sublimed with the less Minerals and Salts, and that Mercury it self, which is in its Nature cold and moist, may be made a Powder by Nature hot and dry, as he saith, this is indeed of no benefit to our Philosophical Work: but suppose a Man may make such a Powder, as

he

he ſpeaks of, out of Mercury, namely, dry and hot by ſublimation with ſaline Things, yet theſe Purgations are vain and impertinent, yea hurtful as to the perfecting of our Work, *&c.* And if it be ſaid by way of inſtance, that as by Purging the impurities of Mercury, the ſaid *Arnold* dryed it by ſublimation, ſo alſo, as you ſay *Thomas*, moiſtened it by revivification, and made the Mercury hot and moiſt, ſuitable to his own (*humane*) Body in Nature, this indeed impedes not my Reverend Doctor, nor impugnes the Truth of the Philoſophical Art; yea rather the Error appears in this Natural Art: For, as it is clear, *Arnold* teacheth, (if you regard the ſound of Words) that Mercury being thus dryed, by hot Water, into which it is caſt, is revivifyed, and he ſaith, made hot and moiſt, whereas when firſt ſublimed, it was hot and dry: But what Philoſopher can truly ſay, that Mercury, or any other Metal, is by ſimple Water, though never ſo hot and boyling, changed as to its internal quality in Nature, acquires moiſtneſs Natural to it ſelf, and ſo is revivifyed? In this revivification therefore Mercury requires nothing, foraſmuch as common Water decocts not, nor alters it, becauſe it enters it not, and that which enters not, alters not, becauſe every thing to be alter'd muſt firſt be mixed: Some ſuperficial impurities of Mercury, ſuch Water may indeed waſh away from it, but cannot infuſe a new quality into it: For ſuch a Nature as Mercury had when reduced into Powder, and mortified by ſublimations, ſuch a Nature exactly will it keep being revivifyed by Water: This I am willing to ſay with Reverence and Honour to the ſaid *Arnold*, but I conſider and defend the Truth of Nature and Experiment. *About the end of his Epiſtle to* Thomas.

But be it what it will, it conſiſts not with our Prudence to adhere to any Opinions, of what Authority ſoever, but to Truth alone; in which reſpect we ſay Argent vive *is neither cold, nor hot, yet that being of eaſier diſſolution than the reſt of the Metals, it is moſt fit for this kind of* Menſtruums; *and that the Mercurial Waters prepared from it, may by Chymical Liberty be called* Hell-Fires, *though beſides theſe Waters the* Adepts *call alſo other* Menſtruums Infernal Fire, *of which ſort is the* acetum acerrimum *of* Ripley *in the Fifth Kind: But the following Arguments taken out of the Text it ſelf do prove, that* Arnold, Lully*'s Maſter, was as to his reducing of* Argent vive *into the firſt Matter or Eſſence, not ſufficiently underſtood, and miſ-*

obſerved,

observed by Bernhard, *taking* Aqua fervens *for common boyling Water :* Arnold *divided the* Second Book *of his* Rosary *into four Principal Works ; which are,*Solution, Ablution, Reduction, *and* Fixion, *as appears by the* first Chapter *of the aforesaid* Book : *Of the first Work, namely, the* Dissolution *of the* Stone, *in the* second Chapter, *thus :* You must dissolve the Stone (*Gold or Silver*) being dry and thick, into *Argent vive*, that it may be reduced into its first Matter ; and all this is done by *Argent vive* only, it alone having the Power of converting *Sol* and *Luna* into their first Matter ; but *Argent vive* having a terrestrial and adustible feculency in it without inflammation, and substance of aqueity, you must of necessity take away that which is superfluous, and supply what is wanting, if you desire a compleat Medicine ; but the Earthly feculency is to be wholly taken away by sublimation, &c. *This sublimation or depuration of Mercury he describes in the* third Chapter *following :* The Craft (*Way*) therefore of removing the Earthy superfluous substance from it, is to sublime it once or twice with *Vitrum* (*Vitriol formerly so called*) and Salt, till the substance of it becomes most white, having ascended most white, cast it into *Aqua fervens*, till it returns into *Argent vive* ; then take the Water from it, and Work with it, because it is not good to operate with it, except it be first purifyed this way : and therefore saith *Avicen*, The first things to begin with, is the sublimation of Mercury, after that, the solution of it, that it may return into its first Matter, and sublime it wholly : Then put clean Bodies in the same, weighed into this clean Mercury, &c.

If we respect the sound of the Words, Bernard *in his long Argumentation corrected* Arnold *deservedly, but if the Sense of the Words, here is nothing deserving Correction :* Aqua fervens, *the Name of* Arnolds Menstruum, *is the chief and almost only thing concealed by* Arnold *in the whole Practice of his Book, which had he manifested, he would have prostituted all the more secret Chymy ; but that he meant not common boyling Water, is proved by the following considerations.*

1. *Gold or Silver must be dissolved into* Argent vive, *or the first matter, first Being, Essence,* &c. *by* Argent vive, *not common, but Philosophically prepared : Nothing reduceth Gold into a first Matter, but a first Matter ; as here the first Matter of common Mercury, clean Mercury,*

Mercury, or the Mercury of Mercury. The Adepts *have a Rule,* That a first Matter prepares a first Matter; *Therefore as Mercury prepares Mercury; an Essence an Essence; a Magistery a Magistery; so the Philosophers Mercury, or the* primum Ens, *Essence,* &c. *of* Sol *or* Luna, *cannot be prepared but by the Philosophers Mercury,* primum Ens, *or some Essence; wherefore by* Aqua fervens *in this Receipt, we understand the Essence of Mercury, but not in the least common boyling Water.*

2. *Clean* Argent vive, *or the first Matter of Mercury, made of* Argent vive *sublimed by* Aqua fervens, *cannot be running Mercury, because it is in the Form of a Liquor:* For,

First, The dissolution of Gold made with this clean Mercury is to be filtred. Grind time after time, and imbibe, and boyl in Balneo, then distil through a Filter, till it (*meaning the Metal dissolved in the* Menstruum, Chap. 3.) *goes through.*

Secondly, *In the Dissolution of Gold, the Tincture only is extracted, the Body being left.* Be patient, *saith he,* and extract not the Tincture hastily, nor seek to have things perfect hastily or swiftly, for the first Error in this Art is haste, *&c.* Bodies dissolved are reduced to the Nature of a Spirit, and are never separated, as neither Water mixed with Water, and that because Nature rejoyceth in Nature, as the Spouse is joyned with the Bridegroom; but those things which are not dissolved, have not pure parts, except they be mollified. Therefore, my dearest, you want wherewith to operate in the dissolution of the Stone, that is, you must separate their purer parts from them, that the Work may be effected with lighter, the heavier parts being cast away. *Cap.* 3.

Thirdly, *Mercury, or the first Matter of Gold prepared with clean Mercury, is also liquid. Chap.* 3. The beginning of our Work is to dissolve our Stone (*Gold or Silver*) into Mercury, or into a Mercurial Water, *Chap.* 4. *No wonder therefore if Mercury prepared by* Aqua fervens *be called Water:* It is, *saith he,* expedient to dissolve Bodies by Water, that is, by *Argent vive. Cap.* 3.

Fourthly, *Because it extracts an Oyl from every thing.* Put, *saith he,* of the purest Mercury so much as to swim four Fingers, or more, which is better upon the substance of the Body, from which you would extract an Oyl, then kindle a gentle Fire under it till you see the Oyl, that is, the Air of it, by little and lit-

the-tle ascend, or be elevated upon the Mercury; gather it warily, and keep it apart, &c. *Cap.* 10.

3. *This Process of* Arnold *is ordinary, and call'd by the* Adepts, The way of separating the Elements, *which cannot be done without either a Vegetable or Mineral* Menstruum.

4. Aqua fervens *among the* Adepts *is the usual Name of* Menstruum. Dissolve, *saith* Lully, the purest *Sol* in its own *Aqua fervens*, then separate the Phlegm, and the *Sol* will remain below, &c. *Codicil. cap.* 43. *Pag.* 203. That Fire burns Gold more than Elemental Fire, because it contains heat of a terrestrial Nature, and resolves without any fortitude (*force, effervescence, or corrosion*) which common Fire cannot do; we therefore enjoyn you to make the Magistery of the hottest things you can get, and you will have an *Aqua calida*, which resolves every strong thing. *Vade mecum. Pag.* 272.

Which Form of Speech *Bernhard* himself knew, out of *Morienus: Saying*, Know that our *Laton* is red, but of no benefit to us, till it be made white: Know also, that *Aqua tepida: calida*, and *fervens, Synonima's of one* Menstruum) penetrates and whitens, even as it self is (*white*,) and a moist vaporous Fire effects all things: Again *Bendegid, Johannes Mehungus*, and *Haly*: You that seeking Day and Night spend your Mony, waste your Wealth, and Time, tormenting your Wits in vain about the subtilties of Books, I admonish you out of Charity, through Compassion, as a Father moved toward his Son, that you would, I say, whiten the red *Laton* by a white odoriferous *Aqua tepida*, but tear so many Sophistical Books, so many Methods, and leave such great subtilties; believe me, that it may be well with you. *Lib. Alchym.* 770. *Vol. Theat.* 11. *Chym.*

5. *It is by the blackness of the dissolution proved, that* Arnold's Aqua fervens *was a simple Vegetable* Menstruum; the black appearing above, *saith he*, gather apart, because that is the Oyl, and the true sign of dissolution, because this which is dissolved, attains to the end of sublimity, and is therefore separated from the lower parts, ascending upwards, and aspiring to higher places. *Cap.* 3. *Rosarii.*

These things we are willing to say, not impeaching the Reverence and Honour of Bernhard, *but we contemplate and defend the Truth and Experiment of* Arnold.

The

The Ninth KIND.

Vegetable Compounded Menstruums *made of Simple Vegetable* Menstruums, *and Things tinging, being first fixed.*

51. *The* Circulatum majus, *or Metallick* Acetum acerrimum *of* Paracelsus. *Lib.* 10. *Arch. pag.* 38.

IF common Mercury ought to be reduced into the first liquid Being, then is it first to be mortify'd, and deprived of its Form, and that is done by several sublimations with Vitriol and common Salt, that at last it may be made like fixed Cristal: Then dissolve it in its Matrix, namely, in the *primum Ens* of Salt, (*the* Circulatum minus *made of Salt, or the Water of Salt circulated described above in Numb.* 27.) putrify a Month; add to it new *Arcanum* of Salt (*Circulatum minus*) that the impure may be precipitated to the bottom, but the pure turn'd into Cristals: sublime the same in a close Reverberatory, being sublimed, turn it up continually, till it comes to a redness; this sublimation extract with the Spirit of Wine rectifyed to the highest (*Philosophical Wine*) seperate the Spirit of Wine (*by distillation*) the remainder (*the dry Tincture or Crocus of Mercury*) dissolve upon a Marble, (*per deliquium*) and digest for a Month, pour new Spirit of Wine to it, digest for a time, and distil; Then will the *Arcanum* of the *primum Ens*, or first being of Mercury rise over in a liquid substance, which is by the Philosophers called Metallick *Acetum acerrimum*, and in our Archidoxyes *Circulatum majus*: And the same is to be understood of Antimony, Gemms, and all other Metals.

There is a great difference between this and the precedent Kind, though they both treat of Mercurial Waters: The antecedent were made of crude Mercury: This Circulatum *of* Paracelsus, *is indeed made of Mercury, but first fixed: The precedent were most clear; these greater* Circulatums *are indeed most clear, but also most red, and so much better in their Tinctures than the precedent. The Receipt we will consider as divided into its parts, in the first of which* Paracelsus *sublimes* Argent vive *so often, till it be made like fixed Cristal, that is, like mineral or common Cristal, clear and transparent: As this part is common, so it less needs explaining. In his Book,* De Renovat & Restaur. *he takes only Mineral Gold or Antimony for the same Work, which Bodies notwithstanding are more bound up than the open Metal, Mercury; and for this reason it may seem to be fit enough for dissolution in* Circulated Salt *without sublimation: For the illustration of the Receipt, we will add the Description of the said Book.*

Take of mineral Gold or Antimony most finely ground one Pound, of Salt Circulated four Pounds, being mixed, digest them together in Horse-Dung for a Month; from thence will spring a Water, wherefore the pure must be separated from the impure, coagulate it into a Stone, which calcine with Wine cenificated (*lenificated*) and separate again, and dissolve upon a Marble: Let this Water be putrified for a Month, from it will be produced a Liquor, wherein are all such Signs, as in the *primum Ens* of Gold or Antimony, wherefore we deservedly call it the *primum Ens* of those things: It is no otherwise to be understood of Mercury, and other things also.

In the second part, he dissolves Mercury being so sublimed, in Salt Circulated, *the* primum Ens *of* Salt, *the* Arcanum *of* Salt, *the* Water *of* Salt Circulated, (*Synonima's of* Paracelsus *his* Circulatum minus) *putrifies or digests, precipitates with new* Circulated Salt, *filters, and lastly reduceth it into Cristals, or Philosophical Vitriol. In the Receipt of* Lib. de Renov. *he adds the weights of things:* Take, *saith he*, of mineral Gold or Antimony one Pound, of Salt Circulated four Pounds, and then digests, and separates the

the impure from the pure, and coagulates into Criſtals. *Sometimes he diſſolves Bodies by ſome mineral* Menſtruum, *which he draws off two or three times from them, and ſweetens them again by taking away all the acidity ſo far as he is able with common Water: Thus he diſſolves common Sulphur in the ſtrongeſt* Aqua fortis (Paracelſus *his* Aqua regis, *to be deſcribed in the eighteenth Kind) cohobates three times into a black Matter, which he ſweetens with diſtilled Water,* Libro de morte rerum.

For it is much at one, whether Gold or Antimony be diſſolved by the Circulatum minus *only, and reduced into a Philoſophical Vitriol; or whether* Argent vive, *for the abbreviation of time, be in the ſublimation of it firſt impregnated with the acidity of Salts, and ſo made more open for the Work, and then mixed with the* Circulatum minus, *purified by digeſtion and precipitation, and laſtly reduced into a Philoſophical Vitriol; or whether to make the time yet ſhorter, Sulphur be mixed with a mineral* Menſtruum, *that is, an acid, and the* Circulatum minus *mixed together, and then freed from the acid, ſo as with the* Circulatum minus *to be made the ſame Philoſophical Vitriol; for which way ſoever Philoſophical Vitriol is made, it comes to one and the ſame effect: but of theſe Vitriols hereafter in the Receipts of mineral* Menſtruums.

In the third part, he ſublimes the Stones or Criſtals of the Mercury in a cloſe Reverberatory (that is, a Philoſophical Egg) always turning it up, till the Vitriol of the Mercury is at length fixed into a moſt red Precipitate. This part the Sublimations of Sulphur and Antimony in a cloſe Reverberatory will illuſtrate. The ſtrongeſt Aqua fortis *being often drawn off from the Sulphur, the remaining matter being made thereby black, and then ſweetned, he reverberates, that is, ſublimes in a cloſe Reverberatory, and being ſublimed, turns up the cloſe Reverberatory, or Philoſophical Egg ſo oft, and continually till it comes to a redneſs,* as Antimony, *ſaith he,* which will become firſt white (*ſublimate*) then yellow, thirdly red, (*precipitate*) as Cinnabar; which being obtained, you ought to rejoyce, for it is the beginning of your Riches: This reverberated Sulphur gives a moſt deep tincture to any *Lunā*, reducing it into moſt excellent Gold, and preſerves a Man's Body in moſt perfect Health: This reverberated-fixed Sulphur (*obſerve*) is of ſo great Virtue, as is not fitting to declare. *Libro. de morte rerum. pag.* 95.

The Reverberation of Antimony is in *pag.* 67. *Chyr. majoris.*

 thus:

bus: Take of Antimony reduced into a most fine Alcool, (*into Philosophical Vitriol with the* Circulatum minus, *by the way of Mercury in the* Circulatum majus; *or again into a black and sweetned matter by the way of Sulphur*,) what quantity you will, let it be reverberated in a close Reverberatory for the space of one Month (*continually turning up the Reverberatory, till the matter will be no more sublimed*) and it will be Volatile and Light, first White, then Yellow, then Red, lastly of a Purple or Violet Colour: *The Antimony being thus fixed by sublimation, he extracts the tincture, by the Spirit of* Philosophical Wine, *which tincture he calls the most Noble, most Precious, and only not Divine Essence of* Lily.

In the fourth part he dissolves Mercury being precipitated, and extracted by the Spirit of Philosophical Wine, per deliquium, *and digests with new Spirit of* Philosophical Wine, *and cohobates, till it ascends through the Alembick into the* primum Ens *or Essence of Mercury, Mercury Circulated, the* Circulatum majus *prepared from Mercury*, &c.

In the Receipt we observe,

1. *That* Argent vive, *Antimony, Sulphur, yea Gold, Silver, and all the other Metals, being dissolved in some simple Vegetable* Menstruum, *then reverberated, or by sublimation fixed, dissolved* per deliquium, *and distill'd into a liquid substance, are* Argent vive, *Antimony, Sulphur, Gold, Silver*, &c. *Circulated, or the* Circulatum majus *made of Mercury, Antimony, Sulphur*, &c.

2. *That these* Menstruums *are called* Circulatums, *because they were by the ancient Philosophers Circulated for the space of thirty or forty, sometimes sixty Days.*

3. *That these are called the greater* Circulatums, *to be distinguished from the less* Circulatums, *being less excellent, the greater having greater strength, and communicating tincture to things that are dissolved in them.*

4. *That these* Circulatums *are the* first Beings, *or* graduated Essences *of Metals and Minerals, and amongst things Volatile nothing can be more excellent than they, they being exalted from a fixed Essence or* Astrum, *into a much more Noble Essence, called an* Arcanum.

5. *That*

5. *That these* Circulatums *are* Medicines, *or* Medicinal Arcanums.

6. *That these* Circulatums *ore most red.* Sublime the Stones, *saith* Paracelsus, till they come to redness. *He extracts the tincture of* Lily *out of Antimony reverberated to a Purple or Violet Colour ; but makes the Soul of Metals out of Sulphur reverberated, of which thus :* What *Hermes* said, that the Soul alone is the means of joyning the Spirit to the Body, was not impertinently spoken: For Sulphur being that Soul, and maturing and excocting all things, as Fire, it will be also able to bind the Spirit with the Body, and incorporate and unite them together, so as from thence to produce a very Noble Body : The vulgar combustible Sulphur is not to be reputed the Soul of Metals, but the Soul is something more than a combustible and corruptible Body, and therefore cannot be burned by any Fire, being all Fire it self, and indeed it is nothing else but the Quintessence of Sulphur, which is extracted out of Sulphur reverberated by the Spirit of (*Philosophical*) *Wine*, and is of a red Colour, and clear as a Ruby : Which is indeed a great and notable *Arcanum* to transmute white Bodies, and to coagulate running Mercury into fixed and tested Gold : Accept this as commended to you to make you Rich, and you have reason to be content with this only Secret for the transmutation of Metals. *Lib.* 1. *de gener. rerum, Nat. pag.* 87. *If Mercury, Antimony, and Sulphur fixed by reverberation, and the Spirit of* Philosophical Wine *drawn off, be red, and diaphanous as a Ruby, it follows that the same Bodies, volatilized with the Spirit of* Philosophical Wine, *do become more red. From hence we observe, that the* Menstruums *of* Diana *are of divers Colours, sometimes white, milky and opake ; sometimes most clear, sometimes again most red and most transparent ; so that the Arguments of* Bernhard, *denying the diaphaneity of* Menstruums, *may be easily resolved :* Where Fools, *saith he*, do out of the less Minerals extract corrosive Waters, into which they put any sort of Metals, and corrode them : for they think that therefore they are dissolved by a Natural solution, which solution indeed requires permanence together, that is, of the dissolvent, and the dissolved, that from both, as from the Masculine and Feminine Seed a new Species may result: I tell you truly, no Water dissolves a Metallick Species by Natural Reduction, but that which

remains

remains with it in matter and form, and which the dissolved Metals are able to recongeal; which happens not in any sort of *Aqua fortis*, but is rather a defiling of the Composition, that is, the Body that is to be dissolved: Nor is that Water pertinent to Bodies in solution, which remains not with them in congelations; Mercury is of this sort, and not *Aqua fortis*, or that which Fools esteem Mercurial Water, clear and diaphanous: For if they divide and obstruct the Homogeneity of Mercury, how will the first proportion of the Feminine Seed stand and be preserved? *Pag*. 60. *Epist. ad Thomam*. The *Elixir* and *Azoth* (*he goes on*) that is, the Vital Spirit (*Spirit of Life*, Philosophical Aqua vitæ) and fugitive Soul (*animated Spirit*) are not diaphanous nor transparent, nor clear as the Tear of ones Eye, nor any dissolving Spirit. *Pag*. 94. *Ejusd. Epist.* Which cannot be done in a diaphanous, clear and transparent Liquor: because, if the aforesaid *Elixir* and *Azoth*, that is, Spirit and Soul had or could shew any diaphaneity, the Earth would now in proportion have dismissed the Water, and separated it self from it, whereas otherwise it would have inspissated and coagulated the parts of it, caused an opacity in the *Elixir* and *Azoth*, and made the Metallick Form to stand congelable: For in restringing fixed Metallick Species, the restringer must of necessity act upon the restringible, and the congealer upon the congelable, which cannot be done in the aforesaid diaphanous and clear Water: otherwise it is in Vegetables, in which a simple and diaphanous Water is by decoction inspissated in those Vegetables, which notwithstanding vanisheth and evaporates at length by the Tryal of Fire, because it is not permanent and fixed in the Composition, not having an Earth Naturally Homogeneous to it in Composition with it, as *Argent vive* has; which Earth is indeed the cause of permanent fixion in things Homogeneous; wherefore simple Water cannot by congelation be fixed with Vegetables, as Mercury with Metals: It therefore Mercury hath received diaphaneity in the Philosophers Work, it will remain in the quality of an irrestringible substance, and will not be congealed upon *Laton* as to a Metallick Form, Species, and Proportion, which carries the congelation of it self neither with it, nor in it, as Water does Earth, which Earth, as aforesaid, is indeed Mercurial, and the first cause of inspissation, coagulation, and fixation: If there-

fore

fore that Water remains not in Metallick Proportion, how can the like Species be produced from this Composition? They therefore, that think so to extract a clear transparent Water out of Mercury, and work many wonders by it, are in an Error; for suppose they can make such a Water, yet would it be of no advantage to the Work, nor to the Nature and Proportion of it, nor could it restore or erect a perfect Metallick Species; for so soon as Mercury is altered from its first Nature, so soon is it excluded from being an ingredient to our Philosophical Work, because it hath lost its Spermatick and Metallick Nature: By these things therefore it is known, what Truth your Opinion contains, and wherein it is contrary and absurd, you asserting it to be necessary, in order to perfect the great *Elixir*, to have a Gum, in which are all things necessary to it, containing the four Elements, and is a most clear Water as the Tear of an Eye, made Spiritual, which causeth Gold to be a meer Spirit: For one Body penetrates not another, but a pure Spiritual substance congealed, is that which penetrates and tingeth a Body. Be it, as you say, my Honoured Doctor! that Natures are not joyn'd without a Gum, or Oyly Matter, &c.

Had Bernhard *disputed only against every Mercurial Water not permanent, made diaphanous with* Aqua fortis, *or any other vulgar* Menstruum, *and not also against the most clear Mercurial Water of* Thomas de Bononia, *then the Arguments aforesaid had been of great strength; but now the objections against the limpidity of* Menstruums *as well of this as other* Adepts, *are of no validity. The same Earth, which being less than well dissolved, is the cause of opacity in* Bernhard's permanent Menstruum, *the very same exactly dissolved is the cause of limpidity with* Thomas, *inspissating and coagulating the Water, as well, if not better, than if it had been less dissolved. The diaphaneity of* Menstruums *is defended by* Lully, Parisinus, *and most of the* Adepts: Lully *proclaims his* Cœlum Vinosum *to be clear, bright, and resplendent as the Stars of Heaven. In Test. novis. pag.* 8. *Of which very* Menstruum Parisinus *thus, in Appendice Elucidarii, pag.* 273. *Vol.* 6. *Theat. Chym.* Then will you see a Quintessence brighter and clearer than a Diamond, which exceeds the splendor of the Stars, so as to be doubted, whether it be contained in the Glass, or no.

The

The Tenth KIND.

Vegetable Menstruums *compounded made of Vegetable* Menstruums *compounded, and Metallick Bodies.*

52. The *Neapolitan* Menstruum *of* Lully. *In Exper.* 13.

TAke *Luna*, and calcine with common *Argent vive*, that is, by amalgaming, and then grinding the Amalgame with common Salt prepared, then evaporate the Mercury with a most gentle Fire, then take away the Salt with hot Water distilled, and so you will have *Luna* calcined. Take the calcined *Luna*, and pour to it four parts of the Mercurial Water (*described by the three hot Vessels before in Numb.* 46.) and the Vessel being covered with its *Antenotorium* set upon Ashes, so as to boyl gently, and you will perceive a Green or Sea Colour, which Liquor pour warily into another Vessel, so that the Fæces be not disturb'd, the Matter remaining at the bottom dry with an easie Fire, like the heat of the Sun: Then know the weight of the said *Calx*, and pour again four parts of the said Mercurial Water upon one part of the said *Calx*, and the Vessel being covered with its *Antenotorium*, as above, let it boyl again gently, the dissolution pour into another Vessel as before, and joyn it with the first dissolution; but remember to keep the said dissolved Matter continually in Balneo, till the whole Work of dissolution is compleated; repeating the Magistery so oft, till the whole Body of *Luna* be fully dissolved and decanted over, which has indeed hapned to us at the second time, and set it in putrefaction fourteen

fourteen Days: Then put it in an Urinal, with its Receiver and Alembick, very well luted, and distil in a Furnace of Ashes, then increase the Fire, that the Soul of the Body may ascend into its Water: The Vessel being cold, examine the weight of the Earth of *Luna* remaining in the bottom, for I believe of one whole Ounce there will not remain above two Eights (*Drachms*) of the Body not dissolved, the rest will be perfectly dissolved, (that is, distilled;) But if more of the undissolved Earth remains, then pour to it so much of its Water lately distilled, as to be three Fingers above it, and the Vessel being covered with an *Antenotorium*, put it in Balneo for a Natural Day, then taking away the *Antenotorium*, and putting on an Alembick with a Receiver very close, distil by Ashes; at the end of the distillation increase the Fire as before: This repeat, till the whole Body of *Luna* be pass'd through the Alembick by an airy revolution; and thus will you by the Help of God have a *Menstruum*, with which you may dissolve *Sol*.

Annotations.

H*Itherto we have by* Argent vive *acuated either the Spirit of* Philosophical Wine, *or* Menstruums *made with this Spirit, which had so good a faculty of dissolving, that most of the* Adepts *being content with these Mercurial Waters, desisted from inquiring after stronger* Menstruums. *The Mercurial Water, which* Lully *terms Glorious, he saith, is sufficient, yea, a proper* Menstruum *to make the Philosophers Mercury, or Metallick* Sal Armoniack, *out of all Metals and Minerals.* You must know, *saith he*, my Son! that in the Truth and Faith of God, no Sulphur of Nature of any Metal can be sublimed without this Water of common *Argent vive*. *Test. Noviss. Pag.* 12.

But in this Tenth Kind *of* Menstruums, *the* Adepts *made yet other* Menstruums, *adding moreover divers Bodies, according to the intended several uses to the aforesaid Mercurial Waters:* Lully, *to make a more Noble* Menstruum *for the dissolution of Gold, added Silver to the Mercurial* Menstruum: *If perhaps he wanted a* Menstruum *for Pearls, he joyned Pearls with the Mercurial* Menstruum: *If he had a mind to make* Aurum potabile, *he prepared a* Menstruum *out of Gold and Silver, as more suitable to this purpose, yet with some Mercurial* Menstruum, *and so of others, as you will observe in the following Examples.*

53. The precious *Menstruum* for Pearls of *Lully.*

In Comp. Animæ transmut. Pag. Vol. 3. Theat. Chym.

TAke the Liquor of *Lunaria* of the third or second rectification (*Philosophical Aqua ardens rectifyed*) pour it upon *Argent vive*, so as to swim three Fingers above it, and putrefie three Natural Days, and a great part of it will be dissolved with the Water of *Lunaria*, which decant, and pour fresh Liquor upon the Fæces, putrefie in Dung or Balneo, and repeat till all the Mercury is reduced into Water, then joyn all the distillations together, and draw off in Balneo, and when you see it in a manner thick, so as to be half a Pound of the Water of Mercury and *Argent vive*, (*Vegetable and Mineral*) putrifie six Natural Days, then put in Pearls, and they will within ten Hours be dissolved, then exuberate them by the way, which I taught in the exuberation of Metals, till they be converted into a (*Sal Armoniack, or Sulphur Naturæ of Pearls*) whereof dissolve one Ounce in a Pound of its *Menstruum* aforesaid, and distil four times, then put in Pearls, and they will in half a quarter of an Hour be dissolved, by reason of the greater subtilty of the *Menstruum*. *As Silver is joyned to the Mercurial* Menstruum *made by the three Fire-hot Vessels, for the* Neopolitan Menstruum, (*which may be so call'd, because it was reveal'd to* Lully *at* Neapolis *by* Arnold de villa nova) *so this* Menstruum *for Pearls is made of the* Sal Armoniack *of Pearls, and the Mercurial Menstruum, or Glorious Water of Mercury, which if they be Circulated together a convenient time, you will make thereof a* Cœlum perlatum.

54. The

54. The Mercurial compounded *Menstruum* of *Lully*. *In Experim.* 34.

TAke three Ounces of *Luna*, and three Ounces of *Sol*, calcine them ſeverally with Mercury, as in the former Experiments, (*in the Neopolitan* Menſtruum) then evaporate it from the ſaid Metals; being calcined, put them ſeverally in diſtinct ſolutory Veſſels, and put upon them ſo much of the incalcinated *Menſtruum* (*deſcribed before in Numb.* 45.) as will ſwim four Fingers above it: cover the Veſſel with an *Antenotorium*, putrifie in Balneo two Days, and two Days more in Aſhes with a heat like that of the Sun, decant the diſſolution, and dry the remainder: being dryed, pour upon them of the incalcinated *Menſtruum* again as before, putrifying in a cloſe Veſſel in Balneo, then upon Aſhes, and emptying the ſeveral diſſolutions (*of Gold and Silver*) into their ſeveral Veſſels as before: If any thing remains undiſſolved, dry and diſſolve as before, till all the remainder be fully diſſolved, then putrifie both diſſolutions twenty Natural Days, being putrifyed, take the diſſolutions, and put them ſeverally into their Urinals with their Receivers, and having luted the Joynts well, diſtil the Waters of both (*Metals*) in Balneo; in the bottom of the Veſſels will remain the Bodies like melted Honey or Oyl, pour upon thoſe (*Oyls*) again of their own Waters (*The* Menſtruum *now drawn from the Oyls*) diſtilled only by Balneo, ſo as to ſwim three Fingers above the Matter; cover both Veſſels with their *Antenotoriums*, and putrifie for a Natural Day: then take away the *Antenotoriums*, and put on Alembicks, lute well, and diſtil upon Aſhes, laſtly increaſe the Fire, that the Soul or Element of Air may paſs over into both their diſtilled Waters, and laſt of all increaſe the Fire to the higheſt degree, that the Element of Fire may paſs into the Air: But to the Compoſition of *Luna* this Redneſs or Fire is not neceſſary: Diſtillation being compleated, let the Veſſels cool, take the Receivers from them, and keep them very well ſtopp'd, that they may not reſpire, and put diſtinct Schedules or Inſcriptions upon them, that when you have occaſion, you may not take one for the other : Then again to the Earths (*of Gold and Silver, left in distillation*) pour their Waters distilled by Balneo as before, and having put an *Antenotorium* to it, putrifie as before, then distil by Ashes, each Vessel having its own Receiver, wherein you kept the Souls of those Bodies, and thus repeat the Magistery till the Earths are exanimated and destitute of radical moisture: Then take those Earths, grind well, and joyn them together, then put them in a Glass Egg, and keep them in hot Ashes, till I tell you what to do with them : Then take the animated Spirit of *Luna*, and rectifie it seven times in Ashes, then take the animated Spirit of *Sol*, and after the same manner rectifie it seven times in Ashes; the limosities (*remaining Earth*) which the Spirit of *Sol* will in every rectification eject, keep very close, being the Element of Fire (*in the form of an Earth.*) Having rectifyed, take the animated Spirit of *Sol*, and the animated Spirit of *Luna*, and joyn them together, then Circulate in a large Vessel, as that wherein we Circulated the simple *Menstruum :* continue this Circulation sixty Days, in which time you will have a true Mineral *Menstruum* (*not acid, but made of Minerals, as Mercury, Gold, and Silver,*) by which you may operate innumerable Experiments.

Hereto ought to be referred the Menstruum *which is called by* Basilius.

55. The sweet Spirit of Mercury of *Basilius. Cap. 3. Libri de rebus nat. & supernat.*

TAke of Natural Cinabar, or Oar of Mercury, and of the best Oar of Gold equal parts, to which being pulverized and mixed, pour the Oyl of Mercury made of Mercury sublimed, and putrifyed (*that is, Oyl of Mercury sublimed alone, no other Ingredients being added, except the Spirit of* Philosophical Wine, *or some Vegetable* Menstruum, *without which it cannot be made*) digest them for a Month, and you will have a Celestial rather than Terrestrial extraction, draw off the extraction in Balneo, and the Phlegm being taken away, in the bottom will remain a ponderous Oyl, dissolving all Metals in a moment ; to which add of the Spirit of *Wine* (*Philosophical, or Fiery Spirit*

of

of Wine of Basilius) three parts, Circulate in a Pellican to a Blood redness, and incomparable sweetness; being Circulated, pour it upon Tartar calcined to whiteness, and distil the Spirit of Mercury with a strong Fire, the Spirit of Wine remaining with the Tartar.

We must distinguish between this Spirit, and another of the same Name, lest one be taken for the other: For Basilius *prepared also a Spirit of Mercury from the white Spirit of Vitriol, of which you may read in several places, in the Book* de particularibus, *especially in the particular of* Luna; *a Description of which Spirit is lower among the Mineral* Menstruums, *because it is acid: But the other, namely, this our Spirit of Mercury, is most sweet and fragrant, which you have also in the particular of* Luna, *as also in the seventh Chapter of the Book* de rebus nat. & supernat. *where he dissolves the* Crocus *of* Luna *in the white Spirit of Vitriol, as also in the most fragrant Spirit of Mercury.*

Parisinus *for Alchymical Tinctures made a Mercurial compounded* Menstruum, *of his* Circulatum majus, *and the first or middle substance of common* Argent vive, *thus:*

56. The incalcinated *Menstruum* of *Parisinus. Cap. G. Apertoris.*

TAke of the *Circulatum majus* (*described before in Numb.* 50.) one Pound, of Mercury prepared, as we shall teach in the tenth Chapter, two Ounces, mix, and observe that true putrefaction be made with this *Menstruum*: But when first it is incalcinated, that is, mix'd with such Mercury, it is no more used for Men's Bodies, but only as Medicines for Metals, now the said tenth Chapter is this, as followeth:

Of reducing common Mercury into the first Matter or Middle Substance.

Now my Son! we will give you full instruction and demonstration of decocting and reducing common *Argent vive* into its first Matter, or middle substance, and as in the foregoing Chapters we declared the way of reincrudating the two Luminaries,

naries, ſo now we will demonſtrate the ways and means of decocting the ſaid Mercury. Firſt, we will teach the way of diſtinguiſhing good Mercury from bad, ſophiſticated and corrupted, which way is, to take common Mercury, brought out of *Spain* in Skins ſealed, or if you cannot have this, take any other, and put a little of it in a Silver Spoon heated ſo, as to make the Mercury evaporate, and if the remainder of it be of a white or citrine Colour, 'tis good; but if of another Colour, bad, and not at all fit for our Work, becauſe ſophiſticated: Then take of *Roman* Vitriol two Pounds, melt it in a glazed Veſſel, being melted, add one pound of Mercury, and as much of common Salt prepared, ſtir and ſhake till they be all mix'd, evaporating the moiſture with ſuch a heat as that of the Sun; then take out the Matter, grind, and put it in a Sublimatory, and ſublime the Mercury by the uſual degrees of Fire: The Veſſels being cold, take out the ſublimation, to which being put into a Retort, pour of the Vegetable Water without Phlegm (*Philoſophical Aqua Vitæ rectify'd*) about three or four Fingers, let it boyl in Balneo two Hours, then diſtil in Aſhes, that the Vegetable Water may aſcend; then cover the Retort with Aſhes, and increaſing the Fire, the *Mercury vive* will aſcend into the *Aqua ardens*, decant the Water from the Mercury, which again ſublime with new Matters, and that ſix times, always caſting away the Fæces: But take notice that theſe ſeven ſublimations muſt always be tranſacted in Aludels, becauſe you will no other way ſeparate the aduſtible powder aſcending in the Aludels: And to inſtruct you, that you may not err, I will more diſtinctly repeat the method of the ſaid ſeven Sublimations: The way is this, to take a Glaſs Veſſel like one of the narrower ſort of Cucurbits, with its blind Head, perforated in the upper part of it, into this put two parts of Vitriol very well pulverized, of Mercury one part, and of Salt prepared one part, mixing all well, the Matter being now gently dryed, put on a blind Head, or rather an Aludel, yet obſerving not to cover the Cucurbit with Aſhes above one third, the moiſture being evaporated by an eaſie heat, ſtop the Hole of the Aludel with a little Cotton, and increaſing, ſublime, all being cold, take out that which is ſublimed, as well out of the Aludel, as the Cucurbit, in which (*if not yet cold*) diſſolve the Fæces with hot Water, and ſo you will eaſily cleanſe the

the ſaid Veſſel for its uſe. Now mix new Matters with your ſublimation, and ſublime as before, and this repeat ſeven times; then grind the ſublimation into a moſt fine Powder, put it in the aforeſaid Cucurbit with its blind Head, or Aludel, and alſo with its common Alembick, becauſe of the operation differing from the former; the ſublimation being put into a Cucurbit, pour to it of the ſimple Animal or Vegetable *Menſtruum* (*the Animal* Menſtruum *deſcribed in Numb.* 37. *or Vegetable in Numb.* 29.) *but here above he order'd him to take Vegetable Water rectify'd, that is,* Aqua ardens) ſo much, as to be three Fingers above it, cover it with a blind Head, and digeſt in Aſhes twelve Hours, then taking off the blind Head, put on a common Alembick, and draw off the *Menſtruum* in Balneo, lay aſide the Alembick again, and put on an Aludel, ſet the Veſſel in Aſhes ſo deep, as to cover the Matter in the Glaſs, give Fire by degrees, till all the moiſture is exhaled, the Hole in the upper part of the Aludel ſtop with Cotton, increaſe the Fire, that the Mercury may be ſublimed: Sublimation being ended, and the Veſſels cold, take away the Aludel, and what you find ſublimed in it, is not for our purpoſe; for it is that aduſt part, which is no Ingredient to our Magiſtery: Then gather the ſublimation from the ſides of the Cucurbit, which will be clear as Criſtal, and have a care that it be not mix'd with its Fæces, grind, ſift, and put it into the ſame Veſſel, being cleanſed from the Fæces, and pour the *Menſtruum* drawn off in Balneo to it, cover the Veſſel with an Aludel, digeſt twelve Hours as before, lay aſide the Aludel, put on a common Alembick, diſtil in Balneo, lay aſide this Alembick, put on an Aludel, and ſublime in Aſhes, the Fæces, as alſo the aduſtive part being caſt out of the Aludel, gather the middle ſubſtance out of the Cucurbit dexterouſly; with this method you muſt ſublime ſeven times, or till it leaves no Fæces in the Cucurbit: Having obtained this ſign, take the ſaid ſubſtance, grind, and put it in a Glaſs Veſſel, pour to it the ſimple either Animal or Vegetable *Menſtruum*, the height of three Fingers, cover the Veſſel with a blind Head, digeſt gently two Days in Aſhes, then decant the diſſolution into another Veſſel, and that which remains in the Veſſel, dry with a temperate heat, like that of the Sun, to which pour new *Menſtruum*, covering the Veſſel with a blind Head as before, and repeat the ſame method,

till

till all the dissolvible part is dissolved, and in the bottom of the Glass will remain an indissolvible Earth, to be cast away, as nothing worth: Now take away dissolution, that is, your decantations, and distil in Balneo, and the *Menstruum* being distilled, put on an Aludel, and in Ashes sublime the Cristalline substance, which may truly be called the first Matter of Mercury; this is that middle substance, with which we incalcinate our *Menstruum*, (*Circulatum majus, described in Numb.* 50.) and make infinite particulars, as we have taught you before: This also is called the Mineral Stone. Now, my Son! will you be able to proceed by infinite ways, yet following these which I have shewed you; and remember, that Mercury thus reduced, is that, which our Captain *Raymond* speaks of, making mention of the Mineral Stone, as also in the *last Chapter of his Book, nam'd* Vade mecum, and in many other places of his Volumes. This is that Mercury which *Arnold de Villa nova*; treats of in his *Rosarium*, and we declare to you, except Mercury be reduced into the first Matter with the said Vegetable or Animal Water, it is altogether impossible to do any good with it, by reason of its great Corruption, occasioned by the crudity of it.

From the Receipts of this Kind we observe:

1. *That* Menstruums *may and ought to be made according to the designed uses, for they are desired not only to dissolve Bodies promiscuously, but rightly also, that the tinctures of things dissolved may not by any Heterogeneous tinctures of the* Menstruums *be inquinated, but rather illustrated.*

2. *That these* Menstruums *being once compounded, the oftner the Composition is repeated by adding new Matter, are endowed with so much a greater Virtue; whereas on the contrary it is manifest, that common* Menstruums *are this way debilitated.*

3. *That these* Menstruums *are most fragrant, and of exceeding sweetness and redness, yet nevertheless called* Acetum acerrimum, *which dissolves Gold into a Spirit.*

4. *That these* Menstruums *are the Essences or Magisteries of Metals made by Magisteries or Essences, and mix'd together into compounded* Circulatums.

5. *That*

5. *That these compounded* Circulatums *may be made not only of Gold and Silver, but also of imperfect Metals and Minerals.*

6. *That* Sal Armoniack *may be made of Corals, and other arids, as well as Pearls.*

7. *That* Parisinus *his first Matter of Mercury is an Essence rather than a Magistery, it is indeed sooner prepared than the Mercurial* Sal Armoniack *of* Lully, *but is not of the same, but less Virtue.*

8. *That* Parisinus *defends* Arnold de villa nova *in his way of subliming Mercury, (described in the* Rosarium) *against his Consort* Bernhard.

9. *That this first Matter of Mercury is a Poyson; wherefore* Parisinus *the Author gives caution that it is not to be used for humane Medicines, but Metals only, yet if this incalcinated* Menstruum *be Circulated as the rest, it becomes harmless, and an excellent Medicine.*

The Eleventh KIND.

Vegetable compounded Menstruums *graduated, made of the compounded Vegetable* Menstruums, *impregnated with the influences of Heaven and Earth.*

57. The Etherial and Terrestrial Waters of Metals of *Lully* for the making of Pretious Stones.

Canon. 43. *distinct.* 1. *Lib. Quint. Essen.*

TAke the Water of Mercury, made by the way, which we declared in our (*Novissimum*) *Testamentum*, and in *Libro Mercuriorum* (*the Mercurial* Menstruum, *or Glorious Water of common* Argent vive, *described before in Numb.* 44.) and in that Water, Son! you must dissolve one half Ounce of the purest *Luna*, after the filtred dissolution, separate the Water from the Fæces (*distil the* Menstruum *from the Silver through an Alembick*) in which the limosity of the Silver will ascend: This Water, Son! resolves all other Bodies, and *Argent vive* it self, by Virtue of which, Son! Pearls are reformed by the way which I told you in our *Testamentum*, and in the *Compendium super Testamentum & Codicillum missum Regi Roberto.*

The second Water is thus made: Take half an Ounce of Lead, and of the aforesaid Water as much as sufficeth, when you see the Lead dissolved, separate the Water by filtred distillation (*filtre the dissolution of the Lead*) and throw out the Fæces, as nothing

nothing worth, then distil the Water by Balneo (*draw off the* Menstruum *in Balneo*) and keep the Fæces (*the dissolved Lead*) for occasion.

The third Water is thus made: Take of Copper one Ounce, and dissolve it in as much of the first Water as you please, and let it rest in its Vessel, in a cold place, for a Natural Day, then separate the Green Water through a Filtre, and pour out the first Fæces, (*that which remains in the Filtre must be cast away*) then distil the Water through an Alembick, and keep the second Fæces.

The fourth Water is thus made: Take one Ounce of the purest Tin of *Cornwall*, which is purer than any other, and dissolve it in a quantity of the first Water, and distil (*through a Filtre*) that Water (*dissolution*) with its limosity, and the Fæces which remain cast away, then distil the Water through an Alembick, and keep (*the residue, or Tin dissolved*) the second Fæces.

The fifth Water is thus made: Take of the purest Iron one Ounce, and dissolve it in a sufficient quantity of the first Water, then distil through a Filtre, and cast away the Fæces, distil the Water through an Alembick, and keep the second Fæces.

The sixth Water is thus made: Take of the purest Gold one Ounce, and dissolve it as I told you in my *Testamentum*, that is, with pure *Lunaria* (*the simple Vegetable* Menstruum *without* Argent vive *and Silver*) mix'd with such a weight of the fifth Water (*now prepared from Iron*) and do, as you did with the other.

You may also, Son! dissolve all those Metals in this order: Having made the first Water, in it dissolve the Metal, which we commanded you to dissolve after the second way (*to wit Lead*) then do with it as we told you before. In this second Water dissolve the third Metal, (*Copper*) and in the Water of the third Metal dissolve the fourth Metal, (*Tin*) and in the Water of the fourth Metal dissolve the fifth Metal (*Iron*) and in the Water of the fifth Metal dissolve the sixth Metal (*Gold.*)

Take which of those Waters you like best to dissolve a Metal. Son! these limosities of Metals are called Quintessences, or Mineral Mercury, which the Philosophers esteemed in the Alchymical work (*in Alchymical Tinctures*) and the lapidifick, (*in the making of Pretious Stones*) and in the Medicinal Work (*in the preparing of Medicines.*) But Son! in the Alchymical Work those Quintessences ought to be more subtil, and to be done by dividing the Elements as we (*in the third Book of this Volume*) shall declare, but in (*making Pretious*) Stones the Quintessence (*aforesaid*) are not so, in such a subtil Matter, but in Medicine either of them (*this two-fold way of preparing*) may be used.

Having spoken of the Quintessences of Minerals (*of Metallick Waters*) how we are to make them, it is now convenient to speak of the division of them in general. And my Son! do thus; When your Metals are dissolved, you must divide every Water (*being first filtred, and distilled from its remainder*) and every divided Water (*now distilled*) into two parts, and one part of every part you must put with its own Fæces (*the remaining Metal, which the Water had left in distillation*) into a Glass Alembick, and distil a *Limus deserti*, which is Air made out of two Bodies, (*or Metals*) in the Furnace, which we design'd you first with a gentle Fire, shining with great Mineral Lustre, and with great limosity appropriated to receive Celestial Virtues: And put every one of those Waters into a Glass Vessel, with a long Neck and round, and then stop the Mouth of it with common Wax, and after that with Mastick, and every of those Vessels put in the open Air so, as that neither Stone, nor any other hurtful thing may touch the Glass. Son! Take the material Fæces, from which you resolved the *Limus*, which are the second Fæces left in the distillation of the Waters which you put in the Air. (*Take the Caput mortuum from the distillation of every* Limus desertus, *or the third Fæces, for the first remaining in the Filtre were cast away, from the second the* Limus desertus *was distilled; now the Fæces of the* Limus desertus, *are those which he here calls the second*) and put them in a Glass Vessel with a long Neck, which may contain two hands breadth, and put in part of its own Water, which was reserved from that aforesaid limous substance, and stop the Vessels with a Stopple of Wax, and with Leather and Mastick, as you did to the other, and Bury them (*Waters of Metals*) in a Garden, in an Earth half a Yard deep, and put also something about the Neck of the Vessels, which may appear above ground, for the preservation of them, and let them be there for one whole Year: Son! the Waters which are put into the Earth are of one Nature, and those which are put in the Air of another,

ther; for Son! those which are put into the Earth have a hardning, coagulating, and fixing Virtue and Quality; and those which are in the Air, have the Virtue and Property of being hardened, coagulated and fixed: The Year being ended, you will have all that is desired in the World for this Work, &c.

Annotations.

YOu will perhaps wonder, that we have assigned this so high a place to these Menstruums, they being inferior to many Menstruums *of the antecedent Kinds, as to Ingredients, as well as to the method of preparation; but though it be so, nevertheless these* Menstruums *are by being exposed to the Air for a Year, or for so long a time committed to the Earth, made better and more excellent than the aforesaid* Menstruums, *as will appear hereafter by the use of them: We will at present explain the methods of making these Waters: The Waters of the first method he makes thus: He dissolves Lead, Copper, Tin, Iron, and Gold in the Glorious Water of* Argent vive, *acuated moreover with* Luna, *filtres every dissolution, casting away the Fæces, draws off the filtred dissolutions in Balneo to dryness, divides the distilled Waters into two parts, in one of which he dissolves its own Metal left in the drawing off of the dissolution, which he then distills into a Liquor, which he calls* Limus desertus, Quintessence, *or* Mineral Mercury, *and hangs it in the air for a Year, to be his* Etherial Water: *The* Caput mortuum *of the* Limus desertus *he dissolves in the other part of the Water reserved, and Buries it in the Earth for his* Terrestrial Water. In Compendio Animæ transm. pag. 208. Volum. 4. Theat. Chym. *He adds also the Waters of common Mercury and Silver to the rest; the Mercury Water is thus made;* Take of common Mercury one Ounce, and dissolve it in the dissolving Water (*aforesaid*) in the digestion of I. (*Ashes*) distil through a Filtre, regard not the Fæces, but keep the second (*left in the bottom*) after distilling through an Alembick.

The Water of *Luna* is thus made: Take one Ounce of the purest Silver, dissolve it in what quantity of the dissolving Water you please, distil through a Filtre, and cast away the first Fæces, then distil through an Alembick in the digestion of H. (*Balneo*) and keep the second Fæces, you must keep the second

Fæces,

Fæces of all the Waters in their own Veſſels, every one by it ſelf. Moreover (*in Compendio Animæ*) he divides not the diſtilled Waters into equal parts, as *in Libro Eſſentiæ*, but draws off the diſſolutions of Metals by diſtilling one half for the Terreſtrial Water, and diſtils the other half for the Etherial Water. You muſt indeed, *ſaith he*, be cautious in reſolving the *Limus*, becauſe you are to make two Waters or parts of every *Limus*, diſtilling one half of the *Limus*, which you muſt keep apart, becauſe the Terreſtrial Water is made of that firſt part, and you muſt likewiſe diſtil the other (*half*) part, which the Aërial Water is made of, which is hung in the Air as aforeſaid, for a Year, *Pag.* 209. *Volum.* 4. *Theat. Chym.*

The Waters made by the latter method are more compounded than thoſe of the firſt, the firſt were prepared promiſcuouſly with the Lunar Menſtruum, *the ſecond not ſo; for the Water of Lead is made by the Lunar* Menſtruum, *of which Water of Lead is made the Water of Copper; of this Water of Copper is made the Water of Tin; from the Water of Tin he prepares the Water of Iron, but the Water of Gold is made with the Lunar* Menſtruum, *to which is added half of the Water of Iron. O wonderful mixture! I will not ſay, confuſion of Metals! yet doubtleſs the moſt acute Philoſopher had reaſons for it. This method is alſo in* Lapidario, Cap. 9. & ſequentibus.

From the Receipts we obſerve:

1. *That the Etherial Waters are the Eſſences of Metals, expoſed to the influences of the Heavens for a Year.*

2. *That the Terreſtrial Waters are the Bodies of Eſſences, diſſolved in their own* Menſtruums, *and Buried for a Year.*

3. *That the Eſſences of not only Metals, but the whole Mineral Kingdoms do by ſuch a method yield Etherial and Terreſtrial Waters.*

4. *That theſe Waters acquire their principal Virtues by being impregnated with the Stars of Heaven.*

The Adepts *held divers Opinions concerning the Influences of the Heavens. Some would have the Situations, Aſpects, and determinate Times of the Planets to be highly neceſſary to this Work, but others thought the contrary: Amongſt the Affirmers let us hear* Thomas Norton, *an* Engliſh Adept, *who thus in the Sixth Chapter of his Ordinal.* Pag. 99. *of* Theat. Chym. Britannicum.

The

THe Fifth Concord is known well of Clerks,
Between the Sphere of Heaven, and our ſubtil
Nothing in Earth hath more ſimplicity, (Werks;
Than th' Elements of our Stone will be:
Wherefore they being in Work of Generation,
Have moſt Obedience to Conſtellation.
Whereof Concord moſt kindly and convenient,
Is a direct and fiery Aſcendent;
Being Sign common for this Operation,
For multitude of their Iteration:
Fortune your Aſcendent with his Lord alſo,
Keeping th' Aſpect of Shrews them fro;
And if they muſt let, or needly infect,
Cauſe them to look with a Trine Aſpect.
For the white Work may Fortunate the Moon,
For the Lord of the fourth Houſe likewiſe be it done;
For that is *Theſaurum abſconditum* of Old Clerks,
So of the Sixth Houſe for Servants of the Werks:
Save all them well from great Impediments,
As it is in Picture, or like the ſame Intents.
Unleſs then your Nativity pretend Infection,
In contrariety to this Election,
The Virtue of the mover of the Orb is formal,
The Virtue of the Eighth Sphere is here Inſtrumental:
With her Signs and Figures, and parts aſpectual,
The Planets Virtue is proper and ſpecial.
The Virtue of the Elements is here material,
The Virtue infuſed reſulteth of them all:
The firſt is like to a Work-man's Mind,
The ſecond like his Hand ye ſhall find;
The third is like a good Inſtrument,
The remnant like a thing wrought to your Intent:
Make all the Premiſes with other well accord,
Then ſhall your Merits make you a great Lord.

Amongſt the Denyers is Lully *himſelf:* Who thus; we ſay not, that it is the buſineſs of an Artiſt to operate with the Figures and Images of Heaven, by the knowledge of their motions, as many Philoſophers

Philosophers affirm: But it is enough for you to know the influence of the Celestial heat, informed by the Figure of the Heaven and Stars, by reason of which, Virtues are infused into Matter being aptly appropriated, which receives them by the Natural Industry of an Artist with resolution, which is done by Art imitating Nature, *&c.* And in this Point the Philosophers have been mistaken, in reprehending those Men that knew, that the Celestial Virtue is too common to every elemented Nature; for by its great Nobleness it takes determination at any time, because in things mixed it is influenced as well by Art as by Nature, and this is done by reason of the Natural Virtues, which are the subject and proper detainer of it in such a manner, as that it receives such a Virtue, according to the properties of the Matter, and its Kind, which afterwards effects such things by Nature, as are reputed for a Miracle. In like manner let every Artist take Notice, that Nature cannot operate but by the succession of the least particles, nor also can it receive any Virtues but by the succession of its operation, nor can they also do all at once, nor can the Constellations suffer the Station of any time punctually in a certain Virtue, which may not be immediately varied: And it being also granted, that it might, the time of Constellation is so small by reason of the Circles of revolution, as that it may sooner pass from one Virtue to another, *&c. Lib. Essen. dist.* 1. *Pag.* 18.

An ingenious Artist, *saith Paracelsus*, will by diligent animadversion be able to prepare Metals, so that being guided by true reason, he may promote the perfection of transmuting Metals, by his own work or conduct better, than by Courses of the twelve Celestial Signs, and seven Planets, which therefore to observe, will be superfluous, as also the Aspects, the ill or good times, day or hour, the prosperous or unhappy State of this or another Planet, which cannot help, much less hurt in the Art of Natural Alchymy; if otherwise, you have a true possible process, operate when you please; but if there be any defect in you, or your Operations, and Understanding, the Planets and Celestial Constellations will fail you. *Cœlum. Phil. Pag.* 125.

If they alledge, *saith Geber*, that the perfecting of Metals is from a certain situation of one or more Starrs which we know not, we answer, that we regard not this situation and motion; nor also

also is it necessarily requisite for us to know it: because there is not any species of things generable and corruptible, but Generation and Corruption may be dayly and in every instant made from the individuals of it: And it is therefore manifest, that such a position of the Stars is every Day good, and able to perfect, and simply to corrupt all the species whatsoever of Individuals. It is not therefore necessarily expedient for an Artist to expect the place of the Stars, though it might be useful; because it is sufficient for him only to dispose and administer the way of Nature, that She, who is wise, may dispose the situations of those able Bodies agreeing: For Nature can perfect nothing without the motion and position of the Planets. Wherefore if you dispose, and duly consider the Artifice of Nature, whatsoever may be the contingents of this Magistery, it will be perfected under a due position by Nature agreeable to it, without the consideration of it: For when we see a Worm produced from a putrified Dog or other Animal, we do not presently consider the position of the Stars, but the disposition of the ambient Air, and other causes conducing to putrefaction, besides that position: And from such a consideration we know sufficiently, that Worms are produced according to Nature: For Nature finds convenient places for it self, though we may be ignorant of them. *Summa perfect. Lib. 1. parte. 2. Cap. 11.*

Petrus Bonus of Ferraria hath the same Opinion of Influences. As to the ninth reason, *saith he*, we say it is true, that Forms are introduced into things below, by the motion and light of Celestial Bodies, and by their particular Positions and Aspects; but it is not necessary for us to know, nor can we know them, but in a confused manner, as in some things by the Sun, who is the cause of the four Seasons of the Year; Sowing, Reaping, and Planting, being done at certain Seasons; and in some Animals, as Horses, Asses, and Hawks, Conjunctions are made in order to Coition and Generation at some certain Periods of the Sun; but in some these things are done at any time indifferently, as in Man, Pigeons, Hens, &c. Wherefore if we would generate a Worm out of putrifying Flesh, we do not consider any position of the Stars, but only the disposition of the ambient Air, and other causes of putrefaction: Likewise, if we put Eggs in Dung, or such a like place for the production of Chickens, the Form will be given at any time in the place and time predestinated by the Celestial Powers, without our consideration herein: After the same manner in the Generation of Lime and Vitriol, and Gold, and Silver, or Sulphur, and Ceruse, and Minium, and Cinabar, likewise in the Composition of Theriacle, and other Confections, because these things may be done at any time, and any hour; for the Celestial Virtue is very common to all things, and is circumscribed by the Virtues and Dispositions of those things, which are the subject of it in things Elemented and the Elements themselves, because, as aforesaid, the Celestial Vertues do operate in the whole Nature of things capable of Generation and Corruption continually according to the disposition of the Matter, either properly or commonly: Wherefore said *Lilium*, The Work is not caused by the motion of the Powers above, because it may be done at any time. And *Rasis in 70. in Libro Reprehensionis*: Time operates not any thing in this; *and adds* because should time operate in it, it would be of no esteem amongst the People. If therefore all contingents in this Magistery concur rightly in their time, their Form will be introduced under a due Position and Aspect of the Stars, at the time prefixed in the Matter, without any consideration herein: And therefore said *Plato*, According to the merit of the Matter, are the Celestial Virtues infused, &c. But as to those things, in which an accidental, new, and hidden Form is infused by the Celestial Powers, as is manifest in *Arte Imaginum Cœlestium*, it is necessary for us to know and observe the determined Positions and Aspects of the Celestial Bodies, according to the time proposed: Because such a Form is imprinted by such alone, and at such a time and no other, as appears in the Books of Astrology concerning the Election of Hours, Images, and Wars, Buildings, Journey, &c. Wherefore Alchymy being no such Art, therefore is it not expedient for a Man to know these things. *Margar. pretiosa, Pag.* 731: *Vol. 5. Th. Chym.*

The

The Twelfth KIND.

Compounded Vegetable Menstruums *most highly exalted, made of compounded Vegetable* Menstruums *graduated.*

58. The Etherial and Celestial Limes of *Lully*, for the making of Alchymical Tinctures. *In Testam. Novissimo.*

TAke the Sulphur of Gold, (*the Philosophers Mercury made of* Gold, or Sal Armoniack *of* Sol) put it in a Glass Vessel, and pour to it as much as it weighs of the Celestial Vegetable *Menstruum* (*the Cælum Vinosum of* Lully *described in Num.* 30.) which you know already; put it in digestion of Balneo six Days, then distil by Balneo; then pour on new *Menstruum* according to the weight of it, and digest in Balneo six Days, then set it in Ashes one Day, distilling all that can be distilled, and put it with the other distilled before: And again pour on new *Menstruum*, and digest and distil as before; and continue the repetition of this Royal Magistery, till all the said Earth or Sulphur is emptied of its Air, which is done in two and twenty times, if you know how to operate: Then take all the distillations and put them in Balneo, and distil the whole *Menstruum*, and see if all the Air remains in the Form of a Liquor, then will you know that the Earth is emptied of its Air, but if not, repeat with new *Menstruum* in Balneo, digesting and distilling in Ashes as before three times, and then will all our Sulphur be freed from its Air: Then take the Air which you kept, and upon it put its whole *Menstruum*, which is that with which you emptied the

the Air, and pour it upon the Earth of the Sulphur of Gold, and put it in digestion in Balneo eight Days, then distil all the *Menstruum* in the said Balneo for one Day, and another in Ashes, draw off all the Air and Fire, as much as you can, namely, in another Receiver, which you will know, when the Air begins to change the reddish Colour. Keep that Fire apart, and again put the Air with the *Menstruum* drawn from it, or with other, and put it to the Earth in Balneo, and digest six Days, and in the said Balneo distil all the *Menstruum* for one Day, and the Fire in Ashes, separating then every one by it self as you did before, and keep the Fire in Balneo: And again put the Air with the *Menstruum* upon the Earth, in which is the Fire, and digest as before, and this Magistery repeat, till the Earth is well emptied of its Fire, which is done in forty times or repetitions. Then must you sublime the Earth after this manner; Take that Earth which remained after the separation of the Air and Fire, and put it in a Glass Vessel, and pour upon it of the Vegetable *Menstruum*, according to the quantity of the Earth, and set it in Balneo for a Natural Day, then another Day distil in Ashes; and again put of the said *Menstruum* according to the weight of the Earth, and digest in Balneo the space of one Day, and distil in Ashes another Day, and again repeat, digesting in Balneo, and distilling in Ashes, till all the Earth is converted into an impalpable Powder: Then take that, and put of the *Menstruum* upon it according to its weight, and digest in Balneo two Days, then distil in Ashes one Day, and put the distillation in Balneo: Then take the Earth, and put again of other *Menstruum* equal to its weight, digest two Days, and distil as before; proceed in repeating the inhumations and distillations till the Earth has passed through the Alembick together with the *Menstruum*: That Earth being thus mixed with the *Menstruum*, is called *Argent vive* exuberated according to the intention of the Alcyhmists: put therefore those distillations wherein is that Earth, to be distilled by Balneo, and draw off the *Menstruum*, and the Earth will remain dry and prepared in the bottom of the Vessel, which keep: Thus Son! I have you the Elements of the Sulphur of Gold divided with the help of God. Then must you have the Sulphur of Silver, (*the Philosophers Mercury prepared from Silver, or the* Sal Armoniack *of* Luna) and separate the Elements from it, separating the Air

with

with the Menſtrual Water, and the Fire with the Air and Water, and the Earth ſubliming with the *Menſtruum*, and cauſe it to paſs through the Alembick with the ſame *Menſtruum*. Thus have you, my Son! the Elements of the white Sulphur, and the Elements of the red Sulphur ſeparated and divided: Now take the *Menſtruum* or Water with which you ſeparated the Elements of the Sulphurs of Gold and Silver, and for every Pound of the *Menſtruum* in which you diſſolved the Gold, diſſolve one Ounce of Gold; and in the *Menſtruum* wherein you diſſolv'd the Silver, an Ounce of Silver; and put either of them by it ſelf in a Veſſel of Circulation in Balneo or Dung, the ſpace of fifteen Days, and there it will be ſtrengthened into its Menſtrual Nature: This Water, Son! we call Elemented *Menſtruum*, or Water waſhed and drawn from the Fæces of the Earth. Now take the two Elements, namely, the Air and Fire of the Sulphur of Gold, put them together into a Glaſs diſtilling Veſſel, and diſtil in Aſhes with a moſt temperate heat, till you have three parts of five diſtilled in the Receiver, then let it cool, and that which is diſtilled receive by it ſelf, and diſtil it ſeven times, and keep it apart, then diſtil that which you left; when you have diſtilled three parts of five, continue diſtilling the two which remained, till you ſee the Fire congealed at the ſides of the Veſſel, let it cool till the Fire be congealed: And that Fire which you drew off till the Fire was congealed, (*he means that which aſcends as yet moiſt before the ſublimation of the Matter from theſe two parts left*) is called the ſecond Air and Tincture, and we call it our Secret, and our Treaſure, and the Vapour of the Elements: This, my Son! you muſt rectify by ſeven diſtillations or rectifications, and the Earth, which after the diſtillation of the firſt and ſecond Air you drew out of the Veſſels, in which you diſtilled the firſt and ſecond Air, put in the Fire to be congealed, and that Earth is called Fire: Now Son! prepare this Fire after this manner. Put it in a diſtilling Veſſel, and upon it pour its own Water, which is that wherewith you ſeparated the Elements of the Sulphur of Gold, when we commanded to reduce it to a fifth Spirit in the Veſſel of *Hermes*, and ſaid, Take the Water waſh'd from the Fæces of the Earth (*otherwiſe the Elemented* Menſtruum *of* Sol) five parts of its weight, that is, five Ounces of the ſaid Water (*Elemented* Menſtruum *of Gold*) to one Ounce of the ſaid Fire,

Fire, and digest in Balneo eight Days, then distil in Ashes most gently, and again put new Water, namely, five parts, digest and distil as before, repeating this method seven times, and so you have the Fire and Earth (*of the Sulphur of Gold*) calcined by Philosophical calcination; and they are the two Elements of the red Sulphur prepared for the *desert Limes*. And take notice, that you must put the Earth of the white Sulphur, which you calcined and prepared after the separation of the Elements of the red Sulphur with the Earth, which you drew from the Air mix'd with the Fire, and put both with the Fire congealed. Now Son! take the Earth of the Sulphur of Silver, which remained after the separation of the Elements, and prepare it, as you did in calcining and preparing the Earth of Gold, after the separation of the Elements sublimed together with the *Menstruum*, and reduced into an impalpable Powder, and carryed through the Alembick with the same *Menstruum*. You may also prepare the Earth of the Sulphur of Silver with the *Menstruum*, that you used in separating the Elements of the Sulphur of Silver: Then have you the Earths of the Sulphur of Gold and Silver prepared by themselves, which you will know by the sign given you, that is, putting a little of it upon a red hot Plate of *Luna*, the greater part will fume away: Then take those Earths in equal weight and ounces, and put them in a preparing Vessel, then take the *Menstruum*, with which you prepared the Elements of *Luna*, and in one Pound of it, put one Ounce of the Vegetable Sulphur, which we shewed you how to make from the Earth of Wine (*Vegetable* Sal Armoniack *made of the Earth of* Philosophical Wine) and distilling, make the whole pass through the Alembick, and then will you have the *Menstruum*, with which you extracted the Elements of the Sulphur of *Luna*, animated and acuated: Then Son! you must mix and prepare the Earths of the aforesaid Sulphurs (*that is of Gold and Silver*) together, allowing of the said *Menstruum*, now animated and acuated, a fourth part of their weight, digesting and drying, as is done in the making of the Sulphur (*of Nature, or* Sal Armoniack) till they have drank up four parts of the said *Menstruum*, and are disposed to sublimation, which you must sublime with a Fire of the fourth degree: And observe that all those preparations and distillations of the Earths

are

are to be done in Balneo: And thus, Son! have you *our Sulphur or Matter, or Vegetable and Metallick Earth in one Kind united*, for the making of the Glorious, High, and Virtuous Stone, which will transform common *Argent vive* into perfect *Sol* or *Luna*, without the help of Fire, but as the Eye of a Basilisk, which kills Animals by sight alone: But it is your interest Son! to use great diligence, and exquisite Ingenuity in making the Roots of this high and lofty Tree, which Roots we call *desert Limes*, in which the whole Virtue of Heaven and Earth relating to this Magistery will be infused: And the way is this,

Take of the Vegetable (*and Mineral*) *Earth or Sulphur, which you united in one Kind*, by sublimation, which is that which you call'd the *Earth of Sulphur in one Kind united*, put it in a Glass Vessel, and pour so much as it weighs of the *Menstruum*, with which you separated the Elements of the Sulphur of *Luna*, and prepared the said kind of Earth, and put it in a Philosophical Balneo three Natural Days, and in that time it will be all dissolved, which being thus dissolved, put in a common Balneo, and distil the *Menstruum*, and *the Earth united to its kind* will by sublimation remain as an Oyl, which we call the Philosophers Oyntment; and it is one of the Secrets, which we take care to have concealed: Then,

Take of that Oyl or Oyntment aforesaid ten Drachms, and of the rectify'd Air of the Sulphur of *Luna* one Drachm (*not one Ounce: And of the Air of the Sulphur of* Sol *one Drachm*) and distil in a Fire of Ashes, and that which is distilled, which is almost all, is called the Terrestrial *desert Limes*, keep it. Take of the Element of the (*Fire*) Sulphur of Gold already prepared and congealed ten Drachms (*not twenty*) and of the Element of the Air (*Sulphur*) of *Luna* one Drachm, and of the Element of the Air of the Sulphur of Gold another Drachm, and put all in Ashes, and distil; that which is distilled from it, which is almost all, is called the *Etherial desert Limes*; keep it for occasion.

Take of the Element of the Fire of the Sulphur of Gold one Drachm or two, and rectifie it again thus, pouring upon it five parts of its own *Menstruum*, which is that, with which you separated the Elements of the same Sulphur of Gold, and put it to digest in Balneo for one Natural Day, then distil in Ashes what you can: And again pour the said *Menstruum* upon it, digest and

disti-

distil by Ashes, and repeat, till it be all pass'd over by a Fire of Ashes. Then take its weight of the said *Vegetable Earth, united and sublimed together* (*prepared above*) and you must unite them together (*with the distilled Element of Fire*) and not distil, but so lay it aside, and it is called the Terrestrial *desert Limes*, (*of Gold*) not vaporized.

Take of the said Earth (*in one kind united*) one Drachm, and of the Oyl of the Air (*of the Sulphur*) of *Luna* one Drachm, mix them together, and you will make the same Magistery, as you did with the precedent Gold, and it is called the Terrestrial *desert Limes lunificated* (*not*) *vaporized*.

We do now think good to shew the way of celificating and preparing those (*Limes*) in order to receive the Virtues of Heaven and Earth, and the way is this: Take Brass or Iron Cages, and let them be like those wherein Parrots whistle, but the twiggs must be closer, so that no Earth, neither Celestial nor Terrestrial can enter, but only the vapour of Heaven and Earth, which you will have by Influence.

Take the *Limes* (*above mentioned, Terrestrial desert*) made of ten Drachms of the Earth or Sulphur united, which is that which you united with the Earth of the Sulphur of Silver, and reduced into an Oyl or Oyntment; and of one Drachm of the Air (*of the Sulphur*) of *Luna*, and one Drachm of the Air (*of Sol*) mix'd, and that *Limes* put in a Glass Vessel with a long Neck exactly Sealed with the Seal of *Hermes*, and put it in the Cage, and set it one Arm or two deep, and let it stand a Year and half, or at least a Year, covering it well with Earth, and keeping it from all dangers, and in that time will it be made a powerful Water, with wonderful fixative Virtues of the Stone, and it hath admirable Virtues acquired from Heaven, which it attracted from the Vapours of the Earth. Son! depend upon this.

Take the *Limes* (*above declared, Etherial desert*,) which you made of ten Drachms of the Fire of the Sulphur of Gold, and of one Drachm of the Air of the Sulphur of *Luna* (*and one Drachm of the Air of the Sulphur of* Sol) and put it in another Glass Vessel with a long Neck Hermetically Sealed, and put it in another Cage, and hang it in the Air on a Tree, or any private place, free from all Wind, Dust, and Danger; leave it a Year and half, or a whole Year at least, as we said of the other, and

so

ſo will be made a clear Water endowed with the Virtue of hardning, fixing, congealing, penetrating, and making the Stone Volatile, and is called the Mercury of Air of moſt acute penetration.

Take the (*Terreſtrial deſert*) *Limes* of Gold not vaporized, nor celificated (*neither diſtilled through an Alembick, nor circulated*) which is that, that you made (*by meerly mixing*) of one Drachm of the Element of the Fire of the Sulphur of *Sol*, and of one Drachm of *the Earth* (*united in its Kind*) and that (*take alſo the Terreſtrial deſert Limes lunificated, not vaporized*) which you made out of one Drachm of *the Earth of Sulphur united*, and one Drachm of the Air (*of the Sulphur*) of *Luna*, and put thoſe *Limes* every one by it ſelf in a Glaſs Veſſel Sealed, as was ſaid of the other, and put it in the Earth the depth of one Arm for a whole Year in a Cage, and in that time will be made a Water of wonderful Virtue in joyning Bodies, and content your ſelf with this.

Take the *Limes* which you made out of ten Drachms of the Fire or Air, and one of the Earth; and take that which remains of the Air (*of the Sulphur*) of *Luna*, becauſe you took but three Drachms of it, when you made the *Limes*, and let it hang in the Air in a Glaſs Veſſel Sealed, and in a Cage, as you did with the other; and there will it receive the Celeſtial Virtues, which are the means of Conjunction between the *Limes of the Earth, and the Limes of the Fire*, and other *Limes* alſo.

Take the ſecond Air (*the* Menſtruum *Elemented, in which were diſſolved the Air and Fire of the Sulphur of Gold, and gently drawn off, that is, three parts only from five of it*) which is that, which you drew from the Fire congeled, which we call'd Philoſophical Oyl, and Philoſophical Treaſure (*not that, which is alſo called the Philoſophers Oyntment, made of the Earth united in one Kind, but that which was call'd the Vapour of the Elements*) and put it by it ſelf in another Glaſs Veſſel well Sealed, and put it in the Air near the other, which you put for a whole Year.

Take the *Menſtruum* with which you ſeparated the Elements of the Sulphur of *Luna* (*and that* Menſtruum, *wherewith you ſeparated the Elements of the Sulphur of* Sol) and put in every Veſſel, wherein is *Menſtruum* of *Luna* (*and the* Menſtruum of *Sol*) one Drachm of Sulphur (*or Vegetable* Sal Harmoniack) and ſet

 it

it in Balneo, then in Ashes, till you have made it all go over with every *Menstruum* by it self: Then each *Menstruum* being thus recti-fy'd or animated, put in a Glass Vessel Sealed by themselves in their Cages, and hang them in the Air near the other, for a Year.

Take the Oleagineity of *Luna* (*the first, or first Air*) which is that, which you drew from the Earth of *Luna*, when you prepared it for the making of the Sulphur of *Luna*, which we commanded you to keep, and said it should be for the making (*of the Sulphur of Nature*) put it in a Glass Vessel Sealed in the Air, and there it will be made a Fluxible and Virtuous Water of wonderful penetration: And what we said of the white Oyl, we say also of the red incerative Oyl (*of Sol.*) And now Son! you have the Stone (*Menstruum*) divided into eight parts, three in the Earth, and five in the Air.

Annotations.

THe Ten foregoing Kinds of Vegetable as well Simple as compounded Menstruums, *the* Adepts *made by tempering the unctuous Spirit of* Philosophical Wine, *with many sorts of dry Bodies, and by such means produced* Menstruums *adapted equally for every use, and permanent and inseparable, they being of the same Nature with the things that were dissolved. In the Kind immediately antecedent we shew'd you, that all the aforesaid* Menstruums, *whether simple or compound, exalted with so great Labour to the highest degree by tempering them with dry things, may be raised yet higher, and augmented in their Virtues: For what Art cannot do, Nature can; what the Earth cannot do, Heaven can: For* Menstruums *perfected by Art, do, by being exposed to the Influences of the Heavens, attain to very great and incredible Virtues by Nature: In the eleventh precedent Kind, we had* Menstruums *for Pretious Stones, made of the simple Elements of Metals: In this twelfth, he takes the* Sulphur of Nature, Sal Harmoniack, *or* Mercury *of the perfect Metals* Sol *and* Luna, *instead of crude Gold and Silver, and by exposing the Elements of them to the Heaven and Earth, separates them much more Nobly for the best of all Alchymical Tinctures.*

From the Receipts we observe:

1. *That* Limes *in their Compositions are indeed clear, but Clouded with a wearisome multilocution, and disguised by so great a variety*

riety of operations, besides also in respect of time made most tedious on purpose to deter young, and unadvised Practitioners.

2. *That these* Limes *differ from the former* Etherial *and* Terrestrial Waters *in fineness of preparation; these Elements are of the* Sal Harmoniack *or* Philosophical Mercury *of* Sol *and* Luna; *but those Elements of a crude Metal.* For, *said* Lully, Limes for Alchymical Tinctures ought to be of a purer Nature, than those which are for Pretious Stones.

3. *That these* Limes *are Essences graduated, exposed to the Influences of the Heaven and Earth, and consequently are Medicines.*

4. *That the* Sulphurs Naturæ *of imperfect Metals do also by the same method yield* Limes, *as strong in their kind, as the* Sulphurs Naturæ *of Gold and Silver in their kind.*

Hitherto have we treated of Vegetable Menstruums, *now follow those which are called Mineral: But before we proceed further, we are to take notice that by Vegetable* Menstruums *are meant also Animal* Menstruums: *For all the Vegetable* Menstruums *already alleadged, are not called Vegetable in respect of Ingredients; for besides Vegetables, Animals also, and Minerals were made use of in their preparations; but by reason of the Spirit of* Philosophical Wine *produced chiefly from a Vegetable unctuosity; which Spirit, if you knew how to extract out of some Oyly Matter of the animal Kingdom, as the* Adepts *have more than often done: You might with this Animal Spirit transmute the aforesaid Vegetable* Menstruums, *into Animal* Menstruums, *which nevertheless you cannot apply to Mineral* Menstruums; *for though there are also in this Kingdom thin Oyls, swimming upon watrish Liquors, as Oyl of* Petre, Pit-Coals, &c. *Yet these are extraordinary Oyls of this Kingdom, produced either by exorbitancy, or defect of Nature. And therefore such Oyls as these the* Adepts *referred to both the Vegetable and Animal Kingdoms, for they are of one and the same Nature; whereas the Oyls of Minerals and Metals are more dry and masculine, then to produce our feminine* Seed *or* Menstruum: *Now to recite the parts of Animals, and the way of extracting this Spirit of* Philosophical Wine *from them, is not proper to this place, but belongs to a peculiar Book, namely, our fifth (treating more copiously of these things) to be published in due time, when God permits; wherefore not mentioning Animal* Menstruums, *we proceed to the Mineral or Acid* Menstruums.

OF *Mineral* MENSTRUUMS.

The Thirteenth KIND.

Simple Mineral Menstruums *made of the Matter of* Philosophical Wine *only*.

59. The Green Lyon of *Ripley*. *Libro Accurt. Pag.* 383.

TAke the Green Lyon without dissolution in Vinegar (*as sometime the Custom is*) put it in a large Earthen Retort, which can endure the Fire, and distil it the same way as you distil *Aqua fortis*, putting a Receiver under it, and luting the Joynts well, that it may not respire ; then distil first with a gentle Fire, till you see white fumes appear, then change the Receiver, stopping it well, and distil with a great Fire so, as *Aqua fortis* is distilled, thus continuing twenty four Hours, and if you continue the Fire the space of eight Days, you will see the Receiver always full of white fumes, and so you will have the Blood of the Green Lyon, which we call Secret Water, and *Acetum acerrimum*, by which all Bodies are reduced to their first Matter, and the Body of Man preserved from all infirmities. This is our Fire, burning continually in one Form within the Glass Vessel, and not without : Our *Dunghill*, our *Aqua Vitæ*, our *Balneo*, our *Vindemia*, our *Horse-Belly*, which effects wonderful things in the Works of Nature, and is the Examen of all Bodies dissolved, and not dissolved ; and is a sharp Water, carrying Fire in its Belly, as a *Fiery Water*, for otherwise it would not have

have the power of dissolving Bodies into their first Matter. Behold! this is our *Mercury*, our *Sol* and *Luna*, which we use in our Work. Then will you find in the bottom of the Vessel Fæces black as Coals, which you must for the space of eight Days calcine with a gentle Fire, &c.

Annotations.

Hitherto *we have mix'd or tempered the* unctuous Spirit *of* Philosophical Wine *with things* Oyly, Dry-oyly, Oyly-dry, *and* purely Dry, *and reduced them to divers Kinds of Vegetable* Menstruums; *in which we have exhibited* Menstruums *every way absolute and perfect, in Smell, Taste, and Colour incomparable, dissolving without hissing or effervescence, and permanent with things dissolved: Now follow in order, those which are called Mineral* Menstruums, *which though they be of a stinking Smell, of an acid or corrosive Taste, and for the most part of a milky and opake Colour, and dissolve Bodies with very great violence and corrosion, yet nevertheless having the same Spirit of* Philosophical Wine, *as the Vegetable* Menstruums *for their Foundation, are therefore as permanent as they, yea better than they as to the abbreviation of time; for the acidity of Mineral Salts (for which corrosive or acid* Menstruums *are called Minera) lcannot destroy the Nature of the Spirit of Wine, nor the Nature of the Vegetable* Menstruum, *but by corroding makes the particles of dry Bodies more apt to unite themselves with the Oyly Spirit of* Philosophical Wine; *but if that acidity be taken away, it becomes that which it was before, namely, either the Spirit of* Philosophical Wine, *or a Vegetable* Menstruum.

The method which we used in the Vegetable Menstruums, *we will as near as we can observe also in these Mineral* Menstruums: *In the Vegetable we extracted from the* Philosophical Wine *an* Aqua ardens, *from which we did by Circulation separate an Oyl or Essence of Wine, which is our Spirit of Wine, which then by acuating divers ways we reduced into the precedent Kinds of Vegetable* Menstruums; *but in the Mineral we will begin with* Philosophical Grapes, *the Matter it self of* Philosophical Wine, *which is elsewhere called* Green Lyon, Adrop, &c. *Though the Discourse of this Matter appertains not to this place, yet if any thing presents it self to us either in the*

Receipts

Receipts themſelves, or elſewhere, which may tend to a more clear manifeſtation of it, we will not conceal it; but on the contrary have determined to illuſtrate and explain things ſo, as not only to make you more aſſured of the uſe and neceſſity of this Spirit promiſed to you, but moreover alſo, that you may have ſome certain notions beforehand of its Conception, Subſtance, Nativity, &c.

For the elucidation of this Receipt, we will propound ſome other Receipts of the ſame Matter, that being compared together, they may be made the plainer: In the firſt place we will propoſe a Menſtruum *made indeed not of the* Green Lyon *it ſelf, but of the* Green Lyon *diſſolved with an acid, and reduced into a certain Gum.*

60. A *Menſtruum* made of the Gum *Adrop* of *Ripley.* *Libro accurtationum, Pag.* 381.

TAke *Adrop*, that is, the *Green Lyon*, which we ſpoke of before, and diſſolve it in diſtilled Vinegar for the ſpace of ſeven Days, ſhaking well the Veſſel which the Matter is in, three times dayly, then empty the diſſolved Liquor, and diſtil through a Filtre three times from its Fæces, till it be clear as Criſtal, and evaporate the Vinegar with a gentle Fire, till it be thick as Bird-Lime, which you cannot ſtir by reaſon of its Viſcoſity, and being cold, take it out of the Veſſel, and keep it; and again make more of it, and this do, till you have twelve Pounds of this *Green Lyon* or *Adrop* reduced to the Form of a Gum, then have you the Earth extracted from the Earth, and the Brother of the Earth. Then take a Pound of that Gum, and put it in a Glaſs Veſſel of the bigneſs of a Bottle, well luting the Joynts of the Alembick with Glew made of the white of Eggs and Filings well mix'd together.

This Receipt in the Treatiſe of the *Philoſophical Adrop (which is in the ſixth Volume of* Theatrum Chymicum, *and inſcribed to an* anonimous Diſciple of the great *Guido de monte, but differs not from the Books of* Ripley, namely, *the preſent* de Accurtationibus, *and the* Clavis aureæ portæ, *the greateſt part of which is aſcribed to the Famous* Dunſtan, *Archbiſhop of* Canterbury) *is altogether the ſame as to the Senſe, though theſe Words run better in the Tranſlation thus:*

thus: Now take three Pounds of the aforesaid Gum, put it into a Distillatory able to hold about two Measures, and putting on an Alembick, lute the Joynts with luting made of Ale, the white of an Egg, and Wheat-Flower, *Pag.* 552. *Volum.* 6. *Theat. Chym. Which is confirmed with the Process or Receipt of the* Clavis aureæ portæ, *were thus:* Put three Pounds of this Milk (*thickned or Gumn'd*) into a Glass *Pag.* 257. *Clavis aureæ portæ:* and distil in a Sand Furnace, and let the Sand be the thickness of two Fingers under the Vessel, and so round about even to the middle of the Vessel, or till the Matter be covered: put a Receiver to it, making at first a gentle Fire, but not luting the Receiver, till the Phlegm be gone over, and this continue, till you see fumes appear in the Receiver white as Milk; then increasing the Fire change the Receiver, stopping it well, that it may not evaporate, and so continually augment the Fire, and you will have an Oyl most red as Blood, which is airy Gold, the *Menstruum fœtens*, the *Philosophers Sol*, our Tincture *Aqua ardens*, the Blood of the *Green Lyon*, our unctious Humor, which is the last consolation of Man's Body in this Life, the Philosophers Mercury, *Aqua solutiva*, which dissolves Gold with the preservation of its Species, and it hath a great many other Names: And when first the white fumes appear, continue your Fire twelve Hours, in which space if the Fire be strong, will all the Oyl be distilled, which keep well stopp'd to prevent respiring.

This Menstruum *differs from the precedent, forasmuch as in this, the* Green Lyon *is dissolved in Vinegar, but in that, it is all distilled alive, but they are both clearly enough described in themselves; yet the Matter of the* Menstruum *remaining more obscure, and less intelligible to the Reader, we have found out four Reasons in* Ripley, *why it is called* Green Lyon.

First, *saith he*, by *Green Lyon*, the Philosophers means the Sun, which by its attractive Virtue makes things Green, and governs the whole World. *Tract. de. Adrop. Phil. Pag.* 547. *Volum. sexti Theat. Chym. and else where:* The *Green Lyon* is that, by which all things became Green, and grow out of the Bowels of the Earth by its attractive Virtue, elevated out of the Winter Caverns, whose Son is most acceptable to us, and sufficient for all the *Elixirs*, which are to be made of it; for from it may be had the power of the white and red Sulphur not burning, which

is

is the best thing, saith *Avicenne*, that Alchymists can take, thereby to make Gold and Silver. But these Words may suffice a Wise Man to know and obtain the *Green Lyon*. *Medulla Phil: Pag.* 139.

Secondly, It is moreover also called Green, because that Matter is as yet sharp and unripe, that is, not yet fixed or perfected by Nature, as common Gold. The Philosophers *Green Lyon* therefore is green Gold, *Gold vive*, which is not as yet fixed, but left imperfect by Nature, and for this reason hath it the Virtue of reducing all Bodies into their first Matter, and making those Bodies which are fixed Spiritual and Volatile. *Tract. de Adrop. Pag.* 547.

Thirdly, It may also be called *Lyon*, because as all other Animals give place to a *Lyon*, so all Bodies yield to the power of *Gold vive*, which is our Mercury. *Tract. Adrop. Pag.* 548.

Fourthly, This Noble Infant is called *Green Lyon*, because when it is dissolved, it is cloathed with a Green Garment. Yet out of the *Green Lyon* of Fools (*Vitriol*) is with a violent Fire extracted that which we call *Aqua fortis*, in which the said *Lyon* ought to be elixirated. *Medulla Philos. Pag.* 139.

These things spoken of the Green Lyon, *are also to be understood of* Adrop, *being a Synonymous term of the same Matter :* Take, *saith Ripley*, *Adrop*, that is, the *Green Lyon*. *Now as to* Adrop *he declared as followeth :* Adrop, *saith he*, is Gold and Silver in power but not in sight, as *Rhasis* saith, and our Gold and Silver, according to the Philosophers, is not common Gold and Silver, for our Gold and Silver are airy, which in order to be well fermented, ought to be joyned with the beloved (*common Gold*,) Forasmuch as the Philosopher saith, That *Adrop* in its profundity is airy Gold, and *Adrop* it self is called Leprous Gold. And to these Sayings seems to assent *Guido*, the Greek Philosopher, speaking of the Mercurial or Menstrual Spirit (*the Spirit or Blood of the* Green Lyon) which is extracted out of the Natural *Adrop* by Art, where he writes : And that Spirit is *Sol* extracted out of the Philosophers *Solary Water*, *Arsenick*, and *Luna :* And in the same place presently adds ; The Body is the ferment of the Spirit, and the Spirit the ferment of the Body, and the Earth, wherein lies the Fire, dries, imbibes, and fixeth the Water ; and the Air, wherein lies the Water, (*the Air which lies in the Water*,

it

it ought to be read according to the Doctrine of separating the Elements) washeth, tingeth, and perfecteth the Earth and Fire; and so *Guido*'s Saying, that they tinge and perfect, ought to be understood, that the Stone (*the* Menstruum *drawn from* Adrop, *or the* Green Lyon) is sufficient for the compleating of it self into an *Elixir*, and that no Exotick or Heterogeneous Matter, as he affirms, is or ought to be introduced to it, but all the parts of it are co-essential and concrete, because the Philosophers meaning was to compleat that work in a short space above the Earth, which Nature scarce perfecteth in a thousand Years under the Earth: Unskilfully therefore according to the Opinion of the Philosophers, as *Guido* saith, do they proceed, that seek to obtain a ferment from common Silver and Gold for our select Body: For that Matter, in which is *Argent vive* clean and pure, not (*most, is ill read*) throughly brought to perfection by Nature, is, as *Guido* affirms, after compleat purification, a thousand times better than the Bodies of *Sol* and *Luna* vulgarly decocted by the Natural heat of the Sun. *Concord. Lully & Guidon. Pag.* 323.

A certain Philosopher saith, *He goes on Discoursing of the same.* Adrop; A fume (*white*) is drawn from its own Mines, which if rightly gathered, and again sprinkled upon its own Mines, will there make a fixation, and so the true *Elixir* will in a short space of time be produced from it: And certainly without those Liquors or Spirits, that is, the Water and Oyl of Mercury (*Menstruum*) this Alchymical Body which is *Neutral* or *Adrop*, is not purged: And that is the Alchymical Body, which is called Leprous Body, that is, black (*at the beginning of the Work*) in which, as saith *Vincentius* in his *Speculum Naturale*, are Gold and Silver in power, and not in aspect; which in the Bowels of it is also airy Gold, to which no Man can attain, except the unclean Body be first cleansed, which is without doubt after its compleat dealbation, and then it is a thousand times better than are the Bodies of common Gold and Silver decocted by Natural heat: The first Matter of this Leprous Body is a viscous Water inspissated in the Bowels of the Earth: Of this Body, according to the Judgment of *Vincentius*, is made the great *Elixir* for the red and white, the Name whereof is *Adrop*, otherwise called, the Philosophers black Lead, out which *Raymund* commands us to extract an Oyl of a Golden Colour, or such like: *Raymund* adds,

 But

But this Oyl is not neceſſary in the Vegetable Work (*namely, for the inceration of the Vegetable Stone*) becauſe ſolutions and coagulations are there ſoon made; and if you can ſeparate it from its Phlegm, and after that ingeniouſly find out the Secrets of it, you will in thirty Days be able to perfect the Philoſophers Stone: For this Oyl makes Medecines (*Tinctures*) penetrable, ſociable, and amicable to all Bodies, and in the World there is not a greater Secret. *Medul. Phil. Chym. pag.* 131.

Ripley *hath here recited various Synonima's of this* Adrop: *We for a time will follow the* Green Lyon *by the way of* Philoſophical Lead, *as we are directed by* Ripley *in theſe very Words:* Firſt, underſtand, when *Avecenn* ſaith, that Gold and Silver are in Lead by Power, and not by ſight, and they are left by Nature crude and half cocted, and therefore that ought to be perfectly ſupplyed by Art, which is left imperfect by Nature, and by way of a ferment digeſting and cocting that which is left crude: For a ferment therefore take perfect Gold, for a little (*paululum, not paulatim*) of their fixed ſubſtance (*thoſe fixed Bodies*) will draw and convert much of Bodies not fixed to the perfection of Gold and Silver. And thus will Art help Nature, that in a little ſpace of time that may be done above the Earth, which is not in a thouſand Years done under the Earth: And by this means you will underſtand, how Lead contains in it the greateſt Secrets of this Art: For it hath in it *Argent vive*, clean, pure, odoriferous, not brought by Nature to perfection: And this *Argent vive* is the Baſis and Ground-Work of our pretious Medicine, as well for Metallick as Humane Bodies, ſo as to be the *Elixir* of Life, curing all infirmities: Which the Philoſopher meant, ſaying, There is in Mercury whatſoever Wiſe Men ſeek: From this are the Soul, Body, Spirit, and Tincture drawn: Moreover alſo in this Mercury is the Philoſophers Fire, always burning equally within the Veſſel, and not without: It hath alſo a great attractive Virtue and Power in diſſolving *Sol* and *Luna*, and reducing the ſame into their firſt Matter: With this Mercury are to be diſſolved the Calxes of the perfect Bodies in congealing the aforeſaid Mercurial Spirit, &c. *Pupilla, Pag.* 295. But have a care that you operate not with (*common*) *Saturn*, becauſe commonly it is ſaid, Eat not of the Son, whoſe Mother is corrupted, and believe, that many Men err in *Saturn*. Hear what *Avicenn* ſaith,

Saturn

Saturn will be always *Saturn*; yea operate not with the Earth of (*Philosoph.*) *Saturn*, which the Spirit of it has despised, and relinquished for the worst Sulphur: Operate only with the fume of it to congeal Mercury, yet not as Fools, but as the Philosophers do, and you will have a very good Work. *Phil. Cap.* 2. *Pag.* 188. The whole composition we call our Lead; the quality of the splendor proceeds from *Sol* and *Luna*, and in short, these are our *Menstruums* wherewith we calcine perfect Bodies naturally, but no unclean Body is an Ingredient, one excepted, which is by the Philosophers commonly called *Green Lyon*, which is the means of joyning the Tinctures between *Sol* and *Luna* with perfection, as *Geber* himself attesteth, *Libro.* 42. *portar. Pag.* 12. To manifest this thing to you, you must know, that it is one of those, which are of the seven Days (*Planets*) and the meanest of the same, out of whose Body is artificially extracted Blood, and a vaporous Humor, which is called the Blood of the *Green Lyon*, from which is produced a Water, called *White of an Egg*, and *Aqua Vitæ*, *May-Dew*, and by many other Names, which to avoid prolixity, we now omit. *Phil. Cap.* 3. *Pag.* 190.

The method of extracting the Blood of the Green Lyon *out of* calcined Lead, *or* Philosophical Minium *is this that followeth.*

61. A *Menstruum* made of the red Lead of *Ripley*.

In pupilla Alchym. pag. 303.

TAke of Lead calcined or rubifyed, or the best *Minium*, that is, *Mineral Antimony*, prepared, what quantity you please, yet with this consideration, that you must have so many quarts of distill'd Vinegar, as you have pounds of the aforesaid calcined Lead: To this Vinegar pour the aforesaid Lead in a large Earthen Vessel well glazed, then for the space of three Days stir the Matter strongly with a Wooden *Spatula* six or seven times a Day, cover it well from Dust, and let it not be put to the Fire by any means during all this time, after which separate all that is clear and cristalline by a Filtre into another Vessel, then put it into a Brass Skillet to a gentle Fire, that all the Phlegmatick

Water may evaporate, till a very thick Oyl is left in the bottom of the Vessel, which suffer to cool; which being done, the Matter will become like Gum, so as to be cut with a Knife, hereof put four Pounds into a Glass Cucurbit with an Alembick, the Joynt being well luted with a Paste made of the Scales of Iron, Flower, and the whites of Eggs well beaten together: put the Vessel in a Furnace of Sand, and not in Ashes, and let the Vessel be buried in the Sand even to the middle of it, and let the Sand be two Fingers thick under the bottom of the Vessel; then put a Receiver to it, but not luted, till you have drawn out all the Phlegmatick Water with a most gentle Fire, which Water throw away: When you see a white fume appear, then lute the Receiver, which must be two foot long; which being drawn out, strengthen the Fire as much as you can, and continue it till you have distilled all that can be extracted in twelve Hours, and so will you have the Blood of the *Red Lyon*, most red as Blood, which is our Mercury, and our Tincture now prepared, to be poured upon its ferment, that is, upon the Calxes of most pure Gold, &c. But if you would use it for the white Work, you must distil your Mercury three times with a slow Fire, always reserving the Fæces apart in every distillation, and then will you have your Mercury most white as Milk: And this is our *Virgins Milk*, whitened *Menstruum*, and our *Argent vive* Philosophically exuberated; with which by Circulation make an Oyl out of the Calxes of *Luna*, and proceed in all things, as you did with the red Mercury upon the Calxes of Gold, and you will have a white *Elixir*, which will convert any Metal into perfect *Luna*: But the Golden Oyl ought to be perfected and tempered, and well united with artifical Balsom, by the way of Circulation, till out of them is made a most clear and resplendent Golden Liquor, which is the true *Aurum potabile*, and *Elixir* of Life more pretious for Mens Bodies, then any other Medicine of the World.

The like Menstruum Ripley *hath in his* Medulla Philosophiæ Chymicæ.

62. The

62. The Simple stinking *Menstruum* of *Ripley.* *Medulla Phil. Chym. pag.* 170.

TAke the sharpest Juice of Grapes, and being distilled, dissolve into a clear Cristalline Water, the Body being well Calcined to a Redness, which is by the *Philosophers* called *Sericon;* of which make a Gum, which is like Allum in taste, and is by *Raymund* called *Azoquean Vitriol.* Out of this Gum with a slow Fire is drawn first a weak Water, which hath its taste no sharpness, no more than Spring-water: And when a white Fume begins to appear, then change the Receiver, and Lute strongly, that it may no way expire; and so you will have your *Aqua ardens, Aqua vitæ,* and a resolvitive *Menstruum*, which before was resolvible: This is the Potential Vapour, able to dissolve, putrifie, and also purifie Bodies, divide the Elements, and by its attractive Virtue exalt its own Earth into a wonderful Salt: And they that think there is any other Water, besides this which we speak of, are mistaken in this Work: this Water hath a most sharp taste, and partly also a stinking smell, and therefore is called *stinking Menstruum;* and it being a very Airy Water, it therefore ought to be put upon its Calxes in less then an Hour after it is distilled or rectified; but when it is poured upon the aforesaid Calxes, it begins to boyl up, and then if the Vessel be well stopp'd it will not leave working, though no Fire be administred to it from without, till it be dryed up in the Calx; wherefore you must apply no greater quantity of it than scarce to cover the Calxes, then proceed to the full compleating of it, as in the work of the compounded Water. And when the Elixir is reduced to a purple Colour, let it be dissolved in the same *Menstruum*, being first rectified into a thin Oyl, upon which fix the Spirit of our Water by Circulation, and then hath it the Power of converting all Bodies into most pure Gold, and to heal all Infirmities of man's Body, more than all the Potions of *Hippocrates* and *Galen*, for this is the true *Aurum Potabile,* and no other, which is made of Artificial Gold Elemented, turned about by the Wheel of Philosophy; *&c.*

The same Menstruum *is had in the* Vade Mecum *of* Ripley.

63. The

63. The *Menstruum* of *Sericon* of *Ripley*. In *Vade Mecum*, commonly called the *Bosom-Book*.

TAke of *Sericon* or *Antimony* thirty Pounds, out of which you will have twenty Pounds or thereabout of Gum, if the Vinegar be good; dissolve each pound of that *Sericon* in two measures (a Gallon) of Vinegar twice distilled, and having stood a little while in digestion, stir the matter often every day, the oftner the better, with a clean stick, filtre the Liquor three times, throw away the Fæces, to be taken away as superfluous, being no Ingredient to the Magistery, for it is the damned Earth: Then evaporate the filtred Liquors in *Balneo Mariæ* with a temperate heat, and our *Sericon* will be coagulated into a Green Gum, call'd our *Green Lyon*, dry that Gum well, yet with care, lest you burn the Flowers, or destroy the Greens of it: Then take the said Gum, put it in a strong Glass Retort well luted, and with a moderate Fire distil a weak Water to be cast away: But when first you perceive a white fume ascending, put to it a Glass Receiver large, and of sufficient capacity, whose Mouth is exactly joyned to the Neck of the Retort, which must be very well luted, lest any of the fume be lost or evaporate out of the Receiver: Then increase the Fire by degrees, till a red fume ascends, and continue a stronger Fire, till bloody drops come, or no more fume appears: Then abate the Fire by degrees, and all being cold, take away the Receiver, and forthwith stop it, that the Spirits may not exhale, because this Liquor is called our blessed Liquor, to be kept in a Glass Vessel very close stopped: Then examine the Neck of the Retort, where you will find a white and hard Ice, in the form of a congealed Vapour, or Mercury sublimate, which gather carefully, and keep, because it contains great Secrets, of which lower: Then take the Fæces out of the Retort, being black as Soot, which are called our *Dragon*, whereof calcine one Pound, or more, if you please, in a Potters, Glass-makers, or Philosophical Furnace, into a white Snowy Calx, which keep pure by it self, it being called the Basis and Foundation of the Work, *Mars*, our white fixed Earth, or Philosophers Iron: Now take the residue of the

Fæces,

Fæces, or black Dragon, and sift it on a Marble, or any other Stone, and at one of the ends light it with a live Coal, and in the space of half an Hour the Fire will run over all the Fæces, which it will calcine into a very Glorious citrine Colour; these citrine Fæces dissolve with distilled Vinegar, after the aforesaid manner, filtre also three times as before, then evaporate the dissolution into a Gum, and distil the *Menstruum*, which is now called *Sanguis Draconis*, or *Dragons Blood*, and repeat this Work in all things as before, till you have reduced all, or the greater part of the Fæces into our Natural or Blessed Liquor, all which Liquors pour to the first Liquor or *Menstruum*, called the *Blood* of the *Green Lyon*; the Liquor being thus mix'd, putrefie it in a Glass Vessel the space of fourteen Days: Then proceed to the separation of the Elements, because in this Blessed Liquor you have now all the Fire of the Stone, hidden before in the Fæces; which Secret has been hitherto kept wonderfully close by the Philosophers: Now take all the *Menstruum* being putrifyed, put it in a *Venice* Glass of a fit size, put an Alembick to it, and lute with Linnen Rags dipp'd in the white of Eggs; the Receiver must be very spacious, to keep in the respiring Spirit, and with a temperate heat separate the Elements one from another, and the Element of Air, which is the Oyl (*ardent Spirit, containing a little white Oyl at the top*) will first ascend: The first Element being distilled, rectifie it in another Vessel fit for it, that is, distil seven times, till it burns a Linnen Cloath, being dipp'd in it and kindled; then is it called our rectify'd *Aqua ardens*, which keep very well stopp'd, for otherwise the most subtil Spirit of it will vanish away: In the rectifications of the *Aqua ardens* the Air will ascend in the form of a white Oyl, swimming upon the *Aqua* (*ardens*) and a citrine Oyl will remain, which is distilled with a stronger Fire: Mercury being sublimed, and reduced into Powder dissolv'd *per deliquium*, upon Iron Plates in a cold place; pour a little of the *Aqua ardens* to the Liquor being filtred, and it will extract the Mercury in the form of a Green Oyl swimming a-top; which separate and distil by a Retort, and there will ascend first a Water, and then a thick Oyl, which is the Oyl of Mercury: Then distil the Flood or Water of the Stone into another Receiver, the Liquor will be whitish, which draw off in *Balneo* with a moderate heat, till there remains in the bottom of

the

the Cucurbit a thick Oyly substance, like melted Pitch, keep this Water by it self in a Glass well stopp'd. Take notice, when first the Liquor riseth white, another Receiver must be put to, because that Element is wholly distilled: Two or three drops of that black liquid Oyl being given in the Spirit of Wine, do Cure any Poyson: Now, to this black and liquid Matter pour our *Aqua ardens*, mix them well together, and let the mixture settle three Hours, then decant, and filtre the Liquor, pour on new *Aqua ardens*, and repeat the operation three times, then distil again in Balneo with a gentle heat, and this reiterate thrice, and it will come under the denomination of the rectify'd Blood of Man, which Operators search for in the Secrets of Nature: Thus have you exalted the two Elements, Water, and Air, to the Virtue of a Quintessence; keep this Blood for occasion: Now to the black and liquid Matter or Earth, pour the Flood or Water of the Stone, mix them well together, and distil the whole, till the Earth remains very dry and black, which is the Earth of the Stone; keep the Oyl with the Water for occasion: Reduce the black Earth to a Powder, to which pour the aforesaid Man's Blood, digest three Hours, then distil in Ashes with a Fire sufficiently strong, repeat this Work three times, and it will be call'd the rectify'd Water of Fire, and so have you exalted the three Elements, namely, Water, Air, and Fire, into the Virtue of a Quintessence: Then calcine the Earth being black and dry, in the bottom of the Reverberatory, into a most white Calx, with which mix the Fiery Water, and distil with a strong Fire as before; the remaining Earth calcine again, and distil, and that seven times, or till the whole substance of the Calx be pass'd through the Alembick, and then have you the rectify'd and truly Spiritual Water of Life, and the four Elements, exalted to the Virtue of a Quintessence; this Water will dissolve all Bodies, putrefie and purge them: This is our Mercury, our Lunary, but whosoever thinks of any other Water besides this, is ignorant and foolish, never attaining to the desired effects.

This Menstruum *is made of the same Matter as the precedent* Menstruums. *For* Green Lyon, Adrop, Philosophical Lead, Mineral Antimony, Airy Gold, Mercury, *&c. are Synonima's of one and the same Matter: This Matter being dissolved in distill'd Vinegar, and again inspissated into a Gum, in taste like Alum, is by* Ripley

Ripley *in the Description of the antecedent* Menstruum *in Numb.* 62. *called* Lully's Vitriol of Azoth, *or* Vitriolum Azoqueum: *Lully in practica Testamenti*, Cap. 9. Pag. 159. Vol. 4. Th. Chym. *makes a* Menstruum *of* B. C. D. *By* B. *he meant the said* Green Lyon, *or common* Argent vive, *which as he says elsewhere*, is more common to Men, than vulgar *Argent vive.* B. *saith he*, *Pag.* 153. *of the said practica*, signifies *Argent vive*, which is a common substance consisting in every corruptible Body, as appears by the property of it, *&c. By* C. *he intended common Niter.* C. *saith he*, signifies *Salt Peter*, which hath a common (*acid*) Nature, and like *Argent vive* by the property of its strong (*acid*) Nature, *Pag.* 154. 4. *Volum.* aforesaid. *By* D. *he understood Gum* Adrop, *made of the* Green Lyon. D. *saith he*, signifies *Azoquean Vitriol*, which corrupts and confounds all that is of the Nature and Being of common *Argent vive.* In the same place, *Both* C. *and* D. *he calls the purer mediums.* Cap. 58. Theor. Test. pag. 96. You must know Son! *saith he*, our Bath, you may wash the Nature of (*Phil*) *Argent vive* so, as Nature could never do, that is, to make *Argent vive* a compleat *Elixir.* But (*Phil.*) *Argent vive* and Metals being both in Nature, and in your Work, extreams, and extreams not being able to joyn themselves, without the Virtue of a middle disposition, which is between the softness of *Argent vive*, and the hardness of Metal, because there is by reason of that middle disposition a Natural complyance, which is the cause of Conjunction between Body and Spirit, as it is in every thing generated, or in capacity of being generated; In Nature are many *mediums*, whereof two are more pure, and more viscous, the *Green Azoquean Vitriols*, with the stony Nature, which is the Salt and Nature of Stones. By the help my Son! of this contemptible Matter is our Stone, which we have so much sought for, procreated, *&c.*

With the other of these mediums, C, *the stony Nature*, Salt Peter, Salt of Peter, *or* Niter, *we have no business at present* ; *but being solicitous of* D. *Gum* Adrop, *or the* Azoquean Vitriol *of* Lully, *it will be worth while to consult* Lully *himself* : *Of which the Philosopher*, Cap. 59. Theor. Testamenti, *thus* : Son! *saith he*, the *Azoquean Lyon*, which is called (*Azoquean*) *Vitriol*, is by Nature made of the peculiar substance of common *Argent vive*, which is the Natural Root, from whence Metal is procreated in its own

Mine.

Mine. By common *Argent vive, he meant not the Vulgar but Philosophical Argent vive, the natural Root as well of Metals as Minerals.* When we say common Mercury, *saith he,* we speak of that,which the Philosophers understand; and when we name the Vulgar, we speak of that which is known to the Country-men, and sold in Shops. *Cap.* 1. *Lib. Mercuriorum, which the following Synonyma's of this Mercury, namely,* Chaos, Nature, Origo, Green Lyon, Argent vive, Unguent, Oyl, Pasture and Liquor of great Value, *do also testifie in Cap.* 45. *Theor. Test. pag.* 75. *Vol.* 4. *Th. Chym.*

This common *Argent vive, or Green Lyon, must be purged from its Superfluities, before the* Aroquean Vitriol *of* Lully, *or the* Gum Adrop *of* Ripley *can be made of it.* You must *saith he,* my Son! being a Student of this Science, be stedfast, and not search after this or that, because this Art is not perfected with many things; and therfore we tell you, there is but one only Stone, that is Sulphur, and one only Medicine, namely, the composition of Sulphur, to which nothing is to be added, only the Terrestrial and Phlegmatick Superfluities taken away, because they are and ought to be separated from our *Argent vive,* which is more common to men, than Vulgar *Argent vive,* and is of greater Price, Merit, and stronger Union of Nature, from which and the first forms of it, it is necessary to separate, by the known degrees of separation, all that belongs not to the Sal Armoniack of Metals, &c. *Cap.* 18. *Theor. Test. pag.* 33. *Volum* 4. *Th. Chym.* We say there is but one only Philosophical Stone (*volatile not yet fixed, or matter of a* Menstruum) extracted from the things aforesaid by our Magistery. And therefore when it comes newly into the World, you must not add any other Powder, or any other Water, nor any thing incongruous to it, more than that, which is born in it, being radical to its own Nature, and the Mother of it, which feeds and carryed it, that is Sulphur, which formed the Stone in a Celestial Colour: But before you extract (*distil*) it (*the Stone*) throughly, purge, and cleanse it from all its Phlegmatick, Terrestrial, and corruptible Infirmities, which are contrary to its Nature, because they are the death of it, with which it is surrounded, which do mortifie its vivificative Spirit. *Cap.* 7. *Theor. Test. pag.* 20, of the said Volum. It is to be diligently

ligently noted, that one of the two aforesaid Natural Principles (*Sulphur and Argent vive*) is more truly Natural in the whole, and through the whole substance of it, as well within as without, and that is the pure Sulphur, hot and dry, introducing its form, that is, according to which the form of a Metal pursues a pure effect: But the other (*Argent vive*) is unnatural, that is inwardly natural, and outwardly against Nature; but the internal natural part is made proper and also con-natural to it self, because it comes by its own Nature, but the external part is added to it by accident, and is to be naturally separated from it after the corruption (*Putrifaction*) of it; wherefore it is manifest that such *Argent vive* is not in the whole substance of it natural, in the first reception of it, nor is depurated to the full, unless it be depurated by the Ingenuity of Art. *C. 5. p.* 10. *Codicilli.*

As to this Purification of Argent vive, or the Green Lyon, Ripley *thus:* Wherefore saith he, this Mercury (*the corrosive Spirit of common Vitriol*) is by *Raymond* called, Our Fire against Nature: Nevertheless the same thing happens in some measure to this Mercury (*the acidity of Vitriol*) as also to the other (*Vegetable Mercury, or Green Lyon*) which is our natural Fire: For both of them are hidden in the middle or center of their Bodies, that is, between the Phlegmatick Water on one side, and Terrestrial Crassitude on the other side, nor are they obtained without the great Industry of Philosophy, and so those parts can avail us nothing, except only their middle substance: For saith *Raymond*, We take neither of the first Principles, because they are too simple, nor of the last, because they are too gross and feculent, but only of the middle; wherein is the Tincture, and true Oyl, separated from unclean Terrestreity, and Phlegmatick Water: Therefore saith *Raymond* thus; The unctious Moisture, is the near Matter of our Physical *Argent vive, pag.* 289. *Pupillæ Alchym.*

Argent vive, or the Green Lyon, is purified by common Vitriol, as thus: When the *Argent vive* is put in a dry Vitriolated Vapour (*Spirit of Vitriol*) which is a sharp Water, it is presently dissolved by the Incision and Penetration, caused by the sharpness, being manifestly strong, and in dissolving, is converted into the Nature of Terrestrial Vitriol, not taking a Metalick, nor a clear Cœlestial Form, as appears after the evaporation of the

the ſaid Water, and the congelation of it in the form of Yellow Criſtals, which Yellowneſs proceeds from the ſharp Sulphurous Terreſtreity, which was beyond meaſure mixed in the ſaid Water by Atoms, with an Homogeneous Univerſality and ſimplicity, which ſimplicity was taken and bound by the ſaid Terreſtreity, with the alteration of the Light, Clarity, and Lucidity into Obſcurity, *&c. Cap.* 89. *Theor. Teſt.* 141. *Vol.* 4. *Th. Chym.* Son! the thick Vitriolated Vapours from which Vitriol is produced, is very ſharp and pontick, and therefore penetrates the parts of the Sulphur, and *Argent vive* being depurated, and penetrating, tingeth that purify'd Matter, congealing it into the Form of that Vitriolated and yellow Terreſtrial Vapour, which is mixed with them. Wherefore what we have ſaid is manifeſt, that is, This is the great Gate, namely, that the Terreſtrial Virtues muſt not excel the Cœleſtial, but on the contrary, if you will have the thing deſired, *Cap.* 85. *Theor. Teſt. pag.* 137. *of the ſame Volume.* You may remember that you would put nothing with the Menſtrual (*the Matter of the Menſtrunm*) but that which proceeded from it at the beginning of its mixtion; for if you add an incongruous thing, it will preſently be corrupted by the incongruous Nature, nor will you ever have that which you would have. Gold and Silver, and Mercury are diſſolved in our Menſtrual, becauſe it participates with them in proximity and vicinity of the firſt Nature, and from hence will you extract a white Fume, which is our Sulphur, and the Green Lyon, which is your Unguent, and the ſtinking Water, which is our *Argent vive*: But it is requeſite for the Green Lyon to be throughly diſſolved in the *Aqua Fœtens*, or ſtinking VVater, before you can have the ſaid Fume, which is our Sulphur, which Sulphur is indeed the ſame way diſſolved from the Body, congealing the Spirit in the form of a dry Water, which we call Stone, and the higheſt Medium of all our Work, which is the connexion and aggregation of both Natures, that is, of Body and Spirit. Son! This Water is called *Aqua ignis*, or if you had rather Igniſaqua, that *undeclinable Word*, becauſe it burns Gold and Silver better than Elementary Fire can do, and becauſe it contains in it heat of a Terreſtrial Nature, which diſſolves without Violence, which common Fire cannot do. Wherfore we enjoyn you to make the

Magiſtery

Magistery of the hottest things you can get in Nature, and you will have a hot Water, which dissolveth all things, *Cap.* 59. *Theor. Test. Pag.* 98. Of the same Volume.

These Sayings Ripley *comprehends in short, thus*: These Words, *saith he*, may serve a Wise Man in order to know and acquire the *Green Lyon*: But this Noble Infant is called *Green Lyon*, because being dissolved it is Cloathed in a Green Garment. Yet out of the *Green Lyon* of Fools (*Vitriol*) is extracted by a violent Fire, that Water which we call *Aqua fortis* (*Spirit of Vitriol*) in which the said *Lyon* ought to be Elixirated. For all Alchymical Gold is made of Corrosives, &c. *Pag.* 139. *Medulla Phil.*

This Argent vive, Green Lyon, Philosophers Lead, &c. *being purifyed with Vitriol, must be further matured or calcined into a red Colour*, Minium, Lead calcined, Sericon, &c. E. (*that is, Vitriolated* Azoth, *Pag.* 15. *Theor. Test.*) The fourth (*Medium* or *Principle*) is a substance produced from its Mine, and in it, more near to the Nature of Metals, which is by some called *Calcantis*, and *Azoth Vitreus* (*Mercury Vitriolated, or Azoquean Vitriol*) which is the Earth and Mine of Metals, and is by another Name called *Vrisius*, of shining white and red within Black and Green openly, having the Colour of a Venomous *Lizard*, immediately generated out of *Argent vive*, the Matter aforesaid impregnated with the said hot and dry sulphurous Vapour (*of common Vitriol*) in its resolution congealed into a *Lizard*, in which (*Azoth Vitriolated*) is the form and species of the stinking Spirit in its mixtion, the Mineral heat of which is multiplyed, which is the Life of Metal, and is signified by E. *Cap.* 3. *Theor. Testam. Pag.* 125. *Volume.* 4. *Theat. Chym.* *And a little after*: In the Work of Nature is *Argent vive*, but not such as is found upon the Earth, nor will be, till it be first turned into an apostemated and venomous Blood. *In the same place*: You must know Son! that by Art and Nature *Argent vive* is congealed by an acute Water, understand therefore Philosophically, because if it were not sharp and acute, it could not penetrate, which is the first action in dissolution, after which dissolution it is returned into an apostemated Blood, by the mutation of its own Nature into another. Son! there are two things, which ought to stick together by the agreement of contrariety, one pure, the other impure; the impure recedes, Fire being an Enemy, by reason of its Corruption;

the other remains in Fire, because of its purity, being transmuted into Blood, and this is our *Argent vive*, and our whole Secret, cloathed with a tripartite Garment, that is, black, white, and red, and that alone we want for the purpose of our Magistery, *Argent vive* containing all that is necessary for a Quintessence. There is in Mercury whatsoever Wise Men seek; for under the shadow of it lies a fifth substance; for the substance of it is pure and incombustible; and all of it is nothing else but Gold and Silver (*not common Metals, but airy, being in* Mercury, *or the* Green Lyon) melted and fused within and without by Virtue of the Fire (*against Nature*) and afterwards purify'd and separated from all its Original Blemish and Pollution; for that Gold which is incombustible, remains fused and liquid, and imparts its Golden Nature in the said Mercury, &c. *Cap.* 62. *Theor. Test. Pag.* 103. *Volume*, 4. *Th. Chym.*

Out of this Philosophical Minium, calcined Lead, *or* Sericon *only, the* Adepts *sometimes distilled their* Menstruums; *for Example, the first of this Kind in Numb.* 59. *Sometimes they dissolved this* Minium *in distilled Vinegar, which being drawn off, they reduced it into Gum* Adrop, *or* Lully's Azoquean Vitriol, *out of which they then distilled the stinking* Menstruum, *or* Menstruum fœtens, *in Numb.* 60. *Sometimes they dissolved Gum* Adrop per deliquium *first, and then distilled it.* The thirteenth way of practising, *saith Ripley*, as it here appears, is very curious, and that is in *Saturn*, (*Philosophical*) rubified in a Glass Vessel stopp'd, to prevent respiration, with a strong and continual Fire, till it becomes red: Take therefore that rubified *Saturn*, and pour a good quantity of distilled Vinegar upon it, and shake it very often every Day for a Month (*a Week*) then separate the Vinegar by a Filtre, and take only that which is clear without Fæces, and put it in Balneo to distil, and after the separation of the Vinegar, you will find at the bottom of the Vessel a white or sky-Coloured Water, which take, and being put in a Bladder five double, to keep out the Water, dissolve it in Balneo into a cristalline Water; put that Water in a Distillatory, and if you will, separate the Elements from it, or distil the dissolved Water, which rectifie in a Circulatory, and the Earth which remained in the bottom (*in the distillation*) calcine, till it grows like a Sponge, and then is it very fit to reassume its Mercury separated from it, that a new

Generation

Generation may be made, and a Son brought forth, which is called *King of Fire*, and which is so great in the Love of all the Philosophers, *Cap. 17. Philos. Pag.* 220. *Of this Work* Ripley *made mention:* Cap. 4. *of the same Book*, Pag. 194. *Saying*, There is moreover another Work in Gum produced by Vinegar from red *Saturn*, out of which is the separation of the Elements made, after it is dissolved in Bladders: The *Menstruums* of Gum *Adrop*, which way soever made, were called stinking *Menstruums*, because of the stinking smell: This Water, *saith Ripley*, hath a most sharp taste, and partly also a stinking smell, and therefore is called stinking *Menstruum*. *Assa fœtida* also is so called from the smell, which our Mercury hath when it is newly extracted out of its polluted Body, because that smell is like *Assa fœtida*, according to the Philosopher, who saith; That stink is worst before the preparation of this Water, which after the circulating of it into a Quinteſſence, and good preparation, it is pleasant and very delectable, and becomes a Medicine against the Leprosie, and all other Diseases, without which *Gold vive*, you can never make the true *potable Gold*, which is the *Elixir* of Life and Metals, *Adrop. Phil. Pag.* 548. *Volum.* 6. *Theat. Chym.*

These Menstruums *they called* White Fume, *because of their white and opake Colour.* It is also called *White Fume, saith Ripley*, nor without cause, for in distillation a white fume goeth out first, before the red Tincture, which ascending into the Alembick, makes the Glass white as Milk, from whence it is also called *Lac. Virginis*, or *Virgins Milk.* In the same place: *Out of the red Fume or red Tincture, otherwise call'd the Blood of the* Green Lyon, *the* Adepts *did by rectification alone prepare two Mercuries, namely, red and white:* Upon this occasion, *saith Ripley*, I will teach you a general Rule: If you would make the white *Elixir*, you must of necessity divide your Tincture (*the Blood of the* Green Lyon) into two parts, whereof one must be kept for the red Work, but the other distill'd with a gentle Fire; and you will obtain a white Water, which is our white Tincture, our Eagle, our Mercury and Virgins Milk: When you have these two Tinctures, or the white and red Mercury, you will be able to practise upon their own Earth, or upon the Calx of Metals; for the Philosophers say, we need not care what substance the Earth is of, &c. *Adr. Phil. p.* 554. *Vol.* 6. *Theat. Chy.* Roger Bacon *made a two-fold Mercury thus:*

64. The

64. The *Green Lyon* of *Roger Bacon.*

A Raymundo Ganfrido in verbo abbreviato de Leone Viridi. Pag. 264. Thesauri Chymici Baconis.

THe abbreviated most true and approved Word of hidden things being manifested, I have in a short Discourse abreviated to you in the Work of *Luna* and *Sol*; in the first place earnestly requiring the Readers not to expose so Noble a Pearl to be trodden upon by Dogs or Swine; for this is the Secret of all the Philosophers Secrets, the Garden of Delights, Spices, and all Treasures, into which he that hath once entred, will want no more: Now that Word, not without cause desired by many Men, was first declared by our eminent Doctor *Roger Bacon*; afterwards *J. Fryer Raymund Jeffery*, Minister General of the Order of the Fryers Minors, took care to explain the Word, with as much brevity as I could, to the Sons of Philosophy. In the Name of Christ then, take a great quantity of the strongest Vinegar diligently distilled through an Alembick, in which dissolve a good quantity of the *Green Lyon*, being dissolved, distil through a Filtre, and keep it in Glass Cucurbits well stopp'd: If any remarkable part of the *Lyon* remains undissolved, dissolve it with the aforesaid Vinegar, and distil through a Filtre, and being dissolved, joyn it with the other Waters before reserved in the Cucurbits, then take the reserved Waters (dissolutions) and distil them all in *Balneo Mariæ*, applying Alembicks to them well luted, that the Cucurbits may not respire, put Fire under, and receive all the Waters, which will be distilled, but have a care that the dissolved *Lyon* be not altogether congealed in the Cucurbits, but that it may remain liquid or soft; then take all the Cucurbits, and put all that is in them into one Cucurbit, which lute well with its Alembick, and put it in a Furnace of Ashes, as is fitting, and put a gentle Fire under, because of the temper of the Glass, and because of the Heterogeneous moisture, which is in the *Lyon* to be rooted out: And take notice, that must be always

always done with a gentle Fire, but when the Heterogeneous moiſture is gone over, ſtrengthen the Fire by little and little, and have an Eye continually to the Beak of the Alembick, if a red Liquor begins to go over, but if it does not yet go over, continue the aforeſaid Fire till it doth; but when you ſee the red Liquor diſtil, change the Receiver forthwith, and lute it well to the Beak of the Alembick, and then ſtrengthen the Fire, and you will have the Blood of the *Lyon* exceeding red, containing the four Elements, very odoriferous and fragrant (*after due putrefaction*) keep it therefore in a good Phial well ſtopp'd: Then take the Blood, and put it in a Phial cloſe ſtopp'd to putrefie and digeſt, in hot Dung, changing the Dung every five Days, there to be digeſted for the ſpace of fifteen or ſixteen Days, and this is done, that the Elementary parts may be diſſolved, and be fitter to be divided into the four Elements, and that by diſtillation; being putrify'd fifteen or ſixteen Days, take it out, and put it into a fit Cucurbit, to be diſtilled with a gentle Fire in *Balneo Mariæ*; but it is enough for the Water to boyl with the Fire, take the Water (*diſtilled*) and the Fæces, which you find at the bottom of the Cucurbit, keep carefully the Water which you diſtilled, diſtil ſeven times, always reſerving the Fæces which it makes, with the other Fæces reſerved before; and ſo you will have a ſplendid Water, clear and white as Criſtal, and very ponderous, which is ſaid to be the Philoſophers Mercury hidden by all the Philoſophers, and cleanſed and purified from all its ſuperfluities, moſt choice, and moſt pretious; keep it therefore warily and wiſely in a Phial well ſtopp'd: Then take all the Fæces of the Mercury, as I have ſaid, before reſerved, grind them well on a Marble (*with the Phlegm of diſtill'd Vinegar*) dry them in the Sun, and grind again, from time to time imbibing them with the Water of diſtill'd Vinegar upon the Marble, and drying in the Sun, and repeat the operations of grinding, imbibing, and drying, till all the blackneſs and ſuperfluity is driven out of the Fæces, which you will know thus: If the Fæces be red, or reddiſh, or citrine by the aforeſaid imbibitions and ablutions, then it is well done; but if they be yet black, repeat the contritions, imbibitions, and deſiccations, till you have the ſign aforeſaid, and then keep them: Then take a Glaſs Cucurbit, wherein put the aforeſaid Fæces above prepared, with a good quantity of diſtill'd

Vinegar, and ſet it in a Furnace, that is, in *Balneo Mariæ*, put Fire under, and continue it in courſe, till the Fæces aforeſaid be throughly diſſolved by Virtue of the Vinegar and Fire, and being well diſſolved, take the Cucurbit from the Fire, and diſtil them through a Filtre as is fitting, all that Water (*diſſolution of the Fæces*) being thus diſtilled (*filtred*) put it in a new Cucurbit, well ſtopp'd; but if any conſiderable part remains in the Filtre to be diſſolved, take that part, and ſet it again upon the Fire, as you did the firſt Fæces, in *Balneo Mariæ*, till it be diſſolved, that you may diſſolve thoſe Fæces which remained with the Vinegar, as you diſſolved the firſt Fæces in Balneo with Vinegar in a Cucurbit, then diſtil through a Filtre as before, and put it with the other Water diſtill'd before, which you reſerved; then take that new Cucurbit, in which you put the aforeſaid Fæces diſſolved and diſtilled before, and lute it well with its Alembick, ſet it on a Furnace in Balneo, give Fire, and diſtil as is fitting; but have a care that the Fæces be not throughly dryed, but let them be moiſt or liquid: Then take down the Cucurbit from the Furnace, put it upon Aſhes ſifted and well preſs'd, and give it a gentle Fire for the tempering of the Glaſs, and extracting the Heterogeneous moiſture, which it hath from the Vinegar, and ſee often to the Beak of the Alembick, if a Golden or Ruddy Liquor diſtills, if not, continue the Fire till it does; being diſtilled, preſently change the Glaſs being very clean, and lute it very well to the Beak of the Alembick, then ſtrengthen the Fire, receive the Ruddy Oyl, and thus continue the Fire, till all the Liquor be diſtill'd, and ſave the Fæces becauſe they are the Fire, but the Oyl aforeſaid the Philoſophers us'd to call their occult Sulphur; which you muſt rectifie thus: put it again in a Cucurbit, put on an Alembick well luted, then ſet it on a Furnace in Aſhes, adminiſter a gentle Fire, till it diſtils, receive the Liquor which diſtills in a Bottle well ſtopp'd with the Beak of the Alembick, and the remaining Fæces ſave, becauſe they are the Fire: joyn that Fire with the other Fire reſerv'd, and ſo putrefie by diſtilling it ſeven times, and reſerving the Fæces, it makes, as I ſaid before, and ſo you will have your Air or Sulphur well depurated, clear, bright, and perfectly purified, and of a Gold Colour, &c.

The Blood of the Green Lyon *being Fifteen Days putrify'd*, Bacon *cohobated Seven times by Balneo, into a clear and ponderous Water*,

ter, which he call'd the Philosophers Mercury; out of the Fæces left in the rectifications of this Mercury, dissolved in distilled Vinegar, he made a new Gum, out of which he then distilled a Golden Liquor, or ruddy Oyl, which after the Seventh rectification he would have be the Philosophers Air, or Sulphur well depurated, clear and bright: But Ripley *used two ways in rectifying the stinking* Menstruum, *or Green Lyon, for either he divided the fresh Blood of the Green Lyon into two parts, distilling only one half; the distilled part he called,* white Mercury, white Tincture, Virgins-milk, &c. *The other remaining part he calls the* red Mercury, red Tincture, &c. *as it may be seen in his Book called* Adrop Phil. *in the place before alleadged; or putrify'd the whole Menstruum, the Blood together with the white Fume the space of Fourteen Days, which after that he divided into three Substances, a burning Water, a Water thick and white, and an Oyl, of which at length he made a* Vegetable Menstruum, *which is described by* Lully *in* Potestate Divitiarum, *and by* Ripley (*above in Numb.* 35.) *in his* Vade Mecum.

Concerning these three Substances of the stinking Menstruum, Ripley *hath these following Sayings, in his Book named* Terra Terræ Philosoph. *pag.* 319. *where thus:* When therefore you have extracted all the Mercury out of the Gum, know, that in this Mercury are contained three Liquors, whereof the first is a burning Aqua vitæ, which is extracted by a most temperate Balneo: This Water being kindled, flames immediatly, as common Aqua vitæ, and is called our attractive Mercury, with which is made a Cristalline Earth, with all Metallick Calxes also, of which I will say no more, because in this Operation we want it not: After that there follows another Water thick and white as Milk, in a small quantity, which is the Sperm of our Stone, sought by many men; for the Sperm is the Original of men and all living Creatures; whereupon we do not undeservedly call it our Mercury, because it is found in all things and all places; for without it no man whatsoever lives: and therefore it is said to be in every thing. This Liquor, which now you ought to esteem most dear, is that Mercury, which we call Vegetable, Mineral, and Animal, our Argent vive, and Virgins-milk, and our permanent Water: VVith this Mercurial Water we wash away the Original Sin, and pollution of our

Earth, till it becomes white, as Gum, soon flowing; but after the distillation of this aforesaid VVater, will appear an Oyl by a strong Fire; with this Oyl we take a red Gum, which is our Tincture, and our Sulphur vive; which is otherwise called the Soul of Saturn, and Living Gold, our pretious Tincture, and our most beloved Gold; of which never man spoke so plainly; God forgive me therefore, if I have any way offended him, being constrained to gratifie your will.

Some great Mystery of Art is here discovered by Ripley, *for the revealing of which he fears the displeasure of not only the* Adepts, *but of* God *himself:* Lully, *and others have indeed plainly enough declared to their Disciples, though perhaps it may not appear to us being less instructed in the matter, what our Green Lyon is, what common Mercury more common to us than common Argent vive, what the Azoquean Vitriol is, and the Menstruum made thereof; but* Ripley *affirms that no man ever spoke so plainly of the present Secret. The* Adepts *have indeed in their Practicks described the use of (Philosophical) Wine without any veyl of Philosophy; and amongst them* Raymond *and* Arnold *with some others have attained to the knowledge of the same, but (to use* Ripley's *expression in* Medulla) how it might be obtained they said not: *Wherefore they being silent,* Ripley *the first, and indeed the only man of all, declares to us, that the Key of all the more secret Chymy lyes in the Milk and Blood of the* Green Lyon; *that is, that the* stinking Menstruum (*or the parts of it,* Mercury *and* Sulphur, Virgins Milk, *and* the Lyons Blood, white *and* red Mercury) *being fourteen Days digested gently, is the* white *and* red Wine *of* Lully, *and other* Adepts: *Nor was he satisfied in declaring this freely to us, but adds Strength and Light to his Words, in making a* Vegetable Menstruum *the* Rectify'd Aqua vitæ (*described by* Lully *in* Potestate Divitiarum, *and by us in Numb.* 31.) *of the said stinking and corrosive* Menstruum, *by which one only example he was pleased to teach us, that all* Vegetable Menstruums *may be made of the said* stinking Menstruum: *Lully's* rectify'd Aqua vitæ *is made by divers Cohobations upon its own* Caput Mortuum: *We may if we please proceed by another way or method: Distil the* Menstruum Fœtens, *being fourteen Days digested, and first will ascend the* Aqua ardens, *then the* Phlegm, *and in the bottom will remain a* Matter *thick as melted Pitch, which are the Constitutive Principles of all* Vegetable Menstruums.

Let

Let us therefore desist from further pursuit of the said Green Lyon, *which we have pursued through the* Meads *and* Forrest *of* Diana, *through the way of* (Philosophical) Saturn, *even to the* Vineyards *of* Philosophy : *This most pleasant place is allowed the Disciples of this Art, to recreate themselves here, after so much Pains and Sweat, dangers of Fortune and Life, excercising the work of Women, and the sports of Children, being content with the most* red Blood *of the* Lyon, *and eating the* white *or* red Grapes *of* Diana, *the* VVine *of which being purified, is the most secret Secret, of all the more secret* Chymy; *as being the* white *or* red Wine *of* Lully, *the Nectar of the Ancients, and their only desire, the peculiar refreshment of the Adopted Sons; but the Heart-breaking, and Stumbling-block of the Scornful and Ignorant.*

But before we depart hence, I will present you(Paracelsians) *with another Dish, and that not unsavory, which is, that the* Virgins-milk, *or* white Mercury (*otherwise the* white Wine *of* Lully) *extracted out of the* Green Lyon *is by* Paracelsus *that* Glue *of the* Eagle, *or* Green Lyon, *so carefully sought for : For* Eagle *and* Green Lyon *are to the* Adepts *Synonyma's of the same thing: For thus* Ripley *before* : You will obtain the white Water, which is our white Tincture, our Eagle, our Mercury and Virgins-milk. *Consequently therefore*, red Mercury (*or the* red Wine *of* Lully) is the Blood *of the* Red *or* Green Lyon: *For the same Lyon is called sometimes Green (in his Youthful Estate) sometimes red (in his more grown Estate) and therefore the Blood is sometimes said to be of the* Green Lyon, *sometimes of the* Red : *So* Ripley (*in the* Menstruum *described in Numb.* 61.) *saith*; Take the Blood of the Red Lyon being most Red, as Blood, which is our Mercury, and our Tincture now prepared to be poured upon its Ferment, that is upon the Calxes of the purest Gold : also elsewhere; The Blood of the Lyon of a Rosey Colour. *But let us hear* Paracelsus *himself.*

65. The

65. The *Green Lyon* of *Paracelſus.* *Aurei Velleris Germ. p.* 41.

TAke diſtill'd Vinegar, wherein diſſolve the *Green Lyon*, putrefie, filtre the Solution, draw off the Liquor in Balneo to an Oylineſs; this Oyl or Reſidue put in a Retort, diſtil away the moiſture in Sand with a gentle Fire: Then increaſe the Fire, and the *Green Lyon*, being compelled by the ſtrength of the Fire will yield his Glue, or Air; To the *Caput mortuum*, pour its Phlegm (*the moiſture drawn off*) putrefie in Dung (*or Balneo*) and diſtil, as before, and again will aſcend the Spirits; force it ſtrongly, and there will come a tenacious Oyl of a Citrine Colour: Upon the *Caput mortuum* pour again the firſt diſtill'd VVater, putrefie, filtre, and diſtil, as before: Laſtly with a moſt ſtrong open Fire, and there will come over a Bloody Oyl, which is otherwiſe called Fire: The remaining Earth reverberate into whiteneſs, &c.

Hitherto we have had the ſtinking Menſtruums made of Azoquean Vitriol *only, yet ſometimes the* Adepts *have added common Vitriol to it, thus.*

66. The ſtinking *Menſtruum* made of the *Gum Adrop*, and *Common Vitriol* of *Ripley.* *Pag.* 357. *Viatici.*

TAke and Grind the Gum made of *Sericon* with diſtill'd Vinegar, and as much of Vitriol evaporated, and firſt diſtil the VVater with a gentle Fire, then with a ſtrong; receive the Oyl (*blood of the Lyon*) which ſeparate from the VVater, till you have the pure Oyl by it ſelf.

Sometimes inſtead of common Vitriol, they added common Nitre to the Azoquean Vitriol; *thus* Lully *in Practica Teſtamenti made his* ſtinking Menſtruum.

67. The

67. The *stinking Menstruum* made of *Azoquean Vitriol*, and Nitre of *Lully*. *Cap. 9. Pract. Testam. p.* 159. *Vol.* 4. *The. Chym.*

TAke one part of D, (D, *signifies* Azoquean Vitriol, *which destroys and confounds all that is of the Nature and Being of common* Argent vive, *pag.* 154.) and half a part of C, (C, *signifies* Salt Peter *or* Nitre, *pag.* 154 *of the same Volume*) which being very well ground, fitted, and mixed together, put in a Glass Cucurbit in a Furnace, and putting on an Alembick, in which the Spirits are by resolution distilled and condensed; lute the joynts of the Vessels with linnen Cloath, impasted and steeped in luting, made of VVheat-flower, and the whites of Eggs, that the united properties of the three Mercuries, namely, Saltish, Vitriolick, and VVatry, being joyn'd and united together, may be preserved: And observe, that the said Powders put into the Cucurbit exceed not the weight of eight Ounces; and to abbreviate the time, put of the like Powder into two other Cucurbits, according to the weight of eight Ounces in every Cucurbit, and place them upon little long Furnaces, so as I shall declare in the Chapter of Furnaces; put not above three Cucurbits upon one Furnace, for the Fire cannot administer equal heat to more, as the mixtion of Nature requires; and let the said Cucurbits be placed the distance of five or six Fingers one from another, and let the bottoms of the Cucurbits be luted with Potters Clay mix'd well with hair; put fine Ashes well sifted and pressed the thickness of five Fingers under them, and to the Beak of every Alembick put a Glass Phial with a long Neck at the end, because the Receiver of those Phials must not feel the heat of the Furnace, nor the Water of the Phials flow back, nor the Spirits recede or fly away: Then must you provide a good quantity of Saw-dust, whereof take two parts, and half a part of the husks of Grapes, or the powder of dry Fire, and mix it with the said Saw-dust, and with this Composition fill your Furnace, then light your Fire at both ends, and let it burn; for you

you must make no other Fire, till you see six, or ten, or fifteen; or twenty drops of Water distil, and when twenty have distill'd, make your Fire with small Wood dry, and so by little and little make the Fire flame directly to the Matter; and see when it distils, that the Water be clear, and when it is at fifteen Points, and the Water clear, and the fumes subtil, continue that Fire equally: And if you see it returned from fifteen to twelve Points, or less, strengthen the Fire, and continue it according to the Point of its distillation, and then thirdly, strengthen your Fire one Point further, and continue it till nothing more distills, and then let the Fire go out, stop your Furnace, and let the Matter cool; and if the Water be clear, without any disturbed Colour, or without muddiness, take and keep it, and stop the Phial with warm Wax, that nothing may respire, nor the Air enter, because the Spirits which are subtil, would presently be corrupted by the Air. Remember, when you begin to make the Fire of dry Wood, that your Vessels must be covered with the aforesaid Paste, and wrapped about with Linnen Cloaths, and the Phials well luted to the Beaks of the Alembicks with the same luting, putting a Quill between the Beak of the Alembick and the Phial; for whilst the Fire operates, the Air will for the most part go out and respire, when it hath not a Receiver to retain it, for it is hot, and the subject which retains it, is not able to endure an exceeding heat, and therefore it requires some place wherein it may respire; when therefore you hear it blow, open the Quill-hole for it. O Father! how have you made the practice thus tedious! Son! That you may be acquainted with all things both small and great, and that you may have both a general and particular knowledge of Fires, and other operations, as also of all sorts of luting; because it is not our intention to speak any more of them, there being nothing difficult to the wise, circumspect, and intelligent, and that you may hereafter say, that the stinking Menstruum is at your command, which is a mean thing, by which all Bodies are in a short time converted into their first Nature, and it is the pure and proper Original of a wonderful and most commodious thing, but you must know how to apprehend it with a clear understanding, &c.

The like Menstruum *hath* Lully *in his* Magia Naturalis, *which is called*

68. The

68. The Water calcining all Bodies of *Lully*. *Magiæ Naturalis*. *Pag*. 359.

TAke of the Earth, that is, D. (*of Azoquean Vitriol*) five Ounces and a half, and of the Water, that is C. (*of Salt Peter and Niter*) two Ounces and a half, the Sum of which is the weight of eight Ounces, and being all mix'd, grind the Matter fine upon a Marble, then put it in a glaſs Veſſel with an Alembick upon it, and diſtil the whole ſubſtance, firſt making a gentle Fire of Saw-Duſt, taking two parts of it, and one part and a half of Coals ſmall or ground, and a little dry Bran, and light the Fire, and let it kindle of it ſelf, till it begins to diſtil from one Point to twelve (*twenty*) Points, and then you muſt begin to ſtrengthen the Fire with ſmall Wood, making the Fire of the Flame right under the Matter, and ſo continue the Fire till it be returned to twelve or fifteen Points, or alſo to fewer, and then continue the whole Fire according to the Points of its diſtillation, and after that ſtrengthen the Fire one Point further, and continue it till the Alembick loſeth its Colour, or no more diſtils; then ceaſe, and let it cool, gather the Water, keep it in a hot and moiſt place, and have a care that it reſpires not: And remember to have a Quill in the luting of the Beak of the Alembick, and the Neck of the Receiver, that you may ſometimes draw it out, that the Receiver may have vent, for the heat is there ſo quick, that the Veſſel containing the Matter cannot endure it, wherefore it is requiſite ſometimes to be opened and ſometimes ſhut: Take notice, that this Water, though made of a contemptible thing, hath the power of converting Bodies into their firſt Matter, which being joyn'd to the Vegetable Virtue is of much perfection, and muſt be put into practice preſently after it is diſtill'd, that the Spirit which is ſubtil and of a ſtrange Nature, may not be loſt by the Air.

The ſame Menſtruum *is deſcribed in* Lully's *Clavicula under this Title*,

69. The

69. The Stinking *Menstruum* for the dissolution of the Calx of Gold and Silver, in order to the reducing them into *Argent vive*.

Cap. 15. *Clav. Pag.* 299. *Vol.* 3. *Th. Chym.*

TAke of Vitriol two Pounds, of Salt Peter one Pound, of Cinabar three Ounces (*I do not understand by what Error Cinabar has crept in among the other Ingredients of this* Menstruum, *for it is a constitutive not of this, but of the following* Menstruum *for the dissolving of the Philosophers Stone; especially* Lully *himself, in* Cap. 20. Claviculæ, *speaking of the extracting of Mercury from a perfect Body, having made no mention of Cinabar, whereas notwithstanding in the same place he gave a Description of this* Menstruum *in these few Words, saying:* Put of our stinking Menstrual, made of two parts of red Vitriol, and one of Salt Peter, and let the aforesaid *Menstruum* be first distilled seven times, and well rectify'd) let the Vitriol be rubified and pulverized, then put in the Salt Peter and Cinabar, and grind all together, then put the Matter in fit Vessels well luted to be distill'd; let it be distill'd first with a gentle Fire as the Work requires, and as they know how that have done it: Let this Water be distill'd very often, casting away the Fæces which remain at the bottom of the Cucurbit, and so it will be your best distilled *Menstruum*.

Sometimes they added common Vitriol to the Azoquean Vitriol and Nitre: It is thus done.

70. The Stinking *Menstruum* made of Azoquean Vitriol, common Vitriol, and Niter of *Ripley*.

Cap. 1. *Pag.* 143. *Medul. Phil. Chym.*

TAke Vitriol made of the sowrest Juice of Grapes, with the Fire of Nature and Sericon (*Azoquean Vitriol*) joyn'd together in one mass with Natural (*common*) Vitriol a little dryed, together with the *Sol Niter*, and out of these distil a Water, which will first be weak and phlegmatick, not colouring the Vessel, which throw away: Then will ascend a white Fume, which

which will make the Veſſel look like Milk, which muſt be gathered, till it ceaſeth, and the Veſſel is returned to its former colour: For that Water is the Stinking *Menſtruum*, wherein is our Quinteſſence, that is, the white Fume, which is called the Fire againſt Nature, without which our Natural Fire could not ſubſiſt, whereof we will ſay more in its proper place: And theſe, namely, the Mineral and Vegetable Water, being mix'd together, and made one Water, do operate contraries, which is a thing to be admired; for this one diſſolves and congeals, moiſteneth and dryeth, putrefies and purifies, diſſipates and joyns, ſeparates and compounds, mortifies and vivifies, deſtroyeth and reſtoreth, attenuates and inſpiſſates, makes black and white, burneth and cooleth, begins and ends. Theſe are the two Dragons fighting in the Gulf of *Sathalia*, this is the white and red Fume, whereof one will devour the other: And here the diſſolving Veſſels are not to be luted, but onely ſtopp'd ſlightly with a Linnen Cloth and Maſtick, or common Wax: For this Water is a Fire and a Bath within the Veſſel, and not without, which, if it feels any other ſtrong Fire, will be preſently elevated to the top of the Veſſel, and if it finds no reſt there, the Veſſel will be broken, and ſo the compoſition will be left fruſtrated. So much as this compounded Water diſſolves, ſo much it congeals and elevates (*is congealed and elevated*) into a glorious Earth: And ſo it is the ſecret diſſolution of our Stone, which is alwayes done with the congelation of its own Water: And becauſe this Fire of Nature is added to the Water againſt Nature, ſo much therefore as it loſt of its Form by the Fire againſt Nature, ſo much it recovers by the Water of Nature, that our work by the Fire againſt Nature, may not be deſtroyed or annihilated.

From the Receipts we obſerve.

1. *That the* Menſtruums *of this kind, being made of the very matter of* Philoſophical Wine, *or* Philoſophical Grapes, *are the firſt of all other* Menſtruums, *either Mineral or Vegetable.*

2. *That the* milky Liquor *or* Spirit, Virgins Milk, white Mercury, *the* White Wine *of* Lully, *and the* Glew *of the* Green Lyon, *called by* Paracelſus *the* Glew *of the* Eagle, *are terms*

 ſynonymous;

ſynonymous; and that the Red Liquor, Blood *of the* Green Lyon, Red Mercury, *the* Philoſophers Sulphur, *and the* Red Wine *of* Lully, *otherwiſe by* Paracelſus, *the* Blood *of the* Red Lyon, *are likewiſe Synonyma's.*

3. *That the acid Mineral* Menſtruums, *are by digeſtion or further elaboration, tranſmuted either into a ſimple Vegetable* Menſtruum, *or into the Heaven or Spirit of* Philoſophical Wine.

4. *That theſe* acid Menſtruums *are to be diſtilled with very great caution, by reaſon of the exceſſive efferveſcence of the* Azoquean Vitriol, *or rather* Spirit *of* Philoſophical Wine, *which is in this* Vitriol *cauſed by the* Acids.

5. *That* Mineral Menſtruums *are the* Heaven, *or* Eſſence *of* Philoſophical Wine *diſſolved in an* Acid, *ſo that having acquired this Spirit, you may make them* ex tempore *by ſimple diſſolution.*

6. *That the* Menſtruums *even now prepared, are preſently to be uſed, leſt they periſh.*

7. *That* Menſtruums *are by diſſolving Bodies coagulated.*

8. *That Metallick Bodies are by theſe* Menſtruums *reduced into running* Mercury.

9. *That theſe are called* Stinking Menſtruums, *becauſe of their ſtinking* ſmell. *By the ſmell alone we eaſily diſtinguiſh theſe from thoſe fragrant* Menſtruums *called* Vegetable. *Thus the unſavoury ſmell of the* Menſtruum *it ſelf proves that* Morienus *uſed the Stinking* Menſtruum. What is the ſmell of it, ſaith King *Calid, by way of Queſtion,* before and after the making of it? *Morienus anſwereth,* Before it is made, the ſent of it is ſtrong and unſavoury; but after the preparation of it, it has a good ſent, according to that which the wiſe man ſaith: This Water reſembles the unpleaſant ſmell of a Body dead, and void of life; for the ſmell of it is ill, and not unlike to the ſmell of Graves: He that can whiten the Soul, and cauſe it to aſcend again, and keep the Body well, and take away all obſcurity from it, and extract the ill ſavour out of it, will be able to infuſe it into the Body, and in the hour of conjunction exceeding Miracles will appear, *Morien.* de Tranſ. Metal. p. 33. *Geber alſo acknowledgeth himſelf to have operated with a mineral* Menſtruum, *Cap.* 25. *Summæ perfect.* The firſt natural Principles, *ſaith he,* out of which Metals are procreated, are the *Stinking Spirit,* that is, Sulphur, and *Water Vive,* which alſo we allow to be called dry Water.

And

And in another Place at the end of his Book de Investigat. *he goes on*; We do by plain and open proof conclude our Stone to be nothing else but a *Stinking Spirit*, and *living Water*, which we also call dry Water, being cleansed by natural decoction and true proportion with such an Union, that nothing can be added or taken from it, to which a third thing ought to be added for the abbreviation of the Work, that is, a perfect Body attenuated.

10. *That* Adrop, *the Name of the Matter of these* Menstruums, *signifies the Philosophers Saturn, or Lead.* The first Matter of this leprous Body, *saith Ripley*, is a viscous Water inspissated in the Bowels of the Earth. The great *Elixir* for the Red and for the White, saith *Vincentius*, is made of this Body, whose Name is *Adrop*, otherwise called *Philosophical Lead*, pag. 132. *Medul. Phil. Chym.*

Our Stone, *saith* Arnold, *in Speculo Alchym.* is called *Adrop*, which is in Latine *Saturnus*, in English *Lead*, and according to the Trojans *Dragon* or *Topum*, that is, Poyson, *Septima Dispos. Speculi*, pag. 596. Vol. 4. *Theatr. Chym.* I have shewed that the Philosophers gave it divers Names, because of the diversity of Colours; but as to their Intention, they had one peculiar Name, that is, *Roman Gold*, or *Adrop*, or *Stone* above all the *Stones* of this world, *Quarta dispositio Speculi*, pag. 594. of the same Volume. *Laton* and *Azoth* are together, and never asunder, but remain always joyned together, but because of the diversity of Colours, the Philosophers call'd them by many Names; and as the Colours are varied and changed, they imposed so many Names; because *Azoth* among the *Indians* is Gold; among the *Hermians* Silver; among the *Alexandrians* and *Macedonians* Iron; with the *Greeks* Mercury; with the *Hebrews* Tin; with the *Tartars* Brass; with the *Arabians* Saturn; and among the *Latines*, and especially among the *Romans* Ognividon, (*by an* Anagram *Dono G vini*, G signifying Philosophical Mercury, or *Sulphur aqueum*;) But that none may err, I say it hath one proper Name, and is commonly called by men; and every one knows the Stone, *Tertia dispos. Specul.* p. 593. of the same Volume.

Some of the Adepts *write not* Adrop, *but* Atrop; *by which Name they have been pleas'd to signifie the Matter of these* Menstruums *to be as it were the Gate of all the most secret Chymy*:

for

for Atrop, *by the inversion of the Letters is read* Porta, *a Gate: Thus* Robertus Valensis *in* Gloria Mundi, *pag.* 305. That you may attain (*saith he*) to the true foundation, I will once again repeat it to you, and call it the first Hyle, that is, the beginning of all things; it is also called the only Holy; apprehend what Elements are in it by those which are repugnant; the Stone of the Philosophers, of the Sun, of Metals, the fugitive Servant, the airy Stone, the Thernian Stone, Magnesia, or the corporal Stone, Marcasite, the Stone of *Sal Gemmæ*, the Stone of *Children*, the golden Stone, the Original of worldly things, *Xelis*, also by inversion *Silex*, a Flint, *Xidar*, by the same inversion *Radix*, *Atrop*, by inversion, *Porta*, a Gate; and it hath also as many other Names, yet is but one only thing.

To Robertus Lully *seems to incline, who has been pleased to call every alteration of the* Azoquean Vitriol, *or Matter of the* Menstruums *of this Kind, the first* Porta *or Gate of the Work; thus he call'd the dissolution of the Matter the first Gate.* In our whole Magistery, *saith he*, there are three principal Spirits necessary, which cannot without the consummation of their resolution be manifested, and they are otherwise called, three *Argent vives*. And because Resolution is so often used for the *First Gate* of our Magistery which we will declare; the said Resolution is divided into three principal parts: The first is Corporal, and is called in the Latine Tongue *Recfage* (*that is, Anagrammatically* facere G; *but by* G, *he means* Sulphur aqueum, *Cap.* 5. *The. Test. pag.* 115. *Vol.* 4. *Theat. Chym. or our* Mercury, *Cap.* 20. *Pract. Test. pag.* 170. *of the same Volume.*) The second is spiritual, and called *Agazoph*. The third is spiritual and corporal, and called *Ubridrugat.* &c.

When the Matter in the Resolution of it appears black, this Blackness (for which some have call'd it Lead) he would have to be a sign of the first Gate. In the first Resolution, *saith he*, lies all the danger, and therefore I give you notice, that you must have the Sulphurs of simple *Argent vives* destroyed by heat, in such manner and form, as that their active property may not be expelled by extraneous heat, and that it may not be separated from its moist Subject, which appears wholly black, full of a noble Spirit: That Blackness demonstrates the sign of *the first Gate* leading into our Magistery, and without it can nothing

thing be done, because it is the Fire of Nature, which is to create the Stone, and which cannot be manifested without the corruption of its Body, *Cap.* 28. *Theor. Test. pag.* 51. *Vol.* 4. *Th. Chym.*

Lastly, He calls the Destillation of this Matter the first Gate *also.* The way of preparing the Stony, and fermentable Spirit is, to take the Juice of *Lunary,* and extract the sweat of it with a small and gentle fire, and you will have in your power one of our *Argent vives* in Liquor, in the form of a white water, which is the ablution and purgation of our Stone, and its whole Nature: And that is one of the most principal Secrets, and is *the first Gate*; as you may understand by the Reasons aforesaid, &c. *Cap.* 9. *Theor. Test. pag.* 21. *of the same Volume,*

Being perswaded by these and the like Quotations, I may affirm, that Atrop *is to be written rather than* Adrop, *because besides the Blackness or Philosophical Lead,* Atrop *signifies the beginning or* first Gate *of the Work.*

11. *That in the Adeptical Chymy are many* Green Lyons, *to be necessarily distinguished one from another.*

By the first the Adepts *meant the Cœlestial Sun, governing the whole World.*

The second is Argent vive, *more common to us than common* Argent vive.

The third is called Argent vive *dissolved into a Green Colour.*

The fourth is Adrop, Azoquean Vitriol, Philosophers Lead, &c.

A fifth is the Stinking Menstruum, *otherwise called the Blood of the* Green Lyon.

A sixth is the Green Lyon *of Fools,* Roman Vitriol, Verdigreece, &c.

The seventh is extraordinary, namely, common Mercury sublimed.

12. *That there are also many* Saturns.

The first is common Lead, the impurest of Metals, and consequently the most remote of all in our Art; which to prove by the Sentiments of the Adepts *is a thing superfluous, finding almost every where amongst the* Adepts *a solemn caution for us to beware of this devourer of Metals and Minerals,* Saturn. Have a care, *saith Ripley, (to bring one Witness for all)* of operating with *Saturn,* because it is commonly said, Eat not of the Son, whose Mother is defiled, and believe me, many Men err in *Saturn.* Hear what *Avicenne* saith,

ſaith, *Saturn* will be always *Saturn*, yea operate not with the Earth of (*Philoſophical*) *Saturn*, which the Spirit of it has deſpiſed, and left for the worſt Sulphur, *&c. Cap.* 2. *Philorcii. pag.* 188.

The ſecond is Adrop, *or* Azoquean Vitriol, *whereof before.*

A third is the firſt Colour or blackneſs of the firſt Work; *of which lower.*

The fourth is Copper, the firſt of Metals; *of which* Arnold in Speculo Alchym. diſp. 8. Pag. 605. Volum. 4. Theat. Chym. *thus*: There were, *ſaith he*, Philoſophers that placed our Science in the ſeven Planets; and our firſt Planet is called *Venus*, the ſecond *Saturn*, the third *Mercury*, the fourth *Mars*, the fifth *Jupiter*, the ſixth *Luna*, the ſeventh *Sol*: The Generation of Copper hath the firſt place after (*the univerſal*) *Mercury*, ſaith *Baſilius*, *Libro de rebus nat. & ſupernat. Cap.* 4. Of all thoſe things, *ſaith Paracelſus*, which proceed from Salts, there is none more nearly allyed to the Mineral Virtue, than Vitriol; the reaſon is, becauſe Salts are Minerals, and all Minerals lie in one Maſs and Ares. Now *Vitriol* in the ſeparation of Minerals, is the laſt thing, to which is immediately ſubſequent the generation of Metals, whereof *Venus* is the firſt, *Lib.* 4. *Philoſ. de Element Aquæ, pag.* 279. *And a little after he ſaith*, The *Marcaſites* and *Cachymys* being thus ſeparated from the firſt Matter of Metals, then follows the firſt Generation, which is of *Venus*, &c. Beſides, by the ſeparation, whereby the nature of the *Marcaſites* and *Cachymys* are expelled, the generations of Copper do immediately concur, imprint themſelves, and are coagulated together, becauſe it is the firſt Metal after the ſeparation of the *Marcaſites* and *Cachymys*. in the ſame Book, *pag.* 281.

The Vitriol of Venus *being the firſt of all things added or joyned to the* Vegetable Mercury *in the making of* Adrop, *is called by* Lully *the* firſt Male. This Fire, *ſaith he*, is that Property of the *Mercury*, which you muſt endeavour to preſerve from burning, being the Tincture of *Vitriol*, with which (*the Vegetable*) *Mercury* ought to be ſublimed, becauſe it is the *firſt Male* of it, and is the augmentation of our Tincture, which is a great addition in virtue and power, when it is joyned with the Tincture of *Sol*; for if you know how to extract the Property of *Mercury* from *Vitriol* and *Salt*, and make them friendly by conjunction, which is done by gentle ſublimations, you will know

one

one of the greatest Secrets of Nature, and the true principal perfection. *Codicil. cap.* 92. *pag.* 202. *So in many places of his* Theoriæ Testamenti majoris, *he means* Vitriol *by his* Male; *in these especially: The* Fire *of our* Male, pag. 50. *The* Virtue *of the* Male, pag. 94. *The* Virtue *of the* Sperm *of the* Male, pag. 108. *The* Heat *of the* Male, pag. 72. *The Female* (*Venus*) *is in this case the* Male, *and is not so hot as the true* (*second*) Male, Gold, Pag. 73. Vol. 4. Theat. Chym. *This* Male *also* Espanietus *mentioneth in the making of his* Menstruum. Take, *saith he*, the winged Virgin compleatly washed and cleansed, impregnated with the spiritual Seed of the *first Male*, &c. *Sect.* 58. Arcani Hermet. Phil.

Paracelsus, *the better to express the Masculine Nature of* Venus, *calls it* Metallus, *a Noun of the Masculine Gender, as* Metallus primus. Take, *saith he*, the Coralline Liquor, I mean that which is very diaphanous, to which add a fifth part of the *Vitriol* of *Venus*, digest them in Balneo for a month; for by this means the Wine of the *first Metal* separates it self aloft, but the feculent part of (*this*) Wine, the *Vitriol* of *Venus* retains (*he means the residue left in the extraction of* Vitriol) and so that *first Metal* (*Metallus primus*) is made a perspicuous, diaphanous, and truly red Wine, &c. Cap. 12. Lib. 3. *De Vita longa*, Pag. 65. *As the* Adepts *call'd* Venus *the first Metal* (Metallus primus) *in the Masculine Gender, so also they changed* Saturnus (Saturn) *a Noun of the Masculine Gender, into* Saturna, *a Noun of the Feminine Gender, to signifie not common Lead, but* Venus, *being a Feminine Noun, of Copper.* I have, *saith Ripley*, a dear and beloved Daughter, named *Saturna*, from which Daughter are both the white and red *Elixirs* assuredly procreated; if therefore you desire this Science, you must extract a clear water from her, &c.

Sometimes to describe by Saturn, *not only* Venus, *but also the Philosophical preparation of* Copper (*that is, to be performed by a* Vegetable Menstruum) *they made it a Vegetable or Herb, that so they might distinguish that which was, from that which was not prepared; Thus* Flamel *in his* Summary: Some unskilful men, and unlearnest Chymists take common Gold, Silver, and Mercury, and handle them so ill, till they vanish away by fume, and thereby endeavour to make the *Philosophers Mercury*; but they do not attain to that, which is the first Matter and true Myne of the Stone: But if they would attain to that, and reap any good, they must betake themselves to the seventh Mountain, where there is no Plain, and from the top downward behold the other six, which they will see at great distance. At the top of this Mountain you will find a triumphant Royal Herb, which some Philosophers call a Mineral, some a Vegetable, and if pure and clean Broth be made thereof, the better part of the work will be hereby accomplished, and this right and subtil *Philosophical Mercury* must you take. *This Place is thus read in* Chortalassæus, *pag.* 313. *Vol.* 6. *Theat.Chym.* Ascend therefore the Mountain, that you may see the Vegetable, Saturnine, Plumbeous and Royal, likewise also Mineral Root, or Herb, take only the Juice of it, and throw away the Husks.

The

The Fourteenth KIND.

Simple Mineral Menſtruums *made of the acid or ſaline* Eſſences *of* Salts.

71. The Water or Oyl of Salt of *Paracelſus*. *Cap.* 3. *Lib.* 10. *Arch. Pag.* 38.

THough there be many ways of extracting the *primum Ens* of Salt, yet this (*method of making* Salt circulated, *the* Circulatum minus *of Salt, the diſſolving* Water, *the* Water *or* Spirit *of* Salt circulated, *deſcribed above in Numb.* 27.) is moſt commodious, and expeditious, and after this is that other way, which we mentioned ſpeaking of the *Elixir* of Salt, namely, that new Salt being mix'd well with the diſſolving Water, which is the diſtilled Spirit of Salt (circulated) muſt be putrefied, and ſo long diſtilled, till the whole ſubſtance of the Salt is diſſolved, and reduced into a perpetual oleoſity, the Body of Phlegm being drawn neatly from it. This way is alſo taught the preparation of the *Arcanum* or Magiſtery of Vitriol and Tartar, as of all other Salts.

Annotations.

WE *take notice that the* Menſtruums *of the antecedent Kind are made of the unctuous Matter of* Philoſophical Wine, *purged, diſſolved, and volatilized with an acid; in the preſent we ſhall obſerve the contrary, namely, that the acid or ſaline* Eſſences *of* Salts *made with the unctuous Spirit of* Philoſophical Wine, *are* Menſtruums *of this fourteenth Kind.* Paracelſus *in the preſcribed Receipt reduced Salts by cohobation alone, with the Water of Salt*

circulated

circulated into a liquid ſubſtance or Oyl, *but the* Oyl *made of common* Salt, *by the method aforeſaid, he commends before the reſt to his Diſciples, for the extractions of Metallick Bodies.* Certainly, *ſaith he*, there cannot be a more Noble and better way, than by the Water or Oyl of Salt, prepared as we have clearly deſcribed in *Alchymia* (*and in Libris Chyrurgicis.*) For this Water fundamentally and radically extracts out of all Metallick Bodies their Natural Liquor or Sulphur, and a moſt excellent *Crocus* as well for Medicinal as Chymical Operations: It reſolves and breaks any Metal whatſoever, converting it out of its own Metallick Nature into another, according to the various intention and induſtry of the Operator. *Manuale de Lap. Phil. pag.* 139.

It will therefore be worth while to explain the way of making this Oyl *of* Salt *more clearly to you: Firſt for the illuſtration of the Receipt we will propoſe the Deſcription of the* Oyl *of* Salt *alleadged by the Author himſelf, in the eighth Book of his Archidoxes, which in the* Elixir *of Salt*, Pag. 31. *we read thus*: Take Salt accurately prepared moſt white, and moſt pure; put it into a Pellican with ſuch a quantity of the diſſolving Water, as to exceed the weight of it ſix times: Digeſt them in Horſe-Dung together the ſpace of a Month, then ſeparate the diſſolving Water by diſtillation, pour it again to it, and ſeparate as before, and that ſo oft, till the Salt is converted into Oyl.

By comparing the Receipts it appears, that Sea-Salt newly made is not to be underſtood by new Salt, but the ſame exquiſitely purifyed: Then it is clear, that the weight of the Water of the circulated Salt omitted in the Receipt of the tenth Book, ought to be ſo determined, as to be ſix times more than the weight of the Salt: Moreover, the time and place of putrefaction omitted in the former proceſs are deſcribed in the other, that is, to be digeſted a Month in Horſe-Dung: Beſides it is from the Receipts obſerved, that all the Salt is not converted into Oyl, the Body of the Salt being drawn as a Phlegm from the Eſſence. *Laſtly, that the Oyls of Vitriol and Tartar may be alſo made by the ſame method.*

The Receipts being thus compared, are not only without all obſcurity, but do by the exuberance of their Light give Light alſo to other Proceſſes, being otherwiſe leſs intelligible. So this Oyl *of* Salt, *as the* Eſſence *or* primum Ens *of Salt explains that more obſcure Deſcription of the* Eſſence *of* Salts, *given in* Libro 4. Archid. Pag. 14. Take Salts,

Salts, and calcine them throughly; if they be Volatile, burn (*sublime*) them, after that resolve them into a tenuity (*per deliquium*) and distil them into a Water (*through a Filter.*) This Water putrefy (*not by it self, but as the Disciples of the Art ought to understand and know, with the Water of Salt circulated*) for a Month, and distil by Balneo, and a sweet Water will ascend (*the Body of the Salt by the way of a Phlegm*) which cast away: That which will not ascend, digest again (*with new dissolving Water*) another Month, and distil as before, and that so oft, till no more sweetness is perceived. By this way you have now the Quintessence of Salt in the bottom, (*like an Oyl*) scarce two Ounces out of a Pound of the burned or calcined Salt. One Ounce of this Salt thus extracted, if common, seasoneth Meat more than half a Pound of another; for the Quintessence of it remains only, and the Body is drawn from it by liquid solution. This way is the Quintessence of all Salts separated.

This Process being thus enlightned by the rayes of the antecedent, reflects no small Light upon the said Receipts, namely, that scarce two Ounces are acquired from one Pound of the Salts.

In Clavi Archidoxorum, Lib. 10. Pag. 37. *Paracelsus has described the* Essences *of* Salts *in these Words:* The way of extracting the Quintessence of Salts, as Vitriol, Salt, Nitre, Tartar, &c. is this: Cohobate with its own Liquor or Water very often, putrify with the Phlegm, and then draw off the Body in the form of Phlegm even to the fixed Spirit: This Spirit dissolve in its own Water, and by a strong heat separate the pure from the impure with the Spirit of Wine. *This Description is most obscure, but made clearer by those aforesaid. The meaning of* Paracelsus *is this: He putrefies the Salts, and cohobates them so often with their own Liquors or Waters, that is, with their own* Circulatums; *common Salt with common Salt circulated; Nitre with Nitre circulated; Vitriol with the Water of Vitriol circulated; Alume with the Water of Alume circulated, the dissolving Water of Alume, the* Circulatum minus *of Alume,* &c. *till they remain at the bottom in the form of an Oyl, which Oyl being either acid or saline, easily makes an effervescence with the unctuous Spirit of* Philosophical Wine, *or its own* Circulatum, *and in this heat lets fall some of its impurities, and so becomes purer, which thing is confirmed by the Description it self of the Water of Salt circulated, where he putrefies Salt, being*

melted

melted and resolved per deliquium, *with the Spirit of* Philosophical Wine, *cohobates, and draws it to an Oleity:* Joyn it, *saith he*, with the Spirit of (*Philosophical*) *Wine*, and the impure will fall to the bottom, which separate, but let the pure be Cristallized in a cold place, pour the distillation to it again, and cohobate so oft, till a fixed Oyl remains at the bottom, and nothing sweet will more distill.

Moreover, this Oyl *of* Salt *as a* Menstruum, *makes his Process in* Chyrurgia *intelligible, which otherwise could not be understood.*

72. The Water of Salt by another Description of *Paracelsus*. *Cap. 2. Tract. 3. part. 2. Chyr. major. Pag. 66.*

TAke Salt without any addition of Art being most white by Nature it self (*Sal Gemmæ*) which must be divers times melted, then being reduced into a most fine Powder mixt with the Juice of *Raphanus*, stir them together; after resolution distil, distil the distillation with an equal quantity of the Juice of *Sanguinea* five times more: In this Water are Plates of *Sol*, being purged by *Antimony*, easily resolved into Powder; this Powder being thus prepared must be washed with sweet Water distilled, till it hath no taste of Salt, for the Salt not entring into the substance of it, is easily washed away.

In this Process Sal Gemmæ *being fused by the method of the Water of Salt circulated, is dissolved in the Juice of* Raphanus, *evaporated and resolved* per deliquium, *then six times distilled with an equal proportion of the Juice of* Sanguinea. *In the antecedent Description of this* Oyl *of* Salt, *this fusion of the Salt, dissolution in the Juice of* Raphanus, *and resolution* per deliquium *is not necessary, because the Water of Salt Circulated is sufficient of it self to separate the Essence of Salt from its Phlegm: But where we use the Spirit of* Philosophical Wine *in making the Water of Salt circulated, without the said previous preparation of the Salt, we should have the Work too tedious: In the mean time both Processes agree in weight of* Menstruum, *for it is all one, whether the Salt be cohobated into an Oyl with six times as much of the dissolving Water, or distilled six times with the Juice of* Sanguinea *in equal weight. One thing that makes mades the latter Process inexplicable, is the unknown Juice of* Sanguinea, *but however it is evident by what hath been said, that either the Spirit of* Philosophical Wine, *or the Water of Salt circulated supplies its place.* Basilius *indeed resolved common Salt with the Spirit of* Philosophical Wine *not into an Oyl; but reduced into it a Green Stone thus:*

Viride Salis of *Basilius.*
In supplemento Libri de conclusion.

TAke common Salt, calcine it well, yet without fusion, reduce it to a Powder, resolve *per deliquium* in a Cellar, or in *Raphanus* made hollow, then distil in Sand with a quick Fire, and a Water will ascend, the residue in the bottom pulverize, and dissolve it in its distilled Water, and distil again; this repeat till all the Salt has ascended, which will be in the fourth or fifth time: Draw off the Phlegm from the distilled Water in Balneo, the remainder put into a Cellar in cold Water, and you will have Cristals, which take out, and dissolve in the Phlegm; then draw off one half, and you will find new Cristals, repeat the Operation four times or more, for the oftner, the more fusible will be the Cristals, which being dryed and pulverized on a Marble, pour to them the rectify'd Spirit of (*Philosophical*) *Wine*, which cohobate from the Salt so oft, till you perceive the Oyl of Salt coagulated into a Green transparent Stone, which reserve.

Paracelsus *in his Receipts appointed the calcination of Salt to be done by the fusion of it; but in this Process* Basilius *prohibits this liquefaction of Salt, wherefore we conclude it to be little essential in the said depuration of Salt, nor do we think it so necessary, for the Salt being resolved* per deliquium *to be distilled, thereby to be made a fusible Salt;* Paracelsus *having taught how to make the same Oyl out of fused Salt, which Oyl* Paracelsus *himself, besides* Basilius, *in many places affirms to be of a Green Colour. Thus we read of the Green Oyl of Salt:* Libro de male curatis, Pag. 170. Chyr. Majoris. *Of the Greens of Salt,* Libro. 4. de Gradibus, Pag. 154.

From

From the Receipts we obſerve,

1. *That theſe* Menſtruums *are the* Eſſences *of Salts not tinging.*

2. *That the Oyls or* Eſſences *of tinging Salts, as* Vitriol, *&c. may alſo be made by the ſame method, and do appertain not to this, but to another Kind.*

3. *That theſe* Menſtruums *are by further digeſtion or cohobation made ſweet, and transmuted into volatile* Arcanums, leſs Circulatums, or Simple Vegetable Menſtruums *of the Fifth Kind.*

4. *That theſe* Menſtruums *do diſſolve Metals into Powder for the extraction of the* Crocus *or* Sulphur *of Metals and Minerals: The way we will borrow from* Ripley *in the Uſe of* Stinking Menſtruums.

Let us, *ſaith he*, proceed, *Pag.* 145. *Medul. Phil. Chym.* to practiſe upon the *Calx* of a (*Metallick*) Body duly calcined: The Body therefore being prepared, pour upon it ſo much of this compounded water (in *Numb.* 70.) as to cover it half an inch, and it will preſently boil upon the *Calxes* of the Body without any external heat, diſſolving the Body, and elevating it in the form of Ice, together with the exſiccation of it ſelf, which muſt be taken away by the hand of the Operator: And the remaining *Calxes* being well dried again by Fire, put ſo much water to them as before, and proceed in all things as before, continuing the ſame way of operating, till all the *Calxes* be well diſſolved: which ſubſtance being well diſſolved, neatly ſeparated, and pulverized, muſt be put into a good quantity of the rectify'd water of the Fire of Nature (*Spirit of Philoſophical Wine*) that in that Veſſel well ſtopp'd it may by the adminiſtration of external heat, together with the excitation of internal heat, be diſſolved into an Oyl, which will ſoon be done, *&c.* When the *Menſtruum* (*of Sericon, in Numb.* 63.) is poured upon the aforeſaid *Calxes* (*of Metals*) it begins to boyl up; and if the Veſſel be well ſtopp'd, it will not leave working, though no external Fire be adminiſtred to it, till it be dried into the *Calx*; wherefore you muſt not put a greater quantity of it than juſt to cover the *Calxes*. *In the ſame place, pag.* 171. For in this Operation the leſs of the Spirit, and the

more

more of the Body is put, the better and ſooner will be the diſſolution, which is made by the congelation of the Water. You muſt have a care therefore, as it is ſaid in the *Roſary*, that the Belly be not too moiſt, becauſe then the Matter would not receive drineſs: And this way muſt be obſerved, till all the water be dried up. *The ſame Place*, pag. 161.

5. *That all the ſharpneſs of this Metallick Powder may be waſh'd away with ſweet water. That the* Menſtruums *of the* Adepts *are permanent, is manifeſt by the ways of making them; but more clearly by the Uſe of them in the Receipts of the following Books: However* Paracelſus *ſeeming to have appointed the contrary by the preſent ablution of the* Menſtruum, *leſt therefore you ſhould fall into the greateſt and moſt dangerous Errour of all the* Adeptical Chymy, *we thought good to communicate to you an Obſervation or two about the permanence of* Menſtruums.

Firſt, *That* Aqua ardens, *the Philoſophical that is, is by digeſtion or circulation divided into Phlegm and Oyl ſwimming upon it, as you obſerved in making the Eſſence or Spirit of* Philoſophical Wine. *You have taken alſo notice that the ſame* Aqua ardens, *or ſame Oyl made of it, is further concentrated, and rejects the remaining Phlegm, but that it ſelf as a meer* Oleoſum, *remains with the inanimated Earths ſo called, in the Preparations as well of Vegetable, as Mineral* Sal-Harmoniacks: *For it is impoſſible for the ſaid Phlegm being the vehicle of the unctuous Spirit to abide with things diſſolved, much leſs be fixed with them, they being ſo contrary to it: wherefore the permanence of* Menſtruums, *but rather of the Spirit of* Philoſophical Wine *is eaſie to be underſtood, namely, as theſe* Menſtruums *are unctuous mixed with dry things, not in the leaſt diluted in their aquoſities, which do all ſeparate themſelves as uſeleſs in fixation. Examples you will have in* Lib. 2. De Aſtris & Arcanis, *and often in* Lib. 3. *of* Philoſophical Tinctures.

Secondly, *Theſe* Menſtruums *do not preſently, or at the firſt time abide with their diſſolutions: For ſometimes, nay more than often, we are forced to pour on and cohabate before any part of it will continue with the diſſolved Body, whereas in the mean time the reſt aſcends unaltered.*

Thirdly, *Nor do the* Menſtruums *perſiſt with all things promiſcuouſly, but are united only to things homogeneous to them, which in reason they should remain with. Thus the* Simple Vegetable Menstruums *do continue with* Essences, *but not with their relinquished white Bodies; whereas the* Compounded Vegetable Menstruums *being sutable to these Bodies, do dissolve them wholly in the making of* Magisteries.

Fourthly, *Yea though every* Menstruum *is either an* Essence, *or a* Magistery, *and one* Essence *prepares another, easily entring and mixing themselves radically one with another, yet so long as they are of different kinds or degrees, are they both separable again, nor do they continue; till one being newly extracted, is raised to the same degree as the other, then do they flow together at length into a mixture not to be separated by Art or Nature.*

Fifthly, *As to these Mineral* Menstruums, *you have observed, that the* Acidity *of them admits of the same reason with the Phlegm or Aquosity of the* Vegetable Menstruums, *so far as it is moist, and therefore to be separated in the fixations of things: But as it consists of the dry Particles of Mineral Salts, (but Salts they are dry things dissolved in Acids) it will fall under two several Considerations.*

In the first, the Acidity of the Menstruum *being perhaps in greater plenty than is necessary, or sticking about the superficies of the thing dissolved, is easily washed away with common Water.*

But in the second, the same Acidity being more artificially mixt, and absorbed by the Aridity of the thing dissolved, is made the cause of venenosity, and now cannot be altered but by Vegetable Menstruums *transmuting it.* Paracelsus *commands the washing not of the* Oyl *of* Salt, *but the sharpness of the* Salt, *which penetrates not into the substance of the Metal, and is easily washed away, but the Unctuosity of the* Salt *being throughly mixed with the unctuous* Spirit *of* Philosophical Wine; *and now united to the Unctuosity of the Metal, common Water cannot touch nor separate. But an Acid received into the bowels of an Arid, he corrects again with the* Spirit *of* Philosophical Wine, *that it may not become the cause of venenosity: Yet there is a place in* Paracelsus, *where he seems to have established a particular Decree against the permanence of* Menstruums. Many several ways, *saith he, Lib.* 4. *Archid. de Essentia, pag.* 12. are found, whereby the Quintessence may be extracted, *viz.* by Sublimation, Calcination, by *Aqua fortisses,* by Corrosives, by Sweet, by Sowr, &c. It may be be done which way you pleaſe: Where this is withal to be obſerved, that every thing added by way of mixture, to the Quinteſſence, for the neceſſity of extraction, muſt be again taken away, and ſo the Quinteſſence remain alone, not mix'd, or polluted with any other Matters: For the Quinteſſence cannot be extracted from Metals, eſpecially Gold, which cannot be ſubdued by it ſelf alone; but ſome fit Corroſive muſt be made Uſe of, which may afterwards be ſeparated from it again; ſo Salt (*diſſolved*) in water, is drawn again from the water left void of Salt: Whereas notwithſtanding it muſt be conſidered, that every Corroſive is not fit for this purpoſe, becauſe they cannot all be ſeparated: For if Vitriol or Alume be mix'd with water, neither can be ſeparated from it again without detriment or corruption, but will leave ſome ſharpneſs behind them, becauſe they are both watry; and two likes concur together, which ought not to be in this place: Wherefore it is to be adviſed, not to put watry to watry, or oyley to oyley, nor reſiny to reſiny, but a thing contrary muſt ſeparate the Quinteſſence, and extract it, as waters extract the Quinteſſences of things oleaginous, and the oleaginous the Quinteſſences of watry things, as we may learn by the Quinteſſences of Herbs: The Corroſives therefore are to be ſeparated again after the ſeparation and extraction of the Quinteſſence, which may eaſily be done; for oyl and water are ſeparated with eaſe; but oyl cannot be drawn from oyl, nor water likewiſe from water without mixing, which being left, would indeed infer very great detriment to the Quinteſſence: For a Quinteſſence ought to be clear and pure without any mixture, ſo as to have an uniform ſubſtance, by virtue whereof to penetrate the whole Body.

Leſt the Eſſence ſhould be defiled by things added for the neceſſity of extraction, he commands no Watry Matter to be extracted by a watry Menſtruum,*an oyley by an oyley,a reſiny by a reſiny,but by ſome contrary. This Rule, if underſtood according to the Letter, is erroneous, for it takes away all the permanence of* Menſtruums *eſtabliſhed upon the Maxime ſo often repeated by the* Adepts; The Diſſolution of the Body, is the Coagulation of the Spirit or *Menſtruum*; and on the contrary: *It takes away, I ſay, all the natural homogeneity of the diſſolvent and the diſſolved; yea*

 is

is repugnant to the Experience of Paracelsus *himself, who had no* Menstruum *but what remained in a radical mixtion with the things dissolved in it, as by the Use of them we shall prove hereafter. Now an Essence is divers ways coinquinated by things added in the extraction of it.*

First, *When a Natural or Seminal* Essence *is extracted by the like Natural* Essence *of another species; For example, the* Essence *of* Saffron *is inquinated and confounded with the virtues of* Cinamom, *in extracting it with the specifick* Essence *of* Cinamom, *and therefore the* Essences *of Vegetables are not to be extracted with a Natural, or rather Artificial* Essence, *or with the* Spirit *of* Philosophical Wine, *not yet specificated.*

Secondly, *An* Essence *is inquinated, when a* Menstruum *or* Essence *is in greater than convenient quantity used in the extraction of another* Essence, *by which quantity the quality of the said* Essence *is washed, wasted, and as it were inquinated; wherefore the superfluity of the* Menstruum *must always be taken away, that the* Essence *may remain by it self alone without any mixture.*

Thirdly, *An* Essence *is inquinated by extracting it with* Air *or* mineral Menstruums *according to some Processes of the Ancients. For an* Acid, *though it cannot be radically mix'd with any* Essence, *being no* Essence *it self, yet is easily absorbed or hidden by the aridity of* mineral Essences, *and so joyned with the said* Essences *by accident, and from a thing otherwise innocent, creates a very strong Poyson: This therefore to remove, the Ancients first washed off that which stuck to the outside of the Body, then transmuted that which was more deeply admitted, by the digestion of* Vegetable Menstruums: *But in the making of* Essences *with* acid *or* mineral Menstruums *according to the reformed Process, otherwise called by* Paracelsus, *the Process of* two Colours, *the said inquination of an* Essence *hath no place. In the beginning of this Process the* acid *being absorbed by the* arid, *becomes indeed the cause of venenosity, as in the Process of the Ancients; but when this Process of* Paracelsus *is by industry and ingenuity raised to such perfection, that no more* Aridity *can remain to hide any* Acidity *in it, but on the contrary, the whole Body is converted into two* Oyls *or* Fats, *from which all* Acidity *may easily be washed away with common Water, then is there no inquination to be feared from* Acids: *The Saying of* Paracelsus, *we suppose is to be referred to this*

Method,

Method, he having there treated of it on purpose, especially having said that the oleaginous Essences *of* Metals *are to be extracted by* Watry, *that is,* acid *or* corrosive Menstruums, *but that the* watry Essences *of Herbs, that is, less oyley in respect of* Metals, *must be made by* Oleaginous, *that is* Vegetable Menstruums, *which things being not in common terms, but obscurely enough delivered, we do therefore leave them to be better explained by his Disciples; but if they were to be understood according to the Letter, it would certainly be an Errour, not indeed to be connived at in the Prince of* Adepts: *But according to the Proverb,* We are Men, *&c. For sometimes good* Homer *himself has nodded, and the Pen of* Paracelsus *has wanted mending.*

The

The Fifteenth KIND.

Simple Mineral Menstruums *made of the Spirit of* Philosophical Wine, *and Acid Spirits, as* Aqua fortis, *S*pirit of Nitre, Spirit of Sulphur, Salt, *&c.* distilled Vinegar, *&c.*

73. Aqua fortis *mixt with the Spirit of Wine of* Paracelsus.

In Tinct. Paracelsica, Pag. 37. Aurei Vel. Germ.

TAke the best Wine (*the red or white of* Lully) rectify till a Linnen Cloath burneth, being dipp'd therein and kindled: This Spirit is called the *Essence of Wine.* Take of *Vitriol* two Pounds, of *Nitre* one Pound, from which distil *Aqua fortis* into the aforesaid *Essence of Wine*, then digest ten Days, that they may be well united.

Annotations.

T*Hat the* Adepts *acuated the Spirit of* Philosophical Wine *divers ways as well with Oyly as Dry things, we have given plenty enough of Examples in the antecedent Kinds of Vegetable* Menstruums; *it shall now be declared in the following* Menstruums, *which ways this Spirit is to be acuated by Acids. In this Fifteenth Kind we will joyn the unctuous Spirit of* Philosophical Wine *with some Acid Spirits, that by the help of their acidity it may dissolve and perfect Arids sooner and easier than before without.* Paracelsus

celsus *in our Receipt intending to asswage the excessive effervescence in dissolving the Spirit of* Philosophical Wine *in* Aqua fortis, *distill'd the* Aqua fortis *into the Spirit of* Wine, *that they might both by degrees be mix'd together, which being thus mix'd one with the other, he digested moreover the space of ten Days. The same* Menstruum *is described by* Trithemius.

74. *Aqua fortis* mix'd with the Spirit of Wine of *Trithemius.*
Pag. 46. Aurei velleris Germ.

TAke of the Spirit of Wine three Pounds, of *Vitriol* and *Nitre* one Pound, distil the Spirits of the *Aqua fortis* into the aforesaid *Aqua vitæ*, digest eight Days.

This quantity of Aqua fortis *is insufficient to dissolve three Pounds of the Spirit of Wine, Ounces perhaps are to be understood for so many Pounds. No Art is here required, provided the Acid and Oyly be mix'd together. In former times the* Adepts *used distilled Vinegar, instead of* Aqua fortis, *for this* Menstruum, *thus:*

75. Vinegar mix'd with the Spirit of Wine of *Basilius.*
Cap. de Wein Essig. in Repet. Lapidis.

DEr Wein Essig. (*Vinegarwine, a single undeclinable Word*) is not the Philosophers Vinegar, which is another Liquor, *viz.* the Matter it self of the Stone, because the Philosophers Stone is made of the Philosophers *Azot*; but *Vinegarwine*, is made of common *Azot* distilled (*common Vinegar*) and Spirit of Wine (*that is, Philosophical.*) And elsewhere, *Libro de particularibus de particul. Veneris.* I spoke even now, *saith he*, Parabolically of this preparation, *in Libro Clavium* (*in Repetitione*) *Capite de Wein Essig.* where I said that common *Azot* (*Vinegar*) is not the Matter of the Stone, but our *Azot* or first Matter extracted out of common *Azot* and Wine, which composition is called the expressed Juice of unripe Grapes, with which the Body of *Venus* is to be dissolved, and reduced into Vitriol (*then into our* Azot,

the

the first Matter of the Stone, Philosophers Mercury, Spirit of Mercury made of Vitriol, &c.) which you must very well observe, that you may be free from many troubles and dangers. The Philosophers Mercury, *saith he, Libro de Conclusionibus, Sect. 2. de Vitriolo Philosophorum,* or first Matter of the Stone must be made by Art, for our *Azot* is not common Vinegar, but extracted by Virtue of common *Azot*.

Though therefore a Philosophical Menstruum *may be made of common* Azot *or distilled Vinegar, and the Spirit of* Philosophical Wine, *as also sufficient and qualified for the dissolutions of some Bodies, yet being less sharp, especially in the Alchymical use of Metals and Minerals, instead therefore of Vinegar the* Adepts *took* Aqua fortis, *the sooner to finish their Operations.* You must know, *saith Isaacus Hollandus,* that our Ancestors laboured in the Art divers ways, and yet came to one and the same end, but their Stone made not projection always alike, one making a deep, another a strong projection, as the Works (*Menstruums*) were sharp, or of a deep Colour: some sweat a long time with pains, before they produced the Stone: others shortned the time by sharpness of Wit, as it is now done every day with sweat and pains. Some of our Ancestors wrought three Years, some four, before they acquired the Stone, for in those days *Aqua fortis* was unknown, and they used nothing but distill'd Vinegar; but now their Successors have found out *Aqua fortis*, which hath much abbreviated the Work. *Cap. 6. Lib. 2. Oper. min. pag.* 423. *Volum.* 3. *Theat. Chym.* Even at that time Bodies were to be opened slowly, namely, by calcination, reverberation, solution in our sharp Vinegar (*Vinegar mix'd with the Spirit of* Philosophical Wine) *which their posterity observing and considering, quickned their Wits, and found out* Aqua fortis, which did much abbreviate the way to them. *Cap. 77. Lib. 1. Oper. min. pag,* 358. of the same Volume.

To make the present Kind of Menstruums, *the* Adepts *dissolved this Spirit of* Philosophical Wine, *not in Vinegar and* Aqua fortis *only, but in any acid Spirit not tinging, as of Salt, Sulphur, &c. It is thus prepared;*

76. The

76. The Spirit of Salt of *Basilius*. *Lib. partic. in particul. Solis.*

TAke of the Spirit of Salt accurately dephlegmed one part, of the best Spirit of (*Philosophical*) *Wine* without any Phlegm, or of the Sulphur of Wine half a part, the Vessels being luted, distil with a strong Fire, so as that nothing remains.

If you add new Spirit of Wine to the distillation, and digest for some time, it becomes sweet: It is therefore requisite to dissolve the Spirit of Wine in the Spirit of Salt without digestion, lest the acidity or brackishness of this Spirit be lost. Guido *sometimes took his* Circulatum *either* minus *or* majus, *instead of the Spirit of* Philosophical Wine, *into which he distilled the Spirit of Salt.*

77. The Spirit of Salt of *Guido*. *Pag. 7. Thesauri Chym.*

TAke of the *less* Vegetable *Menstruum* (*in Numb.* 36.) or the *great* (*in Numb.* 38.) one Pound, put it in a large Receiver. Then take of common *Salt*, or *Sal Gemmæ*, of the Stone of *Tripoly*, of each four Pounds, distil in an Earthen Retort with an open Fire, first gentle, till all the Phlegm is drawn off, then put the Receiver with the *Circulatum* to it, and distil the Spirits, till not a drop of the Oyl of Salt ascends, and you will have an acuated *Menstruum*.

To make these Menstruums *stronger, they sometimes separated or drew off the Acid from the* Oleosum, *that the Spirit of* Philosophical Wine *might remain in the form of Oyl or Ice, thus*:

78. *Aqua fortis* mix'd with the Spirit of Wine of *Lully*. *In Elucidat. Testam. pag.* 147. *Artis aurifer.*

TAke of Vitriol one part, of Nitre one part, of Alume a fourth part, mix them all well together, and distil with a gentle Fire, till the Liquor is gone over, then give a stronger, and lastly most strong, till the Alembick grows white, for then is the *Aqua fortis* prepared. Then take of the aforesaid Water one pound, put it in a large Cucurbit, and pour it upon four ounces of *Aqua Vitæ* (*Aqua ardens*) four times distilled, and put an Alembick on with its Receiver, then will it make great noises, boyling exceeding violently without Fire; and therefore the VVaters ought to be mixed by little and little. Then put it into a less Cucurbit, and put on an Alembick with its Receiver, and distil the Water in Balneo, that a Matter may remain alone at the bottom of the Vessel in the form of Ice; pour back the water, and distil again, and this repeat nine times, then will an Oyl or Matter like Ice remain in the bottom.

This Menstruum *of* Lully *is clear, and therefore requires not our Explanation. But it is described by an Anonymous in* Rhenanus, *thus;*

79. *Aqua fortis* mixed with the Spirit *of* Wine *of an* Anonymous *Author.*

Libro de Principiis Naturæ, & Arte Alchym. pag. 28. *Syntagm. Harm.* Joh. Rhenani.

TAke an equal Quantity of *Niter* and *Alume*, distil the Phlegm, till the strong and dissolving Spirits ascend, and set before them new and clean distilled water, and force the Spirits into it with a most strong Fire. Then take the *Spirits* of *Wine* being well purged, and artificially distilled in Balneo, take four ounces of them to one pound of *Aqua fortis*, put them into a large Cucurbit, apply an Alembick to it, stop, and put it into cold water, and let them boyl till they will boyl no more: Then put it in Balneo, and distil the water, so that the Spirits may remain yet moist; then pour the water first drawn off, to them again, and do as before, and that seven times, continually distilling with a gentle Fire, till nothing more will distil, but the Matter remains like an Oyl in the bottom.

From

From the Receipts we observe these remarkable Things:

1. *That the* Spirit *of* Philosophical Wine *dissolved in an acid Spirit, is a* mineral Menstruum. *Our* Aqua fortis, *our Vinegar, distilled Vinegar, Vinegar mixed with the* Spirit *of* Wine, *our* Spirit *of* Salt, *Sulphur*, &c.

2. *That the* Spirit *of the same* Wine, *is with very great ebullition dissolved in an* Acid,*and therefore you ought to be exceeding careful lest you pour too much of the* Spirit *of* Philosophical Wine *upon the* Aqua fortis, *and* vice versa: *For it would be more safe to distil the* Aqua fortis *upon the* Spirit *of* Philosophical Wine, *as* Paracelsus *adviseth.*

3. *That* Aqua fortis *mix'd with the* Spirit *of* Wine, *may be taken instead of Vinegar mix'd with the* Spirit *of* Wine, *or* Spirit *of* Salt *mix'd with the* Spirit *of* Wine. *&c. in Chymical Works especially.*

4. *That the more these* Menstruums *are abstracted from the Acid debilitated in dissolution, the stronger they are made.*

5. *That the* Adepts used *also corrosive* Menstruums *or* Aqua fortis. *There are some, not only common ignorant Operators, but* Adepts *also, who not knowing the Preparation and Use of these* Menstruums, *have written against these corrosive* Menstruums. Fools, *saith Bernhard*, do out of the less Minerals make and extract corrosive waters, into which they cast the Species of Metals, and corrode them; for they think them to be dissolved by a natural solution; which solution doth indeed require permanence together, that is, of the dissolvent and the dissolved; that from both, as the Masculine and Feminine Seed a new Species may result. Verily I tell you no water dissolves a Metallick Species by a natural reduction, but that which continues in matter and form, and which the Metals themselves, being dissolved, are able to re-congeal. Which Quality is not in *Aqua fortisses*, but is rather injurious to the Composition, that is, of the Body dissolved, *&c.* Yet thus they think they dissolve, mistaking Nature; but they dissolve not, because the *Aqua fortisses* being abstracted, the Body melts, as before; nor will that water be permanent to it, nor is it to that Body as radical Moisture: The Bodies are indeed corroded, but not dissolved, and so

so much the more alienated from a Metallick Species. Wherefore such solutions as these are not the foundation of the transmutative Art, but rather Impostures of Sophistical Alchymists, who think this sacred Art lies in these things, *&c. Epist. ad Thom. de Bononia, pag.* 60. *Artis Aurifer.* So in the Regeneration of Metals, *saith Sendivogius*, Vulgar Chymists proceed amiss, they dissolve Metallick Bodies, either Mercury, or Gold, or Saturn, or Luna, and corrode them with *Aqua fortisses*, and other heterogeneous things not requisite to true Art, then they joyn and force them together, not knowing that man is not generated from the Body of a man dissected, *&c. Tract.* 6. *pag.* 488. *Vol.* 4. *Th. Chym.*

Some do by Art corroding Waters make,
In which Metalline Species they calcine;
But then the Liquor doth the Earth forsake,
Nor by mans Skill together they will combine:
This way to Fools we leave, for nothing fit,
But for to wast ones Thrift, beware of it.

Page 41. of the second Part of the Marrow of *Alchymy*.

These and the like Expressions they reflect against our Mineral *or* Acid Menstruums, *whereas they were written by the Philosophers against* Common *not* Philosophical Aqua fortisses. In that Point, *saith Lully*, they ignorantly err, imagining the Bodies of Metals to be dissolved, and as I said before, reduced to their first Matter or Nature with *Common Aqua fortisses*; but if they had read our Books, they would certainly know that these Liquors are repugnant to the intention of the Philosophers, *&c. Comp. Anim. Transm. pag.* 194. *Vol.* 4. *Th. Chym.* Parisinus, *a faithful Disciple of* Lully, *explains his Meaning thus:* Those things that are objected by us against *Aqua fortisses*, namely, that they are of no efficacy in the Art, and neverthelesss are taught by *Lully*, are to be otherwise understood: For he this way puts a difference between the *Vulgar* and *Philosophical Aqua fortisses*, &c. And therefore *Raymund* rejecting sharp Waters, means the *Aqua fortisses* of separation, but not those of the Philosophers, *Cap.* 6. *Lib.* 1. *Elucid. pag.* 206. *Vol.* 6. *Th. Chym. But it would be meerly superfluous for us, either by Authorities or Arguments to illustrate that which the* Menstruums *themselves will demonstrate.*

The

The Sixteenth KIND.

Simple Mineral Menstruums *made of* Philosophical Vinegar, *and* Volatile Salts, *as* Common Sal Armoniack, Urine, *&c.*

80. The Oyl of *Sal Armoniack* of *Guido.* *Pag.* 11. *Thesaur. Chymiatr.*

TAke of the *Oyl* of *Salt* (*the Menstruum described in Numb.* 71.) half a pound, of (*Common*) *Sal Armoniack* four ounces. Dissolve the Salt in the Oyl, cohobate the Dissolution three times through an Alembick.

Annotations.

IN *the attecedent Kind, the* Spirit *of* Philosophical Wine *was dissolved in* Acids: *Now to make these Oyley-acid* Menstruums *stronger, the* Adepts *added to them* Salts, *that is, Arids dissolved in Acids, and Cristallized. In this present Kind they took* Volatile Salts, *as being of easier preparation, in the following: fixed* Salts, *because of stronger virtue. In the Receipt of* Guido, *there is nothing either difficult or dark, unless you will object against the Ingredients, which cannot be both common, because* Guido *sublimes Gold Philosophically with this* Menstruum. *Whatsoever also you read in the Books of* Practical Chymy, *understand always according to the Letter (we need not admonish you to except the Terms of Art) if so, that which is promised in the Preparation and*

and use may be performed; if not, seek an Analogical sense not in the method and use of preparation, but in the ingredients; according to which Rule either the Oyl of Salt, *or* Sal Armoniack, *or both ought to be Philosophical, because Gold cannot be Philosophically sublimed with Common* Menstruums. *The Oyl of* Salt *of* Paracelsus, *as also the Spirit or Oyl of* Salt *of* Basilius, *wherewith he extracts the Sulphur of* Sol, *do prove the Oyl of* Salt *to be a* Philosophical Menstruum, Cap. 6. de Rebus nat. & supernat.

Probable it is that Guido *meant the same Oyl, for otherwise the Name of Oyl had been improperly attributed by a Philosopher to the thin and common Spirit of* Salt. *But if you think rather that* Guido *meant the common Spirit of* Salt *by the Oyl of* Salt, *you must by* Sal Armoniack *understand not the common, but Vegetable* Sal Harmoniack (*the Spirit of* Philosophical Wine *dryed with some* Salt, *and then sublimed*) *for so you might also make a* Menstruum *of the same if not of stronger Virtue, a species of the following Eighteenth Kind: But if both the Oyl of* Salt *and* Sal Armoniack *be Philosophical, a* Menstruum *will be from thence produced yet stronger than both the precedent: Here you may deviate from the true and genuine sense of the Receipt, but never from Chymical Truth, so long as you are guided by the Spirit of* Philosophical Wine, *but here you must have a great care that you do not transmute (as sometimes through inadvertence you may) the false Receipts of deceitful Distillers into true ones; an impossible into a possible; a lye into truth; and a wicked Man into a Philosopher.*

Sometimes they impregnated common Sal Armoniack *with a Tincture, to make a* Menstruum *higher, thus:*

81. The Water of *Sal Armoniack* of *Isaacus*. *Cap.* 47. 2. *Oper min. pag.* 460. *Vol.* 3. *Theat. Chym.*

TAke *Sal Armoniack*, sublime it with *Roman Vitriol*, one Pound of *Sal Armoniack*, to two Pounds of Vitriol, then grind upon a Stone the Fæces, and sublime again, then throw away the Fæces, and sublime again with two Pounds of new Vitriol, do as before, repeating nine times: pulverize the *Sal Armoniack*, and put the Powder into a Glass, pour upon it distilled Vinegar (Philosophical, or some *Menstruum* of the Fifteenth Kind) so so as only to be dissolved, and no more, than that the *Sal Armoniack* may be turned only into Water as yellow as *Sol*, because the *Sal Armoniack* was sublimed by Vitriol, and that produced the Tincture: And this is that Water of *Sal Armoniack*, which I promised before to teach you how to make.

From the Receipts we observe:

1. *That the Oyl or Essence of* Salt *becomes a stronger* Menstruum *by the addition of Volatile Salts.*

2. *That this ought to be understood also of the* Menstruums *of the fifteenth precedent Kind.*

3. *That these* Menstruums *are the same with the Vegetable* Menstruums *of the fourth Kind, excepting only that they have an Acid added over and above.*

4. *That these* Menstruums *are of most easy preparation, being made by three cohobations only.*

5. *That it is very difficult for a Man to err, being experienced in the more secret Chymy, for he that understands the practice of this Art, will easily explain the Receipt of every* Adept, *be it never so obscure, either by the use, or title, or way of preparing; for it is in a manner impossible, not to draw some Light from one or other of the said three, or direction enough to find the same Receipt more clear in the Writings either of the same or some other* Adept: *And indeed though we sometimes meet with Receipts, which in title, way of preparation, and use, seem to be like the Receipts of vulgar Chymistry, yet a Desciple of our Art will easily determine either for the approbation or reprobation of these Receipts: For there are infallible Signs to distinguish a true from a false* Menstruum; *this one following shall here suffice: The quality of a good* Menstruum *is to dissolve Bodies either gently or violently, and make them not only Volatile, but fat also, yea reduce them into a true Oyl either swimming upon, or sinking under watery Liquors. This Attribute of a* Menstruum *is inconsistent to any common dissolvent, but proper to the Philosophical, and to them alone, being made of the unctuous Spirit of* Philosophical Wine, *which Spirit alone doth by its permanence make the dry Sulphur of a Metal both thinner and fatter: That* Menstruum *therefore in the use of which are promised such things, as cannot be performed by com-*

mon

mon Menstruums, *may be truly called Philosophical, with a caution or two to be observed.*

1. *That the Receipt must be of some known and not suspected Author, not of every smoak-seller, promising great and many things without a Foundation, wherefore every Receipt wanting its Authority, though it may seem like a true one, yet we think ought to be rejected as suspicious.*

2. *That the Receipt must not be alone, described not in one but divers places by the same Author, or at least most clear in its ingredients: For the same Names have one signification with one, but another with another* Adept; *so long therefore as it is not known by collateral places, what an Author means by his Matters, such a Man's Receipts we declare uncertain.*

3. *That the Receipt must import a competent Rule in operating, that is, declare whether Matters are to be volatilized in part or in the whole, but whatsoever are more obscure and concise we lay aside as imperfect.*

The Seventeenth KIND.

Simple Mineral Menstruums *made of Philosophical Vinegar, and fixed Salts not tinging, as well Vegetable as Mineral.*

82. The *Aqua Comedens* of *Paracelsus. Lib.* 10. *Arch. pag.* 37.

BY *Aqua Comedens* (Eating or Corroding Water) we mean Vinegar mix'd with the Spirit of (*Philosophical*) *Wine*, which must be drawn from common Salt so often, till it is dissolved, and comes over by distillation in the Vinegar.

Annotations.

THe Philosophical Vinegar, or Vinegar mix'd with the Spirit of Philosophical Wine, *which you acuated with Volatile Salts in the precedent Kind, is made stronger by the mixing of fixed Salts so called. We have described several Vegetable* Menstruums *made with* Alcali Salts *in their fifth Kind, which if prepared with Philosophical Vinegar instead of the Spirit of* Philosophical Wine, *will produce Mineral* Menstruums *of this Kind, though prepared another way, with this only difference, that they are made more slowly with the Spirit of* Philosophical Wine, *but with Philosophical Vinegar much sooner, yea immediately, if either Common or Philosophical Vinegar be joyned to the Vegetable* Menstruums. Aqua comedens, *or* Eating Water, *is the third* Menstruum *that we have observed to be made of common Salt. The first is in the fifth Kind of Vegetable*

Menſtruums, *where common Salt being fuſed and reſolved* per deliquium, *is by Virtue of the Spirit of* Philoſophical Wine *reduced into the Oyl or Eſſence of Salt, which by being ſometimes cohobated with the ſame Spirit, becomes ſweet, and is tranſmuted into the* Arcanum *of* Salt, *or* Circulatum minus *made of common* Salt. *The ſecond is in the fourteenth Kind, where the aforeſaid Oyl of* Salt *is left in its acid (rather ſaline)* Eſſence. *The third, which is taught in the preſent Kind, agrees with the firſt, except only that it is prepared not with the Spirit of* Philoſophical Wine, *but Philoſophical Vinegar, and ſo, ſooner than that, and in uſe is ſtronger, as a Mineral* Menſtruum. *Diſſolve the* Arcanum *of Salt, or Salt circulated in any Acid not tinging; for example, common Vinegar diſtill'd, Spirit of Niter, Sulphur, Salt, &c. and it will produce the Eating Water by ſimple mixtion; on the contrary, if you weaken, or take away the Acid of the Eating Water, either by precipitating it with common Spirit of Wine, common Water, &c. or digeſting it by it ſelf, you will have the* Arcanum *of Salt, or Water of Salt circulated. That which has been ſaid of common Salt, is alſo to be underſtood of Niter, Alume, and all other Salts not tinging. The Receipt of the Eating Water is clear of it ſelf, except that in the Latin Tranſlation,* a Salis Nitri Spiritu *is read amiſs, the* German *Authors own Writing having it* a Sale communi, Von gemeinen-Saltz: *The Error it is requiſite you ſhould correct.*

Menſtruums *of this Kind are made not only of Mineral Salts not tinging, but alſo of Vegetable* Alcalies, *thus:*

83. The fixative Water of *Trithemius*. *Pag. 37. Aurei Veller. Germ.*

TAke *Aqua fortis* mix'd with the Spirit of Wine, (*deſcribed above in Numb. 74.*) whereto add of the Oyl of Tartar *per deliquium* half a Pound, diſtil the Spirit, throw away the Phlegm, and diſſolve the remaining Earth or Salt in the Spirit.

Keep the ſolution for the fixing of things; but for volatilization the Salt of Tartar muſt be cohobated ſo oft, till it aſcends as the common Salt in the Eating Water.

Hereto is referred the Menſtruum, *called*

84. The

84. The *Aqua Mirabilis* of *Isaacus*. *Cap.* 29. 2 *Oper. Min.* & *pag.* 91. *Manus Phil.*

TAke old Urine, distil with a weak Fire, then a stronger, that whatsoever can, may ascend; rectifie the destillation, taking away all the Fatness or Oyl, till it leaves no Fæces behind it. The *Caput Mortuum* left in the bottom, calcine the space of two hours, but without fusion of the *Salt*, draw all the saltness from the calcined Matter, with common Water; evaporate the Liquor to a thin skin, that the *Salt* may be Cristalized, repeat sometimes, that the *Salt* may be made most pure, which dissolve in the distilled Urine. Then take of this regenerated Urine six pounds, of distilled Vinegar, and *Spirit* of (*Philosophical*) *Wine*, of each three measures, of *Common Salt* two pounds, of *Sal Armoniack* and *calcined Tartar*, of each half a pound, dissolve them all together into an *Aqua Mirabilis*.

The like Water almost hath Basilius, *but that he distils his through an Alembick; the Description of which followeth.*

85. The Resuscitative Water of *Basilius*. *Pag.* 81. *Currus Triumphalis Antim.*

TAke of the *Salt* of Mans Urine clarified and sublimed, of *Sal Armoniack*, and *Salt* of *Tartar*, of each one part, mix the Salts, pour strong (*Philosophical*) Vinegar to them, lute with *lutum sapientiæ*, digest the Salts for a Month in a continual heat, then distil the Vinegar by Ashes, till the Salts remain dry, then mix them with three parts of *Venetian Earth*, force them with a strong Fire through the Retort, and you will have a wonderful Spirit for the making of *Running Mercury* out of *Antimony*. *The same Water we find also, pag.* 39. *of his* Manual Operations.

The Adepts *have sometimes used some crude Oylcy Matter instead of the* Spirit *of* Philosophical Wine *in making these* Menstruums;

ftruums; *thus* Paracelsus *volatilized four Salts into a* Menftruum *of this Kind with Wax diffolved in* Aqua fortis.

86. The Water of *Sallabrum* of *Paracelf.*

Libro de reductione Metallorum in Argentum vivum, five Tractatu 4. Rofarii novi Olympici Bened. Figuli, pag. 24.

TAke notice there is no fhorter Method of reducing Metals into *Mercury*, known to us, than that which we ufed in our Book *de putrefactione quatuor Salium*, which we there called *Sallabrum*, as thus; each of thofe (*Salts, as lower*) muft be converted into a pure Water or Oyl (*per deliquium*) which being mixed in equal weight, are called *Lac Veterum*, or Milk of the Ancients: Which *Philofophical Milk* put into a ftrong Receiver, and diftil the Spirits of calcined Vitriol, calcined Alume, and the beft Niter, *ana*, five times upon it, and the mixture will be called *Flying Eagle*, carrying Metals in its Talons aloft; fuch a Metal being fublim'd, grind to powder, from which draw the Spirit of ftrong Wine being poured to it the height of a Finger, three or four times gently in Balneo, and you will have a quick or running Metal as common Mercury. Now the *Eagle* is made volatile thus: To the *Philofophers Milk* acuated with the faid Spirits, or *Eagle*, pour Wax, being very well liquefied and purged, about the thicknefs of a Finger, diftil the Phlegms together with the Spirits by a Cucurbit in Balneo, which Matter muft be cohobated fo often, till they are all coagulated or well mixed; and you will have the *Philofophers Borax*, which we wrote of in our Book *de virtute Vitrioli*, wherein the *Volatile Eagle* abfconded it felf with its Feathers, namely, *Spirits*. Now take the Calx of what Metal you pleafe, made of *Aqua fortis*, one part, of the *Flying Eagle* half a part, mix, putrefie nine days, the longer the better, then fublime the Matter upon Sand in a Cucurbit well luted, and all the Metal you took will afcend, wherewith proceed as before. *Sallabrum* defcribed in the Book mentioned, (*de putrefactione quatuor Salium*) Take *Sal Niter, Sal Gemmæ,*

common

common Salt, *Pot-Ashes*, an equal quantity of each, dissolve every one by it self, and purge it from all Terrestreity; out of all being mixed together, make a clear and transparent Water, which again coagulate in a clean Vessel, and you will find the Salt of another colour, namely, yellow, penetrating, and sweetning, dissolving and fixing: Love and esteem this Salt, because there are many Secrets in it; for it fixeth the Volatile, and vivifieth the Spirit being dead; and mollifieth the hard and friable, and freeth from any Leprosie and Poyson, fixeth Arsenick, and moreover is the promoter of many famous works to a happy and desired End.

In the first place, let us admonish you to beware of this and such like Menstruums; *for a Mystery lies in these Receipts, which to observe is necessary, lest you begin to doubt the Truth of them after many most dangerous Experiments tried in vain: for you Beginners let this suffice; that it is impossible for Wax, or any other oyley Matter to supply the place of the* Spirit *of* Philosophical Wine. *There would be no need of this* Spirit *in the whole Art, if crude oyley things could perform the same as this most pure and most unctuous Liquor. No man but he that is expert in the Method of preparing the* Spirit *of* Philosophical Wine, *can make these* Menstruums, *whereas all the rest may be made by any Idiot, if he hath but the* Spirit of *this* Wine *given him. The* Adepts *do in these Receipts both prepare and acuate this* Spirit *of* Wine; *no wonder therefore that they either wholly omitted the Mystery, or not sufficiently express'd it in their Compositions; for which reason also these* Menstruums *do appertain to the preparation of the* Spirit *of* Philosophical Wine, *rather than as all the rest to the Use of this* Spirit, *or compositions of these* Menstruums; *nor should I have remembred them here, had they not been detrimental to many men; and that to my own knowledge. The Name* Sallabrum *is given* quasi Salis labrum, or *Salt-Cellar*, *not that Salt is to be contained in this Vessel, as* Candelabrum, *or Candlestick is so called, because Candles are set in it, but rather because the* Essence *or* Fire *of some Metals, or some* Chymcial Light *is either to be reserved, or made in this* Sallabrum, *as* Alume *is by* Isaacus *in* *Man. Philosophor. pag.* 28. *called* Lucerna, *signifying a* Lanthorn.

Concerning this Sallabrum, Thomas Aquinas *in Lilio Benedicto*, *pag.* 1085. *Vol.* 4. *Th. Chym. Thus*;

Adde:

Adde labrum Salis quanta ſit ſexta duorum
Conjunge poneq; ſimul———

In the ſame place he calls this Sallabrum *the Medium of joyning Tinctures, the middle between two Extreams, between hard and ſoft, between Luna and the Spirit, between the Body and Spirit: As the Menſtrual Blood is the Medium between the Sperm of the Male and Female, ſo this our* Salt, *pag.* 1085. Sallabrum *he calls thundring Salt, illuminating Stone, and fatneſs of the Eagle, pag.* 1087. *Sal Alembrot, the Stone Bore* (Borax) *and fatneſs of the Eagle, pag.* 1097. *Tincar, Borax.*

This Sallabrum *or* Saline Labrum *is by* Paracelſus *made of theſe* Salts, *Niter, Sal gemme, common Salt, and Alcali.*

Guido *uſed theſe four following in his reduction of Metals into Mercury: Common Salt, Alcali, Sal armoniac, and Salt of Tartar, pag.* 23. *Theſ. Chym.*

Thomas Aquinas *took the ſame Salts as* Guido, *for his* Labrum Salis. *The Affinity which I obſerve between the Salts of* Paracelſus, *Gemme and Common, I perceive alſo between the Salt of Tartar, and Alcali of* Guido; *but the foundation of the Receipt is not grounded upon theſe four Salts.* Paracelſus *was ſometimes ſatisfied with Niter and common Salt fuſed and reſolved together* per deliquium. *Nor does the Myſtery of the Receipt lie in the Wax, in the room of which if you choſe any oyley thing elſe, you will not err. Inſtead of the ſame, he ſometimes uſed Linſeed-Oyl in the Water of the ſixth gradation; but of this hereafter.*

From the Receipts we obſerve,

1. *That theſe* Menſtruums *are* ſimple Vegetable Menſtruums *of the Fifth Kind diſſolved in* Acids. *Diſſolve any of them in common* Aqua fortis, *and you will have a* Menſtruum *of this Kind; but take away the* Acid, *and it will be a* Vegetable Menſtruum *again, as it was before.*

2. *That theſe* Menſtruums *are by reaſon of the Acidity both ſooner made, and do more powerfully operate than the ſaid* Menſtruums *of the Fifth Kind.*

3. *That*

3. *That they are not always made of the* Spirit *of* Philosophical Wine, *but also with any common Oyley Matter, provided it be undertaken by an Artist expert in the Method of making the* Spirit *of* Philosophical Wine.

4. *That these* Menstruums *do by their own strength without any addition of* Common Argent vive, *reduce* Metals *and* Minerals *into running* Mercury.

5. *That Metals dissolved in these* Menstruums, *and sublimed, are properly enough called* Philosophical Mercuryes, *because as* Common Mercury sublimate, *so these are most easily resuscitated into* running Argent vive.

The

The Eighteenth Kind.

Simple Mineral Menstruums made of *Vegetable Sal Harmoniack*, and *Acids* not tinging.

87. *The* Aqua fortis *of* Isaacus Hollandus. *Cap.* 122. *Oper. Min. pag.* 397. *Vol.* 3. *Th. Chym.*

MAke an *Aqua fortis* with an equal quantity of *Sal Harmoniack*, and *Sal Niter*, dry the *Sal Niter* to a dry Powder, then mix the *Sal Harmoniack* discreetly among the Powder of the *Sal Niter*, so as to be well mixed together, and incorporated one with the other; then distil; not luting the Receiver close to the Beak, before it begins to distil; for if you lute the Receiver at first to the Beak of the Alembick, there are windy wild Spirits in the Matter, which would break the Receiver; but having distilled a little while, lute the Beak without fear, and distil the Water according to Art.

Annotations

Annotations.

BEsides the Philosophers Vinegar, *there is a* Sal Harmoniack, *under the Name of which is comprehended the* Spirit *of* Philosophical Wine, *the root of all* Menstrums, *being concentrated, dried in an Arid, and sublimed into an admirable Salt. This present Kind treats of this Salt, not common* Sal Armoniack, *dissolved in common Acids, not tinging. We have also made indeed* Philosophical Menstruums *before of* common Sal Armoniack, *by the help of* Philosophical Vinegar, *or an Acid mix'd with the* Spirit *of* Philosophical Wine, *but the* Menstruums *of this Kind are stronger than they, the* Spirit *of* Philosophical Wine *being sublimed into a* Vegetable Sulphur *or* Mercury, *is made better, as being acuated either with an* Alcali, *or some fixed* Arid, *and for this reason being dissolved in an* Acid, *it yields also a more noble* Menstruum. Isaac *in our Receipt mixeth* Vegetable Sal Harmoniack *with so much of* Sal Niter, *for the* Vegetable Salt *to be by subsequent distillation dissolved in the Mineral Acid of* Sal Niter; *but because this way of dissolving, is by reason of the sudden ebullition of the oyley and acid, too dangerous, he durst not therefore lute the Receiver close to the Beak, but the like effervescence appearing in the distillation, of* common Sal Armoniack, *and* Sal Niter, *we must prove, that by* Sal Harmoniack Isaacus *meant not the* Common, *but* Philosophical; *which we prove first by the Use of the* Menstruum: *Of which saith* Isaack *thus*; Dissolve your *Sol* in the Water made, and put it in Balneo, with a glass Alembick upon it; kindle the Balneo no more than that you may endure your hand in it, and lute the Receiver very firmly to the Beak, and a little hole being made above in the Alembick, put a glass Funnel therein, whereby other *Aqua fortis* may upon occasion be poured in, and keep the Balneo in that heat aforesaid a day and a night, and when you see your *Aqua fortis* brought to a small quantity (*by distilling*) as it was when you dissolved the *Sol* in it, pour to it new *Aqua fortis* and let it gradually distil a day and a night in Balneo, and when it is thick again, pour *Aqua fortis* again to the Matter, doing in all respects as before; repeat it three times, always pouring to it new *Aqua fortis*, but the third time distil it dry (to siccity) then let the Body cool, and take the Receiver from the Beak, and stop it firmly with wax, remove the Alembick from the Pot, and then take a Drachm or Scruple of the Matter out of the Pot, and put it in a glass Phial, pour common distilled water to it, and set it on a Fornace in Ashes, and let the water boyl half an hour: Then let it cool of its own accord, and stand a day and a night, and a Powder will settle in the bottom of the Vessel; pour off the top of the water gently, and the rest evaporate with a lukewarm heat, to dry your Powder: Being dry, take it out, and heating a silver Plate, put a little of your Powder upon it, and look earnestly whether the Powder fumes not; if you perceive it fume, have a care of your self, for the fume may kill you, &c. *pag.* 397. *of the same Volume. Then he goes on, Cap.* 24. *saying*, Then put your Matter or Powder in it (*the subliming Vessel*) with a large and clean Alembick upon it very well luted, so as to be certain that no Spirits can pierce the luting; for they are subtil beyond description, and should they penetrate, and you receive the fume, you would die. Lute also a large Receiver to the Beak of the Alembick, and let the luting be in every place throughly dry: Then put Fire under the Fornace, first a very small Fire, and sometimes increase it by degrees, till your Matter begins to sublime, which it will do with a little heat; and when you see the Matter ascend, diligently observe to keep the Fire in the same degree, that it may sublime very gently, which will be easily done; for the Matter is sublimed, and ascends with a very little Fire, *pag.* 402. *of the same Volume.*

Gold dissolved in this Aqua fortis *of* Isaack, *and once or twice cohobated, then washed with common Water, becomes so volatile, as to ascend with a very small heat into a most poysonous Sublimate; if any man does the same by as easie a Method with common* Aqua Regis *made of* Sal Armoniack *and* Niter, *we declare he needs not* Menstruums *of this Kind; but that* common Sal Armoniack *is insufficient for such a purpose, even the Novices of vulgar Chymistry have long since experienced.*

Besides the Use of this Menstruum, *the Encomiums of* Sal Harmoniack, *which agree not in the least with the Common of the*

140. *be called* Sal Harmoniack *or dry Water*) Take an example from the Dyers that dye Cloaths, &c. Thus it is with our Stone. Though we have rightly-prepared the Body, Soul and Spirit, if they enter not into one another, they will neither now, nor at any time ever remain together without the Medium of our dry Water. Now Beloved, where now shall we find this Water ? For *Geber* saith, Our water is not Rain-water. *Aristotle saith*, Our water is a dry water. *Hermes saith*, Our water is gathered out of a filthy and stinking *Menstrual Matter*. *Danthynus saith*, Our water is found in old Stables, Houses of Office, and stinking Sinks. And *Morienus*, Our water springs in Mountains and Valleys, and Fools understand not these words, but think it *Mercury* ; it is not *Mercury*, it is a dry water, which causeth all Mineral Spirits, Soul and Body to enter and mix together, and when it has joyned them together, it departs from them, and lets them remain fixed. And this water is found in all things of the world. For if this water was not, in vain should we endeavour to make the Stone : For how should we make one of our prepared Matter enter into another ? As the Apothecaries gather their Herbs together, so ought we to do either in the Vegetable, Animal, or Mineral Kingdom, to make a perfect work or Quintessence, we ought to have a dry water out of every distinct thing. A dry water therefore is in all things, to make themselves perfect. Therefore, saith *Galen*, All things have their own Medicine to make the Stone either in the Mineral, Animal, or Vegetable Kingdom, without the addition of any exotick things. Wherefore when we would make the Stone, or any Fixation, we ought to make that conjunction with our dry water, as was said of the Dyer and Apothecary. Therefore is it, my Beloved ! that so many fall into Errors, because they do not understand nor follow Nature : Therefore did I mention the Dyer and Apothecary, for you to understand Nature, by that rude way, that you may in your own mind perceive that no conjunction

can be made without a Medium.. Wherefore all the works above cited are good, but those two things are not there named, the *Spirit*, that is, and *Dry Water*, weights and way of joyning, wherein consists our whole Art: wherefore I conjure you never to reveal this Secret; for all the Art that is in the world is comprehended in it, to make the perfect work in a short time and little pains, *Cap*. 147, 148, 149. 2. *Oper. Min. pag*. 524, 525. *Vol*. 3. *Theat. Chym*.

Ripley *hath described the same Water thus*;

88. The *Aqua Regis* of *Ripley*. *Pag*. 349. *Viatici*.

MAke a corrosive Water of *Salt Peter* and *Harmoniack*, and put not above four Ounces in the Destillatory, and draw a water with a slow Fire, wherein dissolve and make the Oyl of *Sol*, &c.

This Water Basil Valentine *calls the* Kings Bath, *of which thus, in the elucidation of the second Key*: Take notice, Friend! and seriously consider, because here lies the principal Secret; Make a Bath, have a care that no strange thing enter into it, lest the Noble Seed of Gold be radically destroyed after the dissolution of it: Exactly therefore, and with care examine the things which the second Key informs you of, that is, what Minerals are to be taken for the *Kings Bath*, wherein the King ought to be dissolved, and his external form subverted, that his Soul may appear without blemish: To this purpose will the *Dragon* and *Eagle*, that is *Niter* and *Sal-Armoniack* serve, out of which being united, is made an *Aqua fortis*, as you will be informed in my Manuals, where I shall treat of the Particular of *Sol*.

89. The

89. The *Kings Bath* of *Basilius.*

Lib. Partic. in Particul. Solis.

TAke of *Salt Peter* one part, of *Sal Harmoniack*, one part, of Flints pulverized half a part, mix, and distil. Take notice, that this Water must be carefully and exactly distilled; for it cannot be distilled by the common method: He that is expert in the operations of (*the more secret*) *Chymy*, will know what is to be done. Observe, you must have a strong earthen Retort well luted, in the upper part of which must be a Pipe half a span long, and two fingers broad; put a great Receiver to it, lute well, and increase the Fire by degrees till the Retort grows red hot: Then put in a spoonful of this Matter through the Pipe, and suddenly stop the Pipe with a wet Cloath, and the *Spirits* will pass impetuously into the Receiver; the *Spirits* being asswaged, put in another spoonful of the said Matter, thus proceeding, till no Matter remains, and you will have *Aqua Gehennea*, or Hell-water, dissolving the Calx of Gold in an instant into a thick solution, which we mentioned in the third Part, as also in the second Key, not only dissolving Gold, but reducing the same into volatibility, &c.

This Kings Bath *is described also by* Basilius *in* Revelatione Manualium Operationum, *thus*;

90. A Philosophical Water for the Solution of Gold of *Basilius.*

Labore primo Revelation. Man. Operat.

TAke of *Salt Peter*, and *Sal Armoniack*, of each two parts of Stones washed one part, grind them together, and by a Retort (*with a Pipe*) distil the Water into a large Receiver putting in two or three ounces through the Pipe; the Receiver, must be a big one, and lie in a Vessel full of cold Water, and covered

vered with wet Linnen Cloaths, that the Spirits may cool; for it will be very hot, stop the Joynts of the Retort very close, kindle a Fire, and the Retort being hot, cast in three ounces of Matter, the Pipe being suddenly stopp'd, the Spirits will pass through, and the Receiver will grow white, and drops fall: When the Spirits are setled, put in three ounces more, stopping the Pipe immediately, proceed as before, changing very often with wet Linnen: Continue this Operation till you have water enough, which stop very well, that it may not evaporate; it is the true Water and Mineral Bath for the King.

That Basilius *as well as* Isaacus *used the* Sal Harmoniac *not common* Sal Armoniac, *for his Bath, the Use of the same doth also prove.*

Take of this Water three parts, of the Calx of Gold one part, mix them in a Cucurbit, put it with an Alembick upon hot Ashes to be dissolved; if it be not wholly dissolved, pour out the Water, and pour on new, and that till all the Calx is dissolved in the water, being cold, white Fæces settle in the bottom, which separate; put all the water together, and digest for a day and a night in Balneo, then removing the Fæces, digest the space of nine Days continually, distil the Water, that the Water may remain in the bottom like Oyl, &c. distil so often, till all the Gold has pass'd through the Alembick. *In the same place: This unctious Bath reduceth Gold and all other Metals into Oyls, because it is made of the Oyly Spirit of* Philosophical Wine, *concentrated, and dryed in some Vegetable Alcali; and Spirit of Nitre, whereas on the contrary* Sal Armoniack, *or common* Aqua Regis, *cannot transmute Metals beyond its saline Nature, for that Oleity which it hath not, it cannot give.* Isaacus *for want of a Retort with a Pipe, perhaps not being at that time known, sustained no small loss of Spirits in distilling this* Menstruum, *which* Basilius *did by help of the said Retort endeavour to repair, though that also not without some difficulty.*

The later Adepts, Crinot, Trismosinus, *and* Paracelsus *observing the difficulty of distilling, and the loss of Spirits made it better, who by a plain but better method dissolved the Vegetable* Sal Harmoniack *in Spirit of Nitre or* Aqua fortis, *without any loss, danger, or delay.*

91. The

91. The most strong *Aqua fortis* of *Paracelsus*. *Lib. 3. Arch. de separ. Elem. pag. 7.*

TAke Sal Nitre, Vitriol, and Alume, in equal parts, which distil into *Aqua fortis*, this again pour to its Fæces, and repeat, distil in a Glass, which *Aqua fortis* clarify with Silver, and dissolve *Sal Armoniack* in it.

That Paracelsus *neither by* Sal Armoniack *meant the common, is also demonstrated by the use of the* Menstruum, *which he thus describes:* These things being done, take a Metal reduced into Plates, and there resolve it into Water, in the same Water, then separate by Balneo and pour on again, this repeating, till you find an Oyl in the bottom, of *Sol* or *Gold* a purple, of *Luna* a lazurine; of *Mars* red and very dark; of *Mercury* white; of *Saturn* livid and lead Coloured; of *Venus* altogether green; of *Jupiter* yellow; in the same place. *Whoever dissolved Metals promiscuously with common* Aqua regis, *both Silver and Gold into an Oyl, either purple or lazurine? Not to say any thing of the reduction of all Metals into two Fats red and white, the Essence thereof, and the Dead Body. It is therefore clear from the effect that* Paracelsus *dissolved* Sal Harmoniack *in* Aqua fortis *for his most strong* Aqua fortis.

In making this Menstruum Guido *adds the weight of the* Sal Harmoniack *which* Paracelsus *omits*.

92. The *Aqua Regis* of *Guido*. *Pag. 22. Thesauri Chym.*

TAke Vitriol, common Salt, and Nitre, distil into *Aqua fortis*, take one Pound of this, four Ounces of (*Philosophical*) *Sal Harmoniack*, and distil yet once.

Solomon Trismosinus *sometimes dissolved Metals in common* Aqua fortis, *and to the solution added* Sal Harmoniack. *Thus he volatili-*

volatalized Silver, being dissolved in Aqua fortis, *with the aforesaid Salt.* Lib. 8. Tinct. quinta. pag. 81. Aurei velleris German. Take of pure *Luna* four Ounces, dissolve it in common *Aqua fortis,* draw off the Phlegm, to the remainder add six Drachms of *Sal Harmoniack,* and pour on new *Aqua fortis,* draw off again in Ashes to an oleity, this repeat four times with new *Aqua fortis,* then urge it strongly, and the *Luna* will ascend together with the *Aqua fortis.*

Sometimes he volatilized Gold and Silver together with this Menstruum. In Tinctura Regis Julaton. pag. 16. Aurei veller. Take of the filings of Gold of *Sal Harmoniack,* each two Ounces, to which put four Ounces of the best Silver dissolved in eight Ounces of *Aqua fortis,* draw off to an Oleity, pour on new *Aqua fortis,* and repeat three times with new *Aqua fortis,* and the Gold will ascend with the Silver through the Alembick.

Lully *made his* Aqua Regis *by dissolving Vegetable* Sal Harmoniack *in the acid Water of Mercury sublimate.*

93. The *Aqua Regis* of *Lully.* *In Exp.* 17.

TAke Mercury being twice sublimed with Vitriol, and common Salt prepared, each time with new materials, grind, and if there be one Pound of sublimate, take the whites of nine new laid Eggs, which whites beat so long, that it seems to be Water ; then mix the white with that sublimate, and put it in a Retort with a long Neck, joyn a Receiver to it very close, giving it a Fire of Ashes at the beginning most gentle, till it distils by that degree : The distillation ceasing, increase the Fire, and at last give a most violent Fire, and by this means part of the Mercury will turn into Water, and part into running Mercury, which running Mercury being gone over sublime again, then grind and joyn it with the distilled Water, and distil again as before, repeating the Magistery, till all the sublimate is gone over, and converted into Water: Wherefore you may the same way multiply it as often as you please, always putting new sublimate to the Water, and distilling till it be converted into Water.

Now

Now take this Water, put it in a small Urinal (*Cucurbit*) joyning a Head to it with a Receiver, then distil by Balneo, till the white seems to be gone over mixt with it, which you will thus know; take an Iron or Copper Plate, upon which let one drop of the distillation fall, if it boyls and seems to dissolve, take away the Receiver, joyning another very well luted, and distil by Ashes, and again by Ashes repeat this Magistery seven times: And thus you will have a Mercurial Water, which will serve you in many operations: Take now one Ounce of the Salt of the second Experiment (*Volatile Salt of Tartar, declared in Numb.* 17.) and four Ounces of this Water (*the acid Water now distilled from Mercury sublimate*) mix them together, and the mixture will presently be dissolved; being dissolved, distil by Ashes with a gentle Fire luting the Joynts well, in the last place increase the Fire, that all the Salt may with the Water pass through the Alembick, then again put one other Ounce of the Salt into the same Water, and by distillation pass it all over as before, and thus repeat this Work of distillation four times, in every distillation adding an Ounce of the said Salt to that Water: Then will you have at length a Mineral Water vegetated and acuated, with the augmentation of Virtue and Power proceeding from the said most precious Vegetable Salt, without which is nothing done.

Our Annotations upon the Receipts are:

1. *That the* Menstruums *of this Kind are simple Vegetable* Menstruums *of the sixth Kind, dissolved in Acids. Take away the Acidity, and it will be a* Menstruum *again of the sixth Kind.*

2. *That these* Menstruums *are better made of* Aqua fortis, *it being an Acid stronger than the rest: yet that they may be also made of any other Acid less strong, as distill'd Vinegar, Spirit of Salt, Sulphur*, &c.

3. *That these are the best of all the simple Mineral* Menstruums, *both in the facility of making, and excellency of Virtue.*

4. *That it is much at one, whether the Metal be first dissolved in common* Aqua fortis, *and then the Vegetable* Sal Harmoniack *added, or the said Salt first, and then the Metal.*

5. *That these* Aqua regisses *differ from the common, in that they dissolve all Metals promiscuously, Silver as well as Gold, and reduce the same not into a Calx, but Oyl, which cannot be said of common* Aqua regis.

6. *That Metals dissolved in these* Menstruums *and sublimed, become the greatest Poysons belonging to this Art.*

The

The Nineteenth KIND.

Mineral Menstruums compounded of the Philosophers *Spirit* of *Wine*, and *Acid Spirits* tinging, *Spirit* of *Vitriol*, *Butter* of *Antimony*, &c.

94. Spirit *of* Vitriol *mixt with the* Spirit *of* Wine *of* Lully.

Epist. accurtatoria, pag. 327.

THE *Spirit* of *Vitriol* is more dry and thick, than the *Spirit* of the *Quintessence* of *Aqua ardens*, and great affinity there is between the *Spirit* of *Vitriol*, and the Nature of Gold, because they are both derived from the same Principles with Minerals: The *Spirit* therefore of *Vitriol* being joyned with the *Spirit* of *Aqua ardens*, inspissates it, and makes it suddenly adhere to Gold, so as to be fixed with it; and believe me, this is a very excellent way of Abbreviation.

Annotations.

THis Difference you may observe between the Simple and Compounded Mineral Menstruums; *The Simple dissolve only, but the Compounded do both dissolve and tinge things dissolved; for they are in a wonderful manner exalted by things tinging, and made many degrees better, so as to have enough to serve themselves, and others also, and therefore may deservedly be called graduated, as well as graduatory Waters. Hitherto we have treated of the Simple; In*

Nineteenth Kind, we are to consider them as Compounded, of two Spirits, Oyley and Acid tinging, as in the prescribed Receipt of the Spirits *of* Philosophical-Wine *and* Vitriol *mix'd together, and intimately joyned by two or three distillations. The Preparation is most easie, in which notwithstanding it will not be impertinent to take notice of this one thing ; that both* Spirits *must be without Phlegm, and exquisitely rectified according to the Advice of the following Anonymus.* A burning Oleity is made out of Wine, therefore it participates with Sulphur, and herein is indeed the greatest virtue of the Metallick Nature, which it drew and conceived from the Earth ; and as this Oleity, the Spirits that is, are much more agil than the Spirits of other things ; therefore their Virtues are much more agil than the Virtues of other things : but yet you must know that those Spirits (as saith the Text of Alchymy, and as indeed the truth is) which come out of Vegetables and Animals, conduce not to Alchymy as they are in a Vegetable Nature, but it is requisite for them to attain to a Metallick Nature by many depurations and distillations, and then they are serviceable to it: Therefore is there one only stone, and one foundation necessary to the Art, namely, the Metallick virtue, though sometimes Vegetable and Animal things are taken, yet they do not remain in a Vegetable or Animal Nature, but are transmuted into a Metallick and Sulphureous Nature, which contains a Metallick Virtue. Whereupon, said *Ferrariensis*, cap. 20. *suarum Quæstionum* : It is impossible to coagulate *Argent-vive*, without Sulphur, or something that hath a sulphureous Nature, because Sulphur is the coagulum of *Argent vive*, and if there be sulphureities in Wine, having a burning faculty, it argues there is a Metallick Nature in it : wherefore some do operate in Wine and Gold or Silver, to extract out of the Wine its most subtil Spirit, strengthning the virtue of Gold with it, that so the Spirits may be fixed with it, by which consequently the Tincture of the Gold is dilated and multiplied, and of a certain there is a very great coherence or participation between the Spirits of Wine and the Spirits of Gold, they being both of a hot Nature, and therefore the Spirits of Wine are inseparably fixed with Gold ; yet it is to be noted, that the Spirits of middle Metals, as *Vitriol*, &c. are of larger fixation, and more nearly allied to Gold, both

springing

ſpringing as it were out of one Fountain, namely, out of the Mines of Metals, than the Spirits of Wine; which proceed from a Vegetable Nature; though the Spirits of Wine are more agil and ſubtil. Some therefore do compound the Spirits of them, ſo as to joyn the Spirits of *Vitriol* with the Spirits of *Wine*, to inſpiſſate one with the other, and to make them more eaſily united to Gold: But he that intends to operate with theſe things, muſt take the ſtrongeſt Spirits, and the pureſt Matters, ſo that the Spirits muſt be exactly purified before they are fixed with Gold or Silver. *Anonym. de Principiis Natur. & Arte Alchym. pag.* 30. *Syntagm. Hermon. Rhenani,*

Not only the rectified Spirit of Vitriol, *but every Acid Spirit, is here effectual, provided it be tinging, and mixed with the* Spirit *of* Philoſophical Wine, *thereby to be made a* Menſtruum *of the ſame Kind. 'Tis thus made:*

95. The Butter of *Antimony* mix'd with the *Spirit* of *Wine* of *Baſilius.*

Pag. 88. *Currus Triumphalis Antim.*

TAke of *Common Mercury* moſt purely ſublimed, of *Antimony*, equal parts, grind, mix and diſtil by a Retort, which retains the Spirits, three times; rectifie this Oyl with the *Spirit* of (*Philoſophical*) *Wine*, and it is prepared, and of a Blood-colour; in the beginning it was white, and thickens as Ice or melted Butter. This Oyl hath done many wonderful things; yet the Virtue, Faculty, and Operation of it hath always appeared, making an ill thing good.

This Compoſition, though given by Baſilius, *as a* Medicine, *not as a* Menſtruum, *yet is by* Paracelſus *in Libro de Gradationibus, deſcribed as ſuch.*

6. The

96. The Water of the fourth Gradation of *Paracelsus.*

Libro de Gradationibus, pag. 131.

TAke of *Antimony* one pound, of *Mercury Sublimate,* half pound, distil both together with a violent Fire through an Alembick, and a redness willl ascend like Blood,thick,which tingeth and graduates any *Luna* into *Sol,* and brings this pale Colour to the highest degree, of a permanent Colour.

Though Paracelsus *thought it not always necessary to admonish his Disciples of the* Spirit *of* Philosophical Wine *as an addition in his Compositions, yet nevertheless ought I to declare to you the necessary addition of this* Spirit *in this* Menstruum, *that you may not err; for without it, it would be of no consequence, but rather a dammage to you in the more secret Chymy*:

The Adepts *made sometimes* Menstruums *of this Kind, not with the* Spirit *of* Philosophical Wine, *but the* Matter *of it, namely, some* Vegetable Oleosum, *Thus*;

97. The Water of the sixth Gradation of *Paracelsus.*

Libro de Gradationibus, pag. 132.

TAke of *Sulphur vive,* two pounds, of *Linseed Oyl,* four pounds, boyl them to a Composition (*commonly called the* Liver *of* Sulphur) which must be distilled into an Oyl (*by a peculiar and Philosophical manual Operation, appertaining to the making of the* Spirit *of* Philosophical Wine:) To this must be added again the same quantity of *Sulphur vive,* and boyl'd as before to a Composition, and digested in Horse-dung for a Month, or if longer, better: Then must be added of *Sal Niter, Vitriol, Alume* (*Ingredients of* Aqua fortis) *Flos Æris, Crocus* of *Mars, Cinabar,* (*to increase the Tincture of the* Sulphur) of each half a Verto (*einem halben vierling, that is, a fourth part of half a pound, or two ounces*) distil whatsoever will ascend, and take away the Liquors, the Oyls only being kept (*not*

Oyl,

Oyl, but Oyls, because they are two, White and Red) which must be put into a glass Cucurbit, the *Species* being added, as before, and the *Caput mortuum* pulverized; distil them again together as before; then pour the distillation back to the Fæces, and let it be putrified again for a Month, and distilled again: Then the Colours being evacuated or separated (*the Red from the White*) keep the Red, and rectifie it as is requisite, in which let Plates of *Luna* be digested a due time, and then reduced by cupellation.

Paracelsus *sometimes made this* Oyl *or* Fire *of* Sulphur *by it self, without other tinging things for the graduating of pretious Stones as well as Metals.* It is come to that, *saith he, pag.* 200. *Lib. de Sulph.* that the Spirit of Transmutation hath given his Receipt of making a Liver or Lung out of *Linseed Oyl* and *Sulphur:* The distillation of this Lung or Liver is done many ways; but it is found by operating, that this Liver yields a Milk nothing differing from common Milk, being thick and fat; it yielded also a red Oyl like Blood: This Milk and that Blood confounded not their Colour and Essence by distillation, but remained distinct and separate one from the other, the White setling to the bottom, and the Red ascending to the top: Now Art has been solicitous in making Silver out of the White or Milk, and out of the Red, Gold; but to me it is plain that never any thing could be either by the Ancient or Modern Philosophers done with the White or Milk (*of Sulphur*) I do therefore affirm that Milk to be dead, and nothing contained in it: But as to the Red Oyl which yields the Liver, observe, every Cristal or Beril being first well polished or purified, &c. (See *the fourth Book concerning the Use of this Oyl in the Gradations of Pretious Stones*) exalts Gems even to the highest degree, yea higher than they can be exalted by Nature. Here also note, that all Silver put into it a due time, at length grows black, and leaves a golden Calx, yet not fixed before its exact time, but a volatile and immature thing; but if it hath its time, it performs all things feasible, whereof no more must be here declared. Thus therefore observe of *Sulphur*, if it be taken into degrees, the more subtil, clearer, higher, and of quicker operation it is, the higher and better it is: This way are Metals and Stones made. He that is about to attempt it,

must

must not think, but know himself able; for it is, as to Operation, the most dangerous Labour in all Alchymy, and therefore requires notable Experience, and repeated Practice, nor must he proceed by Hear-say, but by much Experience, *&c.*

Yet not being satisfyed with the strength of this Oyl in this twelfth gradation, he was willing to exalt it yet higher with other tinging things, as Flores Æris, *and* Crocus *of* Mars, *by which* Paracelsus *meant not Common but Philosophical Medicines.* We perceive, *saith he, Lib.* 4. *Archid. de Essentiis, pag.* 16. Verdegrease is accounted the Quintessence of *Venus*, whereas it is not; but the *Crocus* of *Venus* is a Quintessence so to be understood. *Flos Æris* is a (*common*) transmutation with a thick and subtil substance together, extracted out of the whole Complexion of Copper, wherefore it can be no Quintessence; but the *Crocus* of *Venus*, as we have taught, is a true Quintessence, it being a potable thing, without corrosion, and in mixtion divided from the Body, very subtil, yea more than I am minded here to write, to avoid prolixity. So also the *Crocus* of *Mars* and the rust of it has hitherto been esteemed a Quintessence, it not being so; but the (*true*) *Crocus* of *Mars* is the Oyl of *Mars*, (*which is sometimes in a dry form under the Name of an Essence, and called the* Philosophical Crocus *of* Mars *in the second Book of Medicines.*

From the Receipts we observe.

1. *That common Spirit of Vitriol, Butter of Antimony, Arsenick, Tin,* &c. *mix'd with the Spirit of* Philosophical Wine, *are Philosophical Spirit of Vitriol, Philosophical Butter of Antimony,* &c.

2. *That the Menstruums of this Kind, are the same with the Menstruums of the Fifteenth Kind; but with this difference, namely, in that, Philosophical Vinegar not tinging is prepared, but in this, Philosophical Vinegar tinging; because these are made of the Acid Spirits of things tinging, that is* Metals *and* Minerals; *but those of the Acid Spirits of things not tinging, that is, Vegetable Salts, and some Minerals, whose dry part was neither Metal, nor any coloured B.dy.*

3. *That these Menstruums are not only dissolving Waters, but also gradatory, because prepared with things tinging.*

4. *That these Menstruums are the Essences of things tinging, or Magisteries dissolved in an Acid, and consequently Medicines.*

5. *That*

5. *That these* Menstruums, *may be also made of crude Oyls; provided a Man knows the way of preparing the Spirit of* Philosophical Wine.

6. *That the same two Oyls of Sulphur (whereof the Red is an Essence, after the way of* Paracelsus, *that is, the best) which* Paracelsus *elsewhere prepares with the most strong* Aqua fortis, *described before in Numb.* 91. *are here made by the same Author, of a crude oyly matter.*

7. *That* Vegetables *and* Animals *as such, and crude, are not Ingredients in Philosophical Works, but as they are made incombustible, and reduced into a Metallick Nature.* The said separation, *saith the Author of* Via Veritatis, *pag.* 253. You must well observe, for from hence the Ancient Sophi took occasion to inquire into the Three Natures (*Three Kingdoms*) namely, the *Vegetable*, *Animal*, and *Mineral*; and they so much learned from it, that the separation of Natures is nothing else but a defect of coction in Nature: Then they considered them somewhat further, how (for instance) those Essences, which were most weakly cocted by Nature, might be succoured in a Natural way, with common Fire, that the Essences which are now combustible, may by their Liquors (which the Ancients through envy called Mercury, and are black, separated from the Essence) be made perfect by Art, so as that the Essences may remain with the Liquor safe and secure from burning, and the Liquor not be able to separate it self from the Essence: This the Ancients called our Sulphur; for according to this preparation, the Essence is no more *Vegetable*, nor *Animal*, but now by coction made a *Mineral Essence*, and therefore called Sulphur. And afterwards, *pag.* 264. he thus proceeds, One Nature is more cocted by its moisture with its Elementary Fire, than another, whereof the Vegetable Nature is in coction the least, because the Essence of it is easily burned, and the Liquor also is most easily separated from the Elementary Fire, by the help of common Fire. The *Animal* Nature is in coction not much unlike the former (Vegetable Nature) the Essence of it being likewise easily burned, and there-

 fore

fore the Mineral Nature is in coction the highest, because the Metalick Liquor will be more and better united by coction with the Elementary Fire, than the other two aforesaid Natures: Wherefore also, Metals do resist common Fire, better than the other things comprehended under a Vegetable and Animal Nature, as you may see by Metals put into Fire, which do not Flame as Wood; for the Essence of it is not so concted with Liquor, as the Metalick moisture with its Essence; and the conjunction of the Liquor with the Essence is not Metalick, but simply Vegetable, which is consumed in a black Fume. But when the Essence hath attained to coction by Nature, then it remains not a Vegetable, but is now made a Metalick, and is now consumed in a white Fume by common Fire, no otherwise than as you see in perfect Metals, when they are melted in Fire, disperse a white Fume from them. Now consider, *saith* Chortalasseus, *or the Author of* Arca arcani Artificiosissimi, *in his* Cabula Chymica, *pag.* 369: *Vol.* 6. *Th. Chym.* by way of advice; how the aforesaid Speeches of *Vegetables* and *Animals* are to be taken, neither of them must be rejected; for they differ one from the other no otherwise, than that the Vapour is purer, and of greater quantity in one than the other; but you may make the more impure, like to the pure Vapour, for they may by subtil management be so reduced, that those two, that is, the *Animal* and *Vegetable*, in a Watry Body may be taken together with the *Mineral Spirit* or *Vapour*, and then the *Mineral Spirit* separated from the rest with great discretion, which though it shews it self in a small quantity, is notwithstanding of the greatest Virtue, and clearer than the Light at Noon: In this state will that Spirit if you please bring the *Animal* and *Vegetable Spirit*, so as to be like it self. This is the Foundation of the whole Art, that is, for the *Vegetable* or *Animal Spirit* to leave its combustibility, and become Incorruptible, and Immortal: This is the Key to open all Gates; here you have the true first matter of Gems, and Metals: Yet if I consider this thing rightly, it is not the first Matter, but a threefold extraction out of the first matter of Gems; and therefore you ought to to praise God Eternally, and give him thanks in making you worthy of this matter, and vouchsafing you so much understanding, whereby to obtain to your use that which is the deepest in the Earth. I proceed in this first matter; which if you make Liquid, and open by the incombustible *Vegetable Spirit (not common)* you will be able to dissolve Gold, Silver, all Minerals, and Gems in it, and make it melt like Ice in warm Water, destroy, mortifie, and renew it again; by this means I say, visibly obtain, see, touch, and perceive an Astral Spirit (as a Lanthorn, wherein the Eternal Fire, and Virtue of the highest Star of Eternal Wisdom dwelleth) you will I say, with your Eyes behold an inconsumptible Fire, shining Night and Day; Sun, Moon, Stars, Carbuncles, and a Splendor exceeding all manner of Fire; and observe the perfection of the whole Firmament in it. O man, my Creature! how great a Divine Gift, as that which is above all the Heavens, most excellently clear, and is most deep in the Earth, may you in a few Hours time obtain, whereas she hath been a vast time employed in it, and in subtilty is far inferior to you, &c. *The same Author of this first matter in his Rusticus. pag.* 308. *of the said Volume, thus*: This Doctrine certainly is very worthy of Observation; for many Notable Men, do herein err, thinking they have the first matter, when they have obtained the Philosophers Mercury, or Salt of Metals: For the first matter is made when the Man and Woman are joyned together, witness Count *Bernhard*, saying: Then is the Conjunction called the first Matter, and not before; that is, of the Stone, and all Metals; concerning which see *Turba*: For before this is done, we do according to the foundation of Nature, and with good reasons deservedly reject *Animals* and *Vegetables*, as things extraneous, and contrary and ineffectual to our Work, and our Stone we place rightly among *Minerals*.

8. *That both Spirits ought to be warily mixed, because of the danger of overmuch effervescence.*

9. *That these* Menstruums *are by digestion made sweet, and called the sweet Spirit of Vitriol, sweet Butter of Antimony.*

10. *That the Spirit of* Philosophical Wine *is sometimes not expressed in the Receipts of* Menstruums; *but it appears by collateral places, and necessity requires it to be understood.*

The

The Twentieth KIND.

Mineral Menstruums Compounded of the *Spirit* of *Philosophical Wine*, and other tinging things; *Vitriol, Cinabar, Antimony, Lapis Hæmatites*, &c.

98. *Oyl of Vitriol of* Basilius.

Cap. 6. Sect. 2. Libri de Conclusionibus.

TAke *Hungarian* Vitriol, dissolve it in distilled Water, coagulate, cristallize, repeat five times, and so purge it from the Salts, Alume, and Niter: This Vitriol thus purged, distil with the Spirit of (*Philosophical*) Wine to a red Oyl, which ferment with Spiritual Gold; add to it, its part of the Mercury of Stibium, and you have a Tincture for Man, and reducing *Luna* into *Sol. Visitando Inferiora Terræ, Rectificandoq; Invenies Occultum Lapidem, Veram Medicinam.*

Annotations

THE *Antecedent Kind contained* Mineral Menstruums, *compounded of Acid Spirits containing a Metalick Tincture in them; in this present we use the Bodies of these Spirits, to make the* Menstruums *a degree better. For a Tincture, for Example*

ex

extracted out of the dry part or body of Vitriol distilled, with the Spirit of Philosophical Wine *is an Essence, which being in the same distillation dissolved in its own Acid Part, produced a* Menstruum *of this Kind; whereas in the Precedent Kind, that small quantity of Copper, dissolved or contained in common Spirit of Vitriol, and elevated with a violent Fire, is by the Spirit of* Philosophical Wine *reduced not into the Essence, but Magistery, little effectual as well through the smalness of its quantity as Tincture: This present Oyl of Vitriol is not the least esteemed among the Secrets of* Basilius, *and therefore we will a little more exactly consider his most clear description, that by his more abundant Light, we may Illustrate darker places. First,* Basilius *bids us purifie Roman Vitriol by divers solutions, and coagulations; which purification is necessary to separate the Vitriol from strange Dust, Dross, and other impertinent Offals; yet this we think Superfluous, when the Vitriol is purely cristallized, for the Terestreity setling in the dissolution of Vitriol, is not Fæces, but Copper, less dissolved than the rest, and left by the Acid, being too much diluted with common Water: The Vitriol being purified, he enjoyns to be distilled with the Spirit of Wine into a red Oyl.*

He reduced not only Natural Vitriol, but also Artificial Vitriols made of Metals into such Oyls. The Sugar or Vitriol of Saturn *he distills together with the Spirit of Wine into a red Oyl, curing Melancholy, the French Disease,* &c. *Coagulating and fixing Mercury, but, if fixed with the Mercury of Mars, tinging thirty parts of Mercury into Gold. Libro de Conclu. Tract. 2. Sect. 1. Cap. 1, de Sulphure Saturni.* The same way, *saith he,* is a red sweet Oyl tinging Saturn into Gold, to be distilled out of Sugar or Vitriol of *Jupiter,* in the following *Chapter, which he repeats* in *Sect. 2. Cap. 2. de Vitriolis Saturni & Jovis.* Argent vive *he dissolves in* Aqua fortis, *and being reduced into Cristal or Vitriol, distils with the Spirit of Wine rectify'd before with the Salt of Tartar* (the Menstruum described in Numb. 18.) *into a sweet Oyl, curing the French Pox, Old Ulcers, Palsie,* &c. *to be joyned to Martial Tinctures in the Transmutation of Metals. Sect. 2. Cap. 5. de Vitriolo Mercurii: The more fixed Metals, Gold and Silver he distills in Balneo Regis (in Numb. 89.) through an Alembick, which, the* Menstruum *being drawn off, he reduceth into Volatile Vitriols, to be* di-

distilled with the Spirit *of* Wine *into Oyls. Sect. 2. Cap. 1. De Vitriolo Solis et Luna. The more dry Metals, Iron and Copper, he prescribes to be distilled into the same Oyls, but omits the way of distilling. Sect. 1. Cap.* 3. De Sulphuribus Martis & Veneris, *Sect.* 2. *Cap.* 3. De Vitriolo Martis. *Cap.* 4. De Vitriolo Veneris; *but the following Kind of* Menstruum *will prove that they are to be distilled with Philosophical Vinegar: By these places compared together, we are better assured of divers things: First that the Oyl of Vitriol is not any common Acid of Vitriol, though drawn out of Vitriol most exquisitely purify'd, for the same Oyls may be made with the Vitriols of all Metals by the same Spirit of Wine. Secondly, that common Spirit of Wine is altogether useless to this Work; but that the* Philosophical, *or* Menstruum *rather described in Numb.* 18. *is meant by* Basilius *by the Spirit of Wine. Moreover, that the Vitriols of* Saturn *and* Jupiter *do yield sweet Oyls, because made of some weak Acid, namely, common Vinegar, which is easily altered or transmuted by this Philosophical* Menstruum. *But that the Oyls of the other Metals, being made with stronger Acids, either Philosophical Vinegar, or* Mineral Menstruums *do remain Acid, especially the present Oyl of Vitriol, in the distillation of which, the* Spirit *of* Philosophical Wine, *or* Vegetable Menstruum *is dissolved by the Natural Acid, or common Oyl of Vitriol, and with such a prevalent Acidity, ascends in the form of a red Oyl. Lastly, that this Oyl of Vitriol is commended to us by* Basilius *as a* Menstruum *to be fermented with Gold; which we would have you take special notice of; for* Basilius *hath here and there in his Books discovered many notable things concerning the* Meustruum *of Vitriol, but most rarely advised the distillation of it with the* Spirit *of* Philosophical Wine; *yet without which all Processes and Labours, all Endeavours and experiments are vain, and of no importance in the more* Secret Chymy.

For the making this Oyl of Vitriol the Adepts *sometimes dissolved it in the* Spirit *of* Philosophical Wine; *which afterwards being cristallized, they called Vitriol corrected or graduated. Of this correction or graduation of Vitriol* Paracelsus, *thus:* The Description of Vitriol, *saith he*, is to be directed to *Medicine* and *Alchymy*: In *Medicine* it is an excellent Remedy: In *Alchymy* it is good for many other things; but the Art of *Medicine* and *Alchymy*, con-

sists

ſiſts in the preparation of *Vitriol*: For the Crude is not ſuch, but like Wood, out of which any thing may be carved. *Lib. de Vitriolo, pag.* 200. At firſt, *he proceeds*, the Spirit of Vitriol being obtained, the cuſtom was to graduate it to the higheſt, wherewith being exalted, they cured the Epilepſie, whether new or old, in Men and Women, of what condition ſoever, &c. But let us return to the beginning, how the Spirit of Vitriol was found; Firſt they diſtilled the moiſt Spirit of Vitriol by it ſelf from the Colcothar, then they extended its degree by diſtilling and circulating it alone to the higheſt, as the proceſs teacheth: Thus the Water began to be uſed for ſeveral Diſeaſes, as well Internal as External, as alſo for the Falling Sickneſs; ſo a wonderful Cure was performed: But thoſe that came after were much more diligent in the extraction; for they took the *Spirit* of *Vitriol*, corrected as before, and diſtill'd it with the Colcothar eight or ten times with a moſt ſtrong Fire; ſo the dry Spirits were mixed with the moiſt: They urged the work ſo long, continually and without intermiſſion extracting, till the dry Spirits were over, then they graduated both Spirits, the moiſt as well as the dry, in a Phial together their own time: This Medicine they found to be of much greater operation againſt Diſeaſes, that they confounded all the Humoriſts in general: Yet is there ſome correction by Artiſts added by *Spirit* of *Wine*, for better penetration ſake, but of no higher degree: But I will communicate to you my proceſs, which I commend to all Phyſitians, eſpecially for the Epilepſie, which hath the only cure in Vitriol; wherefore even the Charity of our Neighbour, requires us to appoint the more diligent care in that Diſeaſe: Now my Proceſs is for the *Spirit* of (*Philoſophical*) *Wine* to be imbibed by the Vitriol, and then diſtilled, as I ſaid, from the dry and moiſt Spirits, &c. But you muſt further know, that the aforeſaid Receipts of making the moiſt Spirit of Vitriol cannot be more clearly deſcribed; for an Artiſt is required to underſtand it; thoſe ſordid Boylers do not in the leaſt underſtand a thing of ſo great moment. You muſt expect ſufficient information of all things, from Artiſts (*of the more ſecret Chymy*) *Alchymiſts* and *Operators*, ſo alſo to be more inſtructed by the ſame in the way of correcting the *Spirit* of *Wine*.

Baſilius *in his Elucidat.* 12. *Clavium. Where he made the following* Menſtruum *ſpoke of ſuch a graduated Vitriol, not common.* 99.

99. A *Menstruum* of *Basilius* made of *Hungarian Vitriol.*

In Elucid. 12. *Clavium.*

IF you have obtained such a highly graduated and well prepared *Mineral*, called *Vitriol*, most humbly beseech God to give Understanding and Wisdom for the success of your Intention, and when you have calcined it, put it into a *Retort* well luted: Distil it at first with a slow Fire, then increase it, and the *White Spirit* of *Vitriol* will appear in the form of a horrid Fume or Wind, and passeth into the Receiver so long as any of the same Matter is in it: And take Notice, that in this Wind are hidden all the Three Principles, proceeding from one and the same Habitation; it is not necessary therefore to be always diving in pretious Things, because by this Means a nearer way to the Mysteries of Nature lies open, and is obvious to all Men apt to learn Art and Wisdom. Now if you can well and purely separate and free this *Expelled Spirit* by the way of Distillation, from its terrene Moisture, then will you find in the bottom of the Glass Treasure, and the Fundamentals of all the *Philosophers*, hitherto known to few, which is a Red Oyl ponderous as Lead or any Gold whatsoever, as thick as Blood, of a burning and fiery quality, which is the true Fluid Gold of the *Philosophers*, which Nature compacted of the Three Principles, in which are found *Spirit*, *Soul*, and *Body*, and it is *Philosophical Gold*, that (*Spirit of Philosophical Wine*) excepted, with which the Dissolution of it is performed, &c.

Cinabar the Adepts sometimes added to the Vitriol *thus.*

 100. The

100. The Mineral Menstruum of *Isaacus*. *Pag. 59. Manus Philos.*

TAke of the *Roman Vitriol* calcined to Redness, and *Cinaber* an equal quantity, mix and pulverize, then pour *Aqua Vitæ* to them, distill and cohobate upon the *Caput Mortuum* three or four times.

The same Menstruum *hath* Lully *in Magia Naturali*, but *instead of the* Caput mortuum, *he takes new Species in every Rectification.*

101. The Stinking *Menstruum* of *Lully* made of *Vitriol* and *Cinabar*. *Pag. 371. Magiæ Naturalis.*

AFter the Fourth Distillation of the Water aforesaid (*Aqua Vitæ or Ardens made of Philosophical Wine*) Distill seven times with an equal weight of good *Cinabar* and *Vitriol*, putting in new things every time constantly, and drying the Matter of the Stone (*Vitriol* and *Cinabar*) well in every Distillation, before you pour in the Aqua (*Vitæ*) &c.

102. The same Stinking *Menstruum* of *Lully*. *Epist. Accurtatoria Pag. 327.*

THe Vegetable Stone being Distilled (*the Vegetable* Menstruum *or rather* Aqua ardens, *or the* Spirit *of* Philosophical Wine) till the Water is free from Phlegme, and that commonly is in the fifth time, take an equal Weight of *Vitriol* very clear, and of the best *Cinabar*, mix and grind them well together, dry the Matter in the Sun, till all the moisture is exhaled; then cast in your Water, and Distil first with a gentle Fire, and

and strong in the end, as the custom is in preparing the Philosophers Acute Water; and then the Spirits or Quintessence of *Vitriol* and *Cinabar*, which do principally make the Mineral Stone (*Mineral Menstruum*) do mix and joyn together with the Spirit of the Quintessence of *Aqua Ardens*, which Spirit is the Vegetable Stone; and this continue ten Times, beginning after the fifth (*five times after the fifth Rectification of the Spirit of Philosophical Wine*) and so continue the Distillations five times with those Bodies (*Vitriol* and *Cinabar*:) And you must remember to make the things thorough dry, before you put them into the Water, so that all the Water (*all the Phlegme*) must be dried up (*evaporated*) and the Spirits remain, which must be joyned together, because of the strength of the *Aqua Ardens*; and every Distillation you must put in new things.

To Vitriol *and* Cinabar *he sometimes added* Niter; *thus he made this, call'd*

103. The Stinking *Menstruum* of *Lully* made of common *Vitriol*, *Cinabar*, and *Niter*. *In Clavicula. Pag. 299. Vol. 3. Th. Chym.*

TAke of *Roman Vitriol* calcined to Redness three Pounds, of Salt Peter one Pound, of Cinabar three Ounces, grind all together upon a Marble, then put the Matter in a thick and strong Body (*Cucurbit*) and pour *Aqua Vitæ* seven times Rectify'd upon it, and put it in Horse Dung fifteen days, the Vessel being well Sealed: Then Distil with a soft Fire, till you have all the Water in the Receiver, then increase the Fire till the Head (*Alembick*) be red; then strengthen the Fire till the Head (*Alembick*) be white, then let the Vessel cool, take away the Receiver, Seal it very well with Wax, and keep it for occasion: Take Notice that the *Menstruum* ought to be seven times rectify'd by Distillation, every time casting away the Feces, before it be made use of.

Besides the Ingredients of Aqua Fortis and Cinabar, he sometimes adds also Tartar calcined thus,

104. The Stinking *Menstruum* of *Lully* made of *Vitriol, Niter, Alume, Tartar*, and *Cinabar*. *In Experimento* 26.

TAke *Aqua Vitæ* so hot as to burn a Linnen Cloth, then take Vitriol free from all Phlegme, so as to Boyl upon Fire without Liquefaction (*Vitriol calcin'd the common way*) the best Sal Niter, Roch Alume dephlegmed and dried, one Pound of all the aforesaid, of white Tartar calcined, and Cinabar of each half a Pound, grind and sift every one severally through a Sieve; then mix, and put the Matter into a Retort, pouring the aforesaid *Aqua Vitæ* upon it, put a Receiver to it, the Joynts being very close, and the Luting first thoroughly dried: The Receiver must be large, as those, wherein *Aqua Fortises* are commonly distilled: Now the Luting being dried, make a gentle Fire at first, till the Retort grows warm, then continue the Distillation in this degree, that you may pronounce ten words between each drop of the Distilling Water, and when it will Distill no more with that Degree of Fire, increase the Fire so as to return the Distillation again to the same ten Words as at first; and this degree continue, till the Distillation increaseth again, and lastly, increase the Fire with Wood, covering the Retort round about with Tiles above, that it may have a Fire of Reverberation; but this observe, the Retort must first be strengthened on all sides with strong Luting, before this Distillation is begun, and when the Distillation is begun, and when the Distillation is, it ought to be placed in a convenient Fornace, with an open Neck; but it would be best and most commodious in this Work, if the Receiver of this Distilling Water could be handsomly set in a Bason full of cold Water, but if that cannot be, you must at least lay Linnen Cloths dip'd in Water upon the Receiver again and again oftentimes; thus the Receiver may not be broken by the violence of the Spirits, all which particulars mark well. The Distillation being ended, let the

the Veſsels cool, and keep the Receiver with the Water very cloſe ſtopped. Then take the ſame Mineral dried, and prepared as before, in the ſame order and meaſure, which grind together, and put into a Retort, as before, and pour the Water a little before Diſtilled upon it, fit a Receiver to it, the Joynts being very well Luted, as before, and having dried the Luting, put Fire under, the Diſtillation being compleated, take again New Materials of the ſame Weight, and put them again into a Retort with their own Water, and Diſtil, as before, with the ſame Degrees of Fire; which being done, and the Veſſel cold, take away the Receiver, and keep it carefully with its Diſtilled Water firmly ſtopped: For you will have a Phyſical Mineral Water, or Stinking *Menſtruum* with its Form: This Water hath the power of Calcining, and at the ſame time diſſolving all Metals with the preſervation of their Vegetative Form: Many Experiments we have herewith both ſeen and done.

Iſaacus Hollandus to augment the ſtrength of theſe Menſtruums, *did rather add ſome tinging Minerals to the Vitriol, than the Acidity of Niter and Alume. Thus he prepared a* Menſtruum *called,*

105. The Diſſolving Water for *the Red*, of the firſt Deſcription of *Iſaacus*. *Cap.* 103. *Oper. Min.*

TAke of *Roman Vitriol* ſix parts, of *Lapis Hæmatites*, *Crocus Martis*, *Cinabar*, *Æs uſtum*, *Mineral Antimony*, of each one part, being well dried; mix, and putting them into a Retort, pour four Pounds of Rectify'd *Aqua Vitæ* to them, Diſtill and Cohobate three times upon the *Caput Mortuum* pulverized.

The following Menſtruum *being like this, proves it to be of a ſanguine colour.*

106. The

106. The Dissolving Water for the Red of the second Description of *Isaacus*. *Cap.* 45. 3. *Oper. Miner.*

TAke of *Mineral Antimony*, *Æs ustum*, *Crocus Martis*, *Cinabar*, of each two parts, of *Vitriol* the weight of all, being all dried and mix'd together, pour to them of *Aqua Vitæ* most purely rectified, the height of two hands; the Vessel being close luted, digest in Balneo the space of ten days, stirring the Matter three or four times every day, that it may be the better incorporated with the *Aqua Vitæ*; these ten days being ended, and an Alembick put on, Distill with a gentle Fire, but at last with a most strong Fire twelve hours together, that all the tinged Spirits may ascend with the *Aqua Vitæ*: This process repeat, always Distilling the Water with new Matters, till it becomes Red as Blood.

To these two we will add also a third Menstruum *of this sort.*

107. A Dissolving Water for the Red of the third Description of *Isaacus*. *Cap.* 61. 3. *Oper. Min.*

TAke of *Roman Vitriol*, *Cinabar*, of each one part, of *Crocus Martis*, *Lapis Hæmatites*, *Æs ustum*, *Verdegreece*, of each half a part; calcine the *Vitriol* first. If you have a mind, you may extract the Tincture out of *Mineral Antimony* with (*Philosophical Vinegar*), and being separated from the *Vinegar*, add it to the former Species, as also as much *Aqua Vitæ* twelve times rectify'd as sufficeth; the Vessel being well luted, digest in Balneo seven or eight times, then having put on an Alembick, and luted the Joynts well, Distill with a gentle Fire two days, then a stronger two days more, then the space of three days, that the Glass may be hot;

hot; the Glaſſes being cold, take out the *Caput Mortuum*, which being well pulverized, digeſt with the Diſtilled Water for the ſpace of eight days, then Diſtill the firſt day gently, the ſecond more ſtrongly, the third moſt ſtrongly for the ſpace of twenty four hours, that the Glaſs may be red hot; then let it cool, the Diſtilled Water digeſt with new Matters, and Diſtill, as before, and that to be three times repeated.

And as theſe Menſtruums *were for Red Tinctures, ſo alſo he made ſome for White Tinctures, thus,*

108. A Diſſolving Water of *Iſaacus* for *the White.* *Cap.* 76. 3. *Oper. Min.*

TAke of *Roch Alume*, *Lapis Calaminaris*, of the *Calx* of *Eggs*, an equal quantity, pour to them as much *Aqua vitæ* rectify'd from all Phlegme as ſufficeth, and diſtil, as the Diſſolving Water for the Red.

109. Another Diſſolving Water of *Iſaacus* for *the White.* *Cap.* 48. 3. *Oper. Min.*

TAke of *Roach Alume*, *Lapis Calaminaris*, *Calx* of *Eggs*, common *Arſenick*, an equal quantity, being all pulverized, mix, and to the Powder pour as much *Aqua Vitæ* well rectify'd, as to be the ſpace of three hands above the Matter, diſtil with a gentle Fire, then a ſtronger, laſtly, for twenty four hours ſo as to be red hot; cohobate the diſtillation yet four times upon the *Caput Mortuum* reduced into Powder.

Many ſuch Menſtruums *as theſe we meet with in ſeveral places of* Iſaacus, *in the Deſcriptions of which, tho the Addition of* Philoſophical Aqua Vitæ *or* Spirit of Wine *be not always expreſs'd, yet that it is to be underſtood in all of them, is evident by the former Receipts of Diſſolving Waters: The* Menſtruums *following may be Examples, in the firſt place that which is called*

110. A

110. A Red Water Shining Day and Night of the First Description of *Isaacus*. *Cap.* 153. *Lib.* 2. *Oper. Min. Pag.* 528. *Vol.* 3. *Th. Chym.*

TAke the Crocus of *Mars*, *Antimony* as it is dugge out of the Mines, *Red Arsenick*, of each one Pound, of *Auripigment* one Pound, of *Roman Vitriol* three Pounds, of *Sal Niter* as much as the weight of all the rest: Grind all together into an impalpable Powder; mix one Pound of *Sal Armoniack* with them, and being well mix'd, put the Matter in an Earthen Vessel, not glazed within, such as can well endure the Fire, and having put on an Alembick, with a Receiver strongly luted, distil *Aqua Fortis*, as it should be, first with a small Fire, then increasing the Fire by degrees, and a *White Water* will distil, which being distilled, the Alembick will begin to be Red or Yellow; then presently take away the Receiver, and add another, soundly luted, and increase your Fire till a *White Spirit* goes over; it is the *Sal Armoniack* which goes over last of all, and strengthen the Fire so long, till the Alembick be altogether clear: When now the *Red Spirit* goes over, nothing (*of Sal Armoniack*) goes with it, and so soon as it is gone over (*the White Water*) the Spirit and (*dry*) Water (*or Sal Armoniack*) go over together, then the Alembick becomes White within, as if it was full of Snow, and then increase the Fire till the Spirit and Water are driven through the Beak by Exhalation, as a Man casts forth his Breath by force; so the Spirit and dry Water do breath through the Pipe of the Alembick into the Receiver, and increase the Fire, and the Spirit and dry Water being gone over, the Alembick becomes clean, clear, white, and transparent; then let it cool, and take it from the Fire, put the Water into a Glass, and stop it close. Take the *Caput Mortuum*, grind it to a fine Powder, put it in pure clear Water for two hours, let it settle, pour off the clear, and pour it upon pure clear Water again, as before, and let it boyl an hour, as before; then let it settle again, add it again to to the former, cast away the Feces, and that which you poured out (the *Solution*) evaporate, and a yellow Powder will remain, weigh it, add as much *Sal Niter*, and mix them together, put them into a Glass, pour your Distilled Water (*or Menstruum*) upon it, put on an Alembick strongly luted all over, adding a Receiver, and leave it three days upon thee Fornace (*to Digest*) before you put Fire under, then kindle your Fire, and Distill first with a small Fire, then sometimes a greater, till the White Spirit is gone over, then cease, and you have a Red Water shining Day and Night, which dissolves fixed *Luna*, as *Luna* is commonly dissolved, and it will take a *Tincture* as the purest *Sol* that ever was seen, yea, it tingeth all *White Metals* of the colour of *Sol*.

111. A *Red Water* shewing Light by Night of the Second Description of *Isaacus*.

Cap. 44. *Oper. Min. Pag.* 458. *Vol.* 3. *Th. Chym.*

TAke of *Roman Vitriol* three Pounds, of *Cinabar*, *Verdegrese*, *Ceruse*, of each half a Pound, of *Crocus Martis*, *Lapis hæmatites* of each four Ounces, of *Sal Niter* as much, as the whole Mass (*five Pounds*) pulverize and mix them well together; divide the Mass into three parts, and of one part make an *Aqua fortis*, which pour upon the powder of another part; distill *Aqua fortis* again, and pour it upon the third powder, and distill *Aqua fortis* again; which being done, pulverize all the three *Caput Mortuums*. Take the Water of *Sal armoniack*, which I shall teach you below to make (*but we have already declar'd it in Numb.* 81.) wherewith grind the aforesaid powder so fine, as that a Painter may paint with it, then dry it in your Dry Stove in glass Dishes being dried, grind it dry upon a Stone, and put it into an earthen Pot, and pour the *Aqua fortis* (*before distilled*) upon it; distill first with a gentle fire the space of twenty four hours, then increase (*the Fire*) as yet 24 hours more, then increase till it begins to shine, then keep it in the same fiery brightneſs ſix hours more, then let it cool, take it away from the Fire, and ſtop the Receiver well: Then grind and pulverize the *Caput Mortuum* upon a Stone with Vinegar diſtilled, and extract the Salt or Element of Earth out of the Feces; put the Salt into a Glaſs, pour yout *Aqua fortis* upon it, the Alembick and Receiver being very cloſe, put the Glaſs in Sand in a Kettle with Water (*in Balneo*) diſtill all that will diſtill, when no more diſtilleth, let the *Balneo* boil a day and a night whether it drops or no: Then let it cool, remove it from the Fire, put it in Aſhes, uſe firſt a weak Fire for 12 hours, then increaſe the Fire yet 12 hours more; then let it be moderately hot, and let it be ſo for ſix hours; then let it cool, take it from the Fire, and cover it well, and having taken away the Feces or Salt, grind them very ſmall with Diſtill'd Vinegar, put it into a Stone Jugge, and a good part of the Diſtillation being poured to it, put it in *Balneo*, doing as was taught before; ſee if it hath yet any Feces, and make the Salt clear; put it again in a Glaſs, pour on the *Aqua fortis* again, do every way as before, three or four times, and all your Matter or Earth will diſtill with the *Aqua fortis*, then take it from the Fire, ſtop cloſe, and keep it well: For you have a pretious Water, above all the Waters that ever I heard of; and believe me in good faith I have ſeen and done alſo my ſelf wonderful things with this Water: This Water I have reduced to a Red Chriſtalline Stone, which would give light by night, ſo as that my Friends might ſee to eat and drink by it. Keep it well for uſe, and eſteem it as the moſt ſecret Water of all you have.

The Method of making ſuch Shining Menſtruums *is better perceived by the following Water.*

112. A Red and Shining *Aqua fortis* of the Third Description of *Isaacus.*

Cap. 72. 1: *Oper. Min. Pag.* 354. *Vol.* 3. *Th. Chym.*

TAke of *Vitriol* clarified and purified from its Feces, of *Sal Niter*, an equal quantity, distill an *Aqua fortis* out of them according to Art, then take the *Caput Mortuum* out of the Glass, and reduce it to a fine Powder; then grind it upon a Stone, then put it in common Distill'd Water, and draw out all the Salt, then filter it, that you may have it clean from Feces; congeal again, and being congealed, make it an impalpable Powder, aud put the Powder into a Glass, and then pour that *Aqua fortis* again upon the Powder which you distill'd from thence, and distill again all that will distill: Then take out the *Caput Mortuum* again, grind it to Powder as before, and do in all things as before; this Operation repeat, till you have distilled all the Salt within the *Aqua fortis:* Then have you an excellent Red Water shining by night like a clear Fire; then rectifie that Water *in Balneo*, oftentimes distilling, and pouring on again, so as at last to have all the Distillation *in Balneo:* Then is your pretious Water prepared, by which you may multiply and open your (*Philosophical*) Stone. *These* Menstruums *are little different, yea almost the same with the former of* Isaacus, *as to the Ingredients as well as Method of preparation, but the addition of the Spirit of Philosophical Wine which* Isaacus *prescribed in those Dissolving Waters, must of necessity be understood in these his* Aqua fortises; *for without this Spirit all these Waters would be common, of no Vertue and Use.*

From

From the Receipts we observe:

1. *That all Tinging Bodies whatsoever being either naturally or artificially dissolved in an Acid, and reduced into* Salt *or* Vitriol *by the help of the Spirit of* Philosophical Wine, *do yield the present* Menstruums, *by these two Methods; either by repeated Cohobation, or Simple Distillation; but in this latter way it is necessary for the* Salts *or* Vitriols *of the said* Bodies *to be first graduated, that is, by various Dissolutions and Coagulations joyned with the Spirit of* Philosophical Wine, *and then distilled, where Caution must be had, lest in this gradation of the* Vitriol, *the Acid, be by Operations less necessary than convenient debilitated; for so you will easily prepare* Menstruums *unexpectedly of the Eighth instead of this Kind.*

2. *That these* Menstruums *differ from* Menstruums *of the Eighth Kind, these being Acid, but those Sweet. Dissolve a Compounded Vegetable* Menstruum *of the Eighth Kind in Distilled Vinegar, Spirit of Sulphur, Common* Aqua Fortis, &c. *and you will immediately have a* Menstruum *of this Kind; on the contrary, debilitate the Acidity of these* Menstruums, *and they will be transmuted into* Menstruums *of the Eighth Kind.*

3. *That these* Menstruums *are the Essences of Things tinging dissolved in an Acid.*

4. *That* Hungarian Vitriol (*Copper naturally dissolved in an Acid*) *tho artificially purged from Heterogeneous Salts and Feces, does neverthelesss as well as other things tinging, require the Spirit of Philosophical Wine, in order to be reduced into an Oil so excellent in Medicine as well as Alchimy.*

5. *That it is even much at one by what Acid Copper or any other tinging Body is reduced into* Vitriol, *provided it be afterwards graduated, that is, mixed with the Spirit of Philosophical Wine: Wherefore you must once for always take notice, that not only in the Writings of* Basilius *and* Paracelsus, *but of other Adepts also, as in* Via Veritatis, &c. *in several places of which you will meet with these Phrases, Things graduated, corrected, exalted,* &c. *you must understand not Common*

Men-

Menſtruums , *but prepared with the Spirit of* Philoſophical Wine , *and ſo made fit for the Works of the more Secret Chymy.*

6. *That* Roman Vitriol *is reduced into ſo Noble an Oil, not by the Spirit of Common but Philoſophical Wine.*

7. *That theſe* Menſtruums *do by continued Cohobations become moſt red , ſhining by Night ſo , that Men at Supper want no other Light ; permanent and multiplying the* Philoſophers Stone ; *but of theſe in their proper places , namely , the Third and Fourth Books.*

The

The One and Twentieth KIND.

Compounded Mineral Menſtruums *of* Simple Mineral Menſtruums *and* Mercury, *the reſt of the Metals, and other Tinging Things.*

113. The Spirit of *Venus* or Spirit of Verdegreece of *Baſilius.*

Libr. Partic. de Particul. Veneris.

TAke of *Copper* as much as you will, of which make *Vitriol* the common way, or inſtead of it take Common Verdegreece ſold in Shops, which will do the ſame thing; to which being pulverized, pour (*Common*) Diſtilled Vinegar, put it in a heat, decant the Vinegar, being tranſparent and green, to the remainder pour new Vinegar, and repeat the Work, till the Vinegar be tinged, and the Matter remain in the bottom of the Veſſel black; draw off the Vinegar being tinged and gathered together either to drineſs, or to a thin Skin, that the *Vitriol* may be Chriſtallized, and you will have the Verdegreece purified (after *the common way*) to which being pulverized, pour the Juice of Unripe Grapes (*Philoſophical Vinegar in Numb.* 74.) put it in a gentle heat, and digeſting you will have a tranſparent Smagradine gragdine Tincture, with which is extracted the *Red Tincture* of *Venus*, an excellent Colour for Painters. This Tincture being extracted, mix all the Extractions together, and draw off the Phlegme gently, that the *Vitriol* being very clear (*graduated*) may be cristallized in a Cold place, whereof if you have a ſufficient quantity, you have alſo enough Matter for the making of the *Philoſophical Stone*; if perhaps you ſhould doubt to perform ſuch a Myſtery with every (*Natural*) Vitriol whatſoever: Concerning this Preparation we lately ſpoke parabolically in *Libro Clavium*, *Capite de* Wein Eſſig. where we ſaid: That common *Azoth* is not the Matter of our *Stone*, but our *Azoth* or firſt Matter extracted by common *Azoth* and *Wine*, which are the expreſſed Juice of unripe Grapes, whereby the Body of *Venus* is to be diſſolved and reduced into *Vitriol*: This is to be well obſerved, for thus you will free your ſelves from many Difficulties. Now out of this *Vitriol* thus prepared, diſtil a *Spirit* and *Red Oil*, &c.

Annotations.

IN *the* Eighth Kind common Mercury *and* Metals *were either by the Spirit of* Philoſophical Wine, *or by ſome* ſimple Vegetable Menſtruums *converted into compounded* Vegetable Menſtruums. *In the* Twentieth *antecedent* Kind, *tinging* Arids *diſſolved in* Acids *are more eaſily diſtilled together with the* Spirit of Philoſophical Wine *into compounded Mineral* Menſtruums: *But the preſent Kind volatilizeth the ſaid Bodies, not by the Spirit of* Philoſophical Wine; *but* Mineral Menſtruums, *that the* Menſtruums *may be thereby made ſooner, eaſier, and of a higher Kind. In the laſt Kind we diſtilled natural* Vitriol, *being macerated in the Spirit of* Philoſophical Wine, *or, which is much more conducible, diſſolved in the ſame Spirit, and reduced into graduated* Vitriol, *into a* Mineral Menſtruum: *For the natural acidity of* Roman Vitriol *for the corroſion of* Copper, *was in the compoſition of it able and ſtrong enough to diſſolve the Spirit of* Philoſophical Wine *in the making of the ſaid*

Men-

Menſtruum; *but here in Artificial* Vitriols *the matter is otherwiſe; for the dry Bodies of Metals co-operating in their Diſſolutions do debilitate the acid, and therefore* Vitriols, *containing this debilitated acidity, are ſcarce fit either for the diſſolution of the Spirit of* Philoſophical Wine, *or the conſtitution of the preſent* Menſtruum: *Wherefore the* Vitriols *of* Saturn *and* Jupiter *being made with a common acid, do by virtue of the Spirit of* Philoſophical Wine, *yield ſweet Oils, or* Vegetable Menſtruums, *not at all acid or mineral; for that weak acid remaining in the Vitriolification of thoſe ſoft Metals, is wholly tranſmuted in the diſſolution of the Spirit of* Philoſophical Wine, *as alſo in the very Diſtillation of it ſelf, ſo that* Vitriol *being artificially made of Copper and Iron by acids, is diſtilled not by the Spirit of* Philoſophical Wine, *but* Mineral Menſtruums, *into a* Menſtruum *of the preſent Kind; but* Gold *and* Silver *need not only theſe Mineral or Stronger* Menſtruums, *but to be likewiſe volatilized by the ſame, and reduced into* Volatile Vitriols.

Thus *Baſilius in Concluſionibus ſuis. Sect. 2. de Vitriolis. Cap. 1. de Vitriolo Solis & Lunæ: reduced Gold* and *Silver into Volatile Vitriol.* It is requiſite, *ſaith he*, firſt to have our Water made of the cold Salt of the Earth (*Niter*) and the Eagle (*Vegetable Salharmoniack*) wherewith Gold and Silver are made ſpiritual, and coagulated into Criſtal, or Metallick *Vitriol*, by which, *&c.* In *Labore primo Libri Revelationis, ut & in Elucidatione 12 Clavium, this Vitriol of Sol is more exactly thus deſcribed:* Take, *ſaith he*, of this Water (the *Kings Bath or Menſtruum deſcribed above in Numb.* 89.) three parts, of the Calx of Gold one part, mixe, put it in a Cucurbit with an Alembick upon hot Aſhes, to be diſſolved, if it be not all diſſolved, pour off the Water and pour on new, and that, till all the Calx is diſſolved in the Water, when it is cold, white Feces ſettle in the bottom, which ſeparate, joyn all the Water together, and digeſt in Balneo a day and a night; then having taken away the Feces, digeſt the ſpace of nine days continually, diſtill away the Water, that the Matter may remain in the bottom like Oyl, the Water diſtilled from it pour on again being heated, diſtill, as before, pour on again, diſtill, and this repeat ſome

certain

certain times, thus will (*the Menſtruum*) be debilitated, then pour new Water to the Matter like Oyl, digeſt a day and a night, diſtill in Sand to an Oyl, pour on Water again being hot; diſtill, and that ſo oft till all the Gold is come over, but this Diſtillation ought to be done in a low Cucurbit, with a flat bottom, put the Golden Water which came over in a cold place, to criſtallize, ſeparate the Water from them. *Guido made the Volatile Vitriol of Gold out of Gold ſublimed: The Gold he ſublimed thus:* Take of Gold calcined twelve times with three parts of Cinabar, or of Leaf Gold four Ounces, of the Oyl of Salt (*the Menſtruum deſcribed in Numb. 76.*) twelve Ounces, diſſolve in aſhes. Draw off the Oyl of Salt from it ſeveral times, putrifie for a Moneth, then diſtill, and all the Gold will be ſublimed, of a Red Colour in the tenth or twelfth Sublimation; but if it will not be ſublimed, joyn all together, and draw off the Phlegme *in Balneo*, to the remainder add of the Oyl of Tartar *per deliquium* four Ounces gradually, and force it with a ſtronger Fire, and the Gold will aſcend Red with the *Menſtruum*, and be precipitated in the bottom of it; decant the Water from the Gold, upon which kindle Rectified Spirit of (*Common*) Wine eight or nine times, to take away all the Acidity of the Oyl of Salt. *Pag.* 11. *Theſaur. Chym. With Gold thus ſublimed he prepared the graduated* Vitriol *of* Sol *by the following Method.* Take of Gold ſublimed four Ounces and a half, pour to it Radical Vinegar (*mix'd with the Spirit of Wine*) the height of three Fingers, digeſt three days *in Balneo*, decant the Vinegar, and pour on new, till all be diſſolved, which draw off *in Balneo*, but beware of too much; put it in a cold Cellar, and the *Vitriol* of *Gold* will be criſtallized of a Ruby or Granat Colour, more or leſs beautiful, according to the Method of Operating; from which decant the Liquor again to be drawn off to a thin Skin, till you have five Ounces of the *Vitriol. Pag.* 19. *Theſaur. Chym. The ſame way alſo he prepared the Graduated* Vitriol *of* Luna, *Pag.* 31. *as alſo of* Mars, *Pag.* 36. *But* Jupiter, *Pag.* 42. Venus, *Pag.* 45. *and* Saturn, *Pag.* 49. *he calcin'd onely, and reduc'd them with the aforeſaid Vinegar into Graduated* Vitriols, *out of all which* Vitriols *may* Men-

Q q ſtruums

ſtruums *of this Kind be diſtilled*, *as* Baſilius *his Spirit of* Venus.

Iſaacus *diſtilled the Spirit of* Saturn *out of the Graduated* Vitriol *of* Lead, *thus*,

114. The Water of Paradiſe of *Iſaacus*. *In Opere Saturni.*

TAke of *Saturn* ten or fifteen Pounds, which no other Metal is mix'd with, beat it into thin Plates, and have a Bottle half full of Vinegar, lute, put it in a warm Balneo, and every three or four days ſcrape the *Saturn* that is calcined from the Plates, gather about five or ſix Pounds of it, grind this calcined *Saturn* (*Ceruſe*) with diſtilled (*Philoſophical*) Vinegar, upon a Marble, ſo as with a Pencil to ſerve for a Picture, then take a Stone Jugg, and therein pour Diſtilled Vinegar to the calcined *Saturn*, leaving a third part of the Jugg empty, mix very well, ſtop it with a Glaſs or Stone Stopple, ſet it *in Balneo*, ſtir it five or ſix times a day with a Woodden Slice or Spoon, ſtop it again, nor heat the *Balneo* more than that you may endure your hand in it; let it thus ſtand 14 days and nights, then pour off the clear, and pour new Vinegar to the Calx not yet diſſolved; mix, proceed, as before, repeating, till all the Calx of *Saturn* is diſſolved; put the *Saturn* being thus diſſolved *in Balneo*, evaporate the Vinegar with a ſlow Fire, the *Saturn* will be reduced into a Maſs, which move to and fro till it be dry; it will be of a Honey Colour, rub it on a Marble with Diſtilled Vinegar, like Soap, put it again in the Stone Jugge, being very well mixed, in a warm *Balneo* the ſpace of five or ſix days; ſtir it every day with a Woodden Slice, ſtop the Glaſs, let it cool, pour off what is diſſolved into another large Stone Jugge, pour other Vinegar to it, mix very well, put it again *in Balneo*, pour off, and thus proceed, till nothing more will be diſſolved, which you may try by your tongue, for if the Vinegar be ſweet, it is not enough diſſolved; or put a little in a Glaſs Cucurbit, and

let

let it evaporate, if any thing remains, all that will be *Gold* is not dissolved, and that which remains in the Jugge, or Feces, if they be sweet upon the tongue, and you find yet something in the Cucurbit that is not enough dissolved, you may dissolve it by pouring new Vinegar to it. These Solutions coagulate, as before, dissolve in Distilled Vinegar, as before; these Coagulations and Solutions continue, till no more Feces remain in the bottom, but are all things dissolved into a clear and limpid Water; then is *Saturn* free from all its Leprosie, Melancholy, Feces, Blackness, and Superfluities, and is pure, as (now, being exempted from all filth) fusible as Wax, and sweet as Sugar, *&c.* Take half of the Purged *Saturn*, put it in a Stone Jugge, and pour to it four Pounds of Distilled Vinegar, put on an Alembick, and distill the Vinegar *in Balneo*, but the Alembick must have a hole in the top, through which pour new Vinegar, distill, as before, pour on new and draw off, and that till the Vinegar be drawn off as strong as it is poured on, then is it enough, because the Matter hath imbibed as much of the Spirits of the Vinegar, as it needs, and as much as it can retain: Take the Jugge from the Fire, and the Alembick being taken off, put the Matter into a Glass that can endure the Fire, put an Alembick to it, put it in a Copel with Ashes in a Fornace; make first a gentle Fire, increase it by degrees, till your Matter goes over of the Colour of Blood, and thickness of Oyl, sweetness of Sugar, and of a heavenly smell; if the heat diminisheth, keep it while the Matter distills, increase the Fire, till the Glass begins to be Fire hot, keep it in this heat, till nothing more distills; let it cool by it self, take away the Receiver, and stop it very well with Wax, beat the Matter (*Caput mortuum*) in an Iron Mortar, with a Steel Pestle, and then grind it upon a Marble with Distill'd Vinegar (*Vinegar mix'd with the Spirit of Philosophical Wine*) put it in a Stone Jugge two parts full, distill by Balneo, pour on new Vinegar, distill as before, repeat, till the Vinegar distills with the same strength as it was poured on; let them cool, distill the Matter in a strong Glass upon Ashes as before, first with a gentle Fire, then a stronger, as you did before, a Red Oil will go over, as before, *&c.* beat the

 Matter,

Matter, and proceed again, till the Matter will retain no more of the Spirit of Vinegar in the Distillation *in Balneo*, then take the Matter, distil what will distil in a glass Cucurbit upon Ashes, till you have distilled the Matter into a Red Oil, which is the noble Water of Paradise, by which all Fixed Stones may be resolved, and the Stone made perfect. This Water of Paradise the Ancients call'd their sharp, clear, Vinegar, *&c.*

Metals sometimes are not reduced into graduated Vitriols *but by repeated Cohobation made* Menstruums *of this Kind. Thus.*

115. The Mercurial Vinegar of *Trismosinus. Libro Moratosan sive Octo Tincturarum in Secunda Tinctura, Pag. 79. Aur. Vell. Germ.*

TAke *Argent Vive* purged the common way, put it in an Alembick, whereto pour very sharp Vinegar (*Vinegar mix'd with the Spirit of Philosophical Wine described before in Numb. 72.*) three Ounces of Vinegar to one Ounce of Mercury; draw off six times *in Balneo*, then force it to ascend into the Receiver, being distilled, rectifie it, and it will be prepared.

Sometimes instead of Philosophical Vinegar he used the strongest Aqua Fortis *described in Numb. 73.*

116. The Mercurial Water of *Trismosinus. Libr. Octo Tinctürar. in Tinct. quarta. Pag. 80. Aurei Vell. Germ.*

TAke of *Roman Vitriol*, *Sal Niter*, of each one Pound and a half, of (*Vegetable*) *Sal armoniack* four Ounces; of Tiles pulverized one Pound, out of which distil *Aqua fortis* by the Rule of Art. Take of Venetian Mer-

Mercury ſublimed (you muſt have a care of its Venemous Fume) four Ounces, put it in a Cucurbit, pour the ſaid *Aqua fortis* to it, draw off ſtrongly, that the Mercury may be well mixed with the *Aqua fortis*, and it will be prepared.

Albertus Magnus *prepared the ſame* Mercurial Water *thus*,

117. The Mercurial Water of *Albertus Magnus. Libro Compoſitum de Compoſitis. Cap. 5. Pag. 937. Vol. 4. Th. Chym.*

TAke of *Roman Vitriol* two Pounds, of *Sal Niter* two Pounds, of *Alume* calcined one Pound; being well ground and mix'd together put the Matter in a fit Glaſs Phial, and having luted the Joynts very cloſe, that the Spirits may not evaporate, diſtill *Aqua fortis* after the common way, firſt with a weak Fire, ſecondly a ſtronger, thirdly with Wood, that all the Spirits may go over, and the Alembick turn white; then put out the Fire, let the Fornace cool, and keep the Water carefully, becauſe it is the Diſſolvitive of *Luna*, keep it therefore for the finiſhing of the Work, becauſe that Water diſſolves *Luna*, ſeparates Gold from Silver, calcines *Mercury* and the *Crocus* of *Mars*, *&c.* This is the firſt Philoſophical Water (*Common Aqua fortis*) and hath one Degree of Perfection in it. Take of the firſt Water one pound, diſſolve in it two Ounces of (*Vegetable*) *Sal armoniack* pure and clear, which being diſſolved, the Water is preſently otherwiſe qualified, and otherwiſe coloured, becauſe the firſt was of a Green Colour, and the Diſſolvitive of *Luna*, and not of *Sol*, and preſently after the putting in of the *Sal armoniack* the Colour of it is turned to a Citrine, and diſſolveth Gold, Mercury, and Sulphur ſublimed, and tingeth a Mans Skin of a moſt Citrine Colour, keep that Water (*Philoſophical Aqua Regis*) apart. Take of the ſecond Water one Pound, and of *Mercury* ſublimed with *Roman Vitriol*, and common Salt five

Ounces

Ounces and a half, put it to the ſecond Water by little and little gradually, ſeal the Mouth of the Glaſs well, that the Virtue of the *Mercury* put in may not ſuddenly exhale; put the Glaſs in Aſhes temperately hot, and the Water will preſently begin to work upon the *Mercury*, diſſolving it and incorporating; and let the Glaſs ſtand thus in hot Aſhes, and in the diſſolution of the Water, till the Water appears no more, but has wholly diſſolved the Sublimed Mercury: Now the Water acts always upon Mercury by the way of imbibition, till it diſſolves it totally: But take notice, if the Water cannot wholly diſſolve the Mercury put in, then lay aſide the Mercury that is diſſolved by that Water, and that which is not diſſolved at the bottom dry with a gentle Fire, grind, and diſſolve it with new Water as before, and thus repeat this Order, till all the Sublimed Mercury is diſſolved into Water: And then joyn all the ſolutions of that third Water, into one, in a clean Glaſs, and ſtop the Mouth of it well with Wax, and keep it carefully: This is the third Philoſophical thick qualified Water in the third degree of Perfection, and is the Mother of *Aqua Vitæ*, which diſſolves all Bodies into their firſt Matter. Take the third clarifi'd Mercurial Water, qualifi'd in the third Degree of Perfection, putrefie it in the Belly of a Horſe, to be well digeſted in a clear Glaſs with a long Neck, well ſealed the ſpace of 14 days, make it putrefie, and the Feces ſettle at the bottom, then will this Water be tranſmuted from a Citrine to a Yellow Colour, which done, take out the Glaſs, put it in Aſhes with a moſt gentle heat, put on an Alembick with its Receiver, and begin to diſtil by little and little a moſt clear, clean, ponderous *Aqua Vitæ*, *Virgins Milk*, *moſt ſharp Vinegar*, drop by drop, continuing conſtantly a ſlow Fire, till you have diſtilled all the *Aqua Vitæ* gently, then put out the Fire, let the Fornace cool, and keep it diligently apart. Behold this is *Aqua Vitæ*, the *Philoſophers Vinegar*, *Virgins Milk*, by which Bodies are reſolved into their firſt Matter, which is called by infinite Names. The Signs of this Water are theſe, if a Drop be caſt upon a Copper Plate red hot, it will preſently penetrate, and leave a White Impreſſion, it ſmoaks upon Fire, is coagulated in the

Air

Air after the manner of Ice : and when this Water is distilled, the Drops of it do not enter continually as other Drops, but one is distilled one way, another another way ; this Water acts not upon Metallick Bodies, as another strong Corrosive Water, which dissolves Bodies into Water, but if Bodies be put into this Water, it reduceth and resolves them all into *Mercury*, as you shall hear hereafter.

Paracelsus *made this Water by the following Method.*

118. The Mecurial Water of *Paracelsus.*

In Appendice Manualis de Lap. Phil. Pag. 139.

TAke of *Mercury* seven times sublimed with *Vitriol, Sal Niter*, and *Alume*, three pounds of (*Vegetable*) *Sal armoniack* sublimed three times with Salt, clear and white, one Pound and a half, being ground together and alcolized, sublime them in a Sublimatory nine hours in Sand: Being cold, draw off the Sublimate with a Feather, and with the rest sublime, as before : This Operation repeat four times, till no more sublimes, and a Black Mass remains in the bottom flowing like Wax ; being cold take it out, and being ground again, imbibe it often in the Water of *Sal armoniack* prepared according to Art (*the Menstruum described in Numb.* 91.) in a Glass Dish, and being coagulated of it self, imbibe it again, and dry nine or ten times over, till it will scarce any more be coagulated : Being ground finely upon a Marble, dissolve it in a moist place to a clear Oil, which you must rectifie by Distillation in Ashes from all Feces and Sediment. This Water keep diligently as the best of all.

Lully *made his* Mercurial Water *of* Mercury *and the* Stinking Menstruum *thus*,

119. The Stinking Mercvrial Menſtruum of *Lully*. *Pag. 63. Teſtam. Noviſſimi.*

TAke of the Stinking *Menſtruum* four Pounds, and put in one pound of *Mercury Vive*, put the Matter *in Balneo* or Horſe Dung ſix days, and it will be all converted into Water, diſtil by *Balneo*, and you will have a *Mercurial Water*, truly Mineral.

Ripley *followed his Maſter in the way of making the* Mercurial Water, *as followeth.*

120. The Mercurial Green Lion of *Ripley*. *Pag. 310. Pupillæ Alchymicæ.*

TAke *Mercury* ſublimed with *Vitriol* and common Salt, to the quantity of 20 or 40 Pounds (*in my opinion two or four ought to be read*) that you may have enough. Grind it well into Powder, and put it in a Glaſs Veſſel very large and ſtrong, pour to it ſo many Pounds of the moſt ſtrong Water (*the Stinking Menſtruum is the ſtrongeſt Water in the World, Pag. 138. Medullæ*) as there are Pounds of *Mercury:* Shake them ſoundly together, and the Veſſel will become ſo hot, that you can ſcarce touch it; ſtop it well, and let it ſtand nine days in a cold place, ſhaking it ſtrongly three or four times each day: Which done, put the Veſſel in a Fornace of Aſhes, and with a moſt gentle heat diſtil away all the *Aqua Vitæ* (*Menſtruum*) which keep ſafe by it ſelf, then immediately add another Receiver well luted, kindle a moſt ſtrong Fire, and continue it till all the Golden Liquor is wholly diſtilled.

The ſame ways as the Mercurial Waters *are made, may alſo be made* Menſtruums *of this Kind out of the other Metals, thus.*

121. The

121. The Stinking Lunar *Menstruum* of *Lully*. *In Experimento* 29.

TAke of the aforesaid Mineral Water (*described in Numb.* 104.) as you have it in the former Experiment (*Numb.* 26.) six or eight Ounces, dissolve in it one Ounce of *Luna*, which dissolution put into a small Retort to be distilled by Ashes; which Distillation ceasing, increase the Fire as much as possible, and when no more moisture will with this degree of Fire distil, cool the Vessel, receive the Distilled Water, wherein is the Soul of *Luna*; and secure it from respiring.

Thus also Lully *prepares the Water of* Sol.

122. The Stinking Solar *Menstruum* of *Lully*. *In Experim.* 31.

TAke the *Aqua Fortis* or *Mineral Water* (*described in Numb.* 104.) as above, and in every Pound thereof dissolve three Ounces of the Animal Salt prepared and fixed, as you have it in its (*Sixth*) Experiment: Which being dissolved, dissolve therein two Ounces of Gold cemented, as you know, after that putrefie eight days, then distill by *Balneo:* Now that which remains at the bottom, will be like melted Honey, upon which Matter pour again some of its own Water distilled by *Balneo*, so as to swim two fingers above it; putrefie for a natural day, then taking away the *Antenotorium*, put on an Alembick with a Receiver, so close, as not to respire: Distil by Ashes, till no more will distil, then increase the Fire a little, that part of the Air may pass into the Water; and lastly increase the Fire, that also the Element of Fire may pass through the Alembick; and when nothing will distil with this last degree of Fire, cool the Vessel, take away the Receiver with its Distilled Water, and keep it well stopp'd.

Isaacus Hollandus *made a* Mercurial Water *sometimes with the* Mercury *of* Luna, *thus*.

123. Philosophers Vinegar made of the *Mercury* of *Silver* of *Isaacus*.

Cap. 99. 2. Oper. Min. Pag. 492. Vol. 3. Th. Cym.

TAke of the Calx of *Luna* one Pound, of *Sal armoniack*, which must be clear and transparent as Cristal, without moisture, a fourth part, being ground, put them in a Stone Jugge, then take (*Philosophical*) *Vinegar* distilled five or six times from its Phlegme, so as to leave no Feces; empty the Vinegar into another Stone Jugge, and having put on an Alembick, place it in *Balneo*: The Jugge which the ground Calx is in, lute well to the beak of the Alembick, and let the Luting be throughly dried; Then make Fire under the *Balneo*, and distil the Vinegar leasurely upon the Calx of *Luna*; and so many Pounds as you have of the Calx of *Luna*; so many four Pounds of Vinegar distil upon it, and when all the Vinegar is distilled, let it cool gently the space of three days, before you remove the Jugge, for if you remove it sooner, the *Vinegar*, *Luna*, and *Sal armoniack* will run over, and you will retain nothing, so vehement is that Matter, for Cold and Hot do come together; and when you would remove it, have a Glass Stopple ready fitted to the mouth of the Jugge, or Receiver, which you must presently lute to it, that the Virtue may not evaporate: Then set the Jugge in Balneo, let the Fire be no hotter than your hand can well endure in the Water up to the Knuckles, or then may be drunk without burning, and thus keep it the space of six weeks: Then let it be cold, break it, and presently lute an Alembick to the Jugge very firmly, and put a Receiver to the Beak, distil in a temperate *Balneo*, whatsoever will distil, and when now no more distils, take it out, and put it in Ashes, lute the Receiver again to the Beak, and first apply a gentle heat, then sometimes a stronger, till your *Mercury* begins to sublime with the *Sal armoniack*,

as

know how much *Mercury* you ſublimed out of the Calxes of *Luna*, for you knew how much *Sal armoniack* you put into the Jugge: Then put the Sublimate again into a Glaſs, and again ſublime, that you may ſee whether any Feces remain, for you muſt repeat the Sublimation till no Feces remain. Keep this *Mercury* till I teach you what to do with it: You muſt know that in that Veſſel, wherein you ſublimed the *Mercury* with the *Sal armoniack*, is the Body (*commonly called Caput Mortuum*) or Element of Earth with its Oyl or Fire, this take out and weigh, that ſo you may the better know, how much *Mercury* you ſublimed alſo out of it, for you knew how much of the Calx of *Luna* you had in the Jugge, ſo you may certainly know how much you have out of it: Then put your Salt or Earth into a Glaſs, and pour Diſtill'd Vinegar upon it, and diſſolve it into a pure Water, if it yields any Feces, pour off the top gradually, and congeal again, till it leaves no more Feces, then congeal again: Then have you your Salt prepared with your Earth clear as Criſtal. Now take your Sublimed *Mercury* and *Sal armoniack*, and your clear Salt, and grind them together upon a Marble dry, being ground, put all the Matter into a Glaſs-Plate, ſet it on a Tripos or our Calcining Fornace, and there let it ſtand ſix Weeks, and apply ſuch a heat, as if you would keep Lead melted without congealing: Thoſe ſix Weeks being expired, let it cool, then put it in a cold Cellar, and cover it with a Linnen Cloth, that no duſt may fall in, and in the ſpace of ſix or eight days it will be wholly diſſolved into a clear Water. Now you muſt know, this is the Philoſopers clear Vinegar, for when they write our Vinegar; they mean this Water, and when they ſay Philoſophers *Mercury*, they mean this Water, and it is their Vinegar which they write or ſo wonderfully ſpeak of.

From the Receipts we observe:

1. *That Metals and Minerals volatilized with Simple Mineral* Menstruums *are* Menstruums *of this Kind.*

2. *That these* Menstruums *are the same with the* Menstruums *of the Eighth Kind dissolved in Simple Mineral* Menstruums, *but differ from the antecedent Kind, in being made not with the Spirit of* Philosophical Wine, *but* Philosophical Vinegar.

3. *That these* Menstruums *are the* Essences *or* Magisteries *of Things tinging dissolved in Simple Mineral* Menstruums.

4. *That those* Menstruums *being* Mineral *or* Acid, *are in Alchymical Processes better than the Vegetable* Menstruums *of the Eighth Kind, because stronger.*

5. *That the dissolutions of Metals performed by these* Mercurial Menstruums, *have been by the Adepts sometimes called* Amalgamations. You must know, *saith* Isaacus, That this is the best Solution, that ever was found in the World, for herein is no error of Proportion and Weight. For Nature errs not. For when *Mercury* is dissolved, it dissolves other Metals also, as is rightly taught in other places. Nor will it dissolve more than it is able, nor will it receive more of a Body into it, than its Nature can bear. For whatsoever has no need of it, it cannot dissolve. And it is the best *Amalgamation* that can be found. 2. *Oper.Min.Cap.*103.*Pag.* 494. *Vol.* 3. *Th. Chym.* *That* Bernhard in Epistola ad Thomam *treated not of a dry but of this moist* Amalgamation, *I shall prove elsewhere.*

6. *That the* Menstruum *of* Venus, Sol, Luna, *&c. is of the same Virtue, as to the faculty of Dissolving, with the* Menstruum *of common* Argent Vive; *this* Mercurial Menstruum *has been indeed more in use than the other by some Adepts, because of the more easie way of operating upon the Open Body of* Mercury, *tho it be less powerful than the rest in Point of Tinging.*

7. *That there are divers Kinds of Stinking* Menstruums: *The Thirteenth Kind taught us how to distil the most Stinking* Menstruum *of all, out of* Atrop: *For there the Oyly Matter of the*

the Spirit of (Philosophical) Wine *being dissolved in* Vitriol, *is in its Distillation purged from all its Putrid Feculencies*; *but the Twentieth Kind treats of* Menstruums *less stinking*, *being made of the Spirit of Philosophical Wine now purified and sweet* : *The present Kind produceth from the same Matter* Menstruums *of the same Name indeed, but not of the same Stinking Savour, Colour*, &c. *For* Philosophical Vinegar *is*, *by reason of the perfect dissolution of the Spirit of Philosophical* Wine, *Diaphanous*, *not of a Milky Colour*, *but in the Distillation of a* Menstruum *it is made Milky*, *because the Acidity of the said Vinegar being debilitated by the Aridity of a Body dissolved*, *cannot retain the Unctious Spirit of Philosophical* Wine *so well as before*, *but in the precipitation of which the Distilled Liquor becomes Milky*; *for this reason the Adepts sometimes added common* Vitriol *and* Niter *to the Azoquean* Vitriol; *that the said Spirit might the better be dissolved. In a word: The greater quantity of Philosophical Vinegar*, *or any other Mineral* Menstruum *stronger than this*, *is made use of in the making of these* Menstruums, *the less Milky*, *and less Stinking will the* Menstruums *be*, *because made not of the embrionated Stinking Matter of the Spirit of* Philosophical Wine; *but of the same purified by Circulation and Distillation.*

8. *That these*, *as all other* Menstruums, *are by Digestion made sweet and transmuted into Dissolvents of the Eighth Kind.*

The

The Two and Twentieth KIND.

Mineral Menstruums *compounded of the* Philsophers Vinegar, *and other* Simple Mineral Menstruums *and* Things tinging *being first fixed.*

124. The *Menstruum* of *Venus* of *Isaacus Hollandus. Cap.* 82. 3. *Oper. Miner.*

I Will now Son teach you how to make the *Stone*, *which God gives us freely*. You must know it is made divers Ways, but I will teach you the Way which I learnt from my Father. Take of the *Stone which God gives us freely* (*the Vitriol of Venus*) as much as sufficeth, which dissolve in (*Philosophical*) distill'd Vinegar, let the Feces settle, decant the Dissolution from the Feces warily, and filter; draw off the Vinegar with a gentle Fire, that the Matter may remain dry; being dried dissolve it again in Distill'd Vinegar, decant, filter, and draw off, and that to be four times repeated, till no more Feces settle in the Solution: Then distil away the Vinegar with a gentle Fire, till the Matter becomes so dry, as to flie away in the beating of it into Powder, yet retains its Spirits: Now it is prepared for Calcination. You must know Son, that this Matter is in its Nature Stip-

Stiptick and Aſtringent, partly volatile, partly fixed, and ſo diſſolved in Diſtil'd Vinegar, that it may retain the ſubtil Spirit of the Vinegar, and be calcined together with the ſaid Spirit, made more ſubtil, be better opened and diſſolved, for the Spirit of Vinegar diſſolves well before all things. The Vitriol being thus prepared, Put it in a Glaſs Bottle or Egg, lute hermetically, but the Veſſels muſt be fill'd, that there may be no ſpace for the Spirits to elevate themſelves, ſet it on a Tripos, and there let it remain in a temperate heat, to ſubtiliate it ſelf: Then take out the Matter, and pulverize it, put it in a Cucurbit, put on an Alembick with a Receiver to it, and ſo diſtil in Balneo whatſoever will diſtil, it will be diſtilled in about 20 or 25 days: Then lay aſide the Diſtillation, take out the Feces lying at the bottom of the Cucurbit, grind them very fine upon a Stone, put them in a Diſſolving Veſſel, pour all the Diſtilled Water to them, ſeal hermetically, and it will be all diſſolved *in Balneo* without Feces; diſtil the Solution in a Cucurbit through an Alembick *in Balneo* with a moderate heat, that all the Water may ſeparate it ſelf, which keep very choicely; continue the Diſtillation in Aſhes, that you may receive the Element of Air in the form of a very noble Citrine Oyl; and this muſt be done with a ſtrong Fire, lay aſide the Air by it ſelf very well ſtopped near the Water: The Feces being as red as Blood, take out of the Cucurbit, grind them to an Impalpable Powder upon a Stone, put them in a Glaſs Bottle or Egge, ſeal, and ſet it 30 days and nights on a Tripos to be ſubtiliated with a temperate heat, then take out the Matter, grind it to Powder, put it in a Diſſolving Veſſel, pour to it the Element of Water (*above diſtilled*) ſeal, and put it *in Balneo*, to be diſſolved, as before; diſtil the Solution through an Alembick in Aſhes (the Receiver muſt be put into cold Water) increaſe the Fire by degrees, till at length it be hot; ſo let it continue five or ſix days, and in the mean time will aſcend the Element of Fire in the form of a Red Oyl; ſuffer it to be cooling three or four days, then take away the Receiver, keep it very well ſtopp'd, *&c.*

Annota-

Annotations.

WE *have had divers graduated* Vitriols *in the former Receipts, which have yielded us divers* Menstruums. *The* Vitriol *in this Kind is made better than all of them; for it is made of* Vitriol graduated *in a close Vessel, fixed according to Art, and again dissolved in* Philosophical Vinegar, *that by Distillation it may be made a better* Menstruum *than those before. In the Ninth Kind of Vegetable* Menstruums *the graduated* Vitriol *of* Mercury, *made of* Mercury *sublimed and* Salt circulated, *is in a close Vessel reverberated into a Fixed Powder, which Crocus of* Mercury *then volatilized with the* Spirit of Philosophical Wine, *makes a Vegetable* Menstruum. *If the same graduated* Vitriol *of* Mercury *be in a close Vessel reverberated into a Fix'd Precipitate, and then dissolved, not in the* Spirit *of* Philosophical Wine, *but* Philosophical Vinegar, *or some other* Mineral Menstruum, *it will be thereby made a* Menstruum *of this Kind. That which is spoken of the* Vitriol *of* Mercury, *must be also understood of the present* Vitriol *of* Venus *in our Receipt; where* Isaacus *dissolves the said* Vitriol *in* Phiosophical Vinegar, *depurates and graduates, which then he calcines, that is, fixeth upon a Tripos; being fixed it must be dissolved in new* Philosophical Vinegar, *and volatilized, before the Distillation of it, as appears by the Description of the same* Menstruum *elsewhere given.*

125. A Menstruum of Vitriol of *Isaacus Hollandus*. *Cap. 62. 2. Oper. Min.*

TAke a great quantity of *Roman Vitriol*, 10 or 12 Pounds, rather more than less, as much as you will, and dissolve the Vitriol in common Water; let the Feces settle, put the clear Dissolution in a Stone Vessel to be congealed, till a thin skin comes over it, then let it cool and stand three days, and you will have notable Stones of a green colour clear as Criſtal ; take out thoſe Stones, and put them in ſmall Glaſs Veſſels in a clean Balneo to dry, the Balneo muſt have ſuch a heat as is of the Sun in the middle of Summer, and your Stones will be turned into a white Powder, which Powder diſſolve in common Diſtill'd Water, and let the Feces ſettle, decant the clear into a clean Veſſel, as before, and let it be congealed, as before ; this repeat, till you can ſee no Feces left ; when you have thus waſhed and made your Powder white, you may be aſſur'd your *Vitriol* is rightly prepared. Now take the white powder of *Vitriol*, put it in a Glaſs Veſſel with a Neck pretty long, and ſeal the Neck with the Seal of *Hermes* ſo, that no Air can either paſs out or in ; and then put it in a Plate with ſifted Aſhes upon a Fornace, put fire under, and put a Burning Lamp under the Fornace, adding ſuch a heat as the Sun yields in the middle of *March*, and thus keep it, till you ſee your Matter grow yellow, and continue it in the ſame heat, till it be perfectly ruddy, then increaſe the Fire a little, that is, put under one Lamp more, and thus continue it eight or ten days, and then ſee whether your Matter begins not to be red, if it begins to be red, increaſe your Fire, and ſo continue it eight or ten days : But if you gain nothing in redneſs, increaſe your Fire with yet one Lamp, and ſo proceed gradually always one Lamp being kindled, till your Matter be as deep a red, as a Roſe or Ruby ; it being now ſo deeply red, ſuffer it even thus the ſpace of eight or ten days in the ſame heat ; when you ſee your Matter remains in the ſame ſtate, take it out of the Plate with Aſhes, and empty it into another ſtrong Glaſs, pour a good quantity of (Philoſophical) diſtill'd Vinegar upon it, and put it *in Balneo*, let it boil, and ſtir it with a Woodden Spatula three or four times every day, and thus continue it four days and nights, then let it cool, and pour off the clear ; and again pour on Diſtill'd Vinegar, and that repeat three times ; then throw away the Feces, and draw off the Vinegar through an Alembick *in Balneo*, till your Matter become altogether dry ; pour on new Vinegar, and do as before, and that ſo long, till no more Feces remain in the Diſſolution : Then congeal it into a dry Powder, which put into a good thick Glaſs, and putting on an Alem-

 bick

bick with a large Head; distil in order to obtain first Saffron Colour'd Spirits, then a Red Oyl, lastly, white Spirits, then let it cool, take away the Receiver, and keep that truly blessed Oyl which is in it. Take away the Alembick, and in the Pot you will find a Matter white as Snow, and clear as Cristal, *&c.*

The way of making of this Menstruum, we will consider in its several Branches.

The first is concerning the choice of Vitriol, *which Reason requires as well as the antecedent Receipt to be graduated, that is, dissolved either in the Spirit of Philosophical Wine, or Philosophical Vinegar, and Cristallized, for the Calcination of common Vitriol, dissolved in common Water, and purified, in a close Vessel to a most red colour, is altogether Impossible, and of no Efficacy neither; for nothing but the common Acid or common Spirit of Vitriol is extracted out of common Vitriol, be it never so well purified and calcined: Vitriol therefore well Purged in common Water, is to be chosen according to the present Receipt, but after that, according to the antecedent well dissolved in Philosophical Vinegar, that it may be thereby made graduated Vitriol, and the fit Matter of this Menstruum.*

The second Branch treats of the calcination or fixation of this graduated Vitriol *into redness: Concerning which, the former process was too obscure, but the present or later clear enough: This Calcination is the true and Philosophical way of fixing this* Vitriol, *and that chiefly, because citrinity and redness follow blackness and whiteness, the true signs of volatilization as well as fixation, of which* Tho. Isaacus *said nothing in both the Receipts, yet other Adepts have mentioned these Colours in the fixing of Vitriol.* Take that Stone, saith *Ripley, Cap. 7. Phil.* Cupri Stillicidium (*the Green Lyon of Fools, or common Vitriol graduated*) and put it, being ground into a Philosophers Egg, and proceed upon it by the way of Putrefaction, as was declared in the Process of *Rebis*, and continue the Stone upon the Fire, till after blackness and whiteness, it is turned into a red Powder, which many call *Vitriol Rubificated.*

But

But here riseth some doubt, in that the Red Colour of this Calcined Vitriol, *seems to be by* Isaacus *himself called* Volatile, *not in the least fixed.* This Matter, *saith he*, will remain red for ever, and not fixed, for if it should be fixed, it would be altogether corrupted, for it must be Dissolved into Water, and distilled through an *Alembick*, *Cap.* 65. To *disperse this Cloud, you must know, the meaning of* Isaacus *is, that* Vitriol *calcined, or by what way soever reduced into redness, remains red, but not also fixed, because it must be dissolved in* Philosophical Vinegar, *and Distilled through an* Alembick. *For we find the like, if not the same Phrase, concerning the redness and fixity of the* Philosophers Stone, *which will easily remove the aforesaid doubt:* When the Stone is perfect, *saith he*, it ought to remain in that State now and for evermore. After Perfection, it cannot be changed for better nor for worse, but will remain a King for ever. Wherefore, if any Man has prepared the true *Philosophers Stone*, no Multiplication follows after; wheresoever Multiplication follows after Perfection, there is not the *Philosophers Stone*, nor is there a true *Stone*. It may be a Medicine, or other Stone, of which sort are many wherewith Projection is made, but it is not the *Philosophers Stone*, which we here Discourse of. When the aforesaid *Stone* is perfect and prepared, it ought to remain in that State for ever, *Cap.* 127. 1. *Oper. Miner. Pag.* 407. *Vol.* 3. *Th. Chym.*

As to the Permanence of the red colour in the Philosophers Stone, he declares the following Notions: In Multiplication, *saith he*, no blackness intervenes, nor do any Colours of the World shew themselves, nor any Whiteness, nor in Sublimation does any thing shew it self besides redness, nor in fixation does any Colour shew its self except its own, that is, an egregious redness: For the Stone hath no other Colour but redness, for it is one only substance, one single matter, and as the Heaven invincible: You must also know, tho it were sublimed, it would not be deprived of all its fixity, for when the Stone is made and prepared in the utmost vertue of it, then can it not be changed out of its own Essence into another, for if the Stone could be changed or drawn out of its own Essence into another Essence or Nature, it would not be the Philosophers Stone, nor one single Matter, nor a glorified Body; no, no, understand my Discourse rightly, *&c.* *Cap.* 72. 1. *Oper. Min. Pag.* 355. *of the same Volume.*

Isaacus *being perhaps perswaded of an unalterable constancy of redness observed in the Multiplication of the Stone of higher Degree or Kind, concludes the Philosophers Stone to be altogether and absolutely immutable: which Opinion to defend in every part, he has sooner ventured to deny the volatilization it self of the Stone, than give way to the altering of fixity in Multiplication:* You must know, *saith he*, if the Stone were sublimed, yet would it not be deprived of its fixity. *Yea, he has chosen rather to prevert his own Senses (for he himself hath in the same place taught how to volatilize the Philosophers Stone, with some shining Menstruum) and the Sense of the Word Fix (tho upon this Term depends one half of all the Operations in the more secret Chymy) than relinquish this fallacy derived from a* Paralogism. The Stone, *saith he*, may be so often opened as aforesaid, and after that sublimed, and again condensed so as to unite its parts, which we call Fixation; we term it indeed Fixation, but it is not Fixation, but only Condensation, so, as that all the subtil parts of it are again forced into an Union joyntly together, as they were at first, and the Stone will again expect Fire, and we may again make Projection with it, as we did before. *Cap.* 76. *read* 73, 74, 75. *Chapters of the same Book.*

What we have against this Opinion, we will reserve for the Third Book; in the mean time it will be requisite for you to observe this one thing: That the Matter of Calcined Vitriol, as also of the Philosophers Stone, multiplied, remains for ever red, but not fixed, because either of them may be volatilized with Philosophical Menstruums. *But let them be how they will, the Vitriol of Saturn fixed the same way by the same Author, will prove that the graduated Vitriol of Venus, calcined to redness in a close Vessel is fixed.* Take, *saith he*, a Glass Viol, put in it one half of Purged Saturn (*Sugar of Saturn made not with common Distilled Vinegar, but Philosophical*) reserve the other part by it self till you have occasion, put a fit Glass to the mouth of the Viol, and put the Glass in sifted Ashes in a Fornace, of *Tripos Arcanorum*, or on a Fornace wherein

you

you calcine Spirits; give it a Fire as hot as the Sun is at Midsummer, no more, except by chance a little hotter or colder, provided it be not so great as to melt the Lead, for so your Matter would be liquid as Oyl, and should it stand so the space of 12 days, all the Sulphur would fly away, and the Matter be corrupted, for the Sulphur of it is not yet fixed, and on the outside only, and therefore the Matter is most easily melted, and though it be pure, yet is it not fixed; wherefore the Fire must be so gentle as not to melt the Matter; let it stand so the space of Six Weeks, after which take a little, project it upon a hot Iron, if it presently melts and fumes, it is not yet fixed, but if it remains, the Sulphur of it is fixed: Then increase the Fire notably, till your Matter becomes citrine, and so continually till it grows red, still increasing the Fire till it attains to the colour of Rubies; increase till it is red hot, and then is it fixed, and prepared for Infusion, with the Noble Water of Paradise (the *Menstruum described in Numb.* 114.)

Besides this, there is indeed another way also of calcining Philosophical Vitriol, *which is done in an open Vessel; thus graduated Verdigrese is calcined to redness before the Distillation of it, in the preparation of the Spirit of* Venus *of* Basilius, *as we have observed in the precedent Kind, but this belongs not to this place, for the* Calx *remains volatile, not fixed, which way of Calcining was invented meerly for the seperation of the* Phlegme.

The third Branch consists in a new dissolution of this fixed Vitriol *in* Philosophical Vinegar, *for which Reason this* Vitriol *is volatilized again, and made fit for Distillation, in the former Receipt, this Solution is wholly omitted, but more exactly described in the* latter Process.

The fourth Branch is the single, and frequent Distillation in the several ways of making all these Stinking Menstruums, *yet this excepted, that out of this* graduated, fixed, *and again* volatilized Vitriol, *the* Spirit *ascends not* White, *but of a* Saffron Colour (*because more Mature*) *before the Red Oyl; and lastly, the* White Spirit *appears also, being extracted out of the* Salt *or* White Body.

Lastly,

Laſtly, *Theſe words following do prove, that the ſame* Menſtruums *may be alſo made of any other* Metals. But if you would extract an Oyl out of Metals, as has been taught of *Vitriol*; you muſt diſſolve your Metal in *Aqua fortis*, and make it precipitate, and waſh away the Saltneſs of it with common Water, and being dryed, put into a Glaſs with a long Neck, and congealed, and put upon a *Fornace* with Sifted Aſhes, make a Fire under it as for *Vitriol*, till the Metal be alogether red, and till the inſide of it is turn'd outward: Then diſſolve it in Diſtil'd Vinegar, as the *Vitriol*, and *Congeal*, till no more Feces remain: Then diſtil, and the Metal will wholly diſtil into a Red Oyl, and it is the perfect Oyl of the *Philoſophers*, but the Projection of it is not ſo high, as of the Oyl which was firſt Salt: And the Oyl of every Metal you muſt Multiply with the Oyl of *Vitriol*, as aforeſaid: And the Oyl is very eaſily made after the ſame manner out of *Saturn*, and the Projection of it is very high: Give thanks to God, Work, and remember the Poor, diſpenſe the gifts of God to your own Salvation, *Cap.* 80. 2. *Oper. Min. Pag.* 478. *of the ſame Volume.*

All Metals, *ſaith he, Cap.* 67. *of the ſame Work*, even *Jupiter* and *Luna*, will become red as blood, for the inſide of all Metals is red, one more red than another: When therefore they are brought to redneſs, they muſt then be diſſolved (in *Philoſophical Vinegar*) and again congealed, till they be free from any Feces, and yet contain their Elements together perfectly; for when they are brought to that pitch, nothing remains, ſave only Feces; for the Earth (the *Caput Mortuum*) being made ſubtil and liquid, is likewiſe diſſolved, when you have made it ſubtil by Diſſolving and Coagulating ſo, as that no more Feces remain. Thus you may Diſtil it through an *Alembick* into a Red Oyl. As you was here taught concerning *Vitriol*, ſo muſt you alſo do with all Metals, as alſo *Mercury*, when it is diſſolved in *Aqua Fortis*, and precipitated, the Saltneſs waſh'd away and dried, put it in a Glaſs, as was ſaid of *Vitriol*, and done moreover ſo, as was taught before concerning *Vitriol*. And that which is here declar'd of Metal, you may alſo do with *Antimony* (*and all other Minerals.*) Open your Ears, and hearken, and open your Mind, it was never heard that such a Work should be done with so little Pains.

Here I would advise you to take Notice of the difference between the Oyls of Vitriol *and other bodies; the like Oyl is produced from all Metals as from* Vitriol, *yet with this difference, that* Vitriol *in the Distillation of its Oyl, leaves an Earth or Salt behind it, wherewith the Spirit and Oyl of it are fixed into the* Philosophers Stone; *but Metals and the rest of the Minerals not so, they totally ascending into Spirit and Oyl, no* Earth, Salt *or* Caput mortuum *remaining, whereby to be fixed into the Stone:* Vitriol *therefore is that alone, which hath all things in it, relating to the Perfection of it self, whereas the Oyls and Spirits of the rest are forced to borrow fixed bodies elsewhere for their fixations.* You must know, *saith he*, when you would reduce the Salt of *Metals* to an Oyl, the same as hath been said of *Vitriol*, the Elementary Earth of *Metals* will distil together, with the Oyl red as blood, but that the Earth of *Vitriol* does not, the Oyl seperates it self from the Earth: God hath vouchsafed such a blessing, that the *Philosophers Stone* may be made of it alone without Addition, translating all *Metals* into true *Sol*, but the Oyl of it must be fixed with the Earth (its *own Earth or Salt*) but that is not so with *Metals*, the Earth distils together through the *Alembick*, and the whole Body is converted into Oyl, translating all *Metals* into true *Sol*: Herein do all the *Philosophers* agree. An Oyl, *he goes on*, is also made of *Mercury*, and of *Antimony*, but their Earth goes over together, and their whole Body turns into Oyl, and remains an Oyl for ever, and with this Oyl you may do wonderful things, which here to recite would be too long. You know also what is written of *Antimony* and the Oyl of it. Yet must my Son know, That the Oyl of *Mercury* is much better in all works, wherein the Oyl of *Antimony* is used. This is a Secret. *Cap.* 69. and 70. *of the same Work.*

An Example, *That* Metals *wholly ascend into Oyl, he brings in the following Chapter, namely the* 70th, *which we will name.*

126. The

126. The Circulatum Majus of *Isaacus*. *Cap.* 70. 2. *Oper. Min. Pag.* 474. *Vol.* 3. *Th. Chym.*

TAke this *Mercury* (*the* Metals *sublimed in the* Philosophical Menstruums *aforegoing*) Dissolve it in *Aqua Fortis*, with an equal quantity of *Vitriol* and *Niter*, being Dissolved, put the Solution in a Glass Vessel, put on an *Alembick*, set it in Sifted Ashes, give first a gentle Fire, Distil the *Aqua Fortis* from it, then the *Mercury* will sublime upwards into the *Alembick*, when it will sublime no more, take it away; take the *Mercury* out of the *Alembick*, put it in a Glass with a long neck, as you did with the *Vitriol*, put it in a Vessel with Sifted Ashes, light your Lamp under it, so leave it, till it be perfectly red, as hath been taught of *Vitriol*; Dissolve, Congeal, being clean, Distil it into a red Oyl, as hath been said of *Vitriol*, but all the *Mercury* distils into Oyl, so as to leave no Earth.

The Menstruum *immediately antecedent in* Numb. 125, *is in all things clear, except the first Branch of it, wherein is omitted the necessary Dissolution of* Vitriol *in* Philosophical Vinegar, *before the Calcination of it into redness or fixation. The first* Menstruum *of this Kind is imperfect, not indeed in this, but in another Branch, insomuch as it is not therein declared, that* Vitriol *must after the Calcination of it, be again Dissolved in* Philosophical Vinegar. *In this present third, Tho it be said, that it ought to be made according to the rule of the precedent* Menstruums, *there is no mention at all made of* Philosophical Vinegar, *yet without it,* Vitriol *can neither be fixed into redness, nor when fixed, be again Volatalized or Distilled. The Receipts therefore must be compared as often as the Adepts have either through too much fear or envy left us them imperfect: It is enough, if by comparing them together, we can pick out their meaning or intention, being not fully enough expressed in every circumstance, the terms being either too obscure, or altogether omitted. Bodies in this Kind are to be fixed, and then volatilized by* Mineral Menstruums, *as* Mercury *and* Antimony,

Antimony, *in the Ninth Kind, are first fixed, and then distilled in the greater* Circulatums *by vegetable* Menstruums: *This light borrow'd from the said Ninth Kind, will dispel all the Obscurities and Doubts of this Kind.* Vitriol *therefore purged with common Water by Solutions and Coagulations, must first be graduated, that is several times dissolved in* Philosophical Vinegar *and coagulated according to the Receipt in* Numb. 125, *as* Mercury *is dissolved in the Water of Salt, circulated in the* Circulatum majus *of* Mercury. *This* Vitriol *being graduated in a close Vessel, must be fixed into a most red Powder, and being fixed, then dissolved and coagulated in* Philosophical Vinegar, *that it may again become volatile, as* Mercury *being fixed in its own* Circulatum, *is again made volatile by virtue of the Spirit of* Philosophical Wine. *At last the* Vitriol *is to be Distilled into its Spirits. Now by knowing the method, it is manifest that the mystery of the Receipts consists in the* Vinegar, *but to remove all scruple from these most excellent* Menstruums, *we will prove by the very words of* Isaacus *himself, that he meant not a common but* Philosophical Menstruum. Have not I taught you, *saith he*, how to draw all Metals through the *Alembick*, so as to Distil wholly into Oyl, leaving nothing; but that alone does the strong Spirit of Vinegar, and makes them (*Metals*) to be perfectly separated and rectified from their Feces, within and without, as I taught you, and that the inside should be outward, and the outside inward, and then they are so resolved and subtil, that the Elements cannot be separated one from another; if you sought all the means in the world, you would not be able to separate these Elements, by reason of their subtility, cleanness and resolution; and when they have the subtil penetrating Vinegar with them, they pass all together through the *Alembick* with the *Vinegar*; but if you should put them to fire, and any Spirit of Vinegar (*in sufficient quantity*) was present, they (*the Metal and Vinegar*) would be forthwith fixed together; and because the Vinegar is copiously in their clean, open, subtil Body, they distil into Oyl, and the Spirits of the Vinegar are fixed with the Body: Now you must know that the Spirit of Vinegar is more Subtil than all things in the World, yea, a thousand times more subtil than the *Quinteſſence* of *Aqua Vitæ* , it cannot be contained in any Veſſels , but it is eaſily half fixed , and therefore it eaſily fixeth the thing to which it is applied , as it is demonſtrated in the Vegetable (*Work*) where the Diſcourſe is of Wine , and the Nature of it , where you will be ſufficiently inſtructed what Vinegar is , and the Spirit of it, how all things are diſſolved and aſcend. *Cap.* 77. 78. 2. *Oper. Miner. Pag.* 477. *Vol.* 3. *Theat. Chym.* You muſt know , *ſaith he elſewhere*, this is the greateſt Secret in this Art , for the middle parts of Vinegar are of ſo great Virtue as to be incredible , by reaſon of their great Subtility, for every thing they are mixed with, becomes exceeding ſubtil and penetrable , wherefore they make the (*Philoſophers*) Stone a thouſand times more ſubtil than it was before , and more penetrable , and the ſubtil parts mix themſelves with the Stone , for they are of one Nature , and are both clean and ſubtil , and are mixed together , as Water with Water ; and it is a Medicine of that Nature , as to make every thing fixed which it is mixed with , and of its own Nature wherein it is ; and thus are the ſubtil parts (*of Philoſophical Vinegar*) fixed in the (*Philoſophical*) Stone , and are made of one Nature with the Stone , and they make the Stone as fuſible , as an Artiſt can wiſh , as he oftentimes diſſolves the Stone in Vinegar , and congeals it , for as many or few Spirits remain in the Stone , the more fuſible is the Medicine : Wherefore I have taught my Son how to make his Stone ſo fuſible, as thereby to bring *Mercury* to *Sol* and *Luna* ; and it is a great Secret, known to few , peruſe this Lecture diligently ; what vertue there is in Vinegar , and what with the middle matter of Vinegar may be made. *Cap.* 51. 1. *Oper. Min. Pag.* 337. *Vol.* 3. *Th. Chym.*

That Vinegar , which is a thouſand times more ſubtil than the Quinteſſence *of* Aqua Vitæ , *or Spirit of* Philoſophical Wine : *The Spirits of which makes the* Philoſophers Stone *a thouſand times more Subtil : That is of one Nature with it ; and fixeth every thing it is mixed with ; you your ſelves will ſay is no common* Menſtruum, *but another of more excellent quality.* Iſaacus *moreover diſſolves and coagulates the Stone in this Vinegar , ſo oft , till it is converted into Oyl ; which will be no*

more

more congealed. Cap. 51, 59, 107. of the same Book. *With the same Vinegar also he made* Metals *fat, and transmuted them into Oyls, then he dissolved and coagulated Gold so often continually in New Vinegar, till an Oyl was made thereof as red as blood, as* Cap. 54. of the same Book. *Sometimes also he did with the same Vinegar reduce Gold to the consistence of an excellent White Oyl, out of which he then distilled a White Spirit, and a Red Oyl apart, and not immixible together, so subtil, as that he advised the Artist to have a care, lest these Oyls should condense again by too much Rectification, for then being forced with too strong a Fire, the greatest part of them would by reason of their great Subtility penetrate the Glass, and so be lost.* Cap. 126, 128, 1. Oper. Min. Pag. 406. Vol. 3. Th. Chym. *Who can expect such and so great things from Common Vinegar? The same Vinegar, that dissolved the fix'd Metal Gold, and divided it into Spirit and Oyl, the Constitutives of the Stone out of* Sol *alone; the same also is required to dissolve fixed* Vitriol, *and distil it into Spirit and Oyl, the constitutives of the Stone out of* Vitriol *alone, of the making of which in the Third Book of* Alchymical Tinctures.

That this Oyl of Vitriol, *shews light by night, affirms* Trismosinus, *who hath described the said Oyl thus.*

127. The Oyl of *Vitriol* shining by Night, of *Trismosinus.*

Libro Gangeniveron, sive novem Tincturarum in Tinctura prima.

TAke of the best *Hungarian Vitriol* twelve pounds, grind and dissolve it in pure clean Water, or Rain Water distilled, let the Feces settle, decant the Solution into a Glass Dish, placed in a Brass Bason full of Sand, put the said Bason in *Balneo*, and draw off the Water to a thin skin; let it cool, and stand three days in a cold place, and in the mean time you will find green Stones, which take out, the remainder draw off again to a thin skin, and let it Cristallize, and this seven times repeat, put the Stones in a Stove of the same heat as the Sun in Dog-days, and in such a heat they will turn into a White Powder. The *Vitriol* being thus prepared, put it in a *Cucurbit*, with a long neck, well Sealed, in Ashes, under which put a Lamp, so as that the heat exceed not the Sun in *March*, thus leave it, till the *Vitriol* begins to be yellow, being yellow, the Fire of the Lamp increase one Degree, and thus leave it ten days and nights, or till it begins to be red, then again increase the Fire in the Lamp another Degree; and thus continue, till the Matter be altogether red as a *Ruby*, then increase the Fire yet ten days, and the hidden part of the *Vitriol* is now manifest, and prepared in its redness, as a volatile Matter: The redness thus remaining, take the Glass out of the Ashes, and the Matter out of the Glass, and put it in a stronger Glass, to which pour the best Vinegar well rectify'd, stop it well, set it in *Balneo*, so let it stand four days, yet stirring the Matter with a *Spatula* made of *Hasleiwood*, three or four times a day, let it cool, decant the Vinegar into another Glass, pour new upon the Matter, digest in *Balneo*, as before, this repeat with new Vinegar three times, the decanted Vinegar gently draw off, till the Matter remains in the form of a Salt at the bottom, to which, pour new sharp Vinegar, put it four days in *Balneo*, as before, to dissolve, and let that be repeated, till it be free from any sediment: Then coagulate the Matter into a dry Powder, and put it in a Glass Cucurbit, with a wide mouth, and a large *Alembick*, lay the Receiver in a Vessel full of Water, lute the Joynts firm, and distil with an open Fire, but very gently, the space of four hours, after that strongly, and the Spirits will ascend yellow, which are called Air; continue the Fire in the same degree, till the *Alembick* begins to be red; then slow the Fire, that the *Alembick* may be of a blood colour, then increase the Fire still, that the Glass may be burning hot as a red hot Iron, which keep in that heat, till the *Alembick* be made of a Snow Colour, then strengthen the Fire yet more, that the *Alembick* may again be clear and transparent, then let it cool, remove the Receiver, and pour the Oyl into a pure Glass,

Glass, which stop well, and you will have the true Oyl of *Vitriol* shining night and day in dark places, which keep well for your occasion. But you must know there is a White and Beautiful Oyl found in the bottom, which to its red Oyl, *&c.*

This Receipt of Trismosinus *agrees almost in all things with* Isaacus *his Description of the* Menstruum *made of* Vitriol, *so that it seems to me to be borrowed of* Isaacus, *especially because the same phrase of* Isaacus *of the volatile redness of Calcined* Vitriol *is retained: Those things therefore, which were observed before upon the* Menstruum *of* Isaacus, *do also hereto relate; but we added this, because* Trismosinus *does more assure us, that this Oyl shines in darkness, concerning which quality of his* Menstruum, Isaacus *was silent.*

Ripley *made* Menstruums *of this Kind this way.*

128. The Circulatum Majus of *Ripley.*

Pag. 395. Accurtationum.

THe time of true Putrefaction and Alteration is compleated in the space of Six Weeks, but it may be done in a shorter time by half, and that by the acuition of our *Mercurial Waters*, that is, the white and red Water (*the milk and blood of the* Green-Lyon *in* Numb. 59.) with common *Mercury* sublimate, which thus do: Fix and Calcine the *Mercury* sublimate, and dissolve it in our white or red *Mercury* (*of the said* Menstruum) so as to be all one true Water, which Water, being thus acuated, hath the Power of putrifying and altering any Calx of *Metals*, in the space of three Weeks, and that because the two Fires, namely, of Nature and against Nature, are then joyn'd together in that Water.

Common *Mercury* being dissolved in *Philosophical Vinegar*, or any *Mineral Menstruum*, and fixed either by Sublimation as the *Circulatum majus* of *Paracelsus*, or *Calcination*, as the *Vitriol* of *Isaacus* calcined to redness, is then dissolved in a stinking *Menstruum*, and distilled through an *Alembick*. He reduced

reduced all other *Metals* and *Minerals*, the same way as he did *Mercury*, into the greater *Circulatums*, thus.

129. The Metallick *Acetum acerrimum* of *Ripley*. *Pag. 266. Clavis aureæ Portæ.*

HAving therefore these two *Mercuries*, the white and red (*of the Stinking Menstruum*) practice with them either upon their own Earth (or *Caput Mortuum* of the said *Menstruum*) or upon the Calx of *Metals* prepared, for you need not trouble your self about the Earth, provided the substance of it be fixed: Take therefore any of them, being white, and ferment it thus: For the White Work, take the Calx of *Luna*, and the altered Earth (*a Philosophical Calx*, *made of the Mineral Menstruum of* Luna) in equal quantity, grind them together, and temper them with the White *Mercury*, which we call *Lac Virginis* (*in the Description of the* Green Lyon) and sublime them very well, keep and gather that which is not fixed, that is, so much as ascends white, and sticking to the parts of the Glass as *Mercury* sublimate, for this is that our *Mercury* made by sublimation out of the white altered Earth; then grind it upon its own Calxes, tempering, distilling, and subliming it with *Lac Virginis*, till it be wholly fixed, so as to be immovable by Fire: This is the sublimed and fixed *Mercury*, for which fools take that common *Mercury* sublimed with common *Vitriol* and *Salt*, wherein they very much err: put it into a *Circulatory*, and pour *Lac Virginis* upon it, till it be covered, then let it be circulated and distilled through an *Alembick*.

An Example of making the altered Earth of Metals, *and the way of fixing the said Earth he hath given in* Vitriol. Take *Vitriol* calcined to Ashes (*common Colcothar*) grind it to a most fine Powder, put it in an *Urinal*, pour *Lac Virginis* (*the White fume of the* Stinking Menstruum) to it, till it be covered with it, stop the *Urinal* with a Linnen Cloth, and let it stand eight days, then add the same quantity of the former Milk, repeating it from eight days to eight, but when

when it will drink up no more, let it stand in the cold well stopp'd, till a Cristalline Earth appears in the superficies of it, like Eyes of Fish. Seperate this Earth from the thicker parts resided in the bottom, and put it (*this graduated* Vitriol *made not indeed of the Spirit of* Philosophical Wine, *nor* Philosophical Vinegar, *but the* Stinking Menstruum) in a *Philosophical Egg*, to digest (*calcine*) discreetly, till it be perfectly fixed, then increase the Fire, till it be perfectly citrinated, and still increase it, that it may be Rubified in the form and colour of *Sanguis Draconis*.

Lastly, For a conclusion, we will add the Circulatum Majus *of* Isaacus, *made of* Sulphurs, *which being most clear in the graduation, fixation, and volatilization of it, will help to illustrate those things which have perhaps remained more obscure in the antecedent, and make the Receipts in this Kind more clear.*

130. The Circulatum majus of *Isaacus*, made of *Sulphur*.

Cap. 88. 3. *Oper. Min.*

TAke *Hungarian* or *Spanish Sulphur* ten or twelve pounds, prepare it upon a Stone, with (*Philosophical*) Vinegar distilled, as Painters do their Colours, pour a good quantity of the (*aforesaid*) Vinegar upon it, put it in *Balneo*, stir it well with a *Wodden Spatula*, decoct it in a close Vessel in *Balneo* the space of six or eight days, stirring it three or four times a day, then let it cool and settle, filter the tinged Vinegar, pour on new, repeat this Work, till no more Vinegar will be tinged: Draw off all the tinged Vinegar in *Balneo*, that a Powder of a golden Colour may remain at the bottom. This Powder prepare and extract with Vinegar, as before; filter the solution, and draw it off, till at length it leaves no Feces behind it, then draw off the Vinegar, that the rest of the Matter may remain in the form of a Powder. Take of this Powder one part, of Salt prepared one part, of *Roman Vitriol* dried, six

ſix parts, mix them all well, and ſublime by degrees, firſt, with a weak Fire, ſecondly, ſtronger, laſtly, moſt ſtrong for the ſpace of two days; ſublime the ſublimation mix'd with its Feces three times, then caſting away the Feces, ſublime with new Species, and repeat the Work three times, then diſſolve the Sublimation in the Diſſolving Water for the red (*of what Deſcription ſoever in the Twentieth Kind*) the Water being drawn off, ſublime, pour on New Water and ſublime, and that do three times: Then take ſeven parts of this Sublimation, one part of the Calx of *Sol*, and ſublime: This Sublimation being put into a Philoſophical Egg, made of Gold (for one of glaſs would be of little uſe for this purpoſe, becauſe it would become ſoft as wax) ſtop it well, and ſet it upon a Tripos the ſpace of eighteen Weeks to be fixed, but the firſt ſix Weeks with a gentle Fire, the next ſix a ſtronger, the laſt moſt ſtrong: Theſe Eighteen Weeks being ended, take out the Matter (*being fixed*) reduce it to Powder, to which being put in a diſſolving Veſſel, pour an equal quantity of our red burning Water (*of the aforeſaid Diſſolving Water for the red*) ſeal or ſtop the Veſſel very well, let it diſſolve and ſettle, then take it out, and diſtil it through an *Alembick* in *Balneo* with a very ſmall Fire: It is neceſſary for the Receiver, to be well luted, and the *Alembick* muſt have a pipe in the upper part, for it muſt be ſix times diſtilled, always with new Red Water, and your Matter will at length become thick as Honey, which diſtil in Sifted Aſhes by degrees, and an Air will aſcend like Water, then changing the Reciver, an Oyl of a Golden Colour will diſtil gilding the *Alembick*, as alſo the Receiver; let it continue in the ſame heat till the *Alembick* be of a Blood Colour, then take away the Receiver; ſtop it ſuddenly, put another to, and increaſe the Fire for the ſpace of twenty four hours, till the Veſſel grows red hot, in which heat, let it continue twelve hours, and the Matter will aſcend red as blood, and at laſt alſo a red fume: Theſe Spirits no more appearing, let the Veſſels cool, keep the Diſtillation, but the Feces reverberate, &c.

Out

Out of the Receipts these things we observe.

1. THat these Menstruums, made of the graduated Vitriols of Metals, fixed in a close Vessel, have the like place amongst Mineral Menstruums, as the greater Circulatums of Paracelsus, have amongst the vegetable Menstruums. Dissolve the aforesaid Circulatums in any Acid Spirit, and you will presently make Menstruums of this Kind.

2. That these Menstruums are Medicines, call'd Volatile Arcanums, dissolved in an Acid.

3. That the graduated Vitriol of Venus, has some certain peculiar Priviledges above the rest.

1. Because in the Distillations of these Menstruums, it hath a Fixed Body, besides a Soul and Spirit, whereby the two aforesaid must be fixed into the Stone; but all the other Metals and Minerals being reduced into graduated Vitriols, have no Fixed Bodies, and are divided into two parts only, Spirit and Soul; but because the Adepts found it necessary to borrow some Fixed Body elsewhere for the fixing of these, they therefore more than often affirmed the possibility of making the Stone out of Vitriol alone, without any Addition, thus have we heard Isaacus in the antecedent Receipts saying: God hath vouchsafed such a blessing to *Vitriol*, that the *Philosophers Stone* may be made of it alone, without Addition, it translating all Metals into true *Sol*, but the Oyl of it must be fixed with (*its*) Earth (*or Body*) but that is not so with Metals, for their Earth distils together through the *Alembick*.

But who observes not here these Words, Without any Addition, *to be meant of any Foreign Matter, and are so to be understood with some certain restriction? For this most red Oyl of* Vitriol, *shining by night, and which must be fixed with its Salt, into the* Philosophers Stone, *cannot in the least be produced from* Vitriol *alone, and that crude, being not graduated with* Philosophical Menstruums.

Moreover as the like Oyl being distilled from Gold, and fixin the purified, but not volatalized part of it, is called by Isaacus *the Stone of* Sol *alone; whereas notwithstanding, he used his* Philosophical Vinegar *to the making of it; so the Stone may be said to be made out of Vitriol* alone, without Addition, *though the same Vinegar was used in the preparation of it.*

Lastly, *It is manifest by the Kinds of almost all* Menstruums, *that no Acid (that is, dry and incombustible Matter) can be reduced into Oyl, without an* Oyly Menstruum, *because it must receive this unctiosity from the Unctious Spirit of* Philosophical Wine.

2. *Because it is of mean value, and so by the Adepts call'd the* Stone, which God hath given us freely. This Work, *saith Isaacus*, you cannot enter upon with a little Matter, you must have at least four or five Pounds of Matter (*Gold or Silver*) if otherwise, the Work will be insufficient. For it is not the Work of poor men, except the Stone given us by God freely, might happily be obtained; then other Charge is not necessary, more than Vessels, Coals, and Food, till we have prepared the Stone. And the two Stones, which God hath given us freely, for the White and Red Work, require but half the time, as the Matter which is to be taken for preparation sake, for before we come to Sublimation, the Stone given us freely, is already almost brought to fixation. *Cap.* 17. 1. *Oper. Mineral. Pag.* 313. *Vol.* 3. *Th. Chym. The same thing is affirmed by* Basilius: *saying*, There is no moisture in Gold, unless it be reduced into (*graduated*) Vitriol, which would be a Work indeed of no Profit, but much Charge, because of the great quantity of *Vitriol* required to the making of the *Philosophers Stone*; and though there is in *Vitriol* the desired Spirit of Gold, of a white quality, and a Soul and Salt of a glorious Essence, but how many Countreys, Estates and Riches, have been thus consumed, I will not reckon; but this Admonition I give my Disciples, to follow the shorter way of Nature, that they may not also fall into extream and inextricable Poverty. If you intend therefore, *he goes on*, to make the Philosophers Stone out of the *Vitriol* of *Sol*, as many men indeed endeavour, consult with your Purses, and prepare Ten or Twelve pounds of this *Vitriol*, and then you will finish your Work, whereas *Hungarian* or other *Vitriol* would suffice.

3. *Because*

3. *Because it is our Gold full of the Tincture of common Gold.* Green *Vitriol*, saith *Ripley*, being *Stillicidium Veneris (or common Vitriol)* is by many *Philosophers* called *Roman Gold*, because of the abundance of its *Noble Tincture*, which ought to be fermented with common Gold, *Pag.* 140. *Medulla Philos.* For *Vitriol*, *he goes on*, is nothing else but *Stillicidium Cupri (or droppings of Copper)* in the Mynes, wherein Copper is generated, as *Bartholomæus* (an *English Monk* and *Philosopher*) saith; and though it hath an admirable *Tincture* of redness, yet is that *Tincture* polluted with an unclean terrestreity, which is called its original blemish, which hinders Gold and Silver from being made of it. Therefore saith *Raymund*, let not the Terrestrial Virtues over power the Cœlestial Virtues (*of the Sun and the rest of the Stars*) and you will have a good thing in *Vitriol. Pag.* 303. *Pupillæ.*

Arnold *to shew the Golden Nature in common* Vitriol *to his Disciple, resolved to prove it by an Experiment, in* Speculo Alchymiæ, *Pag.* 605. *Vol.* 4. *Theat. Chym. where thus by the way of Dialogue. Disciple*, I wonder, good Master, that you commended Brass so much, I know not whether there be so great a secret in it, I thought it to be a leprous Body, because of that greenness which it hath in it: Wherefore I still admire what you said, that we ought to extract *Argent vive (Menstruum)* out of this Body. *Master*, Son! You must know, that the *Philosophers Brass* is their Gold, and therefore saith *Aristotle* in his Book, Our Gold is not common Gold, because that greenness which is in that Body, is the whole Perfection of it, because that greenness is by our Magistry suddenly turned into most true Gold, as we know by experience; and if you have a mind to try, we will give you a Rule. Take *Æs ustum* well and perfectly rubified (*common to be Sold in Shops*) and let it drink seven times of the Oyl *Duenech* (*Spirit of Philosophical Wine*) as much as it can drink, always assating and reducing (*cohobating and calcining*) then cause it to descend (*melting this* Vitriol *being impregnated with the aforesaid Oyl into a* Regulus) for pure Gold settles as grains (*of Kermes*) red and pure; and you must know that so great a redness descends with it, as to tinge some quantity of Silver of a most true Colour, *&c.*

 To

To alledge all, that the *Philosophers* have said of the Golden Nature of *Vitriol*, would be too much, peruse *Basilius* alone, especially the *fourth* and *fifth* Chapter, *De Rebus Naturalibus & Supernaturalibus*, as also in the *Elucidation of the* 12. *Keyes*, and you will find *Vitriol* more esteemed by him than any Gold, for his Doctrine is that the Tincture of the *Vitriol* of *Venus* and *Mars*, is far better than the *Sulphur* of *Gold*, not indeed in its Kind, for it is one and the same in all, but that this Tincture is in the Natural as well as Artificial *Vitriol* of *Venus* and *Mars* higher, and more noble in Colour, more abundant in Quantity, of easier Separation from its Body, in Preparation, and of less Charge in the use, than the *Tincture* that is in Gold.

4. *Because it is Gold opened, not yet fused, and so of easier preparation.* You have laboured, saith *Isaacus*, a long time, before this Matter is made subtil and spiritual enough to be sublimed: But if you could procure the Stone, which God hath given us freely, there would be no need to prepare it so: But you might presently take it, reduce it to an impalpable Powder, and wash away the uncleanness of it with a common Water, till the Matter came clear from it, then dry it again, and it would be ready for Sublimation, in which respect the Work of it is shorter. *Cap.* 22. *Pag.* 317. *Vol.* 3. *Theat. Chym.* To speak more plainly, *saith Ripley*, I affirm, that the more subtil a Body is, of the easier Dissolution it is. And moreover you must know, that Dissolution ought to be performed by our Vegetable *Menstruum*, or some other Vegetable. And this Vegetable *Mercury* (*Vegetable Menstruum*) cannot penetrate a Body, so as to complete the dissolution of it, except the Body be first made spongy; but no Lead is so spongy, nor so subtil, as Red Lead or Minium (*Vitriol calcined*) and therefore if we would not be frustrated of our expectation, it is necessary for us to take Red Lead, that is, *Antimony* prepared, which is more spongy and subtil, than any other Lead. For the (*Vegetable*) Water will suddenly penetrate into it, and dissolve the most subtil parts of it. But now to declare further concerning the second Body, which is *Roman Vitriol*, you must know, that it is an easier thing to make the separation of the Elements in a thing com-

plexioned,

plexioned, which was never before forced into a hard and compact Substance by the violence of Fire, than to perform the same in a Substance forced into a hard Mass, or in a Metallick and Stony Substance, wherein the Congalative Virtue is extinguished, and therefore in respect to the other is made Intractable, not being soft nor unctious, and consequently less obedient to Solution and Separation; for *Vitriol* is nothing else but, *&c.* Pag. 301. *Pupillæ.*

4. *That the Adepts in the more secret Chymy meant four things chiefly by the* Stone.

1. *The Matter of the* Menstruum *or* Spirit *of* Philosophical Wine, *of which God willing, in the* Fifth Book.

2. *All* Menstruums *whatsoever, made with the* Spirit *of* Philosophical Wine. *Examples enough you will find in the Receipts of* Menstruums *produced to you.*

3. *Every Matter of the* Philosophers Stone; *so Gold and Silver are in many places called* Stones, *but by the* Stones which God hath given us freely *Isaacus meant* Vitriol *for the* Red, *and* Alume *for the* White. *Cap.* 39. 3. *Oper. Miner. Pag.* 67. *He hath besides these two other Stones also made of* Arseniek *and* Auripigment *both graduated, of which see the Six former Chapters,* 1. *Oper.* and *Cap.* 112. and 113. 2. *Oper. Miner. But of these in their proper places.*

4. *Every Alchymical Tincture, tho not in the form of a* Stone, *but* Oyl.

5. *That* Menstruums *made of* Vitriol *or* Venus *are indeed better than the rest in point of Tinging but not Dissolving.*

The Three and Twentieth KIND.

Mineral Menstruums *made of* Mineral Menstruums *compounded*, *and* Metallick Bodies *and other* Tinging Things.

131. *The* Oyl *of* Mars *and* Venus *of* Basilius. *Libro de Conclusion. Sect.* 1. *Cap.* 3.

TAke of *Verdegrese* some Pounds, and with (*Philosophical*) Vinegar distilled make an Extraction, which is cristallized into a Noble *Vitriol*; out of which by a Retort is distilled a Red Oyl, which dissolves *Mars* into *Vitriol*, out of which is the Red Oyl extracted again in a long time, and with a strong Fire; and thus have you the Sulphur of *Mars* and *Venus* together: with this Oyl is *Luna* graduated, and a good part of the Kings Crown obtained, a part dissolved with a part of *Sol* and *Luna* together, and putrified in this Oyl eight days and nights, is changed into good Gold. Praised be God.

Annotations.

THo every Mineral Menstruum *is able enough to dissolve any Body whatsoever, yet the Adepts thought good to acuate them yet more, by the addition of* Metallick Bodies, *that they might the better dissolve and tinge their Dissolutions. In the present Receipt* Basilius *dissolves* Mars *in the Spirit of* Venus, *described before in Numb.* 113. *reduceth it into* Vitriol, *and at last distils it into a Compounded Oyl. Sect.* 2. *Cap.* 4. *This* Menstruum *he calls Oyl of the Salt of* Mars: Now, *ſaith he*, I have taught you how to extract a clear *Vitriol* out of *Venus*, and to diſtil its Red Oyl; this Oyl diſſolves *Mars* into *Vitriol*, and being yet once diſtilled ſtrongly by a Retort, you will have a Noble Tinging Oyl, or Salt of *Mars*, which is a Subject that pays Tribute to the King, and enricheth him. This Oyl diſſolves the Purple Spiritual Gold, and brings it over the Helm, *&c. The Proceſs of this Oyl of the Salt of* Mars, *&c. being by its brevity too obſcure, will be not a little illuſtrated by the following Spirit of* Mercury.

132. *The* Spirit *of* Univerſal Mercury *made of* Vitriol *of* Baſilius.

Labore 2. Libri Revelat.

TAke Common Copper, make *Verdegreſe* of it after the common way, grind it, pour to it a good quantity of Diſtilled Vinegar (*Philoſophical, or Vinegar mix'd with the Spirit of Philoſophical Wine*) ſtir it well, and the *Verdegreaſe* will be diſſolved, let the Feces ſettle, and the Solution will be very pure, clear and green: Draw off the Vinegar in a Cucurbit to thickneſs, and in a cold place a weighty *Vitriol* graduated to the higheſt degree will be criſtallized, which again diſſolve in hot Water, evaporate the Water till it be thick; put it again in a cold place, and the *Vitriol* will be again coagulated: which ſolution and coagulation muſt be three times repeated, and the purification of the *Vitriol* will be perfect: Let the *Phlegm* evaporate from this *Vitriol* in a Calcining Pot, and calcine it till it begins to be red, that is enough. Then take pure Flints, calcine, and being red hot, quench them in Diſtilled Vinegar, repeat ſome certain times, till they be well calcined: Then again calcine, and when they are a little cool, pour to them (*Philoſophical*) Vinegar made hot, and let them be gradually dried. Of theſe little Stones thus prepared, take one part, of the *Vitriol* now calcined two parts, grind and mix, put the Matter in an Earthen Retort, that will not ſuck up the Spirits, or in a Glaſs Retort well luted, put a large Receiver to it, and the Vessel being well luted, kindle a Fire by degrees the space of 24 hours, then give a stronger Fire 24 hours more, and the Green Spirits will come over White, and the Fire being thus continued Red Drops at last: Keep this violent Fire, till all the Spirits and Drops are gone over, then put the Distillation in a *Cucurbit*, and the Vessel being very close, rectifie it in *Balneo* with a most gentle Fire, and the *Phlegme* will ascend, but in the bottom of the *Cucurbit* will remain the Oyl of *Vitriol* red and ponderous. This Work being finished, Take pure Filings of Iron, put them in a *Cucurbit*, pour to them the said Oyl of *Vitriol*, so as to swim above them, add so much distilled Rain Water, till you see that the Oyl dissolves the Iron; then draw of the *Phlegme* by Distillation, and let the remainder cristallize in a cold place into pure *Vitriol*, and thus are *Mars* and *Venus* joyned together: This *Vitriol* calcine it under a Tyle, and stir it with an Iron Hook into a fine reddish Powder: This Powder put into a Glass Retort, well luted, and the Vessels being very close, distil by degrees of Fire, as you distilled the Oyl aforesaid, and first you will have a White Spirit, which is the *Philosophers Mercury*, then a Red Spirit, which is the *Philosophers Sulphur*, an incombustible Oyl compounded of both the *Tinctures* of *Venus* and *Mars* never to be separated, and this is the Blood of the *Green* and *Red Lyon*; with which the King their Father ought to be nourished, draw of the Plegms from this Oyl in *Balneo*, and it is prepared for Gold to be tinged with it. Take the *Caput Mortuum*, which is of a Beautiful Crimson Colour, grind it to a most fine Powder, put it in a Glass, pour (*Philosophical*) Vinegar distilled to it, digest three days in a gentle heat, to extract the Salt, wherein lye the Treasures of the whole World, without which Salt, all labour would be in vain; draw off the *Vinegar* in Ashes, and the Salt will remain in the Glass, to which, pour the aforesaid Oyl (*of Venus and Mars*) in a Glass Retort, and the Salt will be presently dissolved, and then distil with the same violence, as before, and the Oyl will carry its own Spirit of Salt over with it, which rectify once in *Balneo*, and it will be ten times stronger than before; and you have the incombustible Oyl of *Mercury*,

Sulphur,

Sulphur and *Salt*, issuing out of one root prepared; this Oyl is the true first Matter of Metals, and the true root from which Gold is generated.

This Spirit of Mercury, ye searchers of Nature! *has been to my knowledge, detrimental to many unwary men, seeking after it either too inconsiderately, or arrogantly, which to prevent for the future, I will somewhat more clearly manifest the Nature, Qualities, and Original of it. Common Verdegrese reduced into* Vitriol *by Vinegar, then three times dissolved in common Water, and coagulated, must be calcined to redness in an open Vessel, that the superfluous* Phlegm *may be drawn away, and made fitter for the ensuing Distillation. But whoever calcined* Verdegrese *purified, in* Apothecaries Shops, *call'd the flowers of* Verdegrese, *to redness, without the diminution of its Virtues? Who I say has distil'd a most Red Oyl out of this calcined Powder?* Verdegrese *therefore must be dissolved not in common, but* Philosophical Vinegar, *in order to be not only purified, but reduced also into* Vitriol, *graduated to the highest. In the* 20th *Kind*, Basilius *distils the same Red Oyl of* Venus, *ponderous as Lead or Gold, thick as Blood, and of a fiery quality; that is, of extream acidity, out of* Roman Vitriol *being highly graduated, that is, either macerated, or throughly dissolved in the Spirit of* Philosophical Wine. *In the* 21th *Kind, We took Notice, that the same* Vitriol *of* Copper *or* Verdegrese *being purified with common Vinegar, was reduced into a graduated* Vitriol; *not indeed by the Spirit of* Philosophical Wine *alone, but with the juice of Sowre Grapes, that is, mix'd with common Vinegar, or some other stronger Acid, and then distilled into the Oyl of* Venus. *If Metals, Minerals, and all other Acids dissolved in acids, and reduced into* Vitriols, *be so graduated with the Spirit of* Philosophical Wine *or* Philosophical Vinegar, *that the desired Oyls may be drawn from them, the reason why* Vitriols *alone made of* Copper, *should be deprived of the said Priviledge, cannot easily be apprehended: It matters not whether* Vitriol *be graduated according to the method given in* Numb. 113. *or according to the prescription of the present Receipt, for the same Spirit and Oyl is produced either way.*

Now this Oyl of Venus *being made, and diluted in common Water, Iron is reduced into graduated* Vitriol, *which must like the* Vitriol *of* Venus *be also calcined into a Red Colour, and then distilled into a White Spirit and Red Oyl. The Method of this Process is*, in Libro particul. in particulari Martis, *thus*: Take off the Red Oyl of *Vitriol* one part, of *Spring-water* two parts, mix, wherein dissolve the Filings of Steel, filter the Solution warm, then evaporate it gently to the comsumption of a third part, and in a cold place you shall find Cristals sweet as Sugar, the true (*that is graduated*) Vitriol of *Mars*, from which decant the Solution, then draw it off a little, and in a cold place you will have New Cristals, which gently calcine under a Tyle, stirring them continually with an Iron Spatula, into a Powder of a Purple Colour, to which pour (*Philosophical*) distil'd Vinegar; extract the Soul (*Tincture or Essence*) of *Mars*, draw off the Vinegar, and edulcorate the Soul: This is that Soul of *Mars*, which being dissolved in the Spirit of *Mercury*, and united with the Soul of *Sol*, tingeth *Luna* into *Sol*.

But of these below, The Vitriol *of* Mars *being graduated and calcined into a* Purple Powder *in our Receipt, is without the extraction of its Soul distilled into the* Philosophers Mercury, *and* Philosophical Sulphur, *the true Oyl of* Mars *and* Venus, *the* Menstruum *next fore-going in* Numb. 131. *Out of which, to make the present Spirit of* Mercury, *the Salt must be extracted out of the* Caput mortuum, *with* Philosophical Vinegar, *which Salt being mix'd with the Oyl of* Mars *and* Venus, *and distil'd together through an* Alembick, *is call'd the first Matter of* Metals.

Basilius *sometimes used the Salt and Sulphur of* Sol, *instead of the said Salt extracted out of the* Caput mortuum. *Thus*,

133 The Oyl *of* Mars *and* Venus, *acuated with the* Sulphur *and* Salt *of* Sol *of* Basilius.

In Supplemento.

TAke of the Purple Coloured Gold (*the* Crocus *of Sol*, des Konings Purpur Mantel) half an ounce, of the Philosophers Oyl of *Mercury* (*the Oyl of* Mars *and* Venus) one ounce and half, dissolve, to which add of the Salt of *Sol* two drachms; all being resolved into an Oyl, rectifie it by a Retort, that it may be clear and pellucid.

For the Spirit of Universal Mercury, Basilius *took* Copper *dissolved in* Philosophical Vinegar, *and cristallized into graduated* Vitriol, *and with gentle calcination, reduced it into the true Crocus, or Red Powder of* Venus: *But the Iron he dissolved in the Oyl of* Venus (*distilled out of the said* Crocus *of* Venus) *cristallized and calcined into the* Crocus *of* Mars. *For the present* Menstruum *he requireth Gold dissolved in* Balneo Regis (*described in* Numb. 89.) *and reduced into a volatile graduated* Vitriol, *which then being dissolved in Distil'd Water, he precipitates with three times as much of* Argent Vive, *out of the* Menstruum *but the amalgame from thence produced, he gently calcines under a Tyle, into a* Purple Powder *or* Crocus; *as to the making of which here only by the by, but in the following second and third Books, we shall treat more fully of it. The way of making the Salt of* Sol, *he has thus in* Libro particul. in particulari Solis, *described:* Take the White Body of *Sol* left in the extracting of its Soul, (*the Essence extracted out of the* Crocus of *Sol*, *with the sweet Spirit of Salt described in* Numb. 28.) reverberate it gently for half an hour, that it may be made corporal, then pour to it the Corrosive Water of Honey well rectified, which in a gentle heat will extract the Salt in the space of ten days: All the Salt being extracted, draw off the *Menstruum* from it in *Balneo*, edulcorate the Salt, by repeating Cohobations in common Distilled Water; and lastly, Clarify it with the Spirit of (*Philosophical*) Wine, and you will have the Salt of Gold.

Concerning this Water of Honey, Basilius *in Curra triumphali Antimonii*, Pag. 77. *thus*: Out of sweet Honey may be made the strongest Corrosive and Poyson, which is to most men a thing incredible. *The same affirms* Paracelsus, *saying:* The like is to be understood in Honey, which by its elevations is made much sharper than any *Aqua Fortis* and *Corrosive*, and more penetrative than any Sublimate; such a property of sharpness it hath not Naturally, but by elevation, which changeth this Honey into a Corrosive. *Libro* 5. *Archid. Pag*. 18. *and elsewhere*, *Cap*. 14. *de Morbis Tartar*. *Pag*. 319. Honey of it self is innocent, but in the third elevation becomes mortal.

The way of making this Water, is not indeed in the Writings, which we have either of Basilius *or* Paracelsus; *yet easily will a diligent Disciple learn the same, by the Principles of his Art, for either the* Cœlum Mellifluum *of* Parisinus *must be dissolved in distilled Vinegar, or some stronger acid, or crude Honey cohobated in* Philosophical Vinegar, *that is, common, mix'd with the Spirit of* Philosophical Wine, *and the Process will be shorter and better. But this Salt of Gold may be also made without the said Water of Honey, provided the* Menstruum *be so corrosive as to dissolve the remaining Body of the Gold, thus in* Labore tertio Revelat. *he reverberates the* Caput mortuum *of Gold, the space of three days, then calcines it with an equal weight of the Salt of* Tartar, *which he washeth off with Distilled Water, and extracts the Salt out of the dried* Powder *with Vinegar, which drawing off the Vinegar, he clarifies with the Spirit of Wine, that is, he dissolves, filters, draws off, and cristallizeth it into the true* Salt *of* Sol. *In another place, he extracts the* Salt *of* Gold *by the* Spirit *of Universal* Mercury, *as in* Elucidatione 12. Clavium, *where he affirms, that the* Philosophers Stone *cannot be coagulated or fixed without this* Salt; *and that he hath taught the way of making it in the fourth Key. By the* Philosophers *Oyl of* Mercury, *he means the Oyl of* Mars *and* Venus, *not yet reduced into the* Spirit *of Universal* Mercury, *or acuated with its own* Salt, *and the more fixed part indeed of this* Menstruum, *which he calls the* Philosophers Sulphur, *not the more volatile part, which is call'd the* Philosophers Mercury: *With this* Sulphur *he dissolves the*

Soul

Soul *or* Crocus *of* Sol, *and converts it into potable Gold.* Libro de ſupernaturali Medicina. *Yet ſometimes he would have us take the ſame Oyl of* Mercury *for the Oyl of* Roman Vitriol, *the* Menſtruum *deſcribed in* Numb. 98. So in Libro de particular. in particulari Solis, *he reduceth the white Body of the King (Gold, left in the extraction of the* Soul *or* Crocus *of* Sol) *with* Philoſophical Sulphur, *which is the ſecond Principle in order, and the* Spirit *of* Mercury *(a little before call'd the White Spirit of* Vitriol)*into pure and malleable Gold, as it was before, not in the leaſt defective in colour and virtue.*

Sometimes he acuates the Spirit of Univerſal Mercury, *with the* Sulphur *and* Salt *of other* Metals: *Thus,*

134. *The* Spirit *of* Univerſal Mercury *acuated with the* Sulphur *and* Salt *of* Luna *of* Baſilius.

Libr. partic. in particul. Lunæ.

THe Sulphur of *Luna* being extracted and edulcorated, dry the remainder of the Calx of *Luna*, to which pour the ſame Corroſive Water of Honey, that you uſed for the *Salt* of *Sol*, digeſt gently the ſpace of four or five days, that the *Salt* of the *Luna* may be extracted, which you will know by the Whiteneſs of the *Menſtruum.* All the Salt being extracted, draw off the Water of Honey, edulcorate the Salt; diſtilling and clarifying it with the Spirit of (Philoſophical) Wine. The remainder left in extracting the Salt of the *Luna* edulcorate, and dry, then pour the Spirit of *Tartar* to it, digeſt fifteen days, and proceed as with the Gold, and you will have the *Mercury* of *Luna* (*of which in the* Second Book, *for here we uſe it not.*) The ſaid Salt of *Luna* hath excellent Virtues for the Body of Man, of which I ſhall treat in a place more convenient. In the mean time the efficacy of the Salt and Sulphur of *Luna* you will learn by the Proceſs following. Take the Lazurine Sulphur of *Luna*, diſſolved in the Spirit of (*Philoſophical*) Wine (*rectified*) and coagulated; put it in a Cucurbit, pour to it double

double the quantity of the Spirit of *Mercury* made of the White Spirit of Vitriol: In like manner take the Salt of *Luna* extracted and clarified, which mix with three times the quantity of the Spirit of *Mercury*, lute both the Glasses, and digest gently in *Balneo* the space of eight days and nights; have a care that none of the Sulphur and Salt be lost, but let them be in the same quantity as they were separated from the Silver. Putrifaction being ended, mix both Dissolutions and distil, *&c.*

He sometimes acuated this Spirit without Metallick Salt,*and* Sulphurs *only thus:*

135. *The* Spirit *of* Universal Mercury *acuated with the* Sulphur *of* Sol *and* Luna *of* Basilius.

Libro particul. in particul. Lunæ.

TAke of the Sulphur of *Luna* one part, of the Sulphur of *Sol* half a part, of the Spirit of *Mercury* six parts, joyn them together, lute well, digest in a gentle heat, and a Liquor will come over of a Red Colour, distil through an Alembick, so as nothing to remain.

This Spirit of Mercury *he fermented not onely with the Sulphurs of the perfect Bodies; but sometimes added to them withal the Sulphur of some imperfect Metal, as* Mars, *thus:*

136. *The* Spirit *of* Universal Mercury *acuated with the* Sulphur *of* Sol *and* Mars *of* Basilius.

Libro partic. in partic. Solis.

TAke of the Sulphur of *Sol* and of the Sulphur of *Mars*, equal parts of each, of the Spirit of *Mercury* the heighth of two Fingers above them, that the Matter may be well dissolved into a Golden Water of a Ruby Colour, being mix'd, distil through an Alembick, that they may become one, as they were at first from one Stem, keep it well, that nothing may evaporate.

Besides

Besides the Sulphur of Mars *he sometimes added also the Sulphur of* Antimony, *thus:*

137. *The* Spirit *of* Universal Mercury *acuated with the* Sulphurs *of* Sol, Mars, *and* Antimony *of* Basilius.

Libro partic. in particul. Antimonii.

TAke of the Sulphur of *Antimony* two parts, of the Sulphur of *Sol* one part., mix. Take of the Sulphur of *Mars* three parts, of the Spirit of *Mercury* six parts, being well luted digest, that the Sulphur of *Mars* may be wholly dissolved; then cast in a fourth part of the Sulphur of *Antimony* and *Sol*, lute again, and digest till they be all dissolved, then add another fourth part of *Antimony* and *Sol*, repeating the Work, as before, till all be perfectly mix'd, and the Matter made like a thick Red Oyl, distil the whole through an Alembick.

Sometimes he fermented this Spirit after an unusual way, namely, without the Sulphur of any perfect Metal, *but meer imperfect onely, thus:*

138. *The* Spirit *of* Universal Mercury *acuated with the* Sulphur *of* Mars, Jupiter, *and* Saturn *of* Basilius.

Libro partic. in partic. Mercurii Vivi.

TAke of the Soul of *Mars* two Ounces, of the Soul of *Saturn* one Ounce, of the Soul of *Jupiter* one Ounce, dissolve them in six Ounces of the Spirit of *Mercury*, being well dissolved, distil them through an Alembick without any Sediment into a Golden Water like to the transparent Dissolution of Gold.

Tho' these Menstruums *of* Basilius *may well deserve the first place among the Dissolvents of the* Adepts, *yet some of the* Adepts *made* Menstruums *not much inferiour to them.* Isaacus Hollandus *not onely the better to dissolve Bodies, but tinge them also deeper, made his* Menstruums *of Tinging* Menstruums, *and common* Mercury, *but being satiated with the Tinctures (Souls, Sulphurs, &c.) of Tinging Things. Thus made he the* Menstruum *call'd,*

139. *A* Compounded Mercurial Water *for the* Red Work of *Isaacus.*

Cap. 43. 3. Oper. Miner.

TAke *Argent Vive* purged with Salt and Vinegar, which sublime with an equal quantity of *Æs ustum, Crocus* of *Mars*, *Crocus* of *Venus*, and *Lapis Hæmatites*; of *Roman Vitriol* the weight of all, and a little Salt, and repeat the Sublimation seven times, every time with new Species, and the *Mercury* will be sublimed for the Red. Take of *Æs ustum*, *Cinabar*, *Crocus* of *Mars*, *Venus*, *Lapis Hæmatites*, *Antimony*, equal parts of each; of *Roman Vitriol* the weight of all, mix, and reduce to a fine Powder, to which pour of *Aqua Vitæ* compleatly rectifi'd (*Spirit of Philosophical Wine*) the height of two hands breadth, digest in *Balneo* three days, stirring the Matter daily, then draw off the *Aqua Vitæ* with a gentle Fire, then increase the Fire gradually; lastly, force with a most strong Fire for the space of Twelve hours, that all the Spirits may ascend: This Work must be three times repeated with new Matters continually. Take of this Water one Pound, of *Argent Vive* sublimed for the red as much as sufficeth, or you can dissolve, distil, and reserve.

Besides Mercury *he sometimes added also* Sulphur *and* Sal Armoniack *sublimed for the red, thus:*

140. *The*

140. The Philosophers Water made of Three Spirits of Isaacus.

Cap 10. 3. Oper. Min.

TAke of *Roman Vitriol* six parts, of *Lapis Hematites*, *Crocus* of *Mars*, of *Venus*, *Cinabar*, *Æs ustum*, *Mineral Antimony*, of each one part, dry well and mix, put the Matter in a Retort, and pour to it of *Aqua Vitæ* rectifi'd (*Spirit of Philosophical Wine*) four Pounds, distil, and cohobate three times, with the *Caput Mortuum* pulverized: Divide the Water into two parts, whereof save one, in the other dissolve one Ounce of *Salarmoniack*, sublimed to redness, in *Balneo*, which being dissolved, dissolve one Ounce of *Sulphur* prepared: lastly, also put in an Ounce of *Mercury* sublimed for the Red Work: These three being dissolved in the Dissolving Water made of *Aqua Vitæ*, you have a Water, which is deservedly called the *Philosophers Water*, by reason of its admirable and secret Virtues, the Miracles of which must not be described, because not convenient for certain Reasons, &c.

The Preparation of Sulphur, Take of *Sulphur Vivum* 12 Pounds, to which being pulverized, pour distilled (*Philosophical*) Vinegar, let them boyl gently in *Balneo*, the Vessel being very close the space of three days; decant the Vinegar being now tinged warily; to the residue, pour New Vinegar, digest, and decant, and so often repeat, till no more Vinegar will be tinged: The tinged Matter distil gently in *Balneo*, to the remainder of a fourth part; from the residue, you will in the space of three or four days in a cold Celler receive Cristals (*the graduated* Vitriol *of* Sulphur) like *Niter*, clear as *Amber*, and of the colour of Gold: The remaining Vinegar evaporate into a Golden Powder, then dissolve the Cristals and Powder in the aforesaid Vinegar, and Cristallize, and that so oft, till the *Sulphur* leaves no Feces behind it: This is a great *Alchymical Secret* for the Purging of *Sulphur*. *The Preparation of* Mercury, Take of

 Roman

Roman Vitriol (*by which the Adepts do more than often mean that which is graduated*) six or eight Pounds, of common Salt two Pounds, mix them together with three Pounds of *Mercury*, purged with Salt and Vinegar, sublime the *Mercury*, and that repeat three times always with new Species, keep the *Mercury*.

The Preparation of Salarmoniack, Take of *Salarmoniack* three Pounds, sublime it thrice with *Roman Vitriol*, and *Lapis hæmatites*, with New Matters every time.

Tho these Menstruums *of* Isaacus *are not so much esteemed, as those before of* Basilius, *as to the Excellency of Preparation, yet are they of no less but the same Virtue with those, as to the quality of tinging, for they are made of the same* Sulphurs, Crocusses, *and* Essences *of* Mars, Venus, Sulphur, *&c. as the compounded* Mineral Menstruums *of* Basilius *were made of.* Lully *acuates the same* Menstruums *with* Metallick Essences, *not indeed already made; but to be made in the preparation of the* Menstruum, *thus with the* Stinking Menstruum, *acuated with* Vegetable Salharmoniack, *he makes the Essence of* Luna, *which being mix'd with the said* Menstruum, *becomes a* Menstruum *of this Kind, and is called.*

141. *The* Compounded Water *of* Silver *of* Lully.

Cap. 10. Practicæ Testamenti majoris. Pag. 161. Vol: 4. Th. Chym.

IN the Power of A (*God*,) take one Ounce of F (*clear* Luna, *Pag.* 171.) well purged and refined: And that Silver being well beaten (*extended with a Hammer*) into Leaves, cut them into small pieces, short and slender, then divide them into two equal parts, and take two dissolving Glasses, the Form and Measure of which, you will see in the *Chapter of Vessels*; and in one of these two, put one Ounce and a half of E (*Menstrual* Pag. 171, *alleadged by us before, in* Numb. 67.) I mean the eighth part of the whole *Menstrual*, then put in presently one part of F, and be careful immediately to stop the Mouth of the Vessel with its Cover, and

lute

and warily, that the Earth of F may not be ſtrained with the Water, nor the Water troubled, and ſtop the ſaid Phial wherein you put the Water of F, and keep it apart. Then upon the Diſſolving Veſſel of that F, which ought to be diſſolved (*the other part of Silver to be diſtilled into a Menſtruum*) put its *Alembick*, which muſt be cloſe and diſcreetly joyned with the luting aforeſaid; then place it upon Sifted Aſhes, and ſetting it on a Fornace, kindle your Fire and diſtil, put the Liquor in a Glaſs Phial, and make a Fire of Saw-duſt, and when the Liquor is in a manner all diſtilled, ſtrengthen the Fire a little with Coals, according to that which is uſed for the exact calcining of an Earth, but keep it from too much heat, for we have ſeen it done by the heat of the Sun; underſtand this well, unleſs you would be made a fool, give this heat continually for eleven hours, then ſtop the Fornace, and go to ſleep, and in the Morning take your Calcinatory (*which is ſo called becauſe of the property of its operation*) and put in the *Menſtrual* often mentioned, wherein G (*our Mercurial* Pag. 171. *or Vegetable Sal armoniack*) was diſſolved (*ſee the Menſtruum below in* Numb. 147.) and you will ſee it operate, and the fume aſcend, and the Metal calcined with *Liquefaction*, but ſtop it better than before with its own ſtopple, which goes in (to the ſaid Calcinatory) and have a care of puting it into any other heat, till it hath operated by its own Virtue, and when it hath wrought and is quiet, lute the joynt well with common Wax, and being ſo luted, put it in a hot *Balneo Mariæ* three Natural days, as you did elſewhere, becauſe it is ſo expedient. Then diſtil the Water, and calcine the Earth (*remaining in the bottom*) as aforeſaid, and repeat ſo oft till all the Earth is diſſolved by this Method in the Form of a Liquor, and the *Diſſolved Limus*, or Oyl by Art diſſolved, which is the Subſtance of a Body depurated by Water, and carried by

 the

the Water of the Wind, always keep apart, and when it is all dissolved (*and distilled*) joyn them together; then putrifie six weeks (*to be circulated*) in a temperate heat, where the Vessel must be very well luted with its Cover, and so ought the Figure of I to be done (*the composition, or compounded Water of* Luna, *Pag.* 171. *of the same Volume.*)

The same way sometimes he prepares the Essence *of Gold with the* Stinking Lunar Menstruum, *by addition of which, he makes the same* Menstruum *more acute, that is more noble.*

142. *The* Stinking Lunar Menstruum *acuated with the* Essence *of* Sol *of* Lully.

In Experimento 30.

TAke the aforesaid Water, wherein you have the Soul of *Luna* (*described in Numb.* 121.) and dissolve in it two Ounces or one and a half of the fixed Salt of *Urine*, as you have it in its Experiment (*the sixth, but produced by us in* Numb. 30.) which being dissolved, dissolve one Ounce of Gold in that Water, putrefie eight days, then separate the Water by *Balneo*, and the Body will remain in the Vessel like melted honey, (upon which Matter pour back so much of the Distilled Water, as to swim two fingers above it, cover the Vessel with its *Antenotorium*, and putrefie in *Balneo* the space of 24 hours, then put on an *Alembick* with a Receiver, lute the joynts well, distil in Ashes; lastly, increase the fire extreamly, and that which comes over, keep very close, for it is the animated *Spirit*, or *Soul* of the *Gold*.

Form

From the Receipts we observe.

1. *That the* Menstruums *of this Kind are more noble than those of the* 20th and 21th *Kinds; there the Essences or Magisteries of* Metals *were dissolved in Simple* Mineral Menstruums, *but here in the same compounded.*

2. *That these* Menstruums *differ not from the* Menstruums *of the Tenth Kind, but in the addition of Acidity; dissolve a* Menstruum *of the said Kind in what Acid you will, and it will be forthwith transformed into a* Menstruum *of this Kind.*

3. *That these* Menstruums *are by Digestion made sweet again, and Vegetable as before.*

4. *That these* Menstruums *are not satiated, but by their Dissolutions augmented, as well in quantity as quality* in infinitum.

5. *That the Spirit of* Universal Mercury, *or first Matter of Metals of* Basilius, *is by him also called* Mercury duplicated, *wherein the Kings Mantle is to be dissolved.* Sect. 1. Cap. de Sulphure Mercurii, Sect. 2. de Vitriolo Phil. *and* Sect. 3. Cap. 4. de Vitriolo Veneris. *In another place,* the Sulphur *of* Mars *and* Venus duplicated. Sect. 1. Cap. 3. de Sulph. Martis & Veneris. *In another place the* Soul of *Mars* and *Venus*, as in Particul. Veneris.

6. *That this* duplicated Mercury is *made much better by adding the Kings* Mantle, *the* Crocus *of* Sol, Luna, *and other* Metals. *That the* Menstruums *of almost all Kinds are promiscuously called* Philosophers Mercuries, *but of these more copiously and more exactly in the* Third Book.

7. *That the Spirit of* Universal Mercury *of* Basilius, *is the same with the* Magisteries *of* Mars *and* Venus, *made after the* Mineral *way; dissolve the Magisteries of* Mars *and* Venus *in the common Spirit of* Vitriol, *and by this simple Dissolution, you will make the same Spirit of* Universal Mercury.

8. *That*

8. *That as* Mars *and* Venus, *so also* Jupiter *and* Saturn, *and the rest of the* Metals, *may be made into the said first* Matters, *that is, of the same Virtues with the first* Matter *of* Mars *and* Venus, *as to the faculty of dissolving:* *But* Mars *and* Venus *are preferred for the excellency and exuberance of their* Tinctures.

The

The Four and Twentieth KIND.

Mineral Menstruums *compounded of* Vegetable *and* Mineral Menstruums *mix'd together.*

143. *The* Vegetable Fire *dissolved in the* Calcinative Water *of* Lully.

Pag. 363. Magiæ Naturalis.

TAke of the Vegetable Water acuated (*the Metallick Soul of* Lully , *described in* Numb. 5.) one Ounce, put it in a Phial with a long Neck, into which you poured three Ounces of the Calcinative Water (*the* Mineral Menstruum *described in* Numb. 68.) and suddenly cover the Phial with its Cover, luted close with Wax, then place it well in a *Balneo*, the space of two Natural days, and in that time, the whole Vegetable will be converted into Clear Water.

Animadversions.

THe *Adepts acuated the Spirit of* Philosophical Wine *divers ways, and reduced it into several as well* Vegetable *as* Mineral Menstruums *in the antecedent Kinds. Now in this* 24th *and last Kind of* Menstruums, *they mix not either common Oyly or Arid, or Acid Matters, with the Unctious Spirit of* Philosophical Wine , *as they did in the aforesaid Compositions of* Menstruums, *but joyn* Vegetable *and* Mineral Menstruums ,

Menstruums, *already perfected together, in order to make* Menstruums *of this Kind. The like* Menstruum *almost is made by* Luly, *and call'd*

144. *The* Vegetable Heaven *dissolved in a* Mineral Menstruum *of* Lully.

Pag. 59. Testam. Novissimi.

TAke of the *Stinking Menstruum* (*described in* Numb. 99.) one Pound; add one Pound, or half a Pound, which will be enough, of *Aqua Vitæ* most perfectly rectified (*Philosophical, described in* Numb. 50.) and acuated with the sublimed Salt of *Tartar*, (*in* Numb. 17.) or Wine: Hold the Vessel in your hands, and do not put it on the ground or any other place, till the fury (*of the ebullition*) is over, and it is a mixture of a Vegetable with a Mineral; seal it with Wax, and let it stand a day, then put it two days in *Balneo*, and distil in Ashes, and you will have a limpid, clarify'd and ponderous Water; then put it in a Circulating Vessel very well sealed; the space of sixteen days in *Balneo* conveniently, till you return, and see the Water well united, and at the Bottom of the Vessel, in the form of a Cristalline Salt, keep it.

The same Menstruum *but of different weight he made elsewhere, he added half a part of the* Vegetable Menstruum *to one part of the* Stinking Menstruum *in the antecedent, but in the following* Menstruum *he takes more of the* Vegetable *than* Mineral Menstruum.

145. Ice *compounded of* Vegetable *and* Mineral Menstruums *of* Lully.

Pag. 68. Testam. Noviss.

TAke of the *Mineral G, or Stinking Menstruum*, three Ounces, and of *Aqua Vitæ* rectify'd and acuated with the Salt of *Tartar* four Ounces, put them together in a Glass,

and

and distil nine times in *Balneo*, and in that time it will be all converted into one, as *Ice.*

Ripley *mix'd vegetable and mineral* Menstruums *thus.*

146. *The* Aqua Mirabilis *of* Ripley. *Pag.* 212. *Philorcii.*

TAke the *Tartar* calcined white as Snow, grind it upon a Marble, and incerate it with *Aqua Vitæ* fortified with its Species, as is premised (*with the* Menstruum *described in* Numb. 8.) till it be as thin paste; then put it in a Circulating Vessel, and circulate the Water, till it is wholly dried up in the Tartar; repeat the same Work, and so continue, till it hath drank off the Water double its part and quantity in weight, which done, grind the Tartar, and lay it upon a Stone, or hang it in a Linnen Bag, and put a Glass under to receive the droppings of it, and this must be done in a place under ground, till all the *Tartar* is distilled into clear Water; out of which, after Distillation and Coagulation, is made a wonderful Salt of Nature, which the *Philosophers* call *Salt-peter*, and incombustible *Sulphur* (*properly the volatile Salt of Tartar*) which fixeth any *Argent Vive:* But to have perfect *Aqua Vitæ* (*requisite for this Work*) put (*Philosophical*) Wine in a Circulatory, for a hundred days, to be circulated with its Species, and then extract *Aqua Vitæ* out of it (*the Menstruum in* Numb. 23.) because if you put to it as much *Salharmoniack* sublimed as *Tartar*, one drop of it, after it is perfected, suddenly kills a *Cancer* in the Flesh of Man, and if it be dropped upon ones hand, penetrates it, and dissolves every Body. Without this Water we profit little in this Art, and he that has this Water, will not in the least doubt of compleating the Art: But this Water is made twice as strong, if an equal quantity of the Mineral Spirit, which is the *Philosophers* acute Water (*the Green Lyon of* Ripley *in* Numb. 59.) be added to it, and then circulated upon the Tartar, and upon the *Sal harmoniack* to spissity,

sity, and then dissolved into Water; which if done, this Water will be of greater value than any Gold, and one of the wonderful things of this World.

Sometimes they mixed Vegetable Salharmoniack, *instead of* Vegetable Menstruum, *with* Mineral Menstruums. *Thus*,

147. *The* Stinking Menstruum *acuated with the* Salharmoniack *of* Lully.

TAke of the vegetable G. (*Vegetable* Mercury *or* Salharmoniack) one Ounce, put it in the Phial with a long neck, wherein you put three Ounces of E before (*the Stinking Menstrumm in* Numb. 67.) and presently stop it with its stopple, sealed with common Wax, that nothing may respire, then distil in a hot *Balneo*, the space of three Natural days, into a clear dissolved Water.

As they added Salharmoniack *to simple* Mineral Menstruums, *so also to the same compounded.*

148. *The Stinking* Lunar Menstruum, *acuated with* Vegetable Salharmoniack *of* Lully.

Cap. 14. *Practicæ Test. Major. Pag.* 163. *Vol.* 4. *Th. Chym.*

IN the power of A (*God*) take one Ounce of the Compounded Water of Silver (*described in* Numb. 141.) distilled through an *Alembick*, and put to it one Ounce of the vegetable G. (*Mercury* or *Salharmoniack*) dissolve, *&c.*

Basilius *mixed these* Menstruums *thus.*

149. *The Spirit of* Mercury *mixed with* Vitriol *and the Fiery Spirit of Wine of* Basilius.

Labor 3. Libri Revelat.

TAke off this Oyl (*the first Matter of* Metals *made out of* Venus *and* Mars, *or Spirit of* Universal Mercury *described in* Numb. 132.) eight Ounces, of the Spirit of Wine rectified to the highest (*the Menstruum described in* Numb. 19.) five Ounces, distil by a Glass Retort, and that three times; always with New Spirit, so as that fifteen Ounces of the fiery Spirit of Wine may be joyned to the eight Ounces of Oyl.

Paracelsus *made the following mix'd* Menstruum *for the* Arcanum Lapidis *or* Antimony.

150. *The mix'd* Menstruum *of* Paracelsus.

Cap. 6. Lib. 10. Archidon. Pag. 39.

WHoever desires to graduate his Metallick Heaven (*Antimony*) to the highest, and reduce it to an Action, must first extract the liquid *primum Ens* Cœlestial Fire, Quintessence of *Mercury*, (*not of* Sol; *as it is ill read in the* Latine)and the Metallick *Acetum acerrimum* (*the Circulatum majus of* Paracelsus *described in* Numb. 51.) out of its life, that is, common *Mercury*, by dissolving it with its Mother, that is, the *Arcanum* of Salt (*Salt circulated in* Numb. 27.) and mix it with the Stomack of *Anthion*, that is, the Spirit of *Vitriol* (*the* Menstruum *described in* Numb. 98.) and in it (*the mix'd* Menstuum) dissolve, digest, *&c.* the coagulated *Mercury* of *Antimony* (*the Regulus of Antimony*.)

From the Receipts we obſerve.

1. THat theſe Menſtruums *are the mixtures of divers* Menſtruums.

2. *And that they may be made of all* Vegetable *and* Mineral Menſtruums, *being mix'd together at the Artiſts pleaſure.*

3. *Yet that they are made the better, the more tinging the* Menſtruums *were.*

4. *That theſe* Menſtruums *do by Digeſtion become ſweet and pure Vegetable* Menſtruums.

EPI-

EPILOGUE.

THese are the things, My Friends! which I promised you; the Menstruums of Diana, hitherto by none but the Adepts described, declared, and rightly applied to Use, and are now by me so manifestly explained, and distributed into their Kinds, that they may be distinctly apprehended even by the meanest Chymists. There are indeed many more Menstruums remaining (for Diana has superfluity of Menstruums) which I have not shewed you; but I thought these sufficient, as Examples to you: You, if you please, may collect more, and appropriate them to their Kinds: But if it be our duty to respect the common Good, I could wish you would communicate to me some of the more rare Manuscripts or Impressions of the Adepts, if you have any in your Studies or Libraries, that they may be of service not only to you, but to all Mankind, or at least signifie their Names to me, that I may either buy, or by entreaty borrow them of you or others; especially you being already well assured, that in Practical Books all Secrets depend upon the Spirit of Philosophical Wine, but that in the Theoretick, they are all most obscure, being figurative, and not in the least to be understood according to the Letter; which, if you keep longer in your Libraries, will be dayly exposed to a thousand dangers, and at length, as nothing worth, being mouldy and rotten, become the Aliment of Time, the Consumer of all things.

In the mean time, despise not these Receipts of Menstruums offered to you, but rather read and peruse them, and every where endeavour to find out the Chymical Truth, but those which you do not either understand, or not esteem, cast away as trivial; for if one only Kind, or any one Receipt of a Kind out of four and twenty, please you, it is sufficient; for we will easily prove that by that one, all the Secrets of the more Secret Chymy may be prepared.

If also you are pleased to object against the Authority, yea Honesty and Sincerity of this or that Adept, as, Paracelsus, Lully, &c. you may leave him, and reject his Receipts, making choice of

any

any other, in whom you may have greater confidence, and we will prove all the rest by his Receipt: Learn therefore the ways of making these Menstruums, *observe their* Orders, Degrees, Matters, Methods *of* Making, *the* Virtues *of* Dissolving, Tinging, Multiplying *themselves,* &c. *and you will acknowledge them to be the best Instruments of all the more* Secret Chymy, *as Keys, without which nothing, and with which all the Secrets of this Art are opened and unlocked.*

To make these Things, which we have declared in the former Discourse, of the Excellencies of the Menstruums, *more easie to you, I will here contract into a Breviary, and reduce them into twelve subsequent and infallible Conclusions.*

I.

That the Descriptions of these *Menstruums* are understood according to the Sound of the Letter.

THat *the Receipts of this Book contain nothing occult, but the* Spirit *of* Philosophical Wine *(the* Use *only of which we promised to define) you will easily vouchsafe us your Assent. Nor yet is it too obscure, but that it may be properly called an* unctuous Spirit, *proceeding from the* White *and* Red Wine *of* Lully, *the Constitutives of the* Menstruum fœtens: *The rest, which seem more obscure, are Terms of Art, for the most part explained in the very Descriptions of the Receipts of things made and produced from this Spirit: But the obscurity, which a shorter or longer description of a Receipt causeth, is by accident, to be easily overcome and removed by any diligent Disciple of this Art.*

II.

That no one of the aforesaid *Menstruums* is prepared without the *Spirit* of *Philosophical Wine.*

A*Mong all these* Menstruums *of the* Adepts *imparted to you, there is not one, which has not the* Spirit *of* Philosophical Wine *for its Basis. There are indeed* Menstruums, *in the Receipts of which, we meet not with the Name of this* Spirit, *yet there it is*

lurking

lurking under the name of this or that Menſtruum. *Other Receipts of* Menſtruums *there are, which do not take the* Spirit *of* Philoſophical Wine *free, but as it were fettered, that is, any Common Oyl; but when in the making of theſe* Menſtruums *the* Spirit *is unfettered, as alſo acuated, ſuch* Menſtruums *cannot in the leaſt be ſaid to be made without it. There are laſtly alſo* Menſtruums, *in the Receipts of which, neither the* Spirit *of* Philoſophical Wine, *nor any Oyley Matter is expreſly mentioned (but theſe are more rare, on purpoſe alledg'd to ſhew us either the Envy or Moroſity of the* Adepts) *whereas notwithſtanding it is by the Uſe of the* Menſtruum, *manifeſt that this* Spirit *is added through neceſſity; for that which is promiſed, could not otherwiſe be effected.*

Finally, There are ſome, which you will affirm may be made with Common Spirit, Common Vinegar, *and* Aqua fortis, *or* Common Sal Armoniack *without the* Spirit *of* Philoſophical Wine: *Suppoſe it ſo; but when you proceed to Practice, and try an Experiment with ſuch a* Menſtruum, *you will ſoon find it not only too weak, but alſo altogether ineffectual, and deſtructive in the more* Secret Chymy: *For it is impoſſible to do that with a common* Menſtruum, *which the* Adepts *have preſcribed by a Philoſophical* Menſtruum. *The Secrets of the more* Secret Chymy *have this Priviledge, that they cannot be made by any man but him that is poſſeſſed of* Philoſophical Wine.

III.

That theſe *Menſtruums* are prepared from any ſort of Matter.

We have demonſtrated that the Menſtruums *aforeſaid are made of divers Oleoſities, Aridities and Acidities of the three Kingdoms. You have obſerved the* ſimple Vegetable Menſtruums *to be made of things neither Tinging nor Acid;* Compounded Vegetable Menſtruums *of things Tinging, not Acid,* Simple Mineral Menſtruums *made of things Acid, and not tinging; the* Compounded, *of things both Acid and Tinging. Wherefore being now better aſſured of your* Menſtrual Matter *hitherto ſo anxiouſly ſought for, you may take crude Mercury, or Vitriol, Niter, common Salt, Salt of Tartar,*

Tartar, or Urine, Rain-Water, May-Dew, the Spirit of the World also, by whatsoever Art obtained, or any other Matter also which you have made choyce of before the rest, for the true and universal Matter of a Menstruum, *in which choyce you will not err ; for it is much at one, whether you make it of Gold or Mercury ; whether of Pearls or Arsenick ; Vegetable or Mineral Salt, provided you proceed according to this or that Kind of* Menstruums, *with consideration also of what Use you would have the* Menstruum, *lest you prepare an Essence instead of a Magistery, or a Poyson for an Antidote : On the contrary, take pure Honey so applauded by* Parisinus, *or the Salt of Tartar, commended by* Ripley ; *or common Salt, esteemed by* Paracelsus, *as the Matrix of Metals ; or Vitriol abounding with the Tincture of Gold, extolled by* Basilius, *or Argent vive magnify'd by most of the* Adepts, *as the open Metal : Take, I say, which of them you please, but you must know it cannot in the least answer your expectation, except it be joyned, that is, corrected, exalted and graduated with the* Spirit *of* Philosophical Wine.

IV.

That these *Menstruums* are also prepared by any Method.

YOU have here had several Methods of Preparation, which if not satisfactory, you may please to invent new ones. Herein is contained nothing secret, if your Matter, *and the* Spirit *of* Philosophical Wine *be, without any possibility of being separated, mixed together, and distilled either in part or whole, through an Alembick: For every* Matter, *by what method soever volatilized and distilled with the* Spirit *of* Philosophical Wine, *is a* Menstruum.

V.

That these *Menstruums* are sufficient also for every Use.

YOU *have now in this Book observed the* Use *of the* Spirit *of* Philosophical Wine, *as also of most* Menstruums *in these ways of making* Menstruums: *hereafter, in the following Books you will perceive them to be sufficient for every purpose. By these means you will make all the Medicines of the* Adepts,*reduce all Metals into running Mercury, or if you had rather, into the Philosophers Mercury, or first Matter of Metals. By these will you make as well universal as particular Transmutatives of Metals, the best of all in respect of deeper Tincture, shortness of Time, and conciseness of Work. Hereby lastly, will you prepare whatsoever curiosity has been left us by the* Adepts, *and prescribed in their Books, so that if they have any Preparations without the* Spirit *of* Philosophical Wine, *you may decline them without any dammage: For these* Menstruums *do volatilize all fixed Bodies, and fix the volatile and volatilized, dissolve the coagulated, and coagulate the dissolved: Under which few Notions are comprehended all the Operations of the more* Secret Chymy.

VI.

That these *Menstruums* are many.

YOU *have observed divers Kinds of* Menstruums, *designed for several distinct Uses. Simple* Vegetable Menstruums *do extract, rather than dissolve Bodies; the Compounded dissolve only, but not extract: That which* Vegetable Menstruums *do, the* Mineral *cannot; and so on the contrary: Of* Vegetable Menstruums *are made Medicines only,not Poysons; but of* Mineral Menstruums, *Poysons only, and not Antidotes withut the singular dexterity of an Artist. An Use different and contrary to its self admits no universal* Menstruum: *The* Spirit *of* Philosophical Wine *is indeed the universal Matter of them all, but there is not one of all the* Menstruums *sufficient for every Use; wherefore, unless*

less you will for the same reason call every one universal, because they all proceed from the Spirit *of* Light, *the universal Basis of all things, we cannot but deny an universal* Menstruum.

VII.

That some *Menstruums* are corrosive.

THat Mineral Menstruums *are corrosive, and therefore dissolve Bodies with ebullition, is clearly manifest by the Receipts aforesaid. I would not have you, being perhaps not sufficiently instructed in the Sayings of the* Adepts, *every where declaring against* Aqua fortisses, *and all Corrosives, either despise, or think ill of them: These are those* Menstruums *by which the ancient* Adepts *abbreviated their Time and Labour in preparing their Tinctures: And* Paracelsus *justly entituled himself to the Monarchy of* Arcanums, *he having been the principal Instrument in compleating not only the Abbreviations of Alchymy, but moreover introducing these* Mineral Menstruums *to Medicinal Use, and that with so much dexterity, that there seems to be now no hope left to his Disciples of mending any imperfection of this Art, as will be demonstrated in the following Books: Besides, these* Menstruums *differ from the* Vegetable Menstruums *no otherwise, than that an* Acidum *is superadded to them, or to the* Spirit *of* Philosophical Wine, *corroding the* Aridum, *and dividing it into Atoms, making way for the* Oleosum, *to be sooner and better incorporated and mixed together, which notwithstanding do by taking away the* Acidum, *return into the same* Vegetable Menstruums *they were before.*

VIII.

That these *Menstruums* are permanent, yea fixed with Things dissolved in them.

IT *is by the former descriptions of* Menstruums, *manifest, that as well the* Spirit *of* Philosophical Wine, *as* Menstruums *made of it, do stick to the things dissolved in them. There is indeed no better Argument to confirm the excellency of* Menstruums, *than that they are homogeneous and permanent with things dissolved, and consequently*

sequently Dissolvents transmutable with the dissolved into a third substance different from both: These Menstruums *therefore are so far from being immutable, that, according to the* Edict *of the whole Crowd of Philosophers, to wit,* The dissolution of the Body is the coagulation of the Spirit, and so on the contrary, *nothing in the more* Secret Chymy, *can be more infallible. Now this permanence of* Menstruums *you have observed not only in the volatilizations of* Menstruums, *but also in the fixations of some, thus you had the fixation of the* Spirit *of* Philosophical Wine *in the greater* Circulatums *of the* Ninth, *and* Two and Twentieth Kinds; *but you will find more in the Preparations of Medicines, as well as Tinctures. They were by an Analogy of the Ancients ill called* Menstruums, *unless also they could be transformed into the substance of an* Embryo, *and yield proper Nutriment and augmentation to the Infant: The* Spirit *of our* Wine *is indeed an absolute* Oleosum, *that is, combustible, but here being throughly mixed with* Aridums, *it becomes incombustible, and despiseth the violence of Fire: It is also moist, and so uncapable of fixation; but the moister and thinner parts, which it contains, are separated in the work of fixation from the more Oyley Particles being now concentrated. So you observed, that, in the Preparations of the* Sal Harmoniacks, *or* Sulphurs *of* Nature, *the* Spirit *of* Philosophical Wine, *as also the* Vegetable, *as well as* Mineral Menstruums *are partly reduced into insipid Water, and partly sticking to the Matters left in the bottom, and fixed: But better Examples you will have both in the Second and Third Books.*

IX.

That *Menstruums* are not satiated with dissolving, but become rather more avidous, and so are by Dissolutions augmented as well in quantity as quality.

T*Hough the* Spirit *of our* Wine *is the Basis, Root, and Center of all* Menstruums, Medicines, Alchymical Tinctures, *and* Pretious Stones, *yet nevertheless doth it dissolve slowly, yea only such Bodies as are homogeneous to it, that is, purely Oyley, as it self is a pure* Oleosum, *and associate the same to it, transmuting* *into its own Nature, and so multiplies its self by this means. Now so soon as this Spirit is transmuted into an* Arido-Oleosum, *it does under the name of a* Simple Vegetable Menstruum, *dissolve* Arido-Oleosums, *that is, the Sulphurs or Tinctures of the Mineral Kingdom, the pure* Aridum *being untouch'd, and left in the form of a white Powder, with which* Essences *the said* Menstruums *or* Essences *may indeed melt together, but not in the least be satiated, because there is an Addition and Multiplication of like Parts: But the same* Vegetable Menstruums *being now compounded of the* Simple, *do no more extract the Tinctures and Essences of Minerals, but dissolve and transmute the whole Mass or Substance of these Bodies into an Oyl swimming above, which is called a* Magistery: *Now this being digested together with its* Menstruum, *at length falls in, is united, and so multiplies the* Compounded Vegetable Menstruum. *For an Example to young Beginners; The* Spirit *of* Philosophical Wine *being a* Menstruum *of the* first Kind, *and acuated with the Oyl of Nutmegs, is hereby made a* Menstruum *of the* second Kind; *or acuated with Honey, if you would have a* Menstruum *of the* third Kind: *distil either of those* Menstruums *with Common* Sal Harmoniack, *and you will have a* Menstruum *of the* fourth; *but if you desire one of the* fifth Kind, *cohobate either of them with the Salt of* Tartar, *and you will have the* Acetum acerrimum *of* Ripley; *or with common Salt, and you will make the* Sal circulatum *of* Paracelsus; *Cohobate Mercury, or any other Mercury, or any other Metal through an Alembick with this Vinegar or Salt, and you will transmute the* Simple Vegetable Menstruums *into the* Compounded Vegetable Menstruums *of the* eighth Kind; *from which you will further prepare* Menstruums *of the* tenth Kind, *by dissolving and volatilizing any other Metal in them. The same Rule you have as to our* Mineral Menstruums: *But the* Common Menstruums *cannot receive beyond their Capacity.*

10. That

X.

That these *Menstruums* are also Secrets of the Second Book.

YOu have in this Book observed that among the Vegetable Menstruums *there is none but what is either an* Essence, *or a* Magistery, *and it will be more copiously demonstrated in the Book of the Preparations of* Medicines: *You have also taken notice by the aforesaid Receipts of them, especially being compared with the following Descriptions of* Medicines, *that* Mineral Menstruums *are the same Medicines, but mixed and dissolved with* Acids.

XI.

That these *Menstruums* are likewise Secrets of the Third Book.

IT *is now partly clear by the Receipts of them, but will be more clear by the Secrets of the Third Book, that the* Simple Menstruums *are the Philosophers Stones not yet fermented; but the* Compounded *are* Menstruums *mixed with the Masculine Seed, and therefore Volatile and Fermented Stones.*

XII.

That these *Menstruums* are in like manner Secrets of the Fourth Book.

THat these Menstruums *do give Light by Night, and consequently, are perpetual Lights, yield also Matters for Pearls, Pretious Stones,* &c. *the Receipts themselves do shew; which will be confirmed by the Fourth Book.*

RIPLEY,

RIPLEY,

Cap. 13. *Philorcii.*

Without these Waters we do little Good in this Art; but he that hath these Waters, will without all doubt compleat the Art.

The End of the First Book.

ERRATA.

EPist. Ded. pag. 5. l.3. *read* these *for* that. Ep. to the Reader, p. 10. l. 10. *r.* have a mind to. Preface. *p.*3. *l.* 20. *for* Vegetative, *r.* Vegetable. *p.*8. *l.*28. *for* Minerals, *r.* Mineral, *p.* ibid. *r.* fixt Vegetable. *p.* ib. *l.* 8. *after* that, *r.* it scarce deserveth. *p.* 12. *l.* 6. *for* mixt, *r.* mix. *p.* 14. *l.*26. *for* is it, *r.* it is. *p.*24. *l.* 12. *dele* of. *p.* 31. *l.* 3. after oyl, *r.* or middle salts, *for* salts or. *p.* 39. *l.* 5. *for* their, *r.* the. *p.* 42. *l.* 33. *for* with, *r.* which. *p.* 45. *l.* 4. *for* the, *r.* a. *l.* 16. *for* that only are they able to do, *r.* that only is able to do this. *p.* 48. *l.* 16. *for* as, *r.* us. *p.* 54. *l.* 11. *for* fly, *r.* flow. *p.* 56. *l.* 14. *for* drive, *r.* dive. *p.* 69. *l.* 24. *for* distil, *r.* distil'd. *p.* 78. *l.* 19. *for* stored, *r.* restored. *p.* 81. *l.* 1. omit the first four lines wholly. *p.* 95. *l.* 1. *for* the latter is, *r.* it. *p.* 119. *l.* ult. *dele* to. *p.* 127. *l.* 12. *for* Metallick of, *r.* Metals. *p.* 128. *l.* 31. *for* extract, *r.* extracting. *p.* 130. *l.* 32. *for* presers, *r.* preserves. *p.* 138. *l.* 21. *for* wherefore, *r.* whereof. *p.* 146. *l.* ult. *r.* for an *Aurum potabile*, he prepares a *Menstruum* out of Gold and Silver thus. *p.* 152. *for* away, *r.* all the. *p.* 177. *l.* pen. *for* out, *r.* out of. *p.* 181. *l.* 8. *for* its, *r.* in. *p.* 182. *l.* 14. *for* greens, *r.* greenefs. *p.* 199. *l.* 33. *for* fire, *r.* Firr. *p.* 215. *l.* 5. *for* into it, *r.* it into. *l.* ult. for greens, *r.* greenness. *p.* 246. *l.* 22. *for* Water, *r.* Matter. *p.* 261. *l.* 3. *after* Wine, *r.* and Salts. *p.* 296. *l.* 27. *dele* and when the Destillation is. *p.* 301. *l.* 14. *for* shewing, *r.* shining. *p.* 306. *l.* 2. *after* Menstruums, *r.* made. *p.*326. *l.*27. *for* Tho, *r.* tho. *p.*349. *l.*30. *for* Acids, *r.* Arids. *p.* 351. *l.* 33. *for* repeating, *r.* repeated.

Books Printed for, and Sold by *Tho Howkins* in *George-Yard* near *Lombard-Street.*

CLavis *Horologiæ*, or, The *Art of Dyalling*; with an Explication of the Pyramidical Dyal set up in His Majesties Garden at *Whitehal*, Anno 1669. Illustrated with 40 Copper Cuts. in *Quarto.* By *John Holwell.*

A *Cabalistical Dialogue* in Answer to the Opinion of a Learned Doctor in Philosophy and Theology, That the World was made of nothing. By *F. M. Van-Helmont.* in *Quarto.*

Trigonometry made easie, fitted to the meanest Capacity; it being the Foundation of *Astronomy*, *Surveying*, *Navigation*, &c. in *Octavo.* By *John Holwell.*

Mellificium Mensionis, or the *Marrow of Measuring*, wherein a new and ready way is shewed how to measure *Glazing*, *Painting*, *Plaistering*, *Masonry*, *Joyners*, *Carpenters*, and *Brick-layers Work*, in six Books; and Illustrated with Copper Cuts: the like not heretofore Published. The Second Edition, Corrected, in *Octavo*, By *Venterus Mandey.*

The *Royal Catholick English School.* Containing a Catalogue of all Words in the Bible, beginning with one Syllable, and proceeding by degrees to eight, divided and not divided, &c. in *Octavo.* By *Tobias Ellis.*

Dr. *Everard's Works* in *Octavo.*

The *Paradoxal Discourses* of *F. M. Van-Helmont*, concerning the *Macrocosm* and *Microcosm*, &c. in *Octavo.*

The *Narrow Path of Divine Truth*, described, from living Practice and Experience of its three great steps, *viz. Purgation*, *Illumination* and *Union*, according to the Testimony of the Holy Scriptures, &c. By *F. M. Van Helmont*, in *Twelves.*

The *Artless Midnight Thoughts* of a Gentleman at Court. The Second Edition, with Additions, in *Twelves.*

The *Young Man's Companion*; or a very Useful Manual for Youth, &c. The Second Edition with Additions. By *William Mather*, in *Twelves.*

www.ingramcontent.com/pod-product-compliance
Lightning Source LLC
Chambersburg PA
CBHW031351290326
41932CB00044B/876

* 9 7 8 3 3 3 7 3 2 9 8 2 2 *